P-PA

Philology and Linguistics
(General). Greek Language
and Literature. Latin Language
and Literature

Library of Congress Classification
2010

Prepared by the Policy and Standards Division

LIBRARY OF CONGRESS
Cataloging Distribution Service
Washington, D.C.

LIBRARY OF CONGRESS

This edition cumulates all additions and changes to Subclasses P-PA through Weekly List 2010/06, dated February 10, 2010. Additions and changes made subsequent to that date are published in weekly lists posted on the World Wide Web at

<http://www.loc.gov/aba/cataloging/classification/weeklylists/>

and are also available in *Classification Web*, the online Web-based edition of the Library of Congress Classification.

Library of Congress Cataloging-in-Publication Data

  Library of Congress classification. P-PA. Philology and linguistics (general). Greek language and literature. Latin language and literature / prepared by the Policy and Standards Division, Library Services. — 2010 ed.
       p. cm.
  "This edition cumulates all additions and changes to subclasses P-PA through Weekly list 2010/06, dated February 10, 2010. Additions and changes made subsequent to that date are published in weekly lists posted on the World Wide Web ... and are also available in *Classification Web*, the online Web-based edition of the Library of Congress classification"— T.p. verso.
  Includes index.
  ISBN 978-0-8444-9507-1
  1. Classification, Library of Congress. 2. Classification—Books—Philology.
3. Classification—Books—Linguistics. 4. Classification—Books—Greek language.
5. Classification—Books—Greek literature. 6. Classification—Books—Latin language.
7. Classification—Books—Latin literature. I. Library of Congress. Policy and Standards Division. II. Title. III. Title: Philology and linguistics (general). IV. Title: Greek language and literature. V. Title: Latin language and literature.

  Z696.U5P6 2010
  025.4'64—dc22

                                                                    2010008586

For sale by the Library of Congress Cataloging Distribution Service,
101 Independence Avenue, S.E., Washington, DC 20540-4910.
Product catalog available on the Web at **www.loc.gov/cds**.

PREFACE

Class P: Subclasses P-PA was originally published in 1928 and reissued with supplementary pages in 1968 under the title *Philology. Linguistics. Classical Philology. Classical Literature*. A supplement with the title *Byzantine and Modern Greek Literature. Medieval and Modern Latin Literature* was published in 1942 and reissued in 1968 with supplementary pages of additions and changes. The 1997 edition incorporated all supplementary material into the main text. The 2005 edition cumulated all additions and changes from the period 1997-2005. This 2010 edition includes additions and changes that have been made since 2005. Captions for Greek authors and titles in PA3819-4500 and PA5301-5649 now include Greek characters, which were provided by Lucas Graves of the staff of the Policy and Standards Division.

In the Library of Congress classification schedules, classification numbers or spans of numbers that appear in parentheses are formerly valid numbers that are now obsolete. Numbers or spans that appear in angle brackets are optional numbers that have never been used at the Library of Congress but are provided for other libraries that wish to use them. In most cases, a parenthesized or angle-bracketed number is accompanied by a "see" reference directing the user to the actual number that the Library of Congress currently uses, or a note explaining Library of Congress practice.

Access to the online version of the full Library of Congress Classification is available on the World Wide Web by subscription to *Classification Web*. Details about ordering and pricing may be obtained from the Cataloging Distribution Service at

<http://www.loc.gov/cds/>

New or revised numbers and captions are added to the L.C. Classification schedules as a result of development proposals made by the cataloging staff of the Library of Congress and cooperating institutions. Upon approval of these proposals by the weekly editorial meeting of the Policy and Standards Division, new classification records are created or existing records are revised in the master classification database. Weekly lists of newly approved or revised classification numbers and captions are posted on the World Wide Web at

<http://www.loc.gov/aba/cataloging/classification/weeklylists/>

Janis Young, senior cataloging policy specialist in the Policy and Standards Division, is responsible for coordinating the overall intellectual and editorial content of class P and its various subclasses. Kent Griffiths, assistant editor of classification schedules, is responsible for creating new classification records, maintaining the master database, and creating index terms for the captions.

Barbara B. Tillett, Chief
Policy and Standards Division

February 2010

OUTLINE

	Philology. Linguistics
	Periodicals. Serials
	Cf. P215+ Phonology and phonetics
	Cf. P501+ Indo-European philology
1.A1	International or polyglot
1.A3-Z	American and English
2	French
3	German
7	Scandinavian
9	Other
(10)	Yearbooks
	see P1+
	Societies
	Cf. P215+ Phonology and phonetics
	Cf. P503 Indo-European philology
11	American and English
12	French
13	German
15	Italian
17	Scandinavian
18	Spanish and Portuguese
19	Other
	Congresses
	Cf. P505 Indo-European philology
21	Permanent. By name
23	Other
	Museums. Exhibitions
24	General works
24.2.A-Z	Individual. By place, A-Z
	Collected works (nonserial)
	Cf. P511+ Indo-European philology
25	Monographic series. Sets of monographic works
26.A-Z	Studies in honor of a particular person or institution. Festschriften. By honoree, A-Z
27	Collected works, papers, etc., of individual authors
29	Encyclopedias. Dictionaries
29.5	Terminology. Notation
	Cf. P152 Grammatical nomenclature
	Theory. Method
	General works
	see P121+
33	General special
	Relation to anthropology, ethnology and culture
	Including Sapir-Whorf hypothesis
	Cf. GN1+ Anthropology
35	General works
35.5.A-Z	By region or country, A-Z

	Theory. Method
	Relation to education -- Continued
40.8	General works
40.85.A-Z	By region or country, A-Z
	Communism and linguistics see HX550.L55
41	Other (Relation to history, etc.)
	Cf. JZ1253.5 Relation to international relations
	Relation to classical philology see PA37
	Classification of languages see P203+
47	Textual criticism
49	Addresses, essays, lectures
	Cf. P125 Linguistics
	Study and teaching. Research
	Including foreign language study and teaching in general and its methodology
	For individual foreign language study and teaching, see PA-PM
	For foreign language study and teaching (elementary or public school) see LB1578+
51	General
53	General special
	History see P61+
53.15	Aids and devices. Materials development
53.2	Audio-lingual method. Audiovisual aids
53.25	Bilingual method
53.255	Communicative competence
	Cf. P37.5.C64 Psycholinguistics
53.26	Comprehension
	Cf. P37.5.C66 Psycholinguistics
53.27	Composition and exercises. Rhetoric
53.28	Computer-assisted instruction
53.285	Computer network resources
	Including Internet resources
53.29	Conversation
53.295	Curriculum planning
53.296	Dictation
53.2963	Dictionaries
53.2965	Discourse analysis
53.2967	Distance education
53.297	Drama
53.298	Educational games
53.3	Error analysis
53.4	Examinations. Ability testing
53.4115	Fluency
53.41155	Foreign study
53.4116	Frames
53.4117	Gesture
53.412	Grammars. Textbooks

	Study and teaching. Research -- Continued
53.77	Self-instruction
	Cf. P53.445 Independent study
53.774	Semiotics
53.775	Sex differences
53.777	Similarity
53.78	Simulation methods
53.8	Social aspects
53.815	Statistical methods
53.818	Students with disabilities
53.82	Task analysis
53.85	Teacher training
53.855	Technological innovations
	Textbooks see P53.412
53.86	Translating
53.88	Variation in language
53.9	Vocabulary teaching
57.A-Z	By region or country, A-Z
59.A-Z	By school, A-Z
	Biography of language teachers
59.3	Collective
59.4.A-Z	Individual, A-Z
	Subarrange each by Table P-PZ50
	Vocational guidance
60	General works
60.2.A-Z	By region or country, A-Z
	History of philology
61	General works
62	Historiography
	By period
63	Ancient
65	Medieval
67	Renaissance
	Modern
69	General works
71	16th-18th century
	History of comparative philology
	Cf. P541+ Indo-European philology
73	General works
75	19th century
77	20th century
81.A-Z	By region or country, A-Z
	Biography of philologists
83	Collective
85.A-Z	Individual, A-Z
	Subarrange each by Table P-PZ50

Communication. Mass media
>Class here comprehensive works including both the primary techniques of language, pictures, etc., and the secondary techniques of the press, radio, television, etc.
>For radio broadcasting see PN1991+
>For television broadcasting see PN1992+
>For motion pictures see PN1993+
>For news media see PN4699+
>Cf. B832.3.A+ Private language problem
>Cf. BF637.C45 Psychology
>Cf. E98.C73 Indians of North America
>Cf. HE8689+ Radio and television broadcasting

87	Periodicals. Societies. Serials
87.2	Congresses
	Collected works (nonserial)
87.25	Series of monographs, collections of papers, etc. by various authors
87.3.A-Z	Studies in honor of a particular person or institution. Festschriften. By honoree, A-Z
87.4	Collected works of individual authors
87.5	Dictionaries
88.8	Directories
90	General works
91	General special
91.2	Juvenile works
91.25	Addresses, essays, lectures
	Communication of information about the mass media
91.27	General works
91.28	Computer network resources
	Including the Internet
	Study and teaching. Research
91.3	General works
91.5.A-Z	By region or country, A-Z
91.6	Vocational guidance
	By region or country
92.A-Z	Individual regions or countries, A-Z
92.2	Developing countries
	Biography
92.5.A1	Collective
92.5.A2-Z	Individual
	Special aspects
93	Content analysis
93.4	Aesthetics
	Audiovisual aids. Visual communication
	Cf. LB1042.5+ Audiovisual education
	Cf. NC730+ Graphic arts
93.5	General works

	Communication. Mass media
	Special aspects
	Audiovisual aids. Visual communication -- Continued
	Presentation graphics software
93.52	General works
93.53.A-Z	Individual programs, A-Z
93.55	Communication models (General)
93.6	Simulation methods
93.7	Mathematical models. Statistical methods
94	Influence. Moral, ethical or religious aspects
	For mass media in religion (General) see BL638+
	For mass media in Christianity see BV652.95+
94.5.A-Z	Relation to special groups of people, A-Z
	Aboriginal Australians see P94.5.A85+
94.5.A37-.A372	African Americans (Table P1)
94.5.A38-.A382	Aged. Older people (Table P1)
94.5.A45-.A452	Alien (Foreign) workers (Table P1)
94.5.A46-.A462	Amish (Table P1)
94.5.A7-.A72	Arabs (Table P1)
94.5.A75-.A752	Asian Americans (Table P1)
94.5.A76-.A762	Asians (Table P1)
94.5.A85-.A852	Australians, Aboriginal (Table P1)
94.5.B55-.B552	Blacks (Table P1)
94.5.C55-.C552	Children (Table P1)
	Class here general works on the relation between the mass media and children, as well as works limited to children's mass media
	For works on the influence and effects of the media on children see HQ784.M3
94.5.C57-.C572	Chinese Americans (Table P1)
94.5.C83-.C832	Cuban Americans (Table P1)
94.5.F34-.F342	Family (Table P1)
	Foreign workers see P94.5.A45+
94.5.F74-.F742	French-Canadians (Table P1)
94.5.G38-.G382	Gays (Table P1)
94.5.G57-.G572	Girls (Table P1)
94.5.H58-.H582	Hispanic Americans (Table P1)
94.5.I48-.I482	Immigrants (Table P1)
94.5.I53-.I532	Indians (Table P1)
94.5.I82-.I822	Italian Americans (Table P1)
94.5.M44-.M442	Men (Table P1)
94.5.M47-.M472	Mexican Americans (Table P1)
94.5.M55-.M552	Minorities (Table P1)
	Including race relations
94.5.M67-.M672	Mormons (Table P1)
	Older people see P94.5.A38+
94.5.P57-.P572	Pirates (Table P1)

Communication. Mass media
  Special aspects
    Relation to special groups of people, A-Z -- Continued

94.5.P64-.P642	Police (Table P1)
94.5.S68-.S682	South Asians (Table P1)
94.5.W47-.W472	West Indian Americans (Table P1)
94.5.W65-.W652	Women (Table P1)
94.5.Y68-.Y682	Young adults (Table P1)
94.5.Y72-.Y722	Youth (Table P1)

> Class here general works on the relation of the mass media
> and youth, as well as works limited to the depiction of
> youth in the media
> For works on the influence and effects of mass media
> on youth see HQ799.2.M35

Relation to culture. Intercultural communication
> Cf. GN345.6 Anthropology

94.6	General works
94.65.A-Z	By region or country, A-Z
94.7	Interpersonal communication

> Class here general works on interpersonal communication as
> well as works from the linguistic viewpoint
> For works on psychological aspects see BF637.C45
> For works on social aspects see HM1166+

Oral communication. Speech
> Cf. PN4001+ Oratory and public speaking

95	General works
	Study and teaching. Research
95.3	General works
95.4.A-Z	By region or country, A-Z
95.43.A-Z	By region or country, A-Z
95.45	Conversation

> Cf. BJ2120+ Etiquette

95.455	Dialogue

> Cf. P40.5.D53+ Sociolinguistics
> Cf. PN1551 Dialogue as a literary form

95.46	Listening

> Cf. BF323.L5 Listening (Psychology)

95.48	Interviewing
95.5	Paralinguistics
95.52	Questioning
95.53	Silence

> Cf. BJ1499.S5 Ethics

95.535	Small group communication (General)

> For sociological works, see HM133

95.54	Social aspects

> For sociological works, see HN

95.55	Speech acts

	Communication. Mass media
	Special aspects
	Oral communication. Speech -- Continued
95.6	Whistle speech
	Written communication see P211+
	Political aspects. Policy
	For radio and television broadcasting see HE8689.7.P6
	For radio broadcasting see HE8697.8+
	For television broadcasting see HE8700.75+
	For government publicity see JF1525.P8
95.8	General works
95.815	Communication planning
95.82.A-Z	By region or country, A-Z
	Mass media and music see ML3849
	Mass media and theater see PN2041.M37
	Mass media in education see LB1042.5+
	Mass media in missionary work see BV2082.M3
	Mass media in religion see BV652.95+
	Social aspects (U.S. mass media) see HN90.M3
	Social aspects (other countries) see HN101+
96.A-Z	Other, A-Z
96.A22-.A222	Accidents (Table P1)
96.A37-.A372	Africa (Table P1)
	Aged see P94.5.A38+
96.A39-.A392	AIDS (Disease) (Table P1)
	Albania
96.A4	General works
96.A412A-.A412Z	By region or country, A-Z
96.A42-.A422	Alcoholism (Table P1)
96.A44-.A442	Alternative mass media (Table P1)
96.A53-.A532	Animals (Table P1)
96.A56-.A562	Anthropology (Table P1)
96.A66-.A662	Apocalypse (Table P1)
	Arab countries
96.A7	General works
96.A712A-.A712Z	By region or country, A-Z
96.A72-.A722	Archival resources (Table P1)
96.A75-.A7512	Armed forces (Table P1)
	Arts and communication see NX180.C65
	Arts and mass media see NX180.M3
96.A79-.A792	Astronautics (Table P1)
96.A82-.A822	Astronomy (Table P1)
96.A83-.A832	Audiences (Table P1)
96.A86-.A862	Authorship (Table P1)
96.A87-.A872	Automobiles (Table P1)
96.B37-.B372	Batman (Fictitious character) (Table P1)
96.B46-.B462	Bioterrorism (Table P1)

Communication. Mass media
Special aspects
Other, A-Z -- Continued

96.B53-.B532	Black English (Table P1)
96.B64-.B642	Body, Human (Table P1)
96.B87-.B872	Business (Table P1)
	Cf. HD59+ Industrial public relations
96.C35-.C352	Celebrities (Table P1)
96.C4-.C42	Censorship (Table P1)
96.C43-.C432	Characters and characteristics (Table P1)
96.C44-.C442	Charisma (Personality trait) (Table P1)
96.C45-.C452	Chimurenga War (Zimbabwe), 1966-1980 (Table P1)
96.C57-.C572	Cities and towns (Table P1)
	Congo (Democratic Republic) see P96.Z34+
96.C68-.C682	Courtesy (Table P1)
96.C74-.C742	Crime and criminals (Table P1)
96.C76-.C762	Criticism (Table P1)
96.C77-.C772	Croft, Lara (Fictitious character) (Table P1)
96.D36-.D362	Data processing (Table P1)
96.D37-.D372	Dean, James, 1931-1955 (Table P1)
96.D38-.D382	Debates and debating (Table P1)
96.D4-.D42	Detectives (Table P1)
96.D45-.D452	Developing countries (Table P1)
96.D47-.D472	Deviant behavior (Table P1)
	Dinosaurs see P96.M6+
96.D62-.D622	Documentary mass media (Table P1)
96.E25-.E252	Economic aspects (Table P1)
	Including ownership
96.E29-.E292	Education (Table P1)
96.E57-.E572	Environment (Table P1)
96.E75-.E752	Ethnic relations (Table P1)
96.E86-.E862	Europe (Table P1)
96.E87-.E872	European Union (Table P1)
96.F36-.F362	Fantasy (Table P1)
96.F46-.F462	Feminism (Table P1)
96.F65-.F652	Folklore (Table P1)
96.F67-.F672	Forecasting (Table P1)
96.G44-.G442	Gender identity (Table P1)
96.G45-.G452	Genetics (Table P1)
96.G455-.G4552	Genres (Table P1)
96.G46-.G462	Geographical myths (Table P1)
96.G47-.G472	Geography (Table P1)
96.G48-.G482	Germany (Table P1)
96.G65-.G652	Gossip (Table P1)
96.H42-.H422	Healers (Table P1)
	Including faith healers, spiritual healers, etc.
96.H43-.H432	Health (Table P1)

Communication. Mass media
　Special aspects
　　Other, A-Z -- Continued

96.H46-.H462	Heroes (Table P1)
96.H55-.H552	History and mass media. Relation of mass media to history (Table P1)
96.H59-.H592	Holmes, Sherlock (Table P1)
96.H62-.H622	Homelessness (Table P1)
96.H63-.H632	Homosexuality (Table P1)
96.H65-.H652	Horror (Table P1)
	Human body see P96.B64+
96.H84-.H842	Human cloning (Table P1)
96.H85-.H852	Human rights (Table P1)
96.I34-.I342	Identity (Psychology) (Table P1)
	Imaginary voyages see P96.V68+
	Indians see P94.5.I53+
96.I47-.I472	Information services (Table P1)
96.I5-.I52	International cooperation. International communication (Table P1)
96.I53-.I532	International relations (General) (Table P1)
96.I54-.I542	Interviewing (Table P1)
	For interviewing in relation to oral communication see P95.48
96.I73-.I732	Iraq War, 2003- (Table P1)
96.I84-.I842	Islam (Table P1)
96.I87-.I872	Israel (Table P1)
96.J83-.J832	Judicial power (Table P1)
96.K52-.K522	Kibbutzim (Table P1)
96.K67-.K672	Kosovo Civil War, 1998- (Table P1)
96.L34-.L342	Language (Table P1)
96.L38-.L382	Latin America (Table P1)
96.L47-.L472	Liberalism (Table P1)
96.L5-.L52	Literature (Table P1)
96.L62-.L622	Local mass media (Table P1)
96.M34-.M342	Management (Table P1)
96.M36-.M362	Marketing (Table P1)
96.M38-.M382	Martians (Table P1)
96.M39-.M392	Massacres (Table P1)
96.M4-.M42	Media literacy (Table P1)
96.M45-.M452	Mental illness (Table P1)
96.M46-.M462	Mergers (Table P1)
96.M53-.M532	Mickey Mouse (Table P1)
96.M54-.M542	Militia movements (Table P1)
	Minorities see P94.5.M55+
96.M56-.M562	Miscommunication (Table P1)
96.M6-.M62	Monsters. Dinosaurs (Table P1)
	Mormons see P94.5.M67+

Communication. Mass media
    Special aspects
        Other, A-Z -- Continued

96.M83-.M832	Multiculturalism (Table P1)
96.M84-.M842	Mummies (Table P1)
96.M85-.M852	Murder (Table P1)
96.M94-.M942	Myth (Table P1)
96.N35-.N352	Narrative discourse (Table P1)
96.N37-.N372	National characteristics (Table P1)
96.N48-.N482	Network analysis (Table P1)
96.N67-.N672	Northern Ireland (Table P1)
96.O23-O232	Obesity (Table P1)
96.O24-.O242	Objectivity (Table P1)
96.O35-.O352	Oceania (Table P1)
	Online chat groups see HM1169
96.O65-.O652	Oppression (Psychology) (Table P1)
96.P33-.P332	Peace (Table P1)
96.P55-.P552	Pinocchio (Fictitious character) (Table P1)
96.P65-.P652	Popeye (Fictitious character) (Table P1)
	Pornography see P96.S45+
96.P72-.P722	Propaganda (Table P1)
96.P73-.P732	Psychic trauma (Table P1)
96.P75-.P752	Psychological aspects (Table P1)
	Cf. BF637.C45 Applied psychology of personal communication
96.P83-.P832	Public opinion (Table P1)
96.P84-.P842	Public welfare (Table P1)
96.P85-.P852	Publicity (Table P1)
96.R32-.R322	Radicalism (Table P1)
96.R35-.R352	Rape (Table P1)
96.R36-.R362	Ratings (Table P1)
96.R46-.R462	Reproductive health (Table P1)
96.S25-.S252	Savage, Doc (Fictitious character) (Table P1)
96.S29-.S292	Scandals (Table P1)
96.S33-.S332	Science (Table P1)
96.S34-.S342	Science fiction (Table P1)
96.S43-.S432	Semiotics (Table P1)
96.S45-.S452	Sex. Pornography (Table P1)
96.S48-.S482	Sex differences. Sexism (Table P1)
96.S5-.S52	Sex roles (Table P1)
	Sexism see P96.S48+
	Sherlock Holmes see P96.H59+
96.S63-.S632	Social conflict (Table P1)
96.S64-.S642	Social integration (Table P1)
96.S65-.S652	Social sciences (Table P1)
96.S66-.S662	Sound (Table P1)
96.S68-.S682	South Africa (Table P1)

	Communication. Mass media
	Special aspects
	Other, A-Z -- Continued
96.S7-.S72	Space and time (Table P1)
96.S74-.S742	Stereotype (Psychology) (Table P1)
96.S78-.S782	Storytelling (Table P1)
96.S9-.S92	Suburbs (Table P1)
96.S94-.S942	Superman (Table P1)
96.S96-.S962	Symbolism (Table P1)
96.T37-.T372	Tarzan (Table P1)
96.T42-.T422	Technological innovations. Technology (Table P1)
96.T47-.T472	Terrorism (Table P1)
96.T67-.T672	Torture (Table P1)
96.T7-.T72	Trade unions (Table P1)
96.V35-.V352	Vampires (Table P1)
96.V46-.V462	Vietnam War, 1961-1975 (Table P1)
96.V48-.V482	Villains (Table P1)
96.V5-.V52	Violence (Table P1)
96.V68-.V682	Voyages, Imaginary (Table P1)
96.W35-.W352	War (Table P1)
96.W36-.W362	War on Terrorism, 2001- (Table P1)
96.W48-.W482	West (U.S.) (Table P1)
	Women see P94.5.W65+
96.W62-.W622	World politics (Table P1)
96.W64-.W642	World War II (Table P1)
96.X45-.X452	Xenophobia (Table P1)
96.Z34-.Z342	Zaire. Congo (Democratic Republic) (Table P1)
96.Z56-.Z562	Zionism (Table P1)
	Computational linguistics. Natural language processing
	Cf. P307+ Machine translating
	Cf. PE1074.5 English language data processing
	Cf. QA76.9.N38 Computer science
	Cf. Z695.92 Automatic indexing
	Cf. Z699+ Machine methods of information storage and retrieval
98	General works
	Study and teaching. Research
98.3	General works
98.32.A-Z	By region or country, A-Z
98.45.A-Z	By region or country, A-Z
98.5.A-Z	Special aspects, A-Z
98.5.A87	Automatic abstracting and indexing
	Cf. Z695.92 Automatic abstracting and indexing for information storage and retrieval or in library science
98.5.C65	Connectionism
98.5.C67	Constraints

	Computational linguistics. Natural language processing
	Special aspects, A-Z -- Continued
98.5.D44	Deep structure
98.5.E45	Elliptical constructions. Ellipsis
	Cf. P291.3 Comparative grammar
98.5.G44	Generalized phrase structure grammar
	Cf. P158.35 Comparative grammar
98.5.I57	Internet
98.5.L63	Logic
98.5.N48	Network analysis
98.5.P38	Parsing (Computer grammar)
	Cf. QA267.3 Formal languages
98.5.S45	Semantics
98.5.S65	Space and time
98.5.S83	Statistical methods
98.5.S96	Symbol grounding
	Semiotics. Signs and symbols
99	General works
	Study and teaching. Research
99.3	General works
99.35.A-Z	By region or country, A-Z
99.37.A-Z	By region or country, A-Z
99.4.A-Z	Special aspects, A-Z
99.4.C73	Creativity
	Cf. P37.5.C74 Psycholinguistics
99.4.F53	Fieldwork
99.4.I26	Iconicity
99.4.M48	Metaphor
	Cf. P301.5.M48 Metaphor (General)
99.4.M6	Modality
99.4.M63	Models
99.4.P72	Pragmatics
	Cf. B831.5.A1+ Philosophy
99.4.P78	Psychological aspects
99.4.R44	Relevance
99.4.S62	Social aspects
99.4.S72	Statistical methods
	Nonverbal communication
	Cf. P93.5+ Visual communication
	Cf. P95+ Oral communication (General)
99.5	General works
99.6	Drum language
99.7	Silence
	Language. Linguistic theory. Comparative grammar
	Philosophy, origin, etc. of language
	Cf. P501+ Indo-European philology
	General works

Language. Linguistic theory. Comparative grammar
Philosophy, origin, etc. of language
General works -- Continued

101	Through 1800
103	1801-1880
105	1881-1950
106	1951-2000
107	2001-
112	Popular works

Bilingualism. Multilingualism
    Cf. LB1131+ Mental tests
    Cf. LC3701+ Bilingual schools

115	General works
115.2	Bilingualism and multilingualism in children

    For bilingual education see LC3701+
    Cf. P118+ Language acquisition

115.25	Multilingualism and literature
115.3	Code switching
115.4	Psychological aspects
115.45	Social aspects
115.5.A-Z	By region or country, A-Z

    For works emphasizing individual languages, see PA - PM
    For works emphasizing intercultural relations, see D - F

116	Origin of language

Sign language. Gesture
    For sign language of the Indians see E98.S5
    For systems of speech of the deaf see HV2471+

117	General works
117.5.A-Z	By region or country, A-Z
117.7	Pointing

Language acquisition
    Cf. LB1139.L3 Children's language (General)
    Cf. P115.2 Bilingualism and multilingualism in children

118	General works
118.13	Data processing

Study and teaching

118.15	General works
118.152.A-Z	By region or country, A-Z
118.2	Second language acquisition
118.23	Interlanguage
118.25	Language transfer
118.3	Language awareness in children
118.4	Communicative competence in children
118.5	Parent participation
118.6	Individual differences
118.65	Age factors

	Language. Linguistic theory. Comparative grammar
	Philosophy, origin, etc. of language
	Language acquisition -- Continued
118.7	Literacy
	Cf. LC149+ Education
118.75	Testing
119	Sound symbolism. Onomatopoeia
	Political aspects. Language policy
	Cf. P40.5.L35+ Language planning
119.3	General works
119.315	Linguistic minorities
	For sociolinguistic studies see P40.5.L56+
119.32.A-Z	By region or country, A-Z
120.A-Z	Other aspects, A-Z
120.A24	Academic language
	Cf. P301.5.A27 Academic writing
120.A35	Aged. Older people
120.C65	Color
	Cf. P305.19.C64 Vocabulary for colors
120.E27	Economic aspects
120.I53	Imaginary languages
120.I56	Indigenous peoples
120.I6	Internet
120.L34	Language awareness
	Cf. P118.3 Language awareness in children
120.M45	Men
120.M65	Motion
120.N37	Native language
	Nonsexist language see P120.S48
	Older people see P120.A35
120.R32	Racism
120.S48	Sex. Sex differences. Sexism. Nonsexist language
120.S53	Space and time (General)
	Cf. P37.5.S65 Psycholinguistics
	Cf. P299.S53 Comparative grammar
120.S9	Sublanguage
120.V37	Variation
	Cf. P408 Colloquial language
120.W66	Women
120.Y68	Youth
	Cf. P410.J88 Juvenile jargon
	Science of language (Linguistics)
	Cf. P1+ Philology. Linguistics
	Periodicals, societies, collections, etc. see P1+
121	General works
123	General special
124	Juvenile works

Language. Linguistic theory. Comparative grammar
Science of language (Linguistics) -- Continued

125	Addresses, essays, lectures
	Cf. P49 Linguistics and philology (general)
	Methodology. Linguistic analysis
126	General works
128.A-Z	Special aspects, A-Z
128.B5	Binary principle
128.C37	Categorization
	Cf. P37.5.C39 Psycholinguistics
128.C64	Combination
128.C66	Comparison
128.C664	Complexity
128.C67	Context (General)
	For context in relation to semantics see P325.5.C65
128.C68	Corpora
128.D37	Databases
128.D63	Documentation
128.D86	Dynamics
128.E26	Economy
128.E65	Equivalence
128.E94	Experimental linguistics
128.E95	Explanation
128.F5	Field theory
	For works limited to semantic fields see P325.5.F54
128.F53	Fieldwork
128.F67	Formalization
128.F72	Frames
	Cf. P325.5.F72 Semantic frames
128.F73	Frequency
128.G7	Graphic methods
128.H53	Hierarchy
128.H96	Hypothesis
128.I52	Indeterminacy
128.I53	Informants
128.L35	Language surveys
128.M48	Metalanguage. Second-order language
128.M56	Minimal pairs
128.M6	Models
128.O63	Opposition
128.P37	Paradigm
128.P73	Probabilities
128.P74	Prototype
	For prototypes in semantics see P325.5.P74
128.R43	Realization
	Statistics see P138.5+
128.S94	System theory

Language. Linguistic theory. Comparative grammar
Comparative grammar
General special
Syntax -- Continued

	Language. Linguistic theory. Comparative grammar
	Comparative grammar
	General special
	Other aspects, A-Z -- Continued
299.F63	Focus
	Cf. P325.5.F63 Semantics
299.G44	Genericalness
299.G68	Government
299.G69	Gradation
299.G7	Grammaticality
299.G73	Grammaticalization
299.H66	Honorific
299.I34	Ideophones
	Indefiniteness see P299.D43
299.I57	Interrogative
299.M35	Markedness
299.M6	Modality
299.M64	Modularity
299.N37	Naturalness
299.N4	Negatives
299.N48	Neutralization
299.N85	Null subject
299.O73	Order
299.P37	Parallelism
299.P39	Partitives
299.P4	Passive voice
	Cf. P281 Verb and verb phrase (General)
	Politeness see P299.H66
299.P65	Polysynthesis
299.P67	Possessives (General)
299.Q3	Quantifiers
299.R38	Reciprocals
299.R4	Reduction
299.R44	Reflexives
299.S53	Space and time
	Cf. P37.5.S65 Psycholinguistics
299.S89	Subjectivity
299.S92	Substitution
299.S93	Switch-reference
299.T73	Transmutation
	Style. Composition. Rhetoric. Usage
	Cf. P408 Colloquial language
	Cf. PA181+ Greek and Latin
	Cf. PN173+ Literature (General)
301	General works
	Study and teaching see P53.27
301.3.A-Z	By region or country, A-Z

	Language. Linguistic theory. Comparative grammar
	Style. Composition. Rhetoric. Usage -- Continued
301.5.A-Z	Special aspects, A-Z
301.5.A27	Academic writing
301.5.A38	Advertising
301.5.A44	Allusions
	Argumentation see P301.5.P47
301.5.C45	Clichés
301.5.D37	Data processing
301.5.D47	Description
301.5.D54	Digression (Rhetoric)
301.5.E34	Editing. Revision
301.5.F53	Figures of speech (General)
	Cf. PN227 Literary composition
301.5.I34	Idioms
	Cf. P326.5.I35 Lexicology
301.5.I53	Indirect discourse
301.5.I57	Invention
	Cf. PN221 Literary style
301.5.I73	Irony
	Cf. PN1680 Irony in drama
301.5.M48	Metaphor
	Cf. BH301.M4 Aesthetics
	Cf. P99.4.M48 Semiotics
	Cf. P325.5.M47 Semantics
	Cf. PN228.M4 Literary composition
301.5.M49	Metonyms
301.5.P47	Persuasion. Argumentation
	Cf. PN207 Authorship
301.5.P56	Pleonasm
301.5.P65	Point of view
	Cf. PN3383.P64 Literary technique
301.5.P67	Political aspects
	Cf. PN239.P64 Political composition or literary style
301.5.P73	Propaganda
301.5.P75	Psychological aspects
	Cf. BF456.W8 Psychology of writing
301.5.P86	Punctuation
301.5.R45	Repetition
	Revision see P301.5.E34
301.5.S63	Social aspects
301.5.S73	Statistical methods
	Discourse analysis
302	General works
302.15.A-Z	By region or country, A-Z
302.18	Academic writing
302.2	Cohesion. Coherence

	Language. Linguistic theory. Comparative grammar
	Discourse analysis -- Continued
302.23	Complaints
302.25	Comprehension
	Cf. P37.5.C66 Psycholinguistics
302.26	Computer-assisted instruction
302.27	Connectives
302.28	Constraints
302.3	Data processing
	For text processing (Computer science) see QA76.9.T48
302.35	Discourse markers
302.355	Explanation
302.36	Frames
302.4	Intentionality
302.45	Intertextuality
	For intertextuality in relation to literary criticism see PN98.I58
302.46	Interviewing
302.5	Literary discourse
	Cf. PN80+ Literary criticism
302.6	Mathematical models (General)
	For discourse data processing see P302.3
	For statistical methods see P302.85
302.7	Narrative discourse
302.73	Paraphrase
302.75	Parenthesis
302.76	Perspective
302.77	Political aspects
302.8	Psychological aspects
302.813	Punctuation
302.814	Quotation
302.8147	Reference
302.815	Register
302.82	Repetition
302.83	Sequence
302.84	Social aspects
302.85	Statistical methods
302.86	Sublanguage. Specialized texts
302.865	Technology. Technological innovations
302.87	Verbal self-defense
	For psychological studies see BF637.V47
304	Plays on words
	Vocabulary. Terminology (General)
	For linguistic terminology see P29.5
	For lexicology see P326+
	Cf. P53.9 Vocabulary teaching

	Language. Linguistic theory. Comparative grammar
	Vocabulary. Terminology (General) -- Continued
305	General works
305.15.A-Z	By region or country, A-Z
	Biography
305.16	Collective
305.17.A-Z	Individual, A-Z
	Subarrange each by Table P-PZ50
305.18.A-Z	Special aspects, A-Z
305.18.D38	Data processing
305.18.D39	Databases
305.18.I57	Interdisciplinary approach
305.18.P79	Psychological aspects
305.18.S72	Standardization
305.18.T33	Taboo, Linguistic
305.19.A-Z	Vocabulary for special topics, A-Z
	Class here linguistic works
	For terminology of subjects, see the subject in A-Z, e. g. R123, Medicine
305.19.C64	Colors
305.19.P76	Professions
305.2	Abbreviations. Acronyms
	Translating and interpreting
	For works on translating of a particular language, see the language in P-PM
	Special subjects, prefer B-Z, e. g. T11.5 Technology
	For translating as a literary pursuit see PN241+
306.A1	Periodicals. Societies. Serials
306.A2	Directories
306.A3-Z	General works
306.2	General special
306.5	Study and teaching
306.6	Vocational guidance
306.8.A-Z	By region or country, A-Z
	Biography
306.9	Collective
306.92.A-Z	Individual, A-Z
	Subarrange each by Table P-PZ50
306.93	Multimedia translating
306.94	Translating services
306.945	Consecutive interpreting
306.947	Public service interpreting
306.95	Simultaneous interpreting
306.96	Sublanguage translating
306.97.A-Z	Other topics, A-Z
306.97.D62	Documentation
306.97.N35	Names

Language. Linguistic theory. Comparative grammar
Translating and interpreting
Other topics, A-Z -- Continued

306.97.S63	Social aspects
306.97.T73	Technological innovations
306.97.T78	Thesauri

Machine translating. Data processing
For machine translating of individual languages, see the
language in P-PM

307	Periodicals. Societies. Serials
308	General works
309	General special
310.A-Z	By region or country, A-Z
311	Prosody. Metrics. Rhythmics

Class here technical works only
For works on poetics in a particular language, see the language
For general works about the literary aspects see
PN1031+

Etymology

321	General works

Names. Onomastics
Class here general works on names as well as works on
onomastics proper
For works on names in a particular language, see the
language in P - PM
Cf. D - F, Geographic names
Cf. CS2300+ Personal and family names
Cf. G104+ Geographic names (Universal)
Cf. GT471 House names

321.8	Periodicals. Societies. Serials
321.85	Dictionaries
321.9	Directories
323	General works
323.4.A-Z	By region or country, A-Z
323.5	Special aspects (not A-Z)
323.8	Dictionaries
324	Foreign elements
324.5	Particular words (not A-Z)

Semantics

325	General works
325.45.A-Z	By region or country, A-Z
325.5.A-Z	Special aspects, A-Z
325.5.A46	Ambiguity

Cf. P299.A46 Ambiguity (General)

325.5.A48	Antonyms
325.5.C37	Categorization
325.5.C56	Collocation

	Language. Linguistic theory. Comparative grammar
	Semantics
	Special aspects, A-Z -- Continued
325.5.C6	Comparative semantics
325.5.C62	Componential analysis
325.5.C626	Compositionality
325.5.C63	Connotation
325.5.C65	Context
325.5.D38	Data processing
325.5.D43	Deixis
	Cf. P299.D44 Grammar
325.5.E56	Emotive
	Cf. P325.5.C63 Connotation
325.5.E94	Euphemism
325.5.E96	Evidentials
325.5.F54	Field theory
	For field theory in linguistic analysis see P128.F5
325.5.F63	Focus
	Cf. P299.F63 Comparative grammar
325.5.F67	Forecasting
325.5.F72	Frames
325.5.G45	Generative semantics
325.5.H57	Historical semantics
325.5.H65	Homonyms
325.5.I54	Indexicals
325.5.L48	Lexical competence
325.5.M36	Mathematical models
325.5.M47	Metaphor
	Cf. P301.5.M48 Metaphor (General)
325.5.N47	Network analysis
325.5.O55	Onomasiology
325.5.P35	Paradox
325.5.P37	Paraphrase
325.5.P65	Polysemy
325.5.P74	Prototype
325.5.P78	Psychological aspects
325.5.R44	Reference
	For switch-reference see P299.S93
325.5.S46	Semantic features
325.5.S55	Semantic prosody
325.5.S63	Social aspects
325.5.S78	Statistical methods
325.5.S79	Stereotype
325.5.S96	Synonyms
325.5.U54	Universals
	Lexicology
326	General works

Language. Linguistic theory. Comparative grammar

Lexicology -- Continued

326.45.A-Z	By region or country, A-Z
326.5.A-Z	Special aspects, A-Z
326.5.C74	Creativity
326.5.D38	Data processing
326.5.H57	Historical lexicology
326.5.I35	Idioms
	Cf. P301.5.I34 Rhetoric
326.5.L48	Lexicostatistics
326.5.N49	New words
326.5.P45	Phraseology
	Cf. P296 Syntactic phrases
326.5.P75	Psychological aspects
326.5.R44	Relexification
326.5.S64	Social aspects
	Words, New see P326.5.N49

Lexicography

327	General works
327.45.A-Z	By region or country, A-Z
327.5.A-Z	Special aspects, A-Z
327.5.D37	Data processing
	Specialized dictionaries see P327.5.S82
327.5.S82	Sublanguage. Specialized dictionaries
327.5.T43	Technological innovations
327.5.V37	Variation (in orthography, pronunciation, vocabulary, dialect, etc.)

Comparative lexicography

331	General works
	Collections of words, specimen texts, selections, etc. from various languages not belonging to any one particular group
	Lists of words
341	General works
347	Minor works. Particular words
	e. g. Gallagher, The name of God in 48 languages
	Specimen texts
351	Lord's prayer
	Subarrange by editor or compiler
352	Other Bible extracts
	Cf. BS3 Selections from polyglot Bibles
357	Miscellaneous collections
	Polyglot dictionaries, glossaries, etc.
	Cf. P765 Indo-European philology
361	General works
362	Juvenile works

	Language. Linguistic theory. Comparative grammar
	Comparative lexicography
	Collections of words, specimen texts, selections, etc. from various languages not belonging to any one particular group -- Continued
	Abbreviations. Acronyms
	For abbreviations in a particular language, see the language in P - PM
365	General works
365.5.A-Z	By region or country, A-Z
	Dialectology
	For the study and description of the dialects of a specific language or groups of languages, see PA - PM
	For the study and description of the dialects of a specific place see P375+
	Cf. P40.5.U73+ Urban dialects
367	General works
367.5.A-Z	By region or country, A-Z
368	Standard language. Literary language
	For a specific language or groups of languages, see PA - PM
371	Groups of unrelated languages. General surveys of languages
	Prefer PA - PM, as the case may be, e. g. PJ195 Oriental languages; PJ701+ "Muhammedan" (Arabic-Persian-Turkish) languages
	For the theory of language see P101+
	Linguistic geography
375	General works
	America
376	General works
377	United States
379	Canada
380	Languages of Europe (General)
381.A-Z	Languages of other special areas, A-Z
	e.g.
381.S59	Soviet Union
381.S6	Spain
	Mixed languages (Lingua Franca; Creole; etc.) see PM7801+
(391)	Atlases. Maps
	see class G
408	Colloquial language
	Slang. Argot
409	General works
410.A-Z	Special topics, A-Z
410.B33	Black slang

	Language. Linguistic theory. Comparative grammar
	Slang. Argot
	Special topics, A-Z -- Continued
410.I58	Invective
	Cf. BF463.I58 Psycholinguistics
	Cf. GT3070 Manners and customs
410.J88	Juvenile jargon
410.O27	Obscene words
410.R45	Rhyming slang
	Indo-European (Indo-Germanic) philology
501	Periodicals. Serials
503	Societies
505	Congresses
	Collected works (nonserial)
	Cf. P25+ Philology (General)
511	Series of monographs, collections of papers, etc. by various authors
512.A-Z	Studies in honor of a particular person or institution. Festschriften. By honoree, A-Z
513	Collected works of individual authors
	Collections of words, specimen texts, etc. see P341+
518	Encyclopedias. Dictionaries
	Bibliography, biobibliography see Z7001+
	Theory. Method see P121; P561
525	Linguistic antiquities (archaeological, ethnological, geographical)
	Cf. GN539 Anthropology
	Cf. P35+ Philology (General)
	History
	Cf. P73+ Philology (General)
541	General works
	By period
543	19th century
545	20th century
551.A-Z	By region or country, A-Z
	Biography
(555)	Collected
	Prefer P83+
(557)	Individual
561	General works
563	Compends
565	Outlines. Syllabi. Tables
567	Popular works
569	General special
571	Addresses, essays, lectures
	Cf. P125 Linguistics
572	Proto-Indo-European language

Indo-European (Indo-Germanic) philology -- Continued
  Comparative grammar
    Cf. P201+ Philology (General)

575	General works
577	General special
580	Textbooks
	Phonology. Phonetics
	Periodicals. Societies. Serials see P215+
583	General works
587	Phonetics
589	Laryngeal theory
590	Prosodic analysis
591	Syllabication. Quantity
597	Accent
	Vowels and diphthongs
599	General works
601	Vowel gradation (Ablaut)
605	Consonants
607	Grimm's law. Verner's law
609	Particular sounds (not A-Z)
610	Phonetics of the sentence (Sandhi)
	Cf. P240 Philology (General)
610.5	Transliteration
	Morphology. Inflection. Accidence
611	General works
615	Word formation. Derivation. Suffixes, etc.
	Inflection
621	General works
623	Noun. Declension
625	Verb. Conjugation
627	Adjective. Comparison
	Parts of speech (Morphology and syntax)
	Noun
631	General works
632	General special
633	Gender
635	Number
	Case
637	General works
639	General special
641	Adjective
643	Numerals
645	Article
647	Pronoun
649	Verb
	Particles
655	General works

	Extinct ancient or medieval languages
	Languages of Western Asia
	Elamite -- Continued
943.A1	Periodicals. Societies. Serials
943.A2	Collections of texts. By date
943.A5	Achaemenian inscriptions. By date
	Cf. PJ3834 Babylonian
	Cf. PK6128.A+ Old Persian
	Languages of Asia Minor (Anatolian languages)
944	General works
	Indo-European languages
944.5	General works
	Hittite subgroup
	Hittite
945.A1	Periodicals. Societies. Serials
945.A2	Collections of texts. By date
945.A3A-.A3Z	Individual texts. By title, A-Z
945.A4	Individual texts (that have no title). By date
945.A5-.Z3	General works
945.Z8	Dictionaries, indexes, etc. By date
945.Z9A-.Z9Z	Translations. By language, A-Z, and date
946	Carian
	Cf. P1024 Lelegian
947	Lydian
	Luwian subgroup
949	Luwian. Cuneiform Luwian
950	Hieroglyphic Luwian (Hieroglyphic Hittite)
951	Cilician
952	Lycaonian
953	Lycian
954	Pisidian
955	Sidetic
956	Palaic
	Mysian see P1054.5
	Phrygian see P1057
	Other languages
956.5	Cappadocian
	For the "Cappadocian tables" (Assyro-Babylonian cuneiform texts) see PJ3591.A2+
957	Hattic
958	Hurrian
959	Urartian
	Languages of Southeastern Europe
1001	General works
	Languages of pre-Greek and early Greek civilization
	For archaic elements in classical Greek see PA227+
1021	General works

Extinct ancient or medieval languages
Languages of Southeastern Europe
Languages of pre-Greek and early Greek civilization --
Continued
1023   Pelasgian
1024   Lelegian
                    Cf. P946 Carian
1031   Inscription of Lemnos
                    Cf. P1078 Etruscan
                Minoan and Mycenaean inscriptions of Crete, Greece,
                    etc.
1035   General works
1036   Hieroglyphs. Phaistos Disk
1037   Linear A
1038   Linear B (Mycenaean Greek)
1038.5   Eteocretan
1039   Cypro-Minoan script
1040   Cypriot syllabary. Eteocypriot
                Thracian complex
1053   General works
1054   Thracian
1054.5   Daco-Mysian
1055   Macedonian (Ancient)
1055.5   Paeonian
1057   Phrygian
                Illyrian
                    Cf. PG9501+ Albanian
1061   General works
1062   Messapian. Messapic
                Venetic see P1075
            Languages of Southern and Western Europe
1070   General works
                Indo-European languages
1072   Ligurian
1074   Sicel
1075   Venetic
                Other languages
1078   Etruscan (Table P-PZ15)
1079   Nuraghic
1081   Iberian. Celtiberian
                    Including pre-Roman languages of the Iberian Peninsula
                        (General)
                    For post-Roman languages of the Iberian Peninsula
                        see P381.S6
                    Cf. PH5001+ Basque
1088   Pictish
                    Cf. PB1950 Pictish (Celtic)

Extinct ancient or medieval languages
Languages of Southern and Western Europe
Other languages -- Continued
1091   Raetian

PA1-3049

Classical philology
    Periodicals
1.A1   International or polyglot
1.A3-Z   American and English
2   French
3   German
9   Other
    Societies
11   American and English
12   French
13   German
15   Italian
17   Scandinavian
18   Spanish and Portuguese
19   Other
23   Congresses
    Collections
25   Series of monographs; Collections of papers, etc. by various
              authors
26.A-Z   Studies in honor of a particular person or institution
              (Festschriften). By honoree, A-Z
27   Collected works, papers, etc., by individual authors
31   Encyclopedias. Dictionaries. Indexes
              Cf. DE5 History of the Greco-Roman world
              Cf. DF16 History of ancient Greece
              Cf. DG16 History of Rome
35   Philosophy. Theory. Method
37   Aims, value, scope, relations, etc.
    Criticism. Interpretation (Hermeneutics)
39   General
40   General special. Minor
(42)   Manuscripts, etc. Paleography
              see Z105+
(45)   Higher criticism
              see PA39
47   Textual criticism
49   Interpretation. Hermeneutics
50   Language data processing
    History
51   General works
          By period
53   Antiquity
55   Middle Ages
57   Renaissance (15th-16th century)
             Modern
59   General
61   16th-17th century

	History
	By period
	Modern -- Continued
63	17th-18th century
65	19th century
67	20th century
70.A-Z	By region or country, A-Z
72.A-Z	By university, A-Z
	Study and teaching. Research
	Including works on the teaching of the classical languages in secondary schools, and to undergraduates in colleges
74	General
76	General special. Minor
	For general discussions of the value of classical education see LC1001+
	By period see PA53+
78.A-Z	By region or country, A-Z
79.A-Z	By school, A-Z
	Biography
83	Collective
85.A-Z	Individual, A-Z
	General works
91	Treatises
93	Compends
95	Outlines. Syllabi. Tables
97	Popular works
99	General special
	Greek and Latin languages
111	Comparative grammar
116	General special
119	Examination questions
121	Phonology
131	Orthoepy. Pronunciation
	Morphology. Inflection. Accidence
141	General works
143	Word formation. Derivation. Suffixes, etc.
145	Declension
155	Conjugation
161	Syntax
	Style. Composition. Rhetoric
181	General works
184	Choice of words. Vocabulary
184.3	Translating
	Prosody. Metrics. Rhythmics
185	Treatises
186	Text-books
187.A-Z	Special, by form, A-Z

Greek and Latin languages
   Prosody. Metrics. Rhythmics
      Special, by form, A-Z -- Continued

187.E6	Epic poetry
187.L9	Lyric poetry
188.A-Z	Special, by meter, A-Z
189	Other special
190	Rhythm in prose
191	Etymology
195	Semantics
199	Synonymy
199.5	Homonymy

PA1-3049

PA1-3049

PA1-3049

PA1-3049

Hellenistic Greek. Atticists
  Biblical Greek
    New Testament (and early Christian) Greek -- Continued

895 Treatises on particular early Christian writers (to ca. 600 A.D.)
  For the grammar, etc., of particular Hellenistic authors see PA3818+

(899) Greek, "Vulgar" (non-literary)
  see PA1171+

	Medieval and modern Greek language
	Periodicals
1000	International (Polyglot)
1001	English and American
1002	French
1003	German
1005	Greek
1009	Other
	Societies
1011	English and American
1012	French
1013	German
1015	Greek
1019	Other
1023	Congresses
	Collections
1025	Series of monographs; collections of papers, etc., by various authors
1026.A-Z	Studies in honor of a particular person or institution (Festschriften). By honoree, A-Z
1027	Collected works of individual authors
1031	Encyclopedias. Dictionaries
1033	Philosophy. Theory. Method
1035	Aims, value, scope, relations, etc.
	History of philology
1036	General works
1037	General special
1038.A-Z	By region or country, A-Z
	Biography
1039.A2	Collective
1039.A3-Z	Individual, A-Z
	Subarrange each by Table P-PZ50
	Study and teaching. History
1041	General
1043	Early, to 1453
1044	1453-1800
1045	19th century
1046	20th century
1047.A-Z	By region or country, A-Z
1049.A-Z	By school, A-Z
1050	General works, including history of the language
1050.3	Language acquisition
1050.5	Script
	Grammar
1051	Historical and comparative
	Formal (descriptive)
1053	Early works (to 1800)

	Grammar
	Formal (descriptive) -- Continued
	Modern works
1055	General (Medieval and modern Greek)
1056	Medieval Greek
	Modern Greek
1057	Treatises
1058	Text-books. Exercises, etc.
1059	Conversation. Phrase books. Readers
	Phonology. Phonetics
1061	General works
1063	Pronunciation
1065	Accent
1071	Orthography
1072	Transliteration
1076	Morphology. Inflection. Accidence
	Parts of speech (Morphology and syntax)
1081	Noun
1082	Adjective. Comparison
1083	Numerals
1084	Article
1085	Pronoun
	Verb
1087	General works
1087.5	Aspect
1087.9	Tense
1087.93	Voice
1089	Particles
	Syntax
1091	General works
1093	Sentence
1097	Other
1099	Grammatical usage of particular authors
	Style. Composition. Rhetoric
1101	General works
1103	Readers
1104	Idioms
1105	Letter writing
1105.5	Translating
1106	Prosody. Metrics. Rhythmics
	Etymology. Lexicology
1111	General works
1113	Dictionaries
	Foreign elements
1114	General works
1114.5.A-Z	Special. By language, A-Z
1115	Semantics

1117	Synonymy
	Dictionaries
	To 1450
1123	Contemporary authors
1125	Modern authors
	To 1800
1127	Contemporary authors
1129	Modern authors
	19th-21st centuries
1131	Greek only
1133	Greek-Latin
1137	Greek, with definitions in two or more languages
1139.A-Z	Greek, with definitions in one language. By language, A-Z
1145	Lists of words
	Dialects
1151	General. Greece (Balkan peninsula). Adjacent islands
1153.A-Z	By province, region, island (group of islands), A-Z
1153.A73	Arakhova Parnassou Region
1153.C45	Cephalonia
1153.C7	Crete
1153.C9	Cyprus
1153.E7	Epirus
1153.L4	Lesbos (modern name : Mytilene)
1153.S7	Sporades
1153.T8	Tsaconian (Zaconian)
1155	Asia Minor
1159	Italy
	Greek, "Vulgar" (Non-literary)
1171	General works
1172	Grammar
1175	Etymology. Lexicology. Dictionaries
1177	Miscellaneous
(1179)	Texts
	see PA5070+

PA1-3049

	Latin philology and language
	Periodicals
2001	English
2002	French
2003	German
2004	Italian
2009	Other
	Societies
2011	English
2012	French
2013	German
2014	Italian
2019	Other
(2023)	Congresses
	see PA23
	Collections
2025	Series of monographs. Collections of papers, etc., by various authors
2026.A-Z	Studies in honor of a particular person or institution. Festschriften. By honoree, A-Z
2027	Collected works, papers, etc., of individual authors
(2031)	Encyclopedias. Dictionaries
	see PA31
(2035)	Theory. Method
	see PA35
	History of Latin philology
2041	General works
	By period
2043	Antiquity
2045	Middle Ages
2047	Renaissance
	Modern
2049	General works
2051	17th-18th centuries
2052	19th century-
2055.A-Z	By region or country, A-Z
	Latin language (Exterior history, distribution, etc.)
2057	General works
2057.5	Language data processing
(2059)	Medieval and modern
	see PA2801+
	Study and teaching
2061	General works. History and method
2063	General special. Minor
	By period see PA2043+
2065.A-Z	By region or country, A-Z
2067.A-Z	By school, A-Z

	Grammar
(2069)	Theory, nomenclature, etc.
	see P151+
(2070)	History
	see PA2041+
2071	Historical and comparative
	Formal (descriptive)
(2072)	Ancient authors
	see PA6139; PA6202+
2073	To 1500
2075	16th century
2077	17th-18th centuries
2079	19th century
2080	20th century
2080.2	21st century
	Text-books, exercises, etc.
	Cf. PA2313+ Style. Composition. Rhetoric
2081	History and criticism
2082	To 1500
2084	16th-18th centuries
	1801-1975
2087	Grammars and elementary exercises
	Advanced exercises see PA2315
2087.5	1976-
2088	Comic grammars
	Grammars for special classes of students
2091	Law
2092	Medicine. Pharmaceutics
2093	Other
	Church Latin see PA2801+
(2094)	Exercises in composition
	Elementary see PA2087
	Advanced see PA2315
2094.5	Self-instructors
2095	Readers
	Exercises, etc., selected from particular authors
(2096)	Caesar
	see PA2087
(2097)	Cicero
	see PA2087
2099.A-Z	Other authors, A-Z
2100	Outlines, syllabi, tables, etc.
2101	Quizzes. Examination questions
2103	Teachers' manuals
2107	Conversation. Phrase books
2109	Plays (for reading or acting)
	Phonology

PA1-3049

	Grammar
	Phonology -- Continued
2111	General works
2115	Phonetics
2117	Pronunciation
2118	Syllabication
2119	Accent
2121	Quantity
2123	Orthography. Writing
	Cf. Z105+ Paleography
	Alphabet
2125	General works
2127	Vowels. Diphthongs
2129	Consonants
2131	Particular letters
	Morphology. Inflection. Accidence
2133	General works
2137	Word formation. Derivation. Suffixes, etc.
	Cf. PA2341+ Etymology
	Noun. Declension
2140	General works
2141	First
2142	Second
2143	Third
2144	Fourth
2145	Fifth
2147	Adjective. Comparison
	Verb. Conjugation
2150	General works
2151	First
2152	Second
2153	Third
2154	Fourth
2158	Tables. Paradigms
	Parts of speech (Morphology and syntax)
	Noun
	Cf. PA2140+
2161	General works
2165	General special
	Including special classes of noun, e.g. common nouns, proper nouns, compound nouns, diminutives, etc.
2171	Gender
2176	Number
	Case
2181	General works
2182	General special
2183	Nominative. Vocative

Grammar
   Parts of speech (Morphology and syntax)
      Noun
         Case -- Continued

2185	Genitive
2187	Dative
2189	Accusative
	Ablative
2191	General works
2193	Instrumental
2195	Locative
2201	Adjective
2206	Numerals
2213	Pronoun
	Verb
2215	General works
2225	Person
2231	Number
2235	Voice
	Mood
2240	General works
2245.A-Z	Special, A-Z
2245.P2	Participle
	Tense
2250	General works
2253	Present
2255	Imperfect
2257	Future
2259	Perfect
2261	Pluperfect
2263	Future perfect
2265	Other
2268	Other special
	Particles
2271	General works
2273	Adverb
2275	Preposition
2277	Conjunction
2279	Interjection
2281.A-Z	Other special, A-Z
	Syntax
2285	General works
2287	Outlines, etc.
	Cf. PA2158
2289	General special
	Sentence
2293	Arrangement of words and clauses

PA1-3049

PA1-3049

	Style. Composition. Rhetoric
	Special topics, A-Z -- Continued
2318.A6	Anaphora
2318.F54	Figures of speech
2318.G4	Genera dicendi
2318.I54	Indirect discourse
2318.L43	Legal language
	Litotes see PA2318.U53
2318.M43	Medical language
	For Latin terminology in modern medicine, see class R
2318.P8	Punctuation
2318.T4	Terminology
2318.U53	Understatement. Litotes
2319	Idioms, corrections, errors, etc.
2320	Choice of words. Vocabulary
(2327)	Special authors or groups of authors
	see PA6141+ PA6202+
	Prosody. Metrics. Rhythmics
2329	Treatises, including history
2331	Text-books. Compends
2333	Versification (Gradus ad Parnassum; exercises, etc.)
2335.A-Z	Special by form, A-Z
2335.E6	Epic
2335.L9	Lyric
2337.A-Z	Special by meter, A-Z
2337.H6	Hexameter
2337.S2	Saturnian verse
2338	Other special
(2339)	Special authors or groups of authors
	see PA6141+ PA6202+
2340	Rhythm in prose
	Etymology
2341	Treatises
2342	Dictionaries, exclusively etymological
	Word formation see PA2137
2343	Names
2345	Special elements
	Including foreign words and phrases
2347	Semantics
2349	Synonymy
2350.A-Z	Particular words, A-Z
2350.D46	Desidia
2350.F4	Felicitas
2350.G5	Gloria
2350.M37	Mars
2350.R44	Religio
2350.S54	Signum

	Lexicography
2351	Collections
2353	General works. History. Treatises
(2354)	Biography of lexicographers
	see PA83+
	Ancient and medieval glossaries
	Cf. PA6381.D7 Pseudo-Dositheus
	Cf. PA6385.F4 Festus, S. Pompeius
	Cf. PA6518.N6 Nonius Marcellus
	Cf. PA6965.V3 Verrius Flaccus, M.
	Cf. PA8395.P3 Paulus Diaconus
	Editions
2355.A1-.A5	Collections (Comprehensive)
	Arrange chronologically according to date of appearance
2355.A7-Z	Selected glossaries (three or more). By editor, A-Z
2356	Particular glossaries
(2357)	By language
	see PA2356
2357.1	Special classes of words
	Including noun, verb, etc.
2357.3	Special subjects
	Special authors
2357.5	Bible (Vulgate)
(2357.7)	Other
	see the author, e.g. Vergilius, Cicero
2358	Lists of glosses (compiled from various glossaries)
2359	Treatises (general or restricted to a particular glossary; special features, etc.)
	Dictionaries
2361	Dictionaries with definitions in Latin only
2363	Supplementary dictionaries
2364	Dictionaries with definitions in two or more other languages
2365.A-Z	Dictionaries with definitions in one other language. By language, A-Z
	For Greek-Latin see PA442
2371	Dictionaries of particular periods
	For medieval and modern Greek see PA2887+ PA2904; PA2914
(2375)	Dictionaries of particular authors or groups of authors
	see PA6141+ PA6202+
2379	Dictionaries of names
2383	Foreign words
2387	Special (technical, etc.)
2389	Other lists
2390	Statistics of words
	Ancient languages and dialects of Italy
2391	General (Table P-PZ15)

Ancient languages and dialects of Italy -- Continued

(2392)	Greek
	see PA591; PA227; PA1159
	Illyrian
(2393)	General
	see P1061
(2394)	Messapian. Iapygian
	see P1062
(2395)	Venetic
	see P1075
(2397)	Ligurian
	see P1072
(2399)	Celtic (Gaulish)
	see PB3001+
(2400-2409)	Etruscan
	see P1078
	Italic dialects
2420-2429	General (Table PA1)
	Cf. PA2601+ Vulgar Latin
	Oscan-Umbrian
2440-2449	General (Table PA1)
2450-2459	Oscan (Table PA1)
2460-2469	Umbrian (Table PA1 modified)
2461	Tabulae Iguvinae
	Sabellian
2470-2479	General (Table PA1)
	Special
2481	Aequian (Table P-PZ15)
2483	Marrucinian (Table P-PZ15)
2485	Marsian (Table P-PZ15)
2487	Paelignian (Table P-PZ15)
2489	Sabine (Table P-PZ15)
2491	Vestinian (Table P-PZ15)
2493	Volscian (Table P-PZ15)
2510-2519	Latin-Faliscan. Early (archaic) Latin to ca. 100 B.C. (Table PA1 modified)
	Including treatises on the relation of Latin to the Italic dialects, and works confined to Early Latin
	Cf. PA2057
	Cf. PA2071
	Collections
2510.A2	Texts (Minor. Chrestomathies). By date
	Cf. CN510+ Latin inscriptions
	Cf. PA6119.A1+ Roman literature
2510.A5-Z	Other (Treatises, studies, etc.)
2530	Faliscan (Table P-PZ15)
2540	Praenestian (Table P-PZ15)

PA1-3049

	Ancient languages and dialects of Italy
	Italic dialects -- Continued
(2550)	Sicel
	see P1074
	Vulgar Latin
2601-2699	Language (Table P-PZ4)
2701-2748	Literature (Table P-PZ22)
	Post classical Latin see PA2305+
	Medieval Latin (to ca. 1350 or 1500)
2801-2899	Language (Table P-PZ4)
	Literature
	see PA8035; PA8112; PA8122; PA8200+
	Modern Latin (ca. 1350 or 1550 to ...)
	Class here treatises confined to modern Latin; chiefly works
	devoted to errors, idioms, translations of modern works, etc.
2901-2905	Language (Table P-PZ9)
	Literature
	see PA8040; PA8052; PA8114+ PA8123; PA8450+
	Modern Latin (19th century-)
	Class here treatises, textbooks, phrase books, etc., dealing with
	Latin as a living (universal) language
2911-2915	Language (Table P-PZ9)
	Literature
	see PA8043; PA8117; PA8450+

	Classical literature
(3000)	Generalities: Serial publications, etc.
	see PA1+
	Cf. PA3003
(3000.5)	Theory. Methodology
	see PA35+
	Literary history
3001	General works. Treatises
	Cf. PN611+ Ancient literature
3002.A-.Z3	Compends. By author, A-Z
3002.Z5	Outlines. Tables. Quizzes. Charts
3003	Collected essays, studies, etc.
3004	Single lectures, addresses, pamphlets, etc.
	Biography of Greek and Roman authors
3005	Collected
	Cf. DE7 Greco-Roman world
	Individual Greek authors see PA3818+
	Individual Roman authors see PA6202+
3006	Literary landmarks. Homes and haunts of authors
(3006.9)	Iconography
	see N7586+
(3007)	Women authors. Literary relations of women
	see PA3067; PA6017
3009	Relations to history, civilization, culture, etc.
	Cf. B178 Philosophy
	Cf. DE71 Greco-Roman world
(3009.7)	Representation in art
	see N5605+ NK3835+ NK4645+
3010	Relations of Greek to Roman (or ancient Oriental) literature
	Cf. PA3070
(3011)	Relations to modern literature: influence, etc.
	see PN883; PQ143.A3; etc.
3012	Translations (as subject)
3013	History of literary criticism, study and appreciation of classical literature
	Class here treatises confined to literature proper, especially from the esthetic point of view
	For general discussions of the value of classical education see LC1001+
	For the history of the philological study of literature see PA51+
	Cf. PN883 Comparative literature
3014.A-Z	Special topics, A-Z
	Class here treatises dealing with subjects of a more general nature relating to classical or Greek literature in general
3014.A4	Ambiguity
3014.A5	Anonymous

PA1-3049

Literary history
 Special topics, A-Z -- Continued
3014.A87	Authorship
3014.C38	Catharsis
3014.C6	Comic, The
3014.D4	Debates and debating
3014.E7	Erotic literature
	Falsehood see PA3014.T76
3014.F6	Forgeries
3014.G47	Gesture
3014.I55	Imitation
3014.I7	Irony
3014.L3	Laments
	Landmarks see PA3006
3014.L37	Letters
3014.L47	Light
3014.L49	Literary form
3014.M47	Metaphor
3014.M66	Monologue
3014.N37	Narration
3014.O64	Openings (Rhetoric)
	Parody see PA3033
3014.P3	Patronage
3014.P4	Personification
3014.P43	Pessimism
3014.P6	Plagiarism
3014.P65	Politics
3014.P67	Portraiture
3014.P74	Prejudices
3014.Q7	Quoting (Mode of)
3014.R4	Realism
3014.R45	Religion
3014.R65	Romanticism
3014.S47	Sex
3014.S6	Society
3014.S8	Spiritualism
3014.S96	Sympathy
3014.T66	Tragic, The
3014.T7	Triads
3014.T76	Truthfulness and falsehood

Literary history -- Continued
3015.A-Z   Knowledge, treatment, and conception of special subjects, A-Z
                               Class here works on the treatment of special topics by several
                                   authors of classical or Greek literature in general
                               For works limited to the treatment of special topics in specific
                                   forms such as poetry or drama see the form
                               For works on the treatment of special topics in Roman literature
                                   see PA6029+
3015.A37   Agriculture
3015.A55   Amazons
3015.A58   Anger
3015.A8   Assyria and Babylonia
3015.A83   Astronomy
3015.A96   Autobiography
3015.B35   Bathing customs
3015.B38   Battles
3015.B48   Birthdays
3015.B53   Black Sea Lowland (Ukraine)
3015.B56   Body, Human
                           Boeotia (Greece) see PA3015.V64
3015.C5   Characterization. Characters (General)
3015.C52   Children
3015.C54   Cities
3015.C6   Colors
3015.C62   Consolation
3015.C63   Cooks
3015.C66   Counselling
3015.C75   Crime and criminals
3015.C78   Crying
3015.D43   Death
                           Dining see PA3015.D56
3015.D56   Dinners and dining
3015.D73   Dreams
3015.E28   Earthquakes
3015.E35   Egypt
3015.E46   Emotions
3015.E53   Enemies (Persons)
3015.E94   Eye
3015.F3   Fate and fatalism
3015.F43   Fear
3015.F63   Food
3015.F7   Friendship
3015.G44   Geography
3015.G48   Ghosts
3015.G6   Gods
3015.G7   Greece

PA1-3049

	Literary history
	Knowledge, treatment, and conception of special subjects, A-Z -- Continued
3015.H43	Heroes
3015.H56	Homecoming
3015.H58	Homosexuality
3015.H59	Honor
3015.H6	Hope
3015.H77	Human beings
3015.H8	Humor
3015.I44	Illegitimacy
3015.I55	India
3015.I62	Invective
3015.J43	Jealousy
	"Know thyself" see PA3015.S4
3015.L67	Love
3015.L68	Loyalty
3015.M34	Manual labor
3015.M4	Mental illness
3015.M64	Money
3015.M87	Music
	Nature
3015.N3	General works
3015.N4A-.N4Z	Special. By subject, A-Z
3015.N4A6	Animals (General)
3015.N4B4	Bees
3015.N4B5	Birds
3015.N4D48	Dew
3015.N4D63	Dogs
3015.N4F5	Fish
3015.N4G63	Goats
3015.N4I62	Insects
3015.N4S47	Serpents
3015.N4W64	Wolves
3015.O3	Odors
3015.O43	Old age
3015.O8	Outdoor life
3015.P28	Pastoral literature
3015.P4	Philosophy
3015.P48	Physicians
3015.P62	Poetics
3015.P63	Political science
3015.P78	Psychology
3015.P8	Punishment
	Religion. Mythology. Hero legend
3015.R4	General works
3015.R5A-.R5Z	Special. By subject, A-Z

Literary history
Knowledge, treatment, and conception of special subjects, A-Z
Religion. Mythology. Hero legend
Special. By subject, A-Z -- Continued

3015.R5A37	Achilles
3015.R5A385	Actaeon
3015.R5A4	Agamemnon
3015.R5A53	Aion
3015.R5A6	Amphiaraus
3015.R5A62	Andromeda
3015.R5A64	Antigone
3015.R5A7	Aphrodite
3015.R5A75	Argonauts
3015.R5A8	Athene
3015.R5C37	Cassandra
3015.R5C58	Circe
3015.R5D35	Danaus
3015.R5D5	Dionysus
3015.R5E34	Echo
3015.R5E87	Euthymos
3015.R5H37	Helen of Troy
3015.R5H4	Heracles
3015.R5I63	Iphigenia
3015.R5K8	Kreon
3015.R5M44	Medea
3015.R5M87	Muses
3015.R5O25	Oedipus
3015.R5O7	Orestes
3015.R5O82	Orpheus
3015.R5P45	Pelops
3015.R5P54	Phoenix (Fabulous bird)
3015.R5P74	Priapus
3015.R5P75	Procne
3015.R5P76	Prometheus
3015.R5T47	Theseus
3015.R5T57	Tiresias
3015.R5V67	Voyages to the otherworld
3015.S35	Science
3015.S4	Self-knowledge
3015.S48	Sicily (Italy)
3015.S52	Silence
3015.S55	Slaves
3015.S58	Sleep
3015.S69	Sound
3015.S74	Speech
3015.S8	State

PA1-3049

	Literary history
	Knowledge, treatment, and conception of special subjects, A-Z -- Continued
3015.S82	Statues
3015.S84	Stepmothers
3015.S94	Suicide
3015.T4	Technology
3015.T6	Time
3015.U85	Utopias
3015.V57	Vision
3015.V64	Voiōtia (Greece). Boeotia (Greece)
3015.W46	War
3015.W48	Weaving
3015.W49	Wine
3015.W5	Wisdom
3015.W65	Women
(3016)	Knowledge, and treatment, of people, classes, etc.
	see PA3015
(3017)	Textual criticism, interpretation, etc.
	see PA3520+
	Cf. PA35+
	Christian literature see BR67
	Poetry (including history of poetry and drama)
3019	General works
3020	General special
3021	Special topics
(3021.9)	Textual criticism, interpretation, etc.
	see PA3537+
3022.A-Z	Special forms, A-Z
3022.B8	Bucolic. Pastoral
3022.D47	Descriptive
3022.D5	Didactic
3022.E6	Epic
3022.E62	Epigram. Epitaph
	Cf. CN
	Fable see PA3032
3022.G66	Gnomic
3022.I35	Iambic
	Lyric see PA3019+
	Pastoral see PA3022.B8
3022.P75	Priamel
3022.S28	Satire
	Drama
	Cf. PA3131+ Greek literature
3024	General works
3025	General special.
3026	Special topics

	Literary history
	Drama -- Continued
3027	Tragedy
3028	Comedy
3029	Other
	Including mimus, pantomimus, etc.
(3029.9)	Textual criticism, interpretation, etc.
	see PA3545+ PA6143
	Various literary forms (in prose and verse)
	Dialogue
3030	General works
3031	Special topics
3032	Fable. Myth
	Cf. PA3858 Aesopus
	Cf. PA6566 Phaedrus
	Cf. PN980 Folk literature
3033	Wit and humor. Satire. Parody
	Cf. PA3107.5 Epic parody
3034	Other
	Prose
3035	General works
3036	General special
3037	Special topics
3038	Oratory. Rhetoric
3040	Fiction
3042	Letters. Letter-writing as literature
3043	Biography. Autobiography
(3044.A-Z)	Other, A-Z
(3044.G4)	Geography
	see G82+
(3044.H5)	History
	see DE8+ DF211+ DG205+
(3044.M3)	Mathematics
	see QA22
(3044.M4)	Medicine
	see R135
(3044.M5)	Military science
	see U29; U33; U35
(3044.M9)	Mythography
(3044.P3)	Paradoxography
(3044.P5)	Philosophy
	see B110+ B171+ B265+ etc.
(3044.P8)	Proverbs
	see PN6410+
(3044.9)	Textual criticism, interpretation, etc.
	see PA3556+

PA1-3049

(3049)   Textual criticism, interpretation, etc.
                       see PA3520+
          Collections see PA3300+

	Greek literature
	Class here Greek literature from ancient (classical) times to ca. 600 A.D.
	For Byzantine and modern Greek literature see PA5000+
(3050)	Generalities; serial publications, etc.
	see PA1+
(3050.5)	Theory. Methodology
	see PA35+
	Literary history
	General works. Treatises. Compends
	For works restricted to poetry and drama see PA3092+
(3051.A4)	Ancient
	see the individual authors, e.g. Diogenes Laërtius, Suidas, Photius
3051.A7-Z	Latin (Modern)
	English
3052	Treatises
3054	Compends
3055	French
3057	German
3059	Other
3060	Outlines. Quizzes. Tables. Charts
3061	Collected essays. Lectures. Studies
3062	Single lectures. Addresses. Pamphlets
	Biography of Greek authors
3064	Collected
	For treatises on several authors of like name see the authors, e.g. PA3998.H27, Heraclides
	Individual authors
	see the authors
(3065)	Literary landmarks
	see PA3006
(3066)	Iconography
	see N7586+
3067	Woman authors. Literary relations of women
(3069)	Relations to history, civilization, culture (in general)
	see PA3009
3070	Relations to ancient nations and countries
	Including works on Greek literature written (or translated or quoted) by non-Greek writers.
	Cf. PA3010 Relation of Greek to Roman literature
3071	Relations to modern literature: Influence, translations (as subject), etc.
3071.9	Translations (as subject)
(3072)	History of literary criticism, appreciation and study
	see PA3013

PA3050-4505

	Literary history -- Continued
(3074)	Special topics
	see PA3014
(3075)	Treatment and conception of special subjects
	see PA3015
(3076)	Treatment of special classes
	see PA3015
	Textual criticism, interpretation, etc.
	see PA3520+
	By period
3079	Origins (to ca. 500 B.C.)
	Classic (to ca. 300 or 31 B.C., or 600 A.D.)
	see PA3051+
	Hellenistic (Alexandrian) 300-31 B.C. (or 100 A.D.)
3081	General works
3082	General special
3083	Special topics
3084.A-Z	By form, A-Z
3084.C64	Concrete poetry
3084.F53	Fiction
(3085)	Textual criticism, interpretation, etc.
	see PA3527
	Roman, 31 B.C. to 324 (or 600) A.D.
	For Christian literature see BR67
3086	General works
3087	General special
3088	Special topics
3089.A-Z	By form, A-Z
3089.P64	Poetry
(3090)	Textual criticism, interpretation, etc.
	see PA3531
	Poetry
	Class here works on Greek poetry and works on Greek poetry and drama treated collectively
	General works. Treatises
	Ancient (Greek and Latin)
	see PA3051
	Modern
3092.A2	Latin
3092.A5-Z	English
3093	Other
	Outlines. Quizzes. Tables. Charts see PA3060
	Collected essays. Lectures. Studies see PA3061; PA3092+
	Single lectures. Addresses. Pamphlets see PA3062
	Biography of Greek poets
	Collected see PA3064

PA3050-4505

	Literary history
	Poetry -- Continued
3118.A-Z	Special forms, A-Z
	Bucolic see PA3120.A+
3118.C27	Carmina consolatoria
3118.C29	Carmina figurata
	Carmina popularia see PA3109
3118.D58	Dithyrambus
3118.E65	Epithalamion. Hymenaeus
3118.H8	Hymnus
3118.H87	Hyporchema
3118.N66	Nomos
3118.O3	Oda
3118.P3	Paean
3118.P42	Parthenia
3118.P76	Prosodia
3118.S36	Scolia
3118.T54	Threnoi
	Bucolic. Pastoral
3120.A-.Z3	General works
3120.Z5	General special
3120.Z6	Special topics
3122	Didactic
	Cf. PA3032 Fable. Myth
3123	Epigram
3125	Gnomic poetry
(3129)	Textual criticism, interpretation, etc.
	see PA3537+
	Drama
	General
	Including treatises confined to the classic period, and those confined to tragedy
3131	Treatises
3132	Compends. Outlines, etc.
3133	Collected essays. Lectures, etc.
3134	Single lectures. Addresses
	By period
	see PA3135; PA3185+
	Special topics
3135	Origin
3136	Other
(3157)	Language. Style. Versification
	see PA3547+
(3158)	Versification
	see PA3550
(3159)	Textual criticism, interpretation, etc.
	see PA3545+

	Literary history
	Drama -- Continued
3160	Satyr play
	Comedy
3161	General works
	Including treatises confined to the Old Comedy
3163	Minor works. Single lectures, essays, etc.
	Special topics
(3164)	Origin ("Comus")
	see PA3161
(3165)	Sicilian (Dorian) comedy
	see PA3161
3166	Other
3185	Middle comedy
	New comedy
3187	General works
3188	Special topics
3191	Mimus. Pantomimus
(3199)	Textual criticism, interpretation, etc.
	see PA3553
	Theater and stage
	Class here treatises on the Greek theater, or on the Greek and Roman theater treated collectively
	For treatises dealing mainly or entirely with the Roman theater see PA6073+
	General works
3201.A2	Early works to 1800 (or 1870)
3201.A5-Z	Later 1800- (1870-)
3202	General special
3203	Special topics
3238	Modern representation of ancient drama
	Various literary forms (in prose or verse)
3245	Dialogue
3247	Fable. Myth
3249	Wit and humor. Satire. "Silli." Parody
3251	Other
	Prose
3255	General works
3256	General special
3257	Special topics
(3259)	Technique. Language. Style
	see PA3255
(3261)	Textual criticism, interpretation, etc.
	see PA3556+
	Oratory
3263	General works
3264	Special topics

PA3050-4505

	Literary history
	Prose -- Continued
3265	Rhetoric
3267	Fiction
(3269)	Letters (Letter-writing as literature)
	see PA3042
3271	Biography. Autobiography
3273.A-Z	Other special, A-Z
(3273.A3)	Agriculture
	see S429
(3273.A5)	Astrology
	see QB25
(3273.A6)	Astronomy
	see QB21+
(3273.G4)	Geography
	see G82+
(3273.G7)	Grammatical science
	see PA53
(3273.H5)	History
	see DE9+ DF211+
(3273.L4)	Lexicography
	see PA53
(3273.M3)	Mathematics
	see QA22
(3273.M5)	Medicine
	see R135
(3273.M6)	Metrical and musical science
	see PA53; ML
(3273.M7)	Metrology
	see QC83+
(3273.M8)	Military science
	see U29; U33
3273.M9	Mythography
(3273.N3)	Natural science
	see QH15
3273.P3	Paradoxography
3273.P4	Paroemiography
	Cf. PN6413 Ancient Greek proverbs
(3273.P5)	Pharmacy
	see RS63
(3273.P6)	Philosophy
	see B108+ B171+ B265+ etc.
(3273.R5)	Rhetoric
	see PA3265
3285	Folk literature
	Cf. PA3109 Folk songs

Literary history -- Continued
  Local literature, by region, island, place, etc.
    see classification by form or period, e.g. Attic drama, PA3131+
      Alexandrian poetry, PA3081+
  Collections
    Papyri. Ostraka
      Facsimiles (and originals if classified)

3300.A1	Collections of miscellaneous contents and provenance
3300.A2A-.A2Z	By place where found, A-Z
3300.A3	Literary papyri (miscellaneous)
3300.A4	Literary papyri (single authors)
3300.A5A-.A5Z	Papyri by subject (collected). By subject, A-Z
3300.A6A-.A6Z	Papyri by subject (single). By subject, A-Z
	Latin papyri
3300.L1	Collections of miscellaneous contents and provenance
3300.L2A-.L2Z	By place where found, A-Z
3300.L3	Literary papyri (miscellaneous)
3300.L4	Literary papyri (single authors)
3300.L5A-.L5Z	Papyri by subject (collected). By subject, A-Z
3300.L6A-.L6Z	Papyri by subject (single). By subject, A-Z
3300.O1	Ostraka
	Typographical reproductions and editions
3301	Collections (comprehensive)
	By country and place where preserved (or by owner)
	Class here editions of miscellaneous papyri, published by the several institutions or private libraries who own them.
	For publications of literary papyri see PA3317+
	For particular papyri see PA3323
3303	Egypt
3304	Great Britain and colonies
3305	United States. Canada
3306	France. Belgium. French Switzerland
3308	Germany. Austria. German Switzerland
3309	Holland. Scandinavian countries
3310	Italy
3311	Spain. Latin America
3312	Greece. Balkan Peninsula
3313	Russia
3314.A-Z	Other countries, A-Z
3314.P6	Poland
3315.A-Z	By place where found, A-Z
3316.A-Z	Selections. School editions. By editor, A-Z
	Literary papyri
	Herculanean rolls
3317.A1	Collections and selections. By date

	Collections
	Papyri. Ostraka
	Typographical reproductions and editions
	Literary papyri
	Herculanean rolls -- Continued
3317.A2A-.A2Z	Separate papyri. By editor, A-Z
	For papyri limited to one author see the author, e.g. PA4271.P3, Philodemus
	Criticism, interpretation, etc.
3317.A3-.Z3	General
3317.Z5	Grammatical. Syntactical
3317.Z8	Lexicographical: Glossaries, indices, treatises, etc.
	Other literary papyri
	Collections and selections
3318.A-Z	By place or institution where kept, A-Z
	By form
3319.A2	Poetry
3319.A4	Prose (general or miscellaneous). By date
3319.A5	Oratory. By date
3319.A6-.Z3	Other, A-Z (by subject or form, and date)
3319.B55	Biography
3319.H5	History
3319.L4	Letters
(3319.Z5)	Particular authors
	see the authors
3323	Single papyri
	For papyri limited to one author see the author, e.g. PA4008.H2, Herondas
	Papyri in other languages
3331	Bilingual (or trilingual)
3335	Latin
(3338)	Other languages
	Egyptian
	see PJ1650+
	Coptic
	see PJ2195+
	Hebrew
	see PJ
	Aramaic
	see PJ5201+
	Syriac
	see PJ5601+
	Arabic
	see PJ
	Criticism, interpretation, etc. (Papyrology)
3339	Periodicals. Serials. Collections of treatises by various authors

	Collections
	Papyri. Ostraka
	Criticism, interpretation, etc. (Papyrology) -- Continued
	Treatises
3341	General
3342	General special. Minor. Popular
3343	Special topics
	Language
3367	General works
3369	Glossaries, vocabularies, etc.
	Ostraka
3371.A1	Collections. By date
3371.A5-Z	Criticism, interpretation, etc.
	Inscriptions
	Collections of texts
	see CN350+
3391	Grammar and other linguistic studies
	For studies of dialects see PA500+
	Printed editions
	Including "classical" collections (Greek and Roman). Roman
	authors in separate series are classified in PA6101+
3401	Early (previous to the Bibliotheca Teubneriana, 1850-)
(3402-3404)	Bibliotheca Teubneriana (Greek authors)
	Collections and selections (Prose and poetry)
(3402.A1)	General and miscellaneous
	Poetry. Drama
(3402.A2)	General and miscellaneous
(3402.A3)	Selections, extracts, etc.
	Special
(3402.A5)	Anthologia graeca
(3402.B8)	Bucolic poets
(3402.D5)	Didactic poetry
(3402.E7)	Epic poets
	Drama
(3402.Z6)	Tragedy
(3402.Z7)	Comedy
	Prose
(3403.A1)	General and miscellaneous
(3403.A3)	Selections, extracts, etc.
(3403.A5-Z)	By subject (or title) and date
(3403.A8)	Astronomy (Scriptores astronomi)
(3403.B5)	Biography (Scriptores biographi)
(3403.C5)	Chronica
(3403.E3)	Scriptores ecclesiastici
(3403.E6)	Epistulae (Scriptores epistularum)
(3403.E8)	Scriptores erotici
(3403.F3)	Fabulae romanenses

PA3050-4505

	Collections
	Printed editions
	Bibliotheca Teubneriana (Greek authors)
	Collections and selections (Prose and poetry)
	Prose
	By subject (or title) and date -- Continued
(3403.G3)	Geography (Scriptores geographi)
(3403.G5)	Geoponica (Scriptores geoponicorum)
(3403.G8)	Grammar (Scriptores grammatici)
(3403.H4)	History (Scriptores historici)
(3403.H5)	Historia Alexandri (Scriptores historiarum Alexandri M.)
(3403.H8)	Historia byzantina (Scriptores historiae byzantinae)
(3403.I5)	Inscriptions
(3403.M3)	Mathematics (Scriptores mathematici)
(3403.M4)	Medicine (Scriptores medici)
(3403.M5)	Metrics (or Metrics and music) (Scriptores metrici et musici)
(3403.M6)	Metrology (Scriptores metrologi)
(3403.M7)	Military science (Scriptores rei militaris)
(3403.M8)	Music (Scriptores musici)
(3403.M9)	Mythography (Scriptores mythographi)
(3403.N3)	Natural science (Scriptores rerum naturalium et paradoxorum)
(3403.O5)	Orators
(3403.O8)	Origo Constantinopolis
(3403.P3)	Paroemiographers (Scriptores paroemiorum)
(3403.P4)	"Patres ecclesiastici" see (PA3403.E3)
(3403.P5)	Philosophy (Scriptores philosophi)
(3403.P6)	Physiognomic writers (Scriptores physiognomici)
(3403.P7)	"Prophetarum vitae"
(3403.R5)	Rhetores
(3404.A-Z)	Individual authors, A-Z
3405.A-Z	Other collections. By title, A-Z
	Loeb classical library see PA3611+
(3405.S8)	Scriptorum classicorum bibliotheca oxoniensis
	Collections of poetry and prose
	Poetry
	Including drama
(3405.S8A1)	General and miscellaneous
(3405.S8A11-.S8A19)	Special, by title or catchword title, A-Z, successive Cutter number, and date
	e.g.
(3405.S8A13)	Anthologia graeca
(3405.S8A19)	Drama
	Prose

	Collections
	Printed editions
	Other collections. By title, A-Z
	Scriptorum classicorum bibliotheca oxoniensis
	Collections of poetry and prose
	Prose -- Continued
(3405.S8A2)	General and miscellaneous
(3405.S8A21-.S8A39)	Special, by title or catchword title, successive
	Cutter number, and date
	e.g.
(3405.S8A25)	Historic writers
(3405.S8A4-.S8Z)	Individual authors, A-Z
	School editions (Serial publications)
3411	American
3412	English
3413	French
3414	German
3415	Other
	Selections. Anthologies
	For textbooks see PA260
3416.A1	Ancient and medieval
3416.A2	Early to 1800/1850
3416.A5Z3	Later, 1800/1850+
3416.Z5A-.Z5Z	By subject, A-Z, and date
3416.Z5A7	Art
3416.Z5E7	Erotic literature
3416.Z5G7	Greece
3416.Z5L6	Love
3416.Z5P4	Peace
(3417)	Quotations
	see PN6080
3421.A-Z	Special collections, A-Z
3421.A5A-.A5Z	Anecdota. By editor or title
3421.A5B6	Boissonade. Anecdota graeca
3421.A5B7	Boissonade. Anecdota nova
3421.A5C6	Cramer (Oxford manuscripts)
3421.A5C7	Cramer (Paris manuscripts)
3421.A5P3	Palaiokappa, Konstantinos. Violarium
3421.A5P4	Criticism
3421.A5S3	Schoell and Studemund. Anecdota varia
3421.A5V5	Villoison. Anecdota graeca
3421.G8	Graeco-Jewish writers
(3421.J8)	Judaism
	For Theodore Reinach's Textes d'auteurs grecs et romains relatifs au judaisme see DS102
	By period
	Classic (to 300 or 31 B.C. or 600 A.D.) see PA3401+

PA3050-4505

	Collections
	Printed editions
	By period -- Continued
	Hellenistic (Alexandrian, 300 to 31 B.C., or 100 A.D.)
3423.A-.Z3	General
3423.Z5	Selections. Anthologies
	For textbooks see PA260
3424.A-Z	By form, A-Z
	Roman (31 B.C. or 100 A.D. to 324 or 600 A.D.)
	For Christian literature see BR60+
3427.A-.Z3	General
3427.Z5	Selections. Anthologies
	For textbooks see PA260
3428.A-Z	By form, A-Z
	Poetry
	General
	Including collections confined to the classic period, up to 300 or 31 B.C.
3431.A2	Early to 1800 or 1850/1870. By date
3431.A5-Z	Later, 1800 or 1850/1870- . By editor, A-Z
3432	Collections of fragments
	Selections. Anthologies
3433	General
	For school editions see PA260
3435.A-Z	Special. By subject, catchword title or title, A-Z
3435.L6	Love poetry
3435.P6	Places, Poetry of
3435.P65	Poetry
	By period
	Origins
	see PA3437+
	Classic
	see PA3431+
	Hellenistic (Alexandrian) see PA3423+
	Roman see PA3427+
	Christian
	see BR60+
	Epic. Epic-didactic
	Cf. PA3449.A2+ Didactic poetry
3437	General
3438	Fragments (including Fragments of the cyclic poets)
3439	Selections. Anthologies
	Hellenistic (Alexandrian) see PA3423+
	Roman see PA3427+
3441	Parodies
	Cf. PA3469
	Lyric poetry

PA3050-4505

	Collections
	Printed editions
	Poetry
	Lyric poetry -- Continued
	General
3443.A2	Early to ca. 1800. By date
3443.A5-Z	Later (1800+). By editor, A-Z
3445.A-Z	Special, A-Z
3445.D5	Dithyrambus
3445.E6	Elegiac
3447	Women poets
	Didactic poetry
	Cf. PA3437+ Epic-didactic poetry
3449.A2	General and miscellaneous. By date
3449.A5-Z	Particular
3449.G4	Geography
(3449.O6)	Oracula
	see PA4253.O8+
(3449.P5)	Philosophic poetry
	see PA3501+
	Minor forms
(3451)	Bucolic (Theocritus, Moschus, Bion)
	For collections of the three poets, translations, and
	criticisms of their poems see PA4442+
3453	Gnomic poetry
3455	Mimi
	Cf. PA3465.A2 Comedy fragments
	Epigram
3457.A1	Comprehensive editions
3457.A5-Z	Other collections. By editor, A-Z
	Anthologia graeca
	Ancient collections (lost)
	Medieval collections (Anthologia Planudea.
	Anthologia palatina)
(3458.A1)	Manuscripts (facsimiles)
	see Z114
3458.A2	Editions. By date
3458.A3	Selections. By date
3458.A4-.A59	Particular books. By editor, A-Z (successive Cutter
	number)
	Translations
	see PA3623.A5, etc.
	Criticism, interpretation, etc.
3459.A-.Z3	General. Special topics
3459.Z5	Textual. Interpretation of detached passages
3459.Z6	Grammatical. Syntactical
3459.Z7	Metrical

	Collections
	Printed editions
	Poetry
	Minor forms
	Anthologia graeca
	Criticism, interpretation, etc. -- Continued
3459.Z8	Lexicographical: Glossaries, indices, treatises, etc.
	Drama ("Poetae scenici")
3461.A-Z	General. By editor, A-Z
	Including collections of both tragedies and comedies
3462	Fragments of tragedies
3463	Selections. Anthologies
3464	Satyr play
	Comedies
3465.A1	Editions. By date
3465.A2	Fragments, etc. By date
3466	New comedy
3469.A-Z	Various literary forms (in prose or verse), A-Z
3469.C48	Chreiai
3469.D52	Dialogue
3469.F32	Fable. Myth
3469.P37	Parody. Silli ("Poetae sillographi")
	Cf. PA3441 Parodies in poetic form
	Cf. PA3465 Comedy
	Proverbs see PA3499.P3
3469.S3	Satire
3469.W5	Wit and humor
	Prose
3473	General
	Including collections confined to the classic period, up to 300 or 31 B.C.
	Selections. Anthologies
3474	General
	For school editions see PA260
3475.A-Z	Special. By subject, catchword title, or title, A-Z
	Cf. PA3479+
3475.W5	Wit and humor
	Oratory
	Cf. PA3484 Rhetoric
3479.A1	General. By date
	Including editions of the Oratores attici
(3479.A2)	Oratores attici
	see PA3479.A1
	Selections. Anthologies
3481	General and miscellaneous
	For school editions see PA260

Collections
    Printed editions
        Oratory
           Selections. Anthologies -- Continued

3482	Special
	Including funeral orations
	For orations selected from historical, philosophical,
	rhetorical, etc., writers, see those writers
3484	Rhetoric (Rhetores)
	Other prose writers
	Subarrange by subject (Latin title) A-Z, and date
3487.A-.H	A-H
3487.A4	Scriptores alchemistae
3487.A6	Scriptores astrologi
3487.A8	Scriptores astronomi
3487.B5	Scriptores biographi (et commentariorum)
(3487.D7)	Scriptores doxographi
	see PA3502
(3487.E2)	Scriptores ecclesiastici
	see BR60+
3487.E4	Scriptores epistularum
3487.E7	Scriptores erotici
	Scriptores fabularum
	see PA3469
3487.G3	Scriptores geographi
3487.G5	Scriptores geoponicorum
	Scriptores grammatici
3487.G6-.G69	Previous to 1878
3487.G7-.G79	1878-
	Scriptores historici
3488	General (Comprehensive collections)
3489	Selected authors
	Including Historici graeci minores
3490	Fragments
3491	Selections. Anthologies
	For school editions see PA260
	By period
3492	Early to ca. 300 B.C.
3493	History of Alexander the Great ("Scriptores
	historiarum Alexandri Magni")
3494	Later to ca. 500 A.D.
3496.A-Z	By locality, A-Z
3499.H-.P	H-Ph
3499.I6	Scriptores rerum inventarum
3499.L4	Scriptores lexicographi
3499.M2	Scriptores mathematici

PA3050-4505

Collections
Printed editions
Other prose writers
H-Ph -- Continued

(3499.M3)	Scriptores medici
	see R126.A1
3499.M5	Scriptores metrici (et musici)
3499.M6	Scriptores metrologi
3499.M7	Scriptores rei militaris
3499.M8	Scriptores musici
3499.M9	Scriptores mythologi
3499.N3	Scriptores rerum naturalium et paradoxorum
3499.P3	Scriptores paroemiorum (proverbiorum)
	Scriptores philosophi
3501	General (Comprehensive collections)
3502	General special. Selected authors
	Including scriptores doxographi (collections of philosophical doctrines)
3503	Fragments
3504	Anthologies
	For school editions see PA260
3505	By period
	Including ante-Socratic (pre-Sophistic) period
3507.A-Z	Special schools, A-Z
3507.E7	Epicureans
3507.S7	Stoics
3509	By subject
	Cf. PA3515.P5 Scriptores physiognomici
3515.P-Z	Ph-Z
	Scriptores physici see PA3499.N3
3515.P5	Scriptores physiognomici
3516.A-Z	Anonymous works. By title, A-Z
	Class here works not otherwise provided for in PA3818+
3516.A7	Ars rhetorica
	Ascribed to Cornutus by J. Graeven. From the first edition by Seguier de St. Brisson, the author is known as Anonymus Seguerianus
	Batrachomyomachia (Battle of the frogs and mice) see PA4023.B3
	Certamen Homeri et Hesiodi see PA4009.Z7
	Chionos epistolai see PA3948.C33
	Comparatio Menandri et Philistionis see PA4247
	Periplus maris erythraei see PA4267.P14
	Periplus ponti euxini see PA4267.P143

Criticism, interpretation, etc.
  Class here textual criticism, interpretation, etc. of Greek, or Greek
    and Roman authors
  For works devoted primarily to Roman authors see PA6141+
  General. General special. Special topics
    see PA3001+
  Textual. Interpretation of detached passages (poetry and
    prose)
3520   Early, to 1800
3521   1800-
3523   Language. Style
                Cf. PA181+ Classical philology
                Cf. PA401+ Greek philology
3524   Grammatical. Syntactical
                Cf. PA111+ Classical philology
                Cf. PA251+ Greek philology
3525   Lexicographical
                Cf. PA431+ Greek philology
  By period
    Early and classical (to ca. 300 B.C. or 31 B.C. or 600 A.D.)
      see PA3520+
    Hellenistic (Alexandrian, ca. 300 B.C. to 31 B.C., or 100
      A.D.)
      For general, general special, and special topics see PA3081+

3527.A-.Z3   Textual. Interpretation of detached passages
                  Cf. PA3081+ Greek literary history
(3527.Z5)   Grammatical. Syntactical
                  see PA600+
(3527.Z6)   Metrical and rhythmical
                  see PA666; PA766; PA866
(3527.Z8)   Lexicographical: Glossaries, indices, treatises, etc.
                  see PA681; PA781; PA881
    Roman (31 B.C., or 100 A.D. to 600)
3531.A-.Z3   Textual. Interpretation of detached passages
  Poetry
    General. General special. Special topics
      see PA3092+
    Textual. Interpretation of detached passages
3537.A2   Early, to 1800/1850
3537.A5-Z   1800/1850-
3539   Language. Style
3541   Grammatical. Syntactical
                Cf. PA251+ Greek philology
                Cf. PA111+ Classical philology
3542   Metrical and rhythmical
                Cf. PA185+ Classical philology
                Cf. PA411+ Greek philology

	Criticism, interpretation, etc.
	Poetry -- Continued
3543	Lexicographical: Glossaries, indices, treatises, etc.
	Cf. PA431+ Greek philology
	Drama
	General. General special. Special topics see PA3131+
	Textual. Interpretation of detached passages
3545.A2	Early to 1800
3545.A5-Z	1800-
3547	Language. Style
3549	Grammatical. Syntactical
	Cf. PA251+ Greek philology
	Cf. PA111+ Classical philology
3550	Metrical and rhythmical
	Cf. PA185+ Classical philology
	Cf. PA411+ Greek philology
3551	Lexicographical: Glossaries, indices, treatises, etc.
	Cf. PA431+ Greek philology
	Comedy
	General. General special. Special topics
	see PA3161+
3553.A-.Z3	Textual. Interpretation of detached passages
3553.Z5	Language. Style
3553.Z6	Grammatical. Syntactical
3553.Z7	Metrical and rhythmical
3553.Z8	Lexicographical: Glossaries, indices, treatises, etc.
	Prose
	General. General special. Special topics
	see PA3255+
3556	Textual. Interpretation of detached passages
3557	Language. Style
	For general treatises see PA181+ PA401+
	For rhythm in Greek prose see PA190; PA419
3558	Grammatical. Syntactical
	For general treatises see PA111+ PA251+
(3559)	Lexicographical: Glossaries, indices, treatises, etc.
	see PA431+
	Oratores. Oratores attici
	General. General special. Special topics see PA3263+
3561	Textual criticism. Interpretation of detached passages
3562	Language. Style
3563	Grammatical. Syntactical
	Lexicographical: Glossaries, indices, treatises, etc.
3564.A2	Treatises
3564.A5-Z	Indices, glossaries, etc.
	Translations
3601	Polyglot collections and selections

	Translations -- Continued
3602	Modern Greek
	Latin
3603	Ancient
	Modern
3604.A1	Collections and selections. By date
3604.A3	Poetry
3604.A5	Drama
3604.A8	Prose
(3604.A9)	Individual authors
	see the author
	English
	General and miscellaneous
3606	A-Loe
(3611-3612)	Loeb classical library
(3611.A1-.A39)	Poetry
(3611.A4-.A69)	Drama
(3611.A7-.A99)	Prose
(3612)	Individual authors
3617.L-Z	Loec-Z
3621	Anthologies. Selections. Specimens
	Poetry
	General and miscellaneous
3622.A2A-.A2Z	By various translators (by editor, A-Z)
3622.A5-Z	By individual translators, A-Z
	By form, A-Z
3623.A5	Anthologia graeca
	Bucolic
	Cf. PA4443 Theocritus
	Elegiac and iambic
3623.E5	Epic
	Epigram see PA3623.A5
	Gnomic
	Hymns
	Lyric see PA3622.A2+
	Scolia
3624.A-Z	By subject, A-Z
3624.E75	Erotic poetry
3624.H64	Homosexuality, Male
3624.L7	Love
3625	Women poets
	Drama
	General, or Tragedy alone
	Collected or selected plays
3626.A2A-.A2Z	By various translators. By editor, or date
3626.A5-Z	By individual translators, A-Z
3627	Selections: Extracts, specimens, etc.

PA3050-4505

	Translations
	English
	Drama
	General, or Tragedy alone -- Continued
3628	Stories, paraphrases, etc.
3629	Comedy
	Prose
3631	General and miscellaneous
3632	Anthologies. Selections, etc.
	Oratory
3633	Collections
3634	Selected orations
3637.A-Z	Other, A-Z
3637.E7	Erotic literature
3637.F32	Fables
3637.L4	Letters (Epistulae)
3637.R5	Rhetoric
3641-3647	French (Table PA7)
3651-3657	German (Table PA7)
3661-3667	Italian (Table PA7)
3671.A-Z	Other western languages. By language, A-Z
3681.A-Z	Oriental languages. By language, A-Z
	Individual authors to 600 A.D.
	Subarrange by Tables P-PZ37 or P-PZ38 unless otherwise specified
	Unless otherwise specified, individual topical works by ancient Greek writers are classified in Class PA or in Classes B-Z according to language (for texts) or intent (for critical works)
	Class individual topical works in PA if included in the following categories: 1) Original Greek texts (without translations); 2) Latin translations; 3) Philological or textual criticism and commentaries
	Class individual topical works in B-Z if included in the following categories: 1) Translations with or without the original text, except translations into Latin; 2) Criticism and commentaries dealing primarily with the substance of the topic
3818	A to Achilles
	Achilles Tatius, 3rd century A.D. Leucippe et Clitophon. Leucippe and Clitophon. Ἀχιλλεὺς Τάτιος. Κατὰ Λευκίππην καὶ Κλειτοφῶντα
3819.A2	Editions. By date
	Translations
3819.A4	Latin. By date
3819.A5-.Z3	Other. By language and date
3819.Z5	Criticism
3820	Achilli... to Aelianus

	Individual authors to 600 A.D.
	Achilli... to Aelianus -- Continued
3820.A3	Aedesius (sophist) fl. between 300 and 350 A.D. Αἰδέσιος (Table P-PZ38)
	Aelianus Tacticus, 2nd century A.D. Tactica (De militaribus ordinibus instituendis more Graecorum; De instruendis aciebus). Αἰλιανὸς ὁ Τακτικός. Περὶ στρατηγικῶν τάξεων Ἑλληνικῶν
	For English translations and military commentaries see U101
3820.A5	Editions. By date
3820.A6A-.A6Z	Translations. By language and date
3820.A7	Criticism
3821	Aelianus, Claudius, 3rd century A.D. Aelian. Κλαύδιος Αἰλιανός
	Editions
3821.A2	Collected works. By date
3821.A3	De natura animalium. Περὶ ζῴων ἰδιότητος. By date
3821.A4	Varia historia. Ποικίλη ἱστορία. By date
3821.A43	Epistulae (Epistulae rusticae). Ἐπιστολαὶ ἀγροικικαί. By date
3821.A45	Fragments. By date
	Translations
3821.A5	Latin. By date
3821.A6-.Z3	Other. By language and date
3821.Z5	Criticism
3822	Aelianus (M.) to Aeschines
3822.A4	Aeneas, of Gaza, 6th century A.D. Αἰνείας Γαζαῖος (Table P-PZ38)
3822.A43	Aeneas, of Stymphalus, 4th century B.C. Αἰνέας Στυμφάλιος (Table P-PZ38)
	Aeneas Tacticus, 4th century B.C. Commentarius poliorceticus (Commentarius de toleranda obsidione). Peri tou pōs chrē poliorkoumenous antechein. Αἰνείας ὁ Τακτικός. Περὶ τοῦ πῶς χρὴ πολιορκουμένους ἀντέχειν
	For English translations and military commentaries see U101
3822.A5	Editions. By date
3822.A6A-.A6Z	Translations. By language and date
3822.A7	Criticism
3822.A75	Aenesidemus, of Cnossus, skeptic, fl. ca. 30 B.C. Αἰνησίδημος (Table P-PZ38)
3823	Aeschines, ca. 389-314 B.C. Αἰσχίνης
	Editions of Aeschines and Demosthenes combined are classified with Demosthenes; combinations of one or two orations, with the author first named on the title page
3823.A2	Editions. By date

PA3050-4505

	Individual authors to 600 A.D.
	Aeschines, ca. 389-314 B.C. Αἰσχίνης -- Continued
3823.A23	In Ctesiphontem. Against Ctesiphon. Κατὰ Κτησιφῶντος
3823.A25	De falsa legatione. Περὶ τῆς παραπρεσβείας
3823.A27	In Timarchum. Against Timarchus. Κατὰ Τιμάρχου
3823.A29	Epistulae (Spurious)
3823.A3-.A69	Translations. By language and date
3823.A7-.Z3	Criticism
3823.Z8	Indices, glossaries, etc. By date
3824	Aeschines (Soc.) to Aeschylus
3824.A4	Aeschines Socraticus, fl. 399-366 B.C. Αἰσχίνης ὁ Σωκρατικός (Table P-PZ38)
	Genuine dialogues lost; the dialogues and letters published under his name are spurious
	Aeschylus. Αἰσχύλος
3825	Editions
(3825.A1)	Manuscripts. Facsimiles
	see Z114; Z115Z
3825.A2	Collected plays. By date
3825.A3A-.A3Z	Selected plays. By editor, A-Z
3825.A4A-.A4Z	School editions. By editor, A-Z
3825.A45	Selections. Quotations. Passages
3825.A5	Cantica (Choral odes). By date
	Single plays
	Oresteia (Agamemnon. Choephori. Eumenides). Ὀρέστεια
3825.A6	Editions. By date
3825.A6A-.A6Z	Criticism
	Agamemnon. Ἀγαμέμνων
3825.A8	Editions. By date
3825.A8A-.A8Z	Criticism
	Choephori. Χοηφόροι
3825.C5	Editions. By date
3825.C5A-.C5Z	Criticism
	Eumenides. Εὐμενίδες
3825.E7	Editions. By date
3825.E7A-.E7Z	Criticism
	Persae. Πέρσαι
3825.P3	Editions. By date
3825.P3A-.P3Z	Criticism
	Prometheus vinctus. Prometheus bound. Προμηθεὺς δεσμώτης
3825.P8	Editions. By date
3825.P8A-.P8Z	Criticism
	Septem contra Thebas. Seven against Thebes. Ἑπτὰ ἐπὶ Θήβαις
3825.S4	Editions. By date

	Individual authors to 600 A.D.
	Aeschylus. Αἰσχύλος
	Editions
	Single plays
	Septem contra Thebas. Seven against Thebes. Ἑπτὰ -- Continued
3825.S4A-.S4Z	Criticism
	Supplices. Suppliants. Ἱκέτιδες
3825.S7	Editions. By date
3825.S7A-.S7Z	Criticism
	Lost plays
3825.Z3	Collections of fragments. By date
(3825.Z5)	Criticism (General, and particular plays)
	see PA3829
3826-3828	Translations
3826	Greek (Modern). Latin
	Greek (Modern)
3826.A1	Collected and selected plays. By date
3826.A11-.A19	Single plays (Latin title). By date
	Latin
3826.A3	Collected and selected plays. By date
3826.A6-.S7	Single plays (Latin title). By date
3827	English
	Collected and selected plays
3827.A1	Early to 1800/1850. By date
3827.A2-.A69	Later. By translator, A-Z (succesive Cutter numbers)
	Single plays (Latin title)
3827.A7A-.A7Z	Oresteia. By translator, A-Z
3827.A8A-.A8Z	Agamemnon. By translator, A-Z
3827.C5A-.C5Z	Choephori. By translator, A-Z
3827.Z5A-.Z5Z	Choral odes, etc. By translator, A-Z
3828.A-Z	Other. By language, A-Z
	e.g.
3828.I7-.I8	Italian
3828.I7A-.I7Z	Collected and selected plays. By translator, A-Z
3828.I8A-.I8Z	Single plays. By Latin title, A-Z, and date
	Interpretation and criticism
3829.A1	Ancient. Scholia. By date
	Modern
	Treatises
3829.A2	Early to 1800
3829.A5-.Z3	Later, 1800-
3829.Z7	Variants. Interpretation of detached passages
3829.Z9	Minor. Popular addresses, essays, lectures
3849	Language. Style. Versification
3849.A-.Z3	General works
(3849.Z5)	Grammar. Syntax

PA3050-4505

	Individual authors to 600 A.D.
	Aeschylus. Αἰσχύλος
	Interpretation and criticism
	Language. Style. Versification -- Continued
3849.Z8	Versification
3849.Z9	Glossaries. Indices. Concordances
3850	Aeschylus (of Knidos) to Aeso...
	Aesop. Αἴσωπος
3851	Editions
(3851.A1)	Manuscripts. Facsimiles
	see Z114
3851.A2	Other. By date
	Special collections or recensions
(3851.A3)	Popular fables and stories, with the "Vita Aesopi"
	see PA3851.A2
3851.A4	"Vita Aesopi"
(3851.A6)	Rhetorical fables
	see PA3851.A2
(3851.A7)	Other
	Including "Syntipas the philosopher" (Pseudo-Syntipas)
	see PA3851.A2
3851.A9	Selections. School editions. By date
3852	Translations and paraphrases: Ancient and medieval
	Greek
	Ancient
	Babrius see PA3941
	Pseudo-Dositheus see PA6381.D7
	Medieval see PA3851
	Latin
(3852.A3A8)	Avianus
	see PA6225
(3852.A3P5)	Phaedrus
	see PA6563+
(3852.A3P8)	Pseudo-Dositheus
	see PA6381.D7
(3852.A3T5)	Titianus, Julius
	see PA6791.T3
	Romulus. "Aesopus latinus"
3852.R6	Editions. By date
(3853)	Medieval derivations
	see classes PA-PT
3855	Translations and paraphrases: Modern
	Class here translations of the ancient fables ascribed to Aesopus. Editions and translations of medieval collections are classified with the literature of the respective language
3855.A2	Latin

	Individual authors to 600 A.D.
	Aesop. Αἴσωπος
	Translations and paraphrases: Modern -- Continued
3855.A5-Z	Other. By language, A-Z, and translator
3855.1	Vita Aesopi
(3855.3)	Paraphrases
	see the author
(3855.5)	Juvenile editions
	see PZ8.2 etc.
3858	Criticism, interpretation, etc. (confined to the Greek fable)
3858.A-.Z3	General (philological and linguistic mainly)
3858.Z5	Textual criticism
3858.Z6	Language. Grammar
3858.Z8	Glossaries. Indices, etc. By date
3860	Aet... to Alc...
	Aethiopis see PA3873.A95
	Aetius Amidenus (Aetius, of Amida), 6th century A.D. Ἀέτιος
	Aëtius doxographus, 1st-2nd century A.D. De placitis. Ἀέτιος. Περὶ ἀρεσκόντων

PA3050-4505

3860.A5	Africanus, Sextus Julius, fl. 200 A.D. Chronographiae (fragments). Chronicles. Ἀφρικανός. Χρονογραφίαι (Table P-PZ38)
3860.A6	Agatharchides. Ἀγαθαρχίδης (Table P-PZ38)
3860.A67	Agathias, Scholasticus, d. 582. Ἀγαθίας ὁ Σχολαστικός (Table P-PZ38)
3860.A7	Agathon (dramatist) fl. 416-407 B.C. Ἀγάθων (Table P-PZ38)
	Albinus Platonicus (Alcinous) 2nd century A.D. Ἀλβίνος
	Cf. B535.A4+ Philosophy
	Introductio in Platonis Dialogos. Εἰσαγωγὴ εἰς τοὺς Πλάτωνος διαλόγους
	In Platonicam philosophiam introductio. Prologos. Εἰς τὰ τοῦ Πλάτωνος δόγματα εἰσαγωγή
3861	Alcaeus, fl. ca. 595 B.C. Ἀλκαῖος (Table P-PZ37)
3862	Alce... to Alex...
	Alcibiades II see PA4279.A77
3862.A2	Alcidamas (rhetor) 4th century B.C. Ἀλκιδάμας (Table P-PZ38)
	Alcinous. Ἀλκίνοος
	see Albinus Platonicus
	Alciphron (sophist) 2nd century A.D. Ἀλκίφρων
3862.A3 date	Collected works. Selections. By date
3862.A3A-.A3Z	Individual works. By title, A-Z
3862.A4	Criticism
3862.A5	Alcman, 7th century B.C. Ἀλκμάν (Table P-PZ38)
3863	Alexander the Great, 356-323 B.C. Ἀλέξανδρος ὁ Μέγας

	Individual authors to 600 A.D.
	Alexander the Great, 356-323 B.C. Ἀλέξανδρος ὁ Μέγας
	Ἀλέξανδρος ὁ Μέγας -- Continued
3863.A2	Ephemerides (fragments)
3863.A3	Epistulae
	Authenticity disputed
	Letter to Aristoteles
	Letters preserved through inscriptions
	Letters addressed to Alexander
	Alexander romance
3863.A5	Collections and selections
	Pseudo-Callisthenes see PA3946.C3
3863.A53-.A59	Minor texts. Spurious letters, etc.
	Epistula Alexandri ad Aristotelem de miraculis Indiae
3863.A56	Texts. By date
3863.A56A-.A56Z	Translations. By language, A-Z
3863.A57	Criticism
(3863.A6)	Oriental and medieval vernacular literature
	see classes PJ, PK, PQ, PR, PT
3863.A8-Z	History and criticism of the romance
3864	Alexander (Aet.) to Anac...
3864.A16	Alexander Aetolus (dramatist) fl ca. 280 B.C. Ἀλέξανδρος ὁ Αἰτωλός
	Alexander Aphrodisiensis, fl. ca. 200 A.D. Alexander of Aphrodisias. Ἀλέξανδρος Ἀφροδισιεύς
3864.A2	Editions (Comprehensive). By date
	Commentarii in Aristotelem
(3864.A2A1)	Collections and selections
	see PA3902
	Commentaries on particular works
	see the individual works in PA3891+
	Scripta minora
3864.A2A5	Collections and selections. By date
3864.A2A6	De anima. De anima mantissa. Περὶ ψυχῆς
3864.A2F3	De fato. On fate. Περὶ εἱμαρμένης
	De intellectu see PA3864.A2A6
3864.A2M4	De mixtione. Περὶ κράσεως καὶ αὐξήσεως
3864.A2Q3	Quaestiones lib. III (Quaestiones naturales; Difficilium physicarum sive naturalium quaestionum et solutionum lib. III). Φυσικαὶ σχολικαὶ ἀπορίαι καὶ λύσεις
3864.A2Q5	Quaestiones morales lib. I. Ἠθικὰ προβλήματα
	Spurious works
3864.A2Z3	De febribus. Περὶ πυρετῶν
3864.A2Z5	De mixtione

	Individual authors to 600 A.D.
	Alexander (Aet.) to Anac...
	Alexander Aphrodisiensis, fl. ca. 200 A.D. Alexander of Aphrodisias. Ἀλέξανδρος Ἀφροδισιεύς
	Spurious works -- Continued
3864.A2Z7	Problemata medica et physica lib. V. Problemata Alexandri Aphrodisiei. Ἰατρικὰ ἀπορήματα καὶ φυσικὰ προβλήματα
3864.A2Z9	Quarundam difficultatum solutiones
	Translations
3864.A3A2	Latin. By date
3864.A3A5-.A3Z	Other. By language, A-Z
3864.A4	Criticism
3864.A42	Alexander Lycopolitanus (Alexander, of Lycopolis). Ἀλέξανδρος Λυκοπολίτης (Table P-PZ38)
3864.A43	Alexander Myndius, 1st century A.D. Ἀλέξανδρος ὁ Μύνδιος (Table P-PZ38)
3864.A45	Alexander Numenii (rhetor, son of the rhetor Numenius) 2nd century A.D. Ἀλέξανδρος ὁ τοῦ Νουμηνίου (Table P-PZ38 modified)
3864.A45A61-.A45A78	Separate works. By title
	e.g. De figuris (excerpts); De materiis rhetoricis (excerpts). Περὶ τῶν τῆς διανοίας καὶ τῆς λέξεως σχημάτων· Τέχνη (ῥητορική) περὶ ἀφορμῶν ῥητορικῶν
3864.A47	Alexander Polyhistor (Alexander, Cornelius, of Miletus, historian) fl. 82 B.C. Ἀλέξανδρος Πολυΐστωρ (Table P-PZ38)
3864.A5	Alexander Trallianus, 6th century A.D. Alexander, of Tralles. Ἀλέξανδρος ὁ Τραλλιανός (Table P-PZ38)
	Cf. PA6611.A3 Medicina Plinii
3864.A54	Alexis, ca. 372-270 B.C. Ἄλεξις (Table P-PZ38)
3864.A6	Alypius (date uncertain). Introductio musica. Ἀλύπιος. Εἰσαγωγὴ μουσική
3864.A65	Ammonius Alexandrinus (grammarian, pupil of Aristarchus) 2nd century B.C. Ἀμμώνιος (Table P-PZ38)
3864.A68	Ammonius Alexandrinus (grammarian) 4th century A.D. (existence doubtful). De adfinium vocabulorum differentia. Ἀμμώνιος. Περὶ ὁμοίων καὶ διαφόρων λέξεων
	A spurious work based on Herennius Philo, De differentia significationis
3864.A7	Ammonius Hermeiou, 6th century A.D. Ammonius, Hermiae. Ἀμμώνιος Ἑρμείου (Table P-PZ38 modified)
3864.A7A61-.A7A78	Separate works. By title

PA3050-4505

95

Individual authors to 600 A.D.
Alexander (Aet.) to Anac...
Ammonius Hermeiou, 6th century A.D. Ammonius,
Hermiae. Ἀμμώνιος Ἑρμείου
Separate works. By title -- Continued
Commentarii in Aristotelem: Analytica priora;
Categoriae; De interpretatione. Εἰς τὰς τοῦ
Ἀριστοτέλους Κατηγορίας ὑπόμνημα· Ὑπόμνημα εἰς
τὸ Περὶ ἑρμηνείας Ἀριστοτέλους
see PA3891+ ; PA3902
Commentarius in Porphyrii Isagogen. Εἰς τὰς πέντε
φωνὰς τοῦ Πορφυρίου ὑπόμνημα see PA4398
Ammonius Saccas, d. ca. 242 A.D. Ἀμμώνιος Σακκᾶς see
B650.A6+

3865	Anacreon, fl. 545-514 B.C. Ἀνακρέων
3865.A1	Editions. Carmina (Anacreontica, including the geniune poems of Anacreon). Anacreontea. By date
3865.A5-.Z3	Translations (including paraphrases of the Anacreontica and genuine poems). By language, A-Z, and date
(3865.Z4)	Adaptations, imitations, etc.
	see the individual authors
3865.Z5	Criticism
3866	Anac... to Ando...
	Anacreontica. Anacreontea see PA3865.A1
3866.A14	Anatolius, Saint, Bishop of Laodicea, fl. 262-280 A.D. Ἀνατόλιος (Table P-PZ38)
3866.A18	Anatolius, Vindonius, of Berytus, 4th century A.D. Ἀνατόλιος (Table P-PZ38)
3866.A2	Anaxagoras, of Clazomenae, ca. 500-428 B.C. Ἀναξαγόρας (Table P-PZ38)
	Cf. B205 Philosophy
3866.A4	Anaximander, b. ca. 610 B.C. Ἀναξίμανδρος (Table P-PZ38)
	Cf. B208 Philosophy
3866.A6	Anaximenes, of Lampsacus (rhetor) ca. 380-320 B.C. Ἀναξιμένης ὁ Λαμψακηνός (Table P-PZ38 modified)
3866.A6A61-.A6A78	Separate works. By title
	e.g. Hellenica (Prima historia); Philippica (Secunda historia); De rebus Alexandri (Historiarum pars tertia); Rhetorica ad Alexandrum. Ἑλληνικά· Φιλιππικά· Περὶ Ἀλέξανδρον· Ῥητορικὴ πρὸς Ἀλέξανδρον
3866.A8	Anaximenes, of Miletus, fl. ca. 546-528 B.C. Ἀναξιμένης ὁ Μιλήσιος (Table P-PZ38)
	Cf. B211 Philosophy
3867	Andocides, fl. 411-391 B.C. Ἀνδοκίδης
3867.A1	Editions. By date
	Separate orations

	Individual authors to 600 A.D.
	Andocides, fl. 411-391 B.C. Ἀνδοκίδης
	Separate orations -- Continued
3867.A14	In Alcibiadem (spurious). Κατὰ Ἀλκιβιάδου
3867.A15	De mysteriis. Περὶ τῶν μυστηρίων
3867.A2-.A69	Translations. By language (alphabetically)
3867.A7-.Z3	Criticism
	Including criticism of particular orations
3867.Z8	Lexicography: Glossaries, indices, etc. By date
3868	Andr... to Antiphon
3868.A4	Andronicus, of Rhodes, fl. ca. 70 B.C. Ἀνδρόνικος Ῥόδιος
	(Table P-PZ38)
	Anthologia graeca
	see PA3458.A2+
	Antigonus. Ἀντίγονος
3868.A47	General. Treatises on the various authors known by this name
3868.A471	Antigonus (biographer). Vitae philosophorum. Ἀντίγονος
	Identical with Antigonus Carystius?
3868.A473	Antigonus (historian) fl. ca. 260 B.C. Italica (lost). Ἀντίγονος
3868.A475	Antigonus (periegetes). Periegesis Macedonica (lost). Ἀντίγονος
	Antigonus (sculptor, and writer on art). Ἀντίγονος
	Identity with Antigonus Carystius disputed
3868.A48	De toreutice (lost)
3868.A481	De tabulis pictorum (lost)
3868.A49	Antigonus Alexandrinus (Antigonus, of Alexandria, grammarian) 1st century B.C. Lexicon Hippocrateum (lost). Ἀντίγονος ὁ Ἀλεξανδρεύς
3868.A5	Antigonus Carystius (Antigonus, of Carystus, paradoxographer) fl. ca. 240 B.C. Ἀντίγονος ὁ Καρύστιος (Table P-PZ38 modified)
	Identical with Antigonus the biographer, historian or sculptor?
3868.A5A61-.A5A78	Separate works. By title
	e.g. Historiarum mirabilium collectio; Vitae philosophorum. Ἱστοριῶν παραδόξων συναγωγή· Βίοι φιλοσόφων
	Historica hypomnemata see PA3946.C6
3868.A51	Antigonus Carystius (the younger; Antigonus of Carystos, poet) fl between 60 B.C. and 40 A.D. Ἀντίγονος ὁ Καρύστιος. Epigrams (Anth. graeca IV, 213; IX, 406)
3868.A55	Antigonus Cumanus (Antigonus, of Cuma, Kyme, Asia Minor). De re rustica (lost). Ἀντίγονος
3868.A58	Antigonus Nicaeensis (Antigonus, of Nicaea, astrologer). Ἀντίγονος ὁ Νικαεύς (Table P-PZ38)

PA3050-4505

Individual authors to 600 A.D.
Andr... to Antiphon -- Continued

3868.A7	Antimachus Colophonius, 5th century B.C. Antimachus, of Colophon. Ἀντίμαχος (Table P-PZ38)
3868.A8	Antiochus, of Ascalon (academician) fl. ca. 86 B.C. Ἀντίοχος (Table P-PZ38)
3868.A83	Antipater, of Sidon, fl. ca. 100 B.C. Ἀντίπατρος Σιδώνιος (Table P-PZ38)
3869	Antiphon (orator) d. 411 B.C. Ἀντιφῶν ὁ Ῥαμνούσιος (Table P-PZ37)
3870	Antiphon (sophist) to Apoll...
	Antiphon, sophist, 5th century B.C. Antiphon, of Athens. Ἀντιφῶν
	Antisthenes (disciple of Socrates), fl. ca. 400 B.C. Ἀντισθένης
	Cf. B293.A3+ Philosophy
	Antisthenes, of Rhodes (historian and peripatetic philosopher) 2nd century B.C. Ἀντισθένης
3870.A2	Antoninus Liberalis, 2nd (?) century A.D. Transformationum congeries. Metamorphōseōn synagōgē. Ἀντωνῖνος Λιβεράλις. Μεταμορφώσεων συναγωγή
	Antoninus, Marcus Aurelius see PA3939
3870.A3	Antonius Diogenes. Ἀντώνιος Διογένης (Table P-PZ38)
3870.A4	Anyte, of Tegea, fl. ca. 300 B.C. Ἀνύτη Τεγεᾶτις (Table P-PZ38)
3870.A5	Aphthonius, 4th to 5th century A.D. Ἀφθόνιος (Table P-PZ38)
3870.A53	Apollodoros, b. ca. 394 B.C. Ἀπολλόδωρος (Table P-PZ38)
3870.A55	Apollodorus (supposed author of the Bibliotheca). Ἀπολλόδωρος (Table P-PZ38)
	Apollodorus, of Artemita, 1st century B.C. Ἀπολλόδωρος
3870.A6	Apollodorus, of Athens, fl. ca. 140 B.C. Ἀπολλόδωρος (Table P-PZ38)
	Numerous fragments
(3870.A7-.A9)	Bibliotheca [mythorum]. Βιβλιοθήκη
	A handbook of mythology, wrongly ascribed to Apollodorus see PA3870.A55
	Apollodorus, of Athens (writer of comedies). Ἀπολλόδωρος Identical with Apollodorus, of Carystus?
3870.A94	Apollodorus, of Carystus (writer of comedies) 4th century B.C. Ἀπολλόδωρος ὁ Καρύστιος (Table P-PZ38) Source of Terentius' Phormio and Hecyra
3871	Apollonius to Apollonius Rhodius
3871.A1	Treatises on the various authors known by the name of Apollonius

	Individual authors to 600 A.D.
	Apollonius to Apollonius Rhodius -- Continued
	Apollonius Archibii
	see Apollonius, sophista
3871.A2	Apollonius Dyscolus, 2nd century A.D. Ἀπολλώνιος ὁ Δύσκολος (Table P-PZ38 modified)
3871.A2A61-.A2A78	Separate works. By title
	e.g. De adverbio; De conjunctionibus; De constructione orationis lib. IV (On syntax); De pronomine (On pronouns). Περὶ ἐπιρρημάτων. Περὶ συνδέσμων. Περὶ συντάξεως. Περὶ ἀντωνυμίας
	For the "Historiae mirabiles" formerly ascribed to Apollonius Dyscolus see PA3871.A95
	Apollonius "Eidographos," fl. ca. 180 B.C. Ἀπολλώνιος ὁ Εἰδογράφος
	Apollonius "Malakos," of Alabanda, fl. ca. 120 B.C. Ἀπολλώνιος ὁ Μαλακός
	Apollonius Molo, of Alabanda (rhetor), fl. 87-78 B.C. Ἀπολλώνιος ὁ Μόλων
3871.A4	Apollonius, of Perga, fl. ca. 200 B.C. Ἀπολλώνιος ὁ Περγαῖος (Table P-PZ38)
	Cf. QA31 Mathematics
3871.A6	Apollonius, of Tyana, 1st century A.D. Ἀπολλώνιος ὁ Τυανεύς (Table P-PZ38)
	His works lost, the letters preserved under his name, most likely spurious
	Cf. PA4272.A3 Philostratus, Apollonii vita
3871.A8	Apollonius, of Tyre (Historia Apollonii regis Tyri) (Table P-PZ38)
	Cf. PA6206.A6 Latin literature
	Cf. PA8320+ Gesta Romanorum
3871.A95	Apollonius, paradoxographus, 2nd (?) century B.C. Ἀπολλώνιος (Table P-PZ38)
	Author of the Historiae mirabiles, wrongly ascribed to Apollonius Dyscolus
3872	Apollonius Rhodius, ca. 295-ca. 215 B.C. Ἀπολλώνιος ὁ Ῥόδιος
	Argonautica. Ἀργοναυτικά
3872.A1	Editions. By date
3872.A13	Selections
3872.A15	Other works (fragments only)
	Translations
3872.A2	Latin. By date
3872.A5-.Z2	Other. By language, A-Z, and date
3872.E5	English
3872.F5	French
3872.G5	German

PA3050-4505

	Individual authors to 600 A.D.
	Apollonius Rhodius, ca. 295-ca. 215 B.C. Ἀπολλώνιος ὁ
	Ῥόδιος -- Continued
	Criticism
3872.Z3	Scholia. By date
3872.Z4	Other
3872.Z5	Grammatical and syntactical
3872.Z6	Versification
3872.Z8	Glossaries, indices, etc.
3873	Apollonius (soph.) to Ari...
(3873.A15)	Apollonius, sophista, fl. ca. 100 A.D. (the son of Archibius).
	Ἀπολλώνιος ὁ Σοφιστής. Lexicon homericum
	see PA4035.A7
	Appianus, of Alexandria, 2nd century A.D. Historia
	Romana. Ἀππιανός. Ῥωμαϊκά
	Editions
3873.A2	Comprehensive. By date
3873.A22	Special books or sections. By date
3873.A225	Fragments
3873.A228	Epistula ad Frontonem
	Authorship doubtful
	Translations
3873.A229	Greek (Modern). By date
3873.A23	Latin. By date
3873.A24A-.A24E	Other, A-Eng. By language, A-Z, and date
(3873.A25)	English
	see DG207.A64
3873.A26	French. By date
3873.A28	German. By date
3873.A3	Italian. By date
3873.A37	Spanish. By date
	Criticism and interpretation
3873.A4A-.A4Z3	General
	For treatises of historical interest see Class DG
3873.A4Z5	Language, style, grammar, etc. By date
3873.A4Z8	Glossaries, indices. By date
	Apsines, of Gadara, fl. 235-238 A.D. Ἀψίνης ὁ Γαδαρεύς
	Aratus, of Sicyon, 271-213 B.C. Ἄρατος
	Fragments only
	For historical treatises see DF236+
	Aratus, of Soli (Solensis), ca. 310-ca. 245 B.C.
	Phaenomena. Ἄρατος Σολεύς. Φαινόμενα
3873.A5	Editions
	Translations
3873.A517	Greek (Modern). By date
	Latin

	Individual authors to 600 A.D.
	Apollonius (soph.) to Ari...
	Aratus, of Soli (Solensis), ca. 310-ca. 245 B.C.
	Phaenomena. Ἄρατος Σολεύς. Φαινόμενα
	Translations
	Latin -- Continued
3873.A519	Ancient. By date
	Cf. PA6227.A4 Avienus, Rufius Festus
	Cf. PA6296.A6 Cicero, M.T.
	Cf. PA6392.G3 Germanicus Caesar
3873.A52	Modern. By date
	Other. By language, A-Z
3873.A53A-.A53E	A-Eng. By language, A-Z, and date
(3873.A54)	English
	see QA31
3873.A56	French. By date
3873.A58	German. By date
3873.A6	Italian. By date
3873.A65A-.A65Z	Slavic. By language, A-Z, and date
	e.g.
3873.A65P7	Polish
3873.A67	Spanish. By date
	Criticism, interpretation, etc.
3873.A7A1-.A7A3	Ancient
3873.A7A5-.A7Z3	Modern
3873.A7Z8	Glossaries, indices. By date
3873.A73	Arcadius, of Antiochia. Ἀρκάδιος (Table P-PZ38)
	. Grammarian of uncertain date, younger than Herodianus, older than Choeroboscus
	Cf. PA4445.T4 Theodosius, of Alexandria
3873.A735	Archestratus, of Gela, 4th century B.C. Ἀρχέστρατος (Table P-PZ38)
3873.A75	Archias, Aulus Licinius, fl. 93-62 B.C. Ἀρχίας (Table P-PZ38)
	Cf. PA6279.A9 Cicero, Pro Archia
3873.A77	Archilochus, fl. between 680-640 B.C. Ἀρχίλοχος (Table P-PZ38)
	Archimedes, d. 212 B.C. Ἀρχιμήδης
3873.A8	Editions. By date
3873.A8A2	Selected works. By date
	Single works
3873.A8A8	Arenarius (De arenae numero). Ψαμμίτης
3873.A8D2	De conoidibus et sphaeroidibus. Περὶ κωνοειδέων καὶ σφαιροειδέων
3873.A8D3	De corporibus fluitantibus lib. II (De insidentibus aquae; De iis quae aquae innatant; De iis quae in humido vehuntur). Περὶ ὀχουμένων

PA3050-4505

Individual authors to 600 A.D.
Apollonius (soph.) to Ari...
Archimedes, d. 212 B.C. Ἀρχιμήδης
Single works -- Continued

3873.A8D4	De lineis spiralibus. Περὶ ἑλίκων
3873.A8D5	De mechanicis propositionibus methodus. Ἔφοδος
3873.A8D6	De planorum aequilibriis lib. II (De planis aequiponderantibus; De centris gravium planorum). Ἐπιπέδων ἰσορροπίαι
3873.A8D7	De sphaera et cylindro lib. II (Theoremata de sphaeris et cylindro). Περὶ σφαίρας καὶ κυλίνδρου
3873.A8D8	Dimensio circuli. Κύκλου μέτρησις
	Methodus see PA3873.A8D5
3873.A8Q3	Quadratura parabolae (Tetragonismus). Τετραγωνισμὸς παραβολῆς
3873.A8S8	Stomachion (fragments). Στομάχιον
3873.A8Z5	Lost works. Fragments
	Spurious and doubtful works
3873.A8Z6	Lemmata (Liber assumptorum). Λήμματα
	Preserved in Arabic only; collection of propositions by some Greek writer of later date including some of Archimedean origin
3873.A8Z7	Problema bovinum. Πρόβλημα βοεικόν
3873.A8Z8	De speculo comburenti
	Translations
3873.A9A2	Arabic. By date
3873.A9A3	Latin. By date
3873.A9A4-.A9A69	Other. By language, A-Z (successive Cutter number)
	Cf. QA31 Mathematics
	Criticism, interpretation, etc.
	For treatises not strictly philological or linguistic see QA31
3873.A9A7	Ancient
	Including Eutocius, of Ascalon
3873.A9A8-.A9Z	Modern
3873.A93	Archytas, of Tarentum, 4th century B.C. Ἀρχύτας (Table P-PZ38)
3873.A95	Arctinus, of Miletus. Ἀρκτῖνος (Table P-PZ38)
	Fictitious name? Reputed author of Aethiopis and Ilii persis (Αἰθιοπίς. Ἰλίου πέρσις)
3873.A97	Aretaeus Cappadox, 2nd century A.D. Ἀρεταῖος (Table P-PZ38)
3873.A98	Arion (mythical poet). Ἀρίων (Table P-PZ38)
3874	Aris... to Aristo...
	Aristaenetus, 5th century A.D. Epistulae eroticae. Ἀρισταίνετος. Ἐπιστολαὶ ἐρωτικαί
3874.A2	Editions. By date

	Individual authors to 600 A.D.
	Aris... to Aristo...
	Aristaenetus, 5th century A.D. Epistulae eroticae.
	Ἀρισταίνετος. Ἐπιστολαὶ ἐρωτικαί -- Continued
	Translations
3874.A3	Latin. By date
3874.A3A-.A3Z	Other. By language, A-Z, and date
3874.A4	Criticism
	Aristaeus
	see Aristeas
	Aristarchus Alexandrinus see PA3874.A5
3874.A48	Aristarchus, of Samos, astronomer, fl. ca. 280 B.C. De magnitudinibus et distantiis solis et lunae. On the sizes and distances of the sun and moon. Ἀρίσταρχος ὁ Σάμιος. Περὶ μεγεθῶν καὶ ἀποστημάτων ἡλίου καὶ σελήνης
3874.A5	Aristarchus, of Samothrace (A. Alexandrinus) 2nd century B.C. Ἀρίσταρχος (Table P-PZ38)
	Commentaries and other works lost
3874.A51	Aristeas, of Proconnesus, Pseudo-Arimaspeia. Ἀριστέας. Ἀριμάσπεια (Table P-PZ38)
(3874.A52)	Aristeas (pseudonym). Epistula (Liber) de interpretatione Septuaginta duorum interpretum. Letter of Aristeas
	see BS744.A7
3874.A54	Aristides (novelist) 2nd to 1st century B.C. Ἀριστείδης (Table P-PZ38)
	Wrongly surnamed "Milesius." Author of erotic novels called "Milesiaca" ("Μιλησιακά") from Miletus, the place of action (now lost)
	For fragments of an ancient Latin version see PA6696.S4 (L. Corn. Sisenna)
(3874.A56)	Aristides, of Athens (philosopher and Christian apologist), 2nd century A.D. Ἀριστείδης
	see BT1116; BR1720
	Aristides, Aelius (rhetor) 2nd century A.D. Αἴλιος Ἀριστείδης
	Editions
3874.A6	Comprehensive, or Orations alone. By date
3874.A6A1	Selected orations or groups of orations. By date
3874.A6A2-.A6Z	Particular orations or treatises, A-Z
	Subarrange by date
	Translations
3874.A7	Latin. By date
3874.A7A-.A7Z3	Other. By language, A-Z, and date
3874.A7Z5	Criticism. By date
3874.A75	Aristides Quintilianus, 3rd (?) century A.D. De musica. Peri mousikēs. Ἀριστείδης Κοϊντιλιανός. Περὶ μουσικῆς

PA3050-4505

Individual authors to 600 A.D.
Aris... to Aristo... -- Continued

3874.A78   Aristippus, of Cyrene, fl. between 435 and 356 B.C.
                  Ἀρίστιππος (Table P-PZ38)
                      No writings extant; spurious letters and sayings ascribed to
                      him
                      Cf. B293.A7+ Philosophy
3874.A8   Aristobulus Judaeus, of Alexandria, 2nd century B.C.
                  Ἀριστόβουλος ὁ Περιπατητικός (Table P-PZ38)
3874.A82   Aristobulus, of Cassandria, 4th to 3rd century B.C.
                  Ἀριστόβουλος ὁ Κασσανδρεύς (Table P-PZ38)
3874.A825   Aristocles (writer on music) 2nd or 1st century B.C.
                  Ἀριστοκλῆς (Table P-PZ38)
                      Identical with Aristocles, of Rhodes?
3874.A828   Aristocles (paradoxographer). Ἀριστοκλῆς (Table P-PZ38)
3874.A83   Aristocles, of Messene (Sicily) peripatetic, 2nd century A.D.
                  Ἀριστοκλῆς Μεσσήνιος (Table P-PZ38)
3874.A84   Aristocles, of Rhodes, grammarian and rhetor, 1st century
                  B.C. Ἀριστοκλῆς (Table P-PZ38)
                      Cf. PA3874.A825 Aristocles (writer on music)
3874.A85   Aristodemus (historian of unknown date). Ἀριστόδημος
                  (Table P-PZ38)
3874.A87   Aristodemus, of Alexandria, 1st century B.C. Ἀριστόδημος
                  Ἀλεξανδρεύς (Table P-PZ38)
3874.A879   Ariston, of Ceos, fl. ca. 225 B.C. Ἀρίστων Κεῖος (Table P-
                  PZ38)
3874.A9   Aristonicus, of Alexandria, fl. between 39 B.C. and 14 A.D.
                  Ἀριστόνικος Ἀλεξανδρεύς (Table P-PZ38)
                      Cf. PA4035.A8 Homer
                  Aristophanes. Ἀριστοφάνης
3875   Comoediae
(3875.A1)   Manuscripts. Facsimiles
                        see Z114 ; Z115Z
3875.A2   Editions. By date
3875.A28A-.A28Z   Selected comedies. By editor, A-Z
3875.A3A-.A3Z   School editions. By editor, A-Z
3875.A35A-.A35Z   Selections. Quotations. Passages. By editor, A-Z
3875.A36   Cantica
3875.A4   Fragments. Editions, by date
                     Separate editions
3875.A6   Acharnenses. Acharnians. Ἀχαρνεῖς
3875.A8   Aves. Birds. Ὄρνιθες
3875.E3   Ecclesiazusae. Ἐκκλησιάζουσαι
3875.E7   Equites. Knights. Ἱππεῖς
3875.L8   Lysistrata. Λυσιστράτη
3875.N8   Nubes. Clouds. Νεφέλαι
3875.P2   Pax. Peace. Εἰρήνη

	Individual authors to 600 A.D.
	Aristophanes. Ἀριστοφάνης
	Comoediae
	Separate editions -- Continued
3875.P6	Plutus. Πλοῦτος
3875.R3	Ranae. Frogs. Βάτραχοι
3875.T5	Thesmophoriazusae. Θεσμοφοριάζουσαι
3875.V5	Vespae. Wasps. Σφῆκες
3875.Z3	Fragments
3875.Z5	Spurious plays
	Translations
	Greek (Modern)
3876.A1	Collections and selections. By date
3876.A11-.A19	Separate plays (alphabetically)
	Subarrange by date
	Latin
3876.A2	Collections and selections. By date
3876.A21-.A29	Separate plays (alphabetically)
	Subarrange by date
3876.A3-.A49	Other languages, A-D
3877	English
3877.A1A-.A1Z	Comprehensive. By translator, A-Z
3877.A2	Selected plays. By date
3877.A3	Selections. Anthologies
3877.A6-.V	Separate plays. By Latin title and date
3878.E-.Z8	Other languages, E-Z, and date
	e.g.
3878.I7-.I8	Italian
3878.I7	Collections and selections
3878.I8A-.I8V	Separate plays
3878.Z9	Imitations. Adaptations
3878.Z99	Illustrations
3879	Interpretation and criticism
	Ancient (Scholia)
3879.A1	Comprehensive (or for various plays)
(3879.A15)	Separate plays
	see PA3875.A6+
3879.A17	By particular authors
	Modern
3879.A2	Early to 1800
3879.A6-Z	1800-
3888	Language. Style. Versification
3888.A-.Z3	General and special. By author, A-Z
	Special
(3888.Z5)	Play at words. Names, etc.
(3888.Z6)	Grammar. Syntax
3888.Z7	Versification

PA3050-4505

Individual authors to 600 A.D.
Aristophanes. Ἀριστοφάνης
Language. Style. Versification
Special -- Continued

3888.Z8	Glossaries. Indices. Concordances
3889	Aristophanes (Byz.) to Aristoteles
3889.A2	Aristophanes Byzantius ca. 250-ca. 180 B.C. Aristophanes, of Byzantium. Ἀριστοφάνης ὁ Βυζάντιος (Table P-PZ38)

Aristotle. Ἀριστοτέλης
Editions

(3890.A1)	Manuscripts (including facsimile reproductions) see Z114; Z115X
3890.A2	Comprehensive. By date
3890.A3	Selected works (Miscellaneous)

Selected works. By group
Class here editions comprising all or several treatises belonging to a distinct group. Class editions of two treatises under the first, especially such as Analytica. Class groups known under special titles (Organon; Parva naturalia) under Separate works

Logic (Organon) see PA3893.O7+

3890.A6	Natural science
3890.A7	Psychological and philosophical
3890.A8	Moral and political writings Cf. PA3893.E5 Ethica
(3890.A9)	Rhetorica and Poetica see PA3893.R3+ PA3893.P5
3890.A99	Selections. Quotations. Passages. Thoughts

Fragments and lost works see PA3893.Z5
Spurious works see PA3894

Separate works
Class here all the works forming part of the corpus associated with Aristotle's name and printed in the standard editions of his works, although some of them were undoubtedly not written by Aristotle

3891	A-D

Analytica (Resolutoria)

3891.A2	Priora lib. II. Prior analytics. Ἀναλυτικὰ πρότερα
3891.A4	Posteriora lib. II (De demonstratione). Posterior analytics. Ἀναλυτικὰ ὕστερα
3891.A5	Criticism

Ars poetica see PA3893.P5
Ars rhetorica see PA3893.R3+

3891.C2	Carmina Including separate editions of the Hymnus in virtutem, also known as "Scolion in Hermiam" (Εἰς Ἑρμείαν)

	Individual authors to 600 A.D.
	Aristotle. Ἀριστοτέλης
	Separate works
	A-D -- Continued
3891.C4	Categoriae (Praedicamenta). Κατηγορίαι
	Chiromantia see PA3894.C5
	De... (Titles beginning with De)
	De amicitia
	A separate treatise De amicitia is lost
	see Ethica lib. VIII-IX
3892.A2	De anima lib. III. Περὶ ψυχῆς
3892.A3	De animalium generatione lib. V. On the generation of animals. Περὶ ζώων γενέσεως
3892.A4	De animalibus historia lib. X (Historia animalium). Περὶ ζώων ἱστορία
3892.A5	De animalium incessu (ingressu, gressu). Περὶ ζώων πορείας
3892.A6	De animalium motu (motione). De motu animalium. Περὶ ζώων κινήσεως
3892.A7	De animalium partibus lib. IV. De partibus animalium. Περὶ ζώων μορίων
3892.A8	De audibilibus (De objecto auditus). Περὶ ἀκουστῶν
	Authorship ascribed to Strato, of Lampsacus
	De auditu physico see PA3893.P3
(3892.B7)	De bona fortuna
	Under this title appear in some manuscripts as independent treatises chapter 8 of Magna moralia II in the Latin translation of Bartholomaeus Messinensis (fl. ca. 1260) or, a combination of that chapter with a Latin translation of Ethica Eudemia VIII,2 (VII,14)
	De causis (De causis causarum, etc.) see PA3894.D2
	De causis proprietatum elementorum (De proprietatibus) see PA3894.D4
3892.C5	De caelo lib. V. Περὶ οὐρανοῦ
3892.C7	De coloribus. Περὶ χρωμάτων
	Authorship doubtful, ascribed to Theophrastus, or Strato, of Lampascus
	De demonstratione see PA3891.A4
3892.D4	De divinatione per somnum. Περὶ τῆς καθ' ὕπνον μαντικῆς
3892.G6	De generatione et corruptione lib. II (De ortu et interitu). Περὶ γενέσεως καὶ φθορᾶς
	De innato spiritu see PA3892.S8
3892.I4	De insomniis (somniis). Περὶ ἐνυπνίων
3892.I7	De interpretatione. Περὶ ἑρμηνείας
3892.I8	De iuventute et senectute. Περὶ νεότητος καὶ γήρως

PA3050-4505

Individual authors to 600 A.D.
Aristotle. Ἀριστοτέλης
Separate works
De... (Titles beginning with De) -- Continued
De lapide philosophorum
see PA3894.T75 PA3894.T8
De lapidibus see PA3894.D5

3892.L4	De lineis insecabilibus. Περὶ ἀτόμων γραμμῶν Authorship doubtful, by some ascribed to Theophrastus
3892.L7	De longitudine et brevitate vitae. Περὶ μακροβιότητος καὶ βραχυβιότητος
3892.M2	De Melisso, Xenophane, Gorgia. Περὶ Μελίσσου, Ξενοφάνους, Γοργίου
3892.M4	De memoria et reminiscentia. Περὶ μνήμης καὶ ἀναμνήσεως

De metallis (Fragments, etc.). Περὶ μετάλλων see
PA3893.Z5A+
De mineralibus, lapidibus metallisque see PA3894.D53

3892.M6	De mirabilibus auscultationibus (De admirandis narrationibus). Περὶ θαυμασίων ἀκουσμάτων

De moribus ad Eudemum see PA3893.E7
De motu see PA3893.P3
De motu animalium see PA3892.A6

3892.M7	De mundo (Epistula de universo ad Alexandrum). Περὶ κόσμου

De natura aut de rerum principiis see PA3893.P3
De naturali auditu see PA3893.P3

3892.N4	De Nilo. Περὶ τῆς τοῦ Νείλου ἀναβάσεως

De objecto auditus see PA3892.A8
De ortu et interitu see PA3892.G6
De perfecto magisterio see PA3894.D55
De physico auditu see PA3893.P3

3892.P5	De plantis lib. II (De vegetabilibus; De vegetabilibus et plantis). Περὶ φυτῶν A compilation from the treatises of Aristotle and Theophrastus, ascribed to Nicolaus of Damascus; the original is lost. The Greek version as given in the editions of Aristotle is a retranslation of the Latin version by Alfred de Sarchel (ca. 1178-ca.1215) which in turn was based upon an Arabic version attributed to Ishak ibn Hunain

De pomo et morte see PA3894.D7
De republica lib. VIII see PA3893.P8
De republica Atheniensium see PA3893.P6
De republica Carthaginiensium
see Politica lib. II, from which it is an extract

3892.R6	De respiratione. Περὶ ἀναπνοῆς

Individual authors to 600 A.D.
    Aristotle. Ἀριστοτέλης
      Separate works
        De... (Titles beginning with De) -- Continued
          De secretiori philosophia Aegyptiorum see PA4364.A2

3892.S2   De sensu et sensibilibus (De sensu et sensato). Περὶ αἰσθήσεως καὶ αἰσθητῶν
          De signis tempestatum see PA3893.V4
          De somniis see PA3892.I4

3892.S4   De somno et vigilia. Περὶ ὕπνου καὶ ἐγρηγόρσεως
3892.S6   De sophisticis elenchis. Περὶ σοφιστικῶν ἐλέγχων
3892.S8   De spiritu (De innato spiritu). Περὶ πνεύματος
3892.V3   De virtutibus et vitiis. Περὶ ἀρετῶν καὶ κακιῶν
3892.V6   De vita et morte. Περὶ ζωῆς καὶ θανάτου
          De Xenophane, Zenone et Gorgia see PA3892.M2

3893   Di-Z
          Dialectica see PA3893.O7+
          Divisiones. Diaireseis. Διαιρέσεις
          Elegiae see PA3891.C2
          Elenchi see PA3892.S6
          Epistula de universo ad Alexandrum see PA3892.M7
          Epistulae see PA3893.Z5A+

3893.E5   Ethica (Editions of the three works on Ethics)
3893.E6   Ethica lib. X (Ethica Nicomachea; De moribus ad Nicomachum). Nicomachean ethics. Ἠθικὰ Νικομάχεια

3893.E7   Ethica Eudemia lib. VII (De moribus ad Eudemum). Ἠθικὰ Εὐδήμεια

3893.E8   Ethica magna lib. II (Magna Moralia). Eudemian ethics. Ἠθικὰ μέγαλα

3893.E9   Criticism of works on ethics
          Historiae animalium see PA3892.A4
          Hymnus in virtutem (Scolion in Hermiam) see PA3891.C2
          Logica see PA3893.O7+
          Magna moralia see PA3893.E8

3893.M3   Mechanica (Problemata mechanica). Μηχανικά
3893.M5   Metaphysica lib. XIII (XIV). Metaphysics. Μετὰ τὰ φυσικά
3893.M7   Meteorologica lib. IV. Μετεωρολογικά
          Nomima barbarica. Νόμιμα βαρβαρικά see PA3893.Z5A+
          Oeconomica see PA4253.O314

PA3050-4505

Individual authors to 600 A.D.
   Aristotle. Ἀριστοτέλης
     Separate works
      Di-Z -- Continued
       Organon (Dialectica, Logica). Ὄργανον
        Class here editions of the entire series or of several parts
         of it
        For editions of single parts see Analytica; Categoriae; De
         interpretatione; De sophisticis elenchis; Topica

3893.O7	Text. By date
3893.O9	Criticism
3893.P2	Parva naturalia

        Pars I: De sensu et sensibilibus; De memoria et
         reminiscentia; De somno et vigilia; De insomniis; De
         divinatione per somnum
        Pars II: De longitudine et brevitate vitae; De iuventute et
         senectute; De vita et morte; De respiratione
        For editions of the single parts see the individual titles

3893.P25	Peplus. Πέπλος

       Philosophia moralis see PA3893.E5
       Philosophia naturalis
        see Physica; Parva naturalia

3893.P3	Physica lib. VIII (Physicae auscultationis lib. VIII; De

        natura aut de rerum principiis; De naturali auditu;
        De auditu physico; Philosophia naturalis). Physics.
        Φυσικὴ ἀκρόασις
        Part II (lib. V-VIII) also entitled De motu (Περὶ κινήσεως)

3893.P4	Physiognomonica. Φυσιογνωμονικά

       Poemata see PA3891.C2

3893.P5	Poetica (Ars poetica). Poetics. Περὶ ποιητικῆς
3893.P6	Politeia Athenaion (Respublica Atheniensium).

        Athēnaiōn politeia. Ἀθηναίων πολιτεία

(3893.P7)	Politiae (Rerum publicarum reliquiae). Πολιτεῖαι

        see PA3893.Z5A+

3893.P8	Politica lib. VIII (De republica). Politics. Πολιτικά

       Praedicamenta see PA3891.C4

3893.P9	Problemata (Problemata physica; Quaestiones).

        Προβλήματα
       Problemata mechanica see PA3893.M3
       Quaestiones see PA3893.P9
       Resolutoria see PA3891.A2+
       Rhetorica lib. III. Rhetoric. Τέχνη ῥητορική

3893.R3	Text. By date
3893.R4	Criticism
(3893.R6)	Rhetorica ad Alexandrum

        see Anaximenes, of Lampsacus
       Rhetorica ad Theodectum see PA3893.Z5A+

Individual authors to 600 A.D.
    Aristotle. Ἀριστοτέλης
      Separate works
        Di-Z -- Continued
          Scolion in Hermiam (Hymnus in virtutem) see
            PA3891.C2
          Secretum secretorum see PA3894.S3
          Sophistici elenchi see PA3892.S6
          Theologia, or Theologia Aegyptiorum see PA4364.A2

3893.T7	Topica lib. VIII. Topics. Τοπικά
3893.V4	Ventorum situs et nomina. Ἀνέμων θέσεις καὶ προσηγορίαι

        Fragments and lost works

3893.Z5	Collections. By date
3893.Z5A-.Z5Z	Separate works, A-Z
3894	Spurious works

          Works ordinarily included in editions of Aristoteles are
            classified with the genuine works

3894.A2	Collections and selections
3894.C5	Chiromantia
3894.D2	De causis (Aphorismi de essentia summae bonitatis; De summo bono; De causis causarum; De esse; De expositione purae bonitatis; De intelligentiis)

          Latin translation of a compilation (in Arabic) of thirty-two
            metaphysical theses, nearly all extracted from the
            Institutio theologica of Proclus, diadochus. Albertus
            Magnus ascribed the book to "David Judaeus quidam"
            (Joannes Hispalensis, aben Daud or Avendeath)

3894.D4	De causis proprietatum elementorum (De proprietatibus elementorum)

         De conservatione sanitatis see PA3894.S3
         De esse see PA3894.D2
         De expositione purae bonitatis see PA3894.D2
         De intelligentiis see PA3894.D2
         De lapide philosophorum
           see PA3894.T75; PA3894.T8

3894.D5	De lapidibus (Lapidarius Aristotelis)
3894.D53	De mineralibus (De mineralibus lapidibus metallisque)

         An Arabic alchemistic commentary (in three chapters)
           appended in Arabic-Latin versions to the fourth book of
           the Meteorologica of Aristoteles, and in medieval
           literature frequently quoted as Meteorum Aristotelis
           liber IV. It was translated into Latin by Alfred of Sarchel
           with title "Liber de congelatis." It has been published
           repeatedly as a work of Avicenna with title De
           congelatione et conglutinatione lapidum
        De morte see PA3894.D7

PA3050-4505

Individual authors to 600 A.D.
Aristotle. Ἀριστοτέλης
Spurious works

3894.D55	De perfecto magisterio
	De physiognomia see PA3894.S3
3894.D7	De pomo (De pomo et morte; De morte)

Pseudepigraphic dialogue in Arabic on immortality between Aristotle and his disciples. No Arabic or Greek manuscripts are known. It is preserved in Persian, Hebrew, and Latin versions

De regimine principum see PA3894.S3
De regimine sanitatis see PA3894.S3
De sanitatis conservatione see PA3894.S3
De secretiori philosophia Aegyptiorum see PA4364.A2
De summo bono see PA3894.D2

3894.E8   Epistulae

Class here letters of spurious oriental or medieval origin only

Epistula Aristotilis ad Alexandrum de conservatione sanitatis see PA3894.S3
Meteorum liber IV see PA3894.D53
Mystica philosophia see PA4364.A2

3894.P4   Problemata Aristotelis ac philosophorum medicorumque complurium

3894.S3   Secretum secretorum (Secreta secretorum sive De regimine principum)

Pseudepigraphic treatise in Arabic purporting to be a translation of the Politica of Aristotle. No Greek text has as yet apparently been found. The chapter on diet has been translated into Latin by Joannes Hispalensis, appearing under various titles: Epistola Aristotelis ad Alexandrum Macedonem de conservatione sanitatis; Epistola de observatione humani corporis; De regimine sanitatis; etc. The title Epistola Aristotelis ad Alexandrum has also been used for the entire work

Theologia (Theologia Aegyptiorum; Mystica philosophia; De secretiori Aegyptiorum philosophia) see PA4364.A2

3894.T75   Tractatulus de practica lapidis philosophici

Not to be confused with the Tractatus Aristotelis... de lapide philosophorum

3894.T8   Tractatus Aristotelis alchymistae ad Alexandrum Magnum de lapide philosophorum

Not to be confused with the Tractatulus de practica [etc.]. The Tractatus was possibly written by one whose real name was Aristoteles, and may not be a treatise falsely ascribed to the Greek philosopher

	Individual authors to 600 A.D.
	Aristotle. Ἀριστοτέλης
	Spurious works -- Continued
3894.Z5	History and criticism
	Class here treatises dealing with all or several of the works listed in PA3894
	Translations
	Greek
(3895.A1)	Ancient (Paraphrases)
	see PA3902
(3895.A15)	Medieval (Paraphrases)
	see PA3902
3895.A2	Modern
	Latin
(3895.A23)	Ancient
	Cf. PA6231.Z2+ Boethius
3895.A3	Medieval
	Modern
3895.A4	Collected works. By date
3895.A41A-.A41Z	Summaries, extracts, etc. By author, A-Z
	Selected works
3895.A42	Miscellaneous. By date
	By group
	Logical (Organon)
	see Separate works
3895.A44	Natural science
3895.A46	Psychological and metaphysical
3895.A48	Moral and political
3895.A49	Rhetoric and Poetics
3895.A5-Z	Separate works, A-Z
(3896)	English
	Classified according to subject in Classes B-Z
3897	French
3898	German
3899	Italian
3900.A-Z	Other languages. By language, A-Z
	Criticism and interpretation
	Ancient and medieval
	Greek
3902.A1	Lists of works (Indices)
	Commentaries. Scholia. Paraphrases
3902.A2-.A49	Collections and selections
	Arrange chronologically by date of publication
	Particular authors
3902.A5	Anonymous

PA3050-4505

Individual authors to 600 A.D.

Aristotle. Ἀριστοτέλης

Criticism and interpretation

Ancient and medieval

Greek

Commentaries. Scholia. Paraphrases

Particular authors -- Continued

3902.A6-.Z3   Other

For the Isagoge of Porphyrius see PA4396.Z2+

Ancient biographies

3902.Z5   Collections. By date

3902.Z5A-.Z5Z3   Particular vitae

3902.Z9   Last will of Aristotle

Latin and Oriental

Latin

(3902.1)   Ancient

see PA6231.Z2+

(3902.2)   Medieval

see B765

Oriental

3902.4   Syriac

3902.5   Arabic

3902.7   Hebrew

3902.9   Armenian

Modern

Class here (1) general treatises, written from a literary point of view, e.g. authenticity, chronology, transmission of the works of Aristoteles, etc. (2) philological and linguistic articles, textual criticism, continuous commentaries without text or with text subordinated to the commentary

For works dealing with the philosophy of Aristotle, including general biography, see B481+

For treatises on special subjects such as political science, or any of the particular sciences, dealt with in the works of Aristotle, see classification with the subject

For philological and linguistic treatises dealing with a particular work of Aristotle see that work

3903.A1   Commentaries (without text or with text subordinated)

Treatises

3903.A2   Early to ca. 1831

3903.A5-.Z3   ca. 1831-

Minor

3903.Z7   Interpretation of detached passages (in various works)

3903.Z8   Single addresses, essays, lectures

Individual authors to 600 A.D.
    Aristotle. Ἀριστοτέλης
      Criticism and interpretation -- Continued
        Language. Style

3925	General
3926	Grammar. Syntax
3926.Z8	Dictionaries. Concordances. Indices. By date

        History of Aristotelianism
          History of Aristotle's philosophy and of his influence on
             various ages, to include history of study and appreciation
             of Aristotle
          see B485; B491

3934	Aristotm... to Arr...
3934.A5	Aristoxenus, of Tarentum, 4th century B.C. Ἀριστόξενος

        Harmonica (Elementa harmonica lib. III) (extracts only).
          Harmonics. Ἁρμονικὰ στοιχεῖα
        Elementa rhythmica (fragments). Elements of rhythm.
          Ῥυθμικὰ στοιχεῖα
        Pythagoricae sententiae (fragments). Πυθαγορικαὶ
          ἀποφάσεις
        Vita Pythagorica (fragments)

PA3050-4505

3934.A8	Arrianus (epic poet) 3rd (?) century A.D. Alexandrias. Ἀρριανός. Ἀλεξανδρίας

        Twenty-four books (fragments)

3935	Arrianus, Flavius, ca. 95-ca. 175 A.D. Arrian. Ἀρριανός
3935.A2	Editions. By date
3935.A25	Selected books or portions of books
3935.A28	Acies contra Alanos. Ἔκτασις κατ' Ἀλανῶν
	Fragment of his Alanica historia (Ἀλανική)
3935.A3	Anabasis Alexandri (De expeditione Alexandri). Anabasis. Ἀλεξάνδρου ἀνάβασις
3935.A39	Bithynica (fragments). Βιθυνικά
3935.A4	Cynegeticus. Κυνηγητικός
3935.A43	De rebus successorum Alexandri. Μετὰ Ἀλέξανδρον
(3935.A48)	Epictetea
	see PA3969
3935.A5	Indica (Historia indica). Ἰνδική
3935.A55	Parthica (fragments). Παρθικά
	Periplus Maris Erythraei see PA4267.P14
3935.A58	Periplus Ponti Euxini. Περίπλους Πόντου Εὐξείνου
	Cf. PA4267.P143 Compilation from Arrianus,
	Menippus, Marcianus, and Pseudo-Seymnus
3935.A6	Tactica. Ars tactica. Τέχνη τακτική
3935.A8-.Z3	Translations. By language, Latin title and date
3935.Z5	Criticism
3935.Z6	Language. Grammar
3935.Z9	Glossaries. Indices. By date

Individual authors to 600 A.D. -- Continued

3936	Arrib... to Ath...
	Artapanus (Jewish historian) 2nd century B.C.? Ἀρτάπανος
3936.A2	Artemidorus, of Daldis (in Lydia) 2nd century A.D. Oneirocritica. Ἀρτεμίδωρος Δαλδιανός. Ὀνειροκριτικά
3936.A23	Artemidorus, of Ephesus (geographer) fl. ca. 100 B.C. Ἀρτεμίδωρος ὁ Ἐφέσιος (Table P-PZ38)
	Artemidorus, of Parion (astrologer) 1st century A.D. Ἀρτεμίδωρος
	Artemidorus, of Tarsus (grammarian) 1st century B.C. Ἀρτεμίδωρος
	Asclepiades, of Bithynia, or Prusa (physician), b. ca. 130 B.C. Ἀσκληπιάδης
3936.A4	Asclepiades, of Myrlia (grammarian) 2nd to 1st century B.C. Ἀσκληπιάδης Μυρλεανός (Table P-PZ38)
	Asclepiades, of Nicaea (grammarian) 3rd century B.C. Ἀσκληπιάδης
3936.A6	Asclepiades, of Samus (poet) 4th to 3rd century B.C. Ἀσκληπιάδης (Table P-PZ38)
	Asclepiades, of Tragilus (historian) 4th century B.C. Ἀσκληπιάδης
	Asclepiades, the younger (pharmacologist) 1st century B.C. Ἀσκληπιάδης ὁ Φαρμακίων
	Asclepiodotus (Neo-Platonist)
	see Asclepiodotus, of Alexandria
3936.A8	Asclepiodotus (philosopher, date unknown). Ἀσκληπιόδοτος (Table P-PZ38)
	Asclepiodotus, of Alexandria (physician) 5th century A.D. Ἀσκληπιόδοτος
	Asclepius, of Tralles, 6th century A.D. Ἀσκλήπιος
3936.A85	Astrampsychus (Table P-PZ38)
	Athenaeus (mechanicus) 2nd century B.C. (or A.D.?) Ἀθήναιος
	Athenaeus (rhetor) 2nd century B.C. Ἀθήναιος
	Athenaeus, of Attalia (physician) fl. between 40 and 70 A.D. Ἀθήναιος
3937	Athenaeus Naucratita, 2nd century A.D. Deipnosophistae lib. XV. Ἀθήναιος Ναυκρατίτης. Δειπνοσοφισταί
3937.A2	Editions. By date
3937.A25	Selected books. By date
3937.A3B1-.A3B15	Individual books
3937.A47	Selections. Quotations. Passages
	Translations
3937.A48	Greek (Modern). By date
3937.A5	Latin. By date
3937.A6	English. By date
3937.A65	French. By date

	Individual authors to 600 A.D.
	Athenaeus Naucratita, 2nd century A.D. Deipnosophistae lib.
	XV. Ἀθήναιος Ναυκρατίτης. Δειπνοσοφισταί
	Translations -- Continued
3937.A67	German. By date
3937.A7A-.A7Z	Other. By language, A-Z
	Subarrange by date
3937.A8-.Z3	Criticism
3938	Athenai... to Aure...
	Athenais see PA3972.E86
	Aurelius, Marcus, Emperor of Rome, 121-180 A.D.
3939	Commentariorum quos sibi ipsi scripsit lib. XII. Meditations.
	Μάρκος Ἀντωνῖνος. Εἰς ἑαυτόν
3939.A2	Editions. By date
3939.A25	Selected books. By date
3939.A3B1-.A3B15	Individual books
3939.A47	Selections. Quotations. Passages
	Translations
3939.A5	Latin. By date
	English see B580+
	Other languages see B582.A+
3939.A8-.Z3	Criticism
	Letters to Fronto (in Latin) see PA6389.F6+
3940	Auto... to Bab...
3940.A8	Autolycus (mathematician) fl. 310 B.C. Αὐτόλυκος (Table
	P-PZ38 modified)
	Cf. QB21 Astronomy
3940.A8A61-.A8A78	Separate works. By title
	e.g. De sphaera quae movetur liber; De ortibus et
	occasibus libri duo (Περὶ κινουμένης σφαῖρας· Περὶ
	ἐπιτολῶν καὶ δύσεων)
3941	Babrius, 2nd century A.D. Βάβριος
3941.A2	Editions
	Translations and paraphrases
3941.A3	Greek (Medieval and modern)
	Latin
(3941.A35)	Ancient
	see PA6225 Avianus
(3941.A37)	Modern
3941.A5-.Z3	Other. By language, A-Z, and date
3941.Z5	Criticism, interpretation, etc.
3941.Z8	Glossaries, indices, etc. By date
3942	Babu... to Bac...
3943	Bacchylides, ca. 505-ca. 450 B.C. Βακχυλίδης
3943.A2	Editions
	Translations and paraphrases
3943.A3	Greek (Medieval and modern)

PA3050-4505

	Individual authors to 600 A.D.
	Bacchylides, ca. 505-ca. 450 B.C. Βακχυλίδης
	Translations and paraphrases -- Continued
3943.A5-.Z3	Other. By language, A-Z, and date
3943.Z5	Criticism, interpretation, etc.
3943.Z8	Glossaries, indices, etc. By date
3944	Bad... to Call...
	Bassus, of Smyrna. Βάσσος
	Bassus, Cassianus see PA3946.C7
	Bassus Lollius
	see Lollius Bassus
3944.B3	Berosus (Berossus), the Chaldean, fl. ca. 300 B.C.
	Babyloniaca. Babylōniaka. Βηρωσός. Βαβυλωνιακά
3944.B38	Bion, of Borysthenes, 3rd century B.C. Βίων (Table P-PZ38)
3944.B4	Bion, of Smyrna (fl. probably towards the end of the 2nd century B.C.). Βίων ὁ Σμυρναῖος
	Class here also editions containing both Bion's and Moschus' poems. Editions of the poems of Theocritus, Bion, and Moschus and fragments of minor poets, are classified with Theocritus
	Boëthus, (Platonist) 2nd century A.D. Βοηθός
	Boëthus, of Sidon (peripatetic) 1st century B.C. Βοηθός
	Boëthus, of Sidon (stoic) 2nd century B.C. Βοηθός
	Boëthus, of Tarsus, poet, 1st century B.C. Βοηθός
3944.B8	Bolus, of Mendes, 3rd century B.C. Βῶλος (Table P-PZ38)
	Published "Commenta" and other treatises as works of Democritus of Abdera
	Cf. PA3948.D8 Pseudo-Democritus
	Brutus, Marcus Junius, d 42. B.C.
3944.B85	Pseudo-Brutus. Epistulae Graecae
3944.C5	Caecilius, of Calacte, 1st century B.C. Καικίλιος Καλακτῖνος (Table P-PZ38)
	Author of a treatise against which Pseudo-Longinus wrote his De sublimitate
	Cf. PA4229.L4+ Pseudo-Longinus. De sublimitate
3945	Callimachus, fl. between 310 and 240 B.C. Καλλίμαχος
	Editions
3945.A2	Hymni and Epigrammata (or Hymni alone). Ὕμνοι. Ἐπιγράμματα
3945.A3	Selections
	Special hymns
3945.A31	I. In Jovem. Εἰς Δία
3945.A32	II. In Apollinem. Εἰς Ἀπόλλωνα
3945.A33	III. In Dianam. Εἰς Ἄρτεμιν
3945.A34	IV. In Delum. Delos. Εἰς Δῆλον

	Individual authors to 600 A.D.
	Callimachus, fl. between 310 and 240 B.C. Καλλίμαχος
	Editions
	Special hymns -- Continued
3945.A35	V. In lavacrum Palladis. Bath of Pallas. Εἰς λουτρὰ τῆς Παλλάδος
3945.A36	VI. In Cererem. Hymnos eis Dēmētra. Εἰς Δήμητρα
3945.A4	Epigrammata. Ἐπιγράμματα
3945.A5	Fragments and lost works. By date
	Including Aetia; Coma Berenices; Hecale; Ibis; Iambi. Αἴτια. Βερενίκης πλόκαμος. Ἑκάλη. Ἶβις. Ἴαμβοι
	Translations
3945.A53	Greek (Modern)
	Latin
(3945.A54)	Ancient
	see PA6274.C6; PA6519.I2
3945.A6	Modern
3945.A8-.Z3	Other. By language, A-Z, and date
3945.Z5	Criticism
3945.Z8	Glossaries. Indices. By date
3946	Callin... to Cass...
	Callinus, of Ephesus, 7th century B.C. Καλλῖνος
	Callippus, of Cyzicus (astronomer) 4th century B.C. Κάλλιππος
	Callisthenes, of Olynthus, ca. 370-327 B.C. Καλλισθένης
	Only fragments extant
3946.C2A1	Collected works
3946.C2A3	Gesta (or Acta) Alexandri. Ἀλεξάνδρου πράξεις
3946.C2A6	Hellenica. Ἑλληνικά
3946.C2A8-.C2Z	Criticism, etc.
3946.C3	Pseudo-Callisthenes
	Legendary and fictitious history of Alexander the Great
	For vernacular medieval versions see Classes PQ, PR, and PT
	Cf. PA6445.I7 Itinerarium Alexandri
	Cf. PA6791.V8+ J. Valerius
3946.C53	Callistratus Aristophaneus (grammarian) 3rd century B.C. Καλλίστρατος ὁ Ἀριστοφάνειος (Table P-PZ38)
3946.C55	Callistratus, sophista (rhetor) 4th century A.D. Καλλίστρατος (Table P-PZ38)
	Callixenus, of Rhodus, 3rd century B.C. Kallixeinos, of Rhodes. Καλλίξεινος
	Carcinus, epic poet. Καρκίνος
	Carcinus, of Akragas, the older (dramatist) fl. 431 B.C. Καρκίνος
	Carcinus, of Akragas, the younger (dramatist) 4th century B.C. Καρκίνος

PA3050-4505

	Individual authors to 600 A.D.
	Callin... to Cass... -- Continued
	Carneades, of Cyrene, 214/3-129/8 B.C. Καρνεάδης see B537
3946.C6	Carystius, of Pergamon, fl. between 125 to 120 B.C. Καρύστιος ὁ Περγαμηνός (Table P-PZ38)
3946.C7	Cassianus Bassus, Scholasticus (geoponic writer) 6th century A.D. Κασσιανὸς Βάσσος (Table P-PZ38)
3947	Cassius Dio Cocceianus, ca. 155-ca. 235 A.D. Δίων Κάσσιος Κοκκηϊανός
	Editions
(3947.A1)	Facsimiles of manuscripts
	see Z114
3947.A2	By date
3947.A3	Selected books or portions
3947.A4	Particular books. By date of publication
3947.A45	Selections. Quotations. Passages
	Translations
3947.A46	Greek (Modern) By date
3947.A47	Latin. By date
(3947.A49)	English
	see DG207.C36
3947.A5-.Z3	Other. By language, A-Z, and date
3947.Z5	Criticism
	For historical treatises see Class DG
3948	Cassius to Demosthenes
	Cassius Dionysius see PA3968.D45
	Cassius Dionysius Longinus see PA4229.L3
	Castor, of Rhodes, historian, 1st century B.C. Κάστωρ
3948.C2	Cebes, 1st (?) century A.D. Tabula. Kebētos Thēbaiou pinax. Κέβης. Κέβητος Θηβαίου πίναξ
	Not identical with Cebes of Thebes, Socratic philosopher
	Celsus, Platonic philosopher fl. 180 A.D. Κέλσος see B538.C2+
	Cephalio (historian) 2nd century A.D. Κεφαλίων
	Cephalio (or Cephalon) of Gergithes, pseud. Κεφαλίων
	see Hegesianax, of Alexandria Troas
3948.C22	Cercidas. Κερκίδας (Table P-PZ38)
	Certamen Homeri et Hesiodi see PA4009.Z7
3948.C23	Chaeremon, 4th cent. B.C. Χαιρήμων (Table P-PZ38)
	Chaeremon, of Alexandria (historian), 1st century A.D. Χαιρήμων
3948.C24	Chaeris (grammarian) 2nd (?) century B.C. Χαῖρις (Table P-PZ38)
	Chamaeleon, of Heraclea (peripatetic philosopher) 4th to 3rd century B.C. Χαμαιλέων

Individual authors to 600 A.D.
Cassius to Demosthenes -- Continued

3948.C26   Chamaeleon, of Heraclea Pontica. Χαμαιλέων (Table P-PZ38)

Charax, of Pergamon, 2nd or 3rd century A.D. Χάραξ Περγαμηνός

Charax, Joannes (grammarian) 6th century A.D. Ἰωάννης Χάραξ

3948.C3   Chariton Aphrodisiensis, 2nd (?) century A.D. De Chaerea et Callirrhoe. Χαρίτων Ἀφροδισιεύς. Περὶ Χαιρέαν καὶ Καλλιρρόην (Table P-PZ43a)

Charon, of Lampsacus (logographer) 5th century B.C. Χάρων

3948.C33   Chion of Heraclea. Χίων
         Fictitious author of a novel in letters

Choerilus (dramatist) 6th century B.C. Χοιρίλος

Choerilus, of Iasos, Caria (epic poet) 4th century B.C. Χοιρίλος

3948.C35   Choerilus, of Samos (epic poet) 5th century B.C. Χοιρίλος (Table P-PZ38)

3948.C38   Choeroboscus, Georgius, grammarian, fl. between 500 and 530 A.D. Γεώργιος Χοιροβοσκός (Table P-PZ38)

Choricius, of Gaza, fl. 526-540 A.D. Χορίκιος

3948.C39-.C393   Christodōros, fl. 5th cent. Ekphrasis. Χριστόδωρος. Ἔκφρασις (Table P-PZ42)

3948.C4   Chrysippus Solensis, 281/77-208/4 B.C. Χρύσιππος (Table P-PZ38)
         Fragments
         Cf. B540+ Philosophy

Cinaethon, of Lacedaemon (date uncertain). Κιναίθων ὁ Λακεδαιμόνιος
         Genealogical poems, lost

Cinesias, of Athens, 5th century B.C. Κινησίας

3948.C5   Cleanthes (Stoic philosopher) 331/0-232/0 B.C. Κλεάνθης (Table P-PZ38)
         Fragments
         Cf. B557.C2+ Philosophy

Clearchus, of Soli, 4th-3rd (?) century B.C. Κλέαρχος

Cleomedes, 2nd century A.D. Κλεομήδης

3948.C63   Cleonides (pupil of Aristoxenus, of Tarentum) fl. ca. 100 A.D. Κλεονείδης (Table P-PZ38)
         Presumably author of Isagoge harmonica (Εἰσαγωγὴ ἁρμονική), falsely ascribed to Euclides or Pappus

3948.C67   Clitarchus (historian) 4th to 3rd century B.C. Cleitarchus. Κλείταρχος (Table P-PZ38)

3948.C7   Colluthus, of Lycopolis, fl. between 491-518 A.D. De raptu Helenae. Rape of Helen. Κόλλουθος. Ἁρπαγὴ Ἑλένης

PA3050-4505

Individual authors to 600 A.D.
Cassius to Demosthenes -- Continued

3948.C73	Colotes, of Lampsacus (Epicurean), 4th to 3rd century B.C. Κωλώτης (Table P-PZ38)
	Comparatio Menandri et Philistionis see PA4247
3948.C75	Conon, fl. between 36 B.C. and 17 A.D. Narrationes. Κόνων. Διηγήσεις
	Fifty mythical tales
3948.C76	Corax, of Syracuse, rhetor, 5th century B.C. Κόραξ (Table P-PZ38)
3948.C77	Corinna, 5th century B.C. Κόριννα (Table P-PZ38)
3948.C8	Cornutus, Lucius Annaeus, fl. 65 A.D. Ἀνναῖος Κορνοῦτος (Table P-PZ38 modified)
	For Latin works see PA6375.C8
3948.C8A61-.C8A78	Separate works. By title
	e.g. Theologiae Graecae compendium (De natura deorum). Ἐπιδρομὴ τῶν κατὰ τὴν Ἑλληνικὴν θεολογίαν παραδεδομένων
	Ars rhetorica see PA3516.A7
3948.C817	Crates. Κράτης (Table P-PZ38)
3948.C82	Crates Mallotes, fl. ca. 167 B.C. Κράτης ὁ Μαλλώτης (Table P-PZ38)
	Cf. PA4035.A7+ Homer
3948.C83	Crates Thebanus, 4th century B.C. Κράτης ὁ Θηβαῖος (Table P-PZ38)
3948.C84	Cratinus (dramatist) 5th century B.C. Κρατῖνος (Table P-PZ38)
3948.C85	Crinagoras, b. ca. 70 B.C. Κριναγόρας (Table P-PZ38)
3948.C86	Critias Atheniensis, fl 415-403 B.C. Κριτίας (Table P-PZ38)
3948.C9	Ctesias, of Cnidus, fl. 415-397 B.C. Κτησίας ὁ Κνίδιος (Table P-PZ38)
3948.C92	Cynaethus, of Chios (Homerida) fl. ca. 504 B.C. Κύναιθος (Table P-PZ38)
	Cf. PA4023.H81 Homer
	Cyranus see PA3998.H5K8
3948.C93	Cypria (epic poem). Κύπρια
3948.C948	"Cyrillus glossator." Lexicon graeco-latinum vetus in calce quorundam Cyrilli scriptorum inventum. Κύριλλος
	Compiler unknown
3948.C95	Cyrillus (Cyril), Saint, Patriarch of Alexandria, d. 444 A.D. Κύριλλος (Table P-PZ38)
	For theological works see BR60+ BR1720
	Collectio alphabetica vocum Grecarum. Λέξεων συναγωγὴ κατὰ στοιχεῖον
	Authorship doubtful
	De dictionibus quae accentu variant significatum see PA4221.J5D5

Individual authors to 600 A.D.
   Cassius to Demosthenes -- Continued

3948.D13   Damascius, of Damascus fl. 529 A.D. Δαμάσκιος ὁ Δαμασκηνός (Table P-PZ38)

3948.D15   "Damigeron magus." De lapidibus. Περὶ λίθων
              Cf. PA4258.D3+ Orpheus

3948.D17   David (Armenian philosopher) 6th century A.D. (Table P-PZ38 modified)

3948.D17A61-   Separate works. By title
  .D17A78
              e.g. Commentarium in Porphyrii Isagogen; Prolegomena philosophiae

3948.D34   Deilochos, of Proconnesus. Δηίλοχος (Δηίοχος) (Table P-PZ38)

          Demeter, Hymn to
            see PA4023.H83 Homer; PA3945.A36 Callimachus
          Demetrius (Jewish historian) 3rd century B.C. Δημήτριος
          Demetrius, of Byzantium (historian) 3rd century B.C. Δημήτριος
          Demetrius, of Byzantium (peripatetic) 1st century B.C. Δημήτριος
          Demetrius, of Callatis (geographer) ca. 200 B.C. Δημήτριος
          Demetrius, of Magnesia, 1st century B.C. (Demetrius Magnes). Δημήτριος ὁ Μάγνης

3948.D4   Demetrius, of Phaleron, ca. 350-ca. 283 B.C. Δημήτριος ὁ Φαληρεύς (Table P-PZ38 modified)
            Fragments only

3948.D5   De elocutione (De interpretatione). Περὶ ἑρμηνείας
            Wrongly ascribed to Demetrius

3948.D55   Demetrius, of Scepsis (historian) fl. 150 B.C. Δημήτριος ὁ Σκήψιος (Table P-PZ38)

          Demetrius Ixion, grammarian, 1st (?) century B.C. Δημήτριος ὁ Ἰξίων
          Demetrius Lacon, fl. ca. 110 B.C. Δημήτριος ὁ Λάκων

3948.D7   Democritus, of Abdera, ca. 460-ca. 370 B.C. Δημόκριτος ὁ Ἀβδηρίτης (Table P-PZ38)
            Cf. B295+ Philosophy

3948.D8   Pseudo-Democritus
            Cf. PA3944.B8 Bolus, of Mendes

          Demophilus (writer of comedies, middle comedy). Δημόφιλος
          Demosthenes. Δημοσθένης

3949.A2   Editions. By date
          Selected orations

3949.A3   Miscellaneous
            Including school editions
          Special groups
           Public orations

PA3050-4505

Individual authors to 600 A.D.
Demosthenes. Δημοσθένης
Selected orations
Special groups
Public orations -- Continued
3949.A4 Collections and selections
Deliberative speeches. Suasoriae. Δημηγορίαι.
Συμβουλευτικοί
Collections and selections see PA3949.A4
Philippics
see PA3950.O3; PA3950.P3+
3949.A5 "Deliberative speeches" (properly so called).
Hellenic speeches. Δημηγορίαι Ἑλληνικαί
Includes three "Hellenic" speeches by Demosthenes,
namely On the symmories, On Megalopolis, On
Rhodes, and two speeches not by Demosthenes,
De republica ordinanda and De foedere
Alexandri
3949.A6 Court speeches (on public questions). Δικανικοὶ
δημόσιοι
Includes On Androtion; On Leptines' law; Against
Aristocrates; On Timocrates; Against Midias, On
the embassy, On the crown
3949.A7 Private (forensic) speeches. Ἰδιωτικοί
Orationes tutoriae see PA3950.A3+
(3949.A88) Epideictic
see PA3950.A13 PA3950.F8
3949.A9 Selections. Quotations. Passages
3950 Particular orations
3950.A13 Amatorius (Declamatio amatoria. Laus Epicratis).
Ἐρωτικός
Spurious
3950.A2 In Androtionem. Kat' Androtiōnos. Κατ' Ἀνδροτίωνος
παρανόμων
3950.A23 In Apaturium. Πρὸς Ἀπατούριον παραγραφή
Authorship disputed
In Aphobum I-III
Including editions of the "Orationes tutoriae", i.e., the three
speeches in Aphobum and the two speeches in
Onetorem
3950.A31 In Aphobum de tutela. Κατὰ Ἀφόβου ἐπιτροφῆς
3950.A32 In Aphobum oratio II. Κατὰ Ἀφόβου β'
3950.A33 Adversus Aphobum de falso testimonio. Πρὸς Ἄφοβον
ὑπὲρ Φάνου ψευδομαρτυριῶν
3950.A4 Criticism
3950.A5 Adversus Aristocratem. Against Aristocrates. Κατὰ
Ἀριστοκράτους

Individual authors to 600 A.D.
   Demosthenes. Δημοσθένης
      Particular orations -- Continued
         In Aristogitonem I-II. Κατὰ Ἀριστογείτονος α′ β′
           I, doubtful; II, spurious

3950.A7	Text. By date
3950.A8	Criticism
3950.B5	In Boeotum de dote. Πρὸς Βοιωτὸν ὑπὲρ προικὸς μητρῴας
	Spurious
3950.B7	In Boeotum de nomine. Πρὸς Βοιωτὸν περὶ τοῦ ὀνόματος
3950.C2	In Calliclem de fundo. Πρὸς Καλλικλέα περὶ χωρίου
3950.C3	In Callippum. Πρὸς Κάλλιππον
	Spurious
3950.C4	De Chersoneso. Περὶ τῶν ἐν Χερρονήσῳ
	Pro Chrysippo see PA3950.P8
	De classibus see PA3950.S9
3950.C5	In Cononem de verberatione. Κατὰ Κόνωνος αἰκείας
	De contributione see PA3950.R3
3950.C6	De corona. On the crown. Ὑπὲρ Κτησιφῶντος περὶ τοῦ στεφάνου
	Cf. PA3823.A23 Aeschines
3950.C8	Pro corona trierarchias. Περὶ τοῦ στεφάνου τῆς τριηραρχίας
	Authorship disputed
3950.D5	In Dionysodorum dati damni. Κατὰ Διονυσοδώρου βλάβης
	Authorship disputed
	Epitaphius see PA3950.F8
	Eroticus see PA3950.A13
3950.E6	In Eubulidem (Appellatio contra E.). Πρὸς Εὐβουλίδην ἔφεσις
	Authorship disputed
3950.E8	In Euergum et Mnesibulum falsos testes. Κατ᾽ Εὐέργου καὶ Μνησιβούλου ψευδομαρτυριῶν
	Spurious
3950.F6	De foedere Alexandri. Περὶ τῶν πρὸς Ἀλέξανδρον συνθηκῶν
	Spurious
3950.F8	Oratio funebris (Declamatio funebris). Ἐπιτάφιος
	Spurious
3950.H3	De Halonneso. Περὶ Ἁλοννήσου
	Original oration lost; oration preserved is presumably by Hegesippus of Sunion
3950.L2	In Lacritum (Adversus Lacriti exceptionem). Πρὸς τὴν Λακρίτου παραγραφήν
	Spurious

PA3050-4505

Individual authors to 600 A.D.
Demosthenes. Δημοσθένης
Particular orations -- Continued

3950.L3 De falsa legatione. Κατ' Αἰσχίνου περὶ τῆς
παραπρεσβείας
Cf. PA3823.A25 Aeschines

3950.L5 In Leocharem (Adversus Leocharem de haereditate).
Πρὸς Λεοχάρην περὶ τοῦ Ἀρχιάδου κλήρου
Spurious

3950.L7 Adversus Leptinem (De immunitate adversus Leptinem).
Περὶ τῆς ἀτελείας πρὸς Λεπτίνην

3950.M2 In Macartatum (Adversus Macartatum de Hagniana
haereditate). Πρὸς Μακάρτατον περὶ Ἁγνίου κλήρου
Spurious

3950.M4 De Megalopolitis. Ὑπὲρ Μεγαλοπολιτῶν

3950.M7 Contra Midiam (In Midiam oratio de alapa). Against
Midias. Κατὰ Μειδίου περὶ τοῦ κονδύλου

3950.N2 In Nausimachum (Exceptio adversus Nausimachum et
Xenopithem). Πρὸς Ναυσίμαχον καὶ Ξενοπείθην
παραγραφή

3950.N5 In Neaeram. Κατὰ Νεαίρας
Spurious

3950.N7 In Nicostratum (Adversus Nicostratum de Arethusii
mancipiis). Πρὸς Νικόστρατον περὶ ἀνδραπόδων
ἀπογραφῆς Ἀρεθουσίου

3950.O2 In Olympiodorum (In O. dati damni). Κατὰ
Ὀλυμπιοδώρου βλάβης
Spurious

Olynthiacae I-III. Ὀλυνθιακοί α' β' γ'

3950.O3 Text. By date
3950.O4 Criticism
3950.O7 Adversus Onetorem I-II. Πρὸς Ὀνήτορα ἐξούλης α' β'
3950.P2 De pace. Περὶ εἰρήνης
3950.P23 In Pantaenetum (Exceptio adversus Pantaenetum).
Against Pantaenetus. Πρὸς Πανταίνετον παραγραφή

3950.P26 In Phaenippum (Adversus Phaenippum de
permutatione). Πρὸς Φαίνιππον περὶ ἀντιδόσεως
Spurious

Philippicae I-XII
Including Olynthiacae 1-3; Philippica I; De pace; Philippica
II; De Halonneso; De Chersoneso; Philippica III;
Philippica IV; Adversus Philippi epistulam; Philippi
epistula

3950.P3 Editions. By date
3950.P4 Selected orations (Miscellaneous)
Separate orations
De Chersoneso see PA3950.C4

Individual authors to 600 A.D.
   Demosthenes. Δημοσθένης
      Particular orations
         Philippicae I-XII
            Separate orations -- Continued
               De Halonneso see PA3950.H3
               De pace see PA3950.P2
               Olynthiacae see PA3950.O3+
               Philippicae (In Philippum) I-IV. Κατὰ Φιλίππου α' β' γ'
                  δ'

3950.P5	I-IV (or I-III)
3950.P51	I (or I-II)
3950.P52	II (or II-III)
3950.P53	III (or III-IV)
3950.P54	IV
	Authorship disputed
3950.P56	Adversus Philippi epistulam. Πρὸς τὴν ἐπιστολὴν τὴν Φιλίππου
3950.P58	Philippi epistula
3950.P6	Criticism
	Including general criticism and criticism of individual orations
3950.P7	Pro Phormione (Exceptio pro Phormione). Ὑπὲρ Φορμίωνος παραγραφή
3950.P8	In Phormionem (Adversus Phormionem de pecunia mutuo data). Πρὸς Φορμίωνα περὶ δανείου
3950.P9	In Polyclem (Adversus Polyclem de trierarchiae sumptibus). Πρὸς Πολυκλέα περὶ τοῦ ἐπιτριηραρχήματος
3950.R3	De republica ordinanda (De constitutione). Περὶ συντάξεως
	Authorship disputed
3950.R6	De Rhodiorum libertate. Περὶ τῆς Ῥοδίων ἐλευθερίας
3950.S5	In Spudiam (Contra Spudiam de dote). Πρὸς Σπουδίαν ὑπὲρ προικός
3950.S7	In Stephanum oratio I. Κατὰ Στεφάνου ψευδομαρτυριῶν α'
	Authorship disputed
3950.S8	In Stephanum oratio II. Κατὰ Στεφάνου β'
	Spurious
3950.S9	De symmoriis (De classibus). Περὶ τῶν συμμοριῶν
3950.T3	In Theocrinem (Delatio in Theocrinem). Κατὰ Θεοκρίνου ἔνδειξις
	Spurious
3950.T5	Adversus Timocratem. Kata Timokratous. Κατὰ Τιμοκράτους

PA3050-4505

	Individual authors to 600 A.D.
	Demosthenes. Δημοσθένης
	Particular orations -- Continued
3950.T7	In Timotheum (Adversus Timotheum de aere alieno). Πρὸς Τιμόθεον ὑπερ χρέως
	Spurious
3950.Z3	In Zenothemin (Exceptio adversus Zenothemidem). Παραγραφὴ πρὸς Ζηνόθεμιν
	Authorship disputed
3950.Z6	Prooemia (Exordia concionum). Προοίμια
3950.Z7	Epistulae. Ἐπιστολαί
	Including De concordia; De reditu suo; De Lycurgi liberis; De Theramenis maledictis; Ad Heracleodorum; Senatui et populo Athenensium. Περὶ τῆς ὁμονοίας. Περὶ τῆς ἰδίας καθόδου. Περὶ τῶν Λυκούργου παίδων. Περὶ τῆς Θηραμένους βλασφημίας. Πρὸς Ἡρακλεοδῶρον. Πρὸς τὴν βουλὴν καὶ τὸν δῆμον τῶν Ἀθηναίων
3950.Z8	Fragments
3950.Z9	Spurious orations
	Class here collections and general treatises only. For particular orations see PA3950
3951	Translations
3951.A15	Greek (Modern)
3951.A2	Latin
3951.A3-Z	Other. By language, A-Z
	English
3951.E5	Collected and selected orations. By date
3951.E5A-.E5Z	Particular orations, by Latin title and translator (successive Cutter numbers)
	French
3951.F8	Collected and selected orations. By date
3951.F8A-.F8Z	Particular orations, by Latin title and translator (successive Cutter numbers)
	German
3951.G5	Collected and selected orations. By date
3951.G5A-.G5Z	Particular orations, by Latin title and translator (successive Cutter numbers)
	Interpretation and criticism
	Ancient
3952.A1	Scholia. By date
	Other
	Treatises on, and lives of Demosthenes
3952.A15	Collections
	Including collections of ancient criticisms of Demosthenes

Individual authors to 600 A.D.
   Demosthenes. Δημοσθένης
     Interpretation and criticism
       Ancient
         Other -- Continued

(3952.A16)   Particular authors
             Cf. PA3965.D17 Didymus Chalcenterus
             Cf. PA3966 Dionysius, of Halicarn.
             Cf. PA4226.Z65 Libanius. Vita et argumenta
                Demosthenis
             Cf. PA4230.D4 Lucianus. Demosthenis
                encomium
             Cf. PA4273 Photius
             Cf. PA4368.V5 Pseudo-Plutarchus. Vitae decem
                oratorum
             Cf. PA4369.D5 Plutarch. Vita Demosthenis
             Cf. PA4487.T35 Tiberius, rhetor
             Cf. PA4500.Z63 Zosimus. Vita Demosthenis
             Cf. PA5365 Suidas
       Modern

3952.A2	Early to 1800/1850
3952.A5-Z	1800/1850-
3964	Language. Style. Technique
3964.A-.Z3	General

           Including treatises on style, rhythm, figures of speech,
             etc.
         Special

3964.Z5	Grammar. Syntax
3964.Z8	Glossaries. Indices. Concordances. By date
3965	Demosthenes (physician) to Dion...
3965.D11	Demosthenes (physician) 1st century A.D. Δημοσθένης (Table P-PZ38)
3965.D112	Demosthenes (jurist) 5th century A.D. Δημοσθένης (Table P-PZ38)
3965.D119	Dexippus (Neo-Platonist) 4th century A.D. Δέξιππος (Table P-PZ38)
3965.D12	Dexippus, of Cos (physician) fl. ca. 390 B.C. Δέξιππος (Table P-PZ38)
3965.D123	Dexippus, Publius Herennius (historian) 3rd century A.D. Π. Ἑρέννιος Δέξιππος (Table P-PZ38)
3965.D128	Diagoras, of Melos. Διαγόρας (Table P-PZ38)
3965.D13	Dicaearchus Messenius, 4th century B.C. Δικαίαρχος ὁ Μεσσήνιος (Table P-PZ38)

          The Descriptio Graeciae formerly ascribed to Dicaearchus is
            by Dionysius Calliphontis

3965.D14	"Dictys Cretensis". Δίκτυς

          Cf. PA6379.D3 Latin literature

Individual authors to 600 A.D.
  Demosthenes. Δημοσθένης (physician) to Dion...
    Didymus (son of Didymus) see PA3965.D17
    Didymus (son of Heraclides) musician and grammarian, fl.
      ca. 60 A.D. Δίδυμος ὁ τοῦ Ἡρακλείδου

3965.D153	Didymus, of Alexandria, metrologist, 1st century B.C. Δίδυμος (Table P-PZ38)
3965.D155	Didymus, of Alexandria, geoponic writer, and physician, 4th century A.D. Δίδυμος (Table P-PZ38)

    Didymus, of Alexandria, grammarian, 1st century A.D. see
      PA3965.D165
    Didymus, of Alexandria, the grammarian, surnamed
      Chalcenterus see PA3965.D17

(3965.D16)	Didymus, of Alexandria, the theologian see BR60+ BR1720

    Didymus, the blind
      see Didymus, of Alexandria, the theologian

3965.D165	Didymus, the younger, grammarian of Alexandria, 1st century A.D. Δίδυμος ὁ Νεώτερος (Table P-PZ38)
3965.D17	Didymus Chalcenterus, ca. 63 B.C.-ca. 10 A.D. Δίδυμος Χαλκέντερος (Table P-PZ38)

      Cf. PA3879.A17 Aristophanes. Scholia
      Cf. PA3952.A1 Demosthenes. Scholia
      Cf. PA3977.A7+ Euripides. Scholia
      Cf. PA4035.D4 Homerus. Scholia
      Cf. PA4276.A1 Pindarus. Scholia
      Cf. PA4416.A7+ Sophocles. Scholia
    Didymus, Ateius (date unknown). Δίδυμος Ἀτήϊος
    Didymus, Claudius, grammarian, fl. ca. 50 A.D.? Κλαύδιος
      Δίδυμος

3965.D18	Dinarchus, fl. 336-292 B.C. Δείναρχος (Table P-PZ38)

    Dio Cassius see PA3947

3965.D2-.D22	Dio, Chrysostom. Δίων Χρυσόστομος (Table P-PZ44)
3965.D25	Diocles, of Carystus, 4th century B.C. Διοκλῆς ὁ Καρύστιος (Table P-PZ38)

    Diodorus Siculus, fl. ca. 60-30 B.C. Διόδωρος Σικελιώτης
      Bibliotheca historica. Βιβλιοθήκη

3965.D3	Editions. By date
	Translations
3965.D4A5	Latin. By date
3965.D4A6-.D4Z	Other. By language, A-Z, and date
3965.D5	Criticism
	For historical treatises see D58
3965.D55	Epistulae
	Spurious

    Diogenes, of Apollonia, 5th century B.C. Διογένης ὁ
      Ἀπολλωνιάτης

Individual authors to 600 A.D.
  Demosthenes (physician) to Dion... -- Continued
    Diogenes, of Seleucia, "the Babylonian," ca. 240-ca. 152 B.C.
    Diogenes, of Sinope, 403-323 B.C. Διογένης see B305.D4+

3965.D6	Diogenes Laertius (probably 3rd century A.D.) De vitis philosophorum lib. X. Lives, teachings, and sayings of famous philosophers. Διογένης ὁ Λαέρτιος. Περὶ βίων, δογμάτων καὶ ἀποφθεγμάτων τῶν ἐν φιλοσοφίᾳ εὐδοκιμησάντων
3965.D74	Diogenianus, of Heraclea (lexicographer) 2nd century A.D. Διογενειανός (Table P-PZ38)
3965.D83	Dionysius. Διονύσιος
	Treatises on various authors known by this name
3965.D85	Dionysius (date uncertain). Διονύσιος
	Author of the Bassarica (Βασσαρικά), to be distinguished from Dionysius Periegetes
3965.D87	Dionysius I, tyrant of Syracuse, d. 367 B.C. Διονύσιος (Table P-PZ38)
(3965.D88)	Dionysius Areopagita. Διονύσιος ὁ Ἀρεωπαγίτης
	see B667.D4
3965.D9	Dionysius Calliphontis, 1st (?) century B.C. Descriptio Graeciae. Διονύσιος. Ἀναγραφὴ τῆς Ἑλλάδος
	Formerly ascribed to Dicaearchus
3965.D93	Dionysius Chalcus, 5th century B.C. Διονύσιος ὁ Χαλκοῦς (Table P-PZ38)
	Dionysius cyclographus see PA3968.D178
3965.D95	Dionysius, of Byzantium (date undertain). Anaplus Bospori. Διονύσιος ὁ Βυζάντιος. Ἀνάπλους τοῦ Βοσπόρου
3965.D97	Dionysius, of Chalcis, historian, 2nd century B.C. (?) Διονύσιος ὁ Χαλκιδεύς (Table P-PZ38)

    Dionysius, of Halicarnassus. Διονύσιος ὁ Ἁλικαρνασσεύς

3966	Editions
3966.A2	Comprehensive
3966.A3	Antiquitates Romanae. Ῥωμαϊκὴ ἀρχαιολογία
	Books I-XI, fragments of XII-XX
3966.A4	Editions of fragments. By date
(3966.A5)	Criticism
	see PA3967.Z4
	Rhetorical treatises
3966.A6	Collections and selections. By date
3966.A7	Fragments. By date
(3966.A9)	Criticism
	see PA3967.Z5
	Particular treatises

PA3050-4505

Individual authors to 600 A.D.
Dionysius, of Halicarnassus. Διονύσιος ὁ Ἁλικαρνασσεύς
Editions
Rhetorical treatises
Particular treatises -- Continued

3966.D2   De admirabili vi dicendi in Demosthene. Περὶ τῆς
                 λεκτικῆς Δημοσθένους δεινότητος
                     Cf. PA3952 Demosthenes
                 De compositione verborum (De structura orationis).
                 Περὶ συνθέσεως ὀνομάτων
3966.D3   Editions
3966.D4   Criticism
                 De Demosthene et Aristotle see PA3966.E6
3966.D43   De Dinarcho. Περὶ Δεινάρχου
3966.D45   De imitatione libri III. Περὶ μιμήσεως
                     Of lib. I only five short fragments are preserved; of lib. II
                         an extract, published in older editions as a
                         separate treatise with title De veteribus scriptoribus
                         censura (Ἀρχαίων κρίσις); lib. III lost
                 De Isaeo iudicium see PA3966.D5
                 De Isocrate iudicium see PA3966.D5
                 De Lysia iudicium see PA3966.D5
                 De Lysiae orationibus see PA3966.F8
3966.D5   De oratoribus antiquis (Commentarii de antiquis
                     oratoribus). Περὶ τῶν ἀρχαίων ῥητόρων
                     ὑπομνηματισμοί
                     Lib. I. De Lysia iudicium; De Isocrate iudicium; De
                         Isaeo iudicium. Λυσίας. Ἰσοκράτης. Ἰσαῖος
                     Lib. II. Fragments only
                         Cf. PA3966.D2 De admirabili vi dicendi in
                             Demosthene
                 De Platone et de praecipuis historicis see PA3966.E8
3966.D6   De Thucydide ad Aelium Tuberonem. Περὶ τοῦ
                     Θουκυδίδου χαρακτῆρος
                     Cf. PA3966.E7 Epistula ad Ammaeum II
                 De Thucydide ad Ammaeum see PA3966.E7
                 De veteribus scriptoribus censura see PA3966.D45
                 Epistulae
3966.E5   Editions (of the three letters)
3966.E6   Epistula ad Ammaeum I (De Demosthene et
                     Aristotele). Ἐπιστολὴ πρὸς Ἀμμαῖον α'
3966.E7   Epistula ad Ammaeum II (De iis quae Thucydidi
                     propria sunt; De Thucydidis idiomatis).
                     Ἐπιστολὴ πρὸς Ἀμμαῖον β' (Περὶ τῶν τοῦ
                     Θουκυδίδου ἰδιωμάτων)
                     Cf. PA3966.D6 De Thucydide ad Aelium
                         Tuberonem

Individual authors to 600 A.D.
   Dionysius, of Halicarnassus. Διονύσιος ὁ Ἁλικαρνασσεύς
     Editions
       Rhetorical treatises
         Particular treatises
           Epistulae -- Continued

3966.E8	Epistula ad Cn. Pompeium Geminum (De Platone et de praecipuis historicis). Ἐπιστολὴ πρὸς Πομπήιον
3966.F8	Lost writings and fragments
	Spurious works
3966.R5	Ars rhetorica. Τέχνη ῥητορική
	Compilation of rhetorical treatises by various authors
	De sublimi see PA4229.L4+
3967	Translations. Criticism, etc.
	Translations
3967.A1	Greek, Modern. By date
3967.A2	Latin. By date
3967.A3-.Z19	Other. By language, A-Z, and date
	e.g.
	English
3967.E5	Complete
3967.E51	Antiquitates
	Rhetorical works
3967.E53	Collections and selections
3967.E54-.E59	Particular works (alphabetically, by title)
	Criticism
3967.Z4	General. Antiquitates
3967.Z5	Rhetorical treatises
	Language. Style, etc.
3967.Z6	General
3967.Z7	Grammar
3967.Z8	Glossaries, indices. By date
3968	Dionysius to Epictetus
3968.D13	Dionysius, of Halicarnassus (ho mousikos), 2nd century A.D. Διονύσιος ὁ Μουσικός (Table P-PZ38)
	Identical (?) with Aelius Dionysius
	Cf. PA3968.D44 Dionysius, Aelius, of Halicarnassus
3968.D14	Dionysius, of Heraclea, 4th to 3rd century B.C. Διονύσιος ὁ Μεταθέμενος (Table P-PZ38)
	Cf. B557 Philosophy
3968.D16	Dionysius, of Miletus (logographer) 5th century B.C. Διονύσιος ὁ Μιλήσιος (Table P-PZ38)

PA3050-4505

Individual authors to 600 A.D.
Dionysius to Epictetus -- Continued

3968.D17   Dionysius, of Mytilene, "Scytobrachion," 2nd century B.C.
Διονύσιος ὁ Σκυτοβραχίων (Table P-PZ38)
     Author of a mythographical cyclus, part of which is the main
       source of Diodorus Siculus, Books 3-4 (history of the
       Argonauts)
     Cf. PA3965.D3+ Diodorus Siculus

3968.D178   Dionysius, of Samos (Dionysius cyclographus) 2nd (?)
century B.C. Διονύσιος ὁ Σάμιος (Table P-PZ38)
Dionysius Periegetes, 2nd century A.D. Διονύσιος ὁ
Περιηγητής
     Orbis terrae descriptio (Periegesis mundi; Ambitus orbis).
       Οἰκουμένης περιήγησις

3968.D2   Editions. By date
        Translations
          Greek paraphrases see PA3968.D4A2

3968.D3   Latin. By date
          Cf. PA6642.A6 Priscianus
        Modern

3968.D31   English. By date
3968.D32   French. By date
3968.D33   German. By date
3968.D36   Other. By date
        Criticism

3968.D4A2   Ancient (Scholia and paraphrases in Greek)
3968.D4A5-.D4Z3   Modern
         For geographical treatises see G87.D7
3968.D4Z5-.D4Z8   Language, grammar, style, etc.
3968.D4Z9   Other works
        Cf. PA3965.D85 Bassarica
Dionysius Scythobrachion see PA3968.D17
Dionysius, the Thracian (Dionysius Thrax) fl. between 170
and 90 B.C. Διονύσιος ὁ Θρᾷξ

3968.D42A-.D42Z   Individual works. By title, A-Z
3968.D43   Criticism
        Cf. PA4396.Z9 Porphyrius De prosodia

3968.D44   Dionysius, Aelius, of Halicarnassus, "Atticista" 2nd century
A.D. Αἴλιος Διονύσιος (Table P-PZ38)
       Cf. PA3968.D13 Dionysius, of Halicarnassus (ho
         mousikos), 2nd century A.D.

3968.D45   Dionysius, Cassius, of Utica, fl. 88 B.C. Διονύσιος Κάσσιος
(Table P-PZ38)
       Translator of Mago's work on agriculture
       Cf. PA4244.M17 Mago, of Carthage
Dionysius Longinus see PA4229.L3

	Individual authors to 600 A.D.
	Dionysius to Epictetus -- Continued

3968.D47   Diophantus, of Alexandria, fl. ca. 250 A.D. Διόφαντος
(Table P-PZ38 modified)

3968.D47A61-
.D47A78   Separate works. By title
       e.g. Arithmetica; De polygonia numeris liber (fragment);
Spurious works. Ἀριθμητικά. Περὶ πολυγώνων ἀριθμῶν

3968.D49   Dioscorides (epigrammatist) 3rd century B.C. Διοσκουρίδης
(Table P-PZ38)

3968.D6   Dioscorides, Pedanius, of Anazarbus, 1st century A.D. De
materia medica. Πεδάνιος Διοσκουρίδης. Περὶ ὕλης
ἰατρικῆς
     Cf. R126.D5+ Medicine

3968.D62   Dioscorus, of Aphrodito. Διόσκορος (Table P-PZ38)

3968.D63   Diphilus, of Sinope (writer of comedies) fl. between 355
and 289 B.C. Δίφιλος (Table P-PZ38)

     Domninus, of Larissa (mathematician) 5th century A.D.
Δομνῖνος

PA3050-4505

3968.D7   Dorotheus, of Ascalon (grammarian) fl. between 30 B.C.
and 37 A.D. Δωρόθεος ὁ Ἀσκαλωνίτης (Table P-PZ38)

3968.D73   Dorotheus, of Sidon, astronomer, fl. between 50 and 300
A.D. Δωρόθεος (Table P-PZ38)

3968.D8   Draco, of Stratonicea (Drakon, grammarian of the
Alexandrian period?). Δράκων Στρατονικεύς (Table P-
PZ38)
     Writings lost; the treatise De metris poeticis (Περὶ μέτρων
ποιητικῶν) is a forgery of Jakob Diassorinos

3968.D9   Duris, of Samos (historian), fl. 301-281 B.C. Δοῦρις (Table
P-PZ38)
     Fragments only

3968.E3   Elias (philosopher) 6th century A.D. Ἠλίας (Table P-PZ38)
     In Aristotelis Categorias commentarium see PA3902.A6+
     In Porphyrii Isagogen commentarium
     Prolegomena philosophiae see PA3902.A6+

3968.E6   Empedocles, of Agrigentum, 5th century B.C. Ἐμπεδοκλῆς
(Table P-PZ38)
     Cf. B218 Philosophy

3968.E65   Epaphroditus, of Chaeronea (grammarian) 1st century A.D.
Ἐπαφρόδιτος (Table P-PZ38)

3968.E7   Ephorus Cumaeus (of Kyme) 4th century B.C. Ἔφορος
(Table P-PZ38)
     Fragments
     Cf. PA3998.H23 Hellenica oxyrhynchia

3968.E8   Epicharmus, ca. 550-460 B.C. Ἐπίχαρμος (Table P-PZ38)
     Cf. PA6382 Ennius. Epicharmus

3969   Epictetus. Ἐπίκτητος
     Cf. B560+ Philosophy

	Individual authors to 600 A.D.
	Epictetus. Ἐπίκτητος -- Continued
3969.A2	Dissertationes. Discourses. Διατριβαί
	lib. I-IV (and editions including Encheiridion)
3969.A3	Encheiridion. Manual. Ἐγχειρίδιον
3969.A31	Paraphrasis Christiana
3969.A33	Fragments
3969.A35	Sententiae (Spurious)
	Translations
3969.A4	Latin
3969.A5-.Z3	Other. By language, A-Z
3969.Z5	Criticism, interpretation
3970	Epicu... to Euc...
3970.E2	Epicurus, 341-270 B.C. Ἐπίκουρος (Table P-PZ38 modified)
	Cf. B570+ Philosophy
3970.E2A61-.E2A78	Separate works. By title
	e.g. De natura (Περὶ φύσεως); Epistulae (Ἐπιστολαί); Testamentum
3970.E22	Epimenides, ca. 500 B.C. (?). Ἐπιμενίδης (Table P-PZ38)
	Eranius Philo see PA4271.P2
3970.E37	Erasistratus, of Ceos, (physician), fl. ca. 258 B.C. Ἐρασίστρατος
	Cf. R126.A+ Medicine (General)
	Eratosthenes, of Cyrene, 3rd century B.C. Ἐρατοσθένης
3970.E4 date	Collected works. Selections. By date
3970.E4A-.E4Z	Individual works. By title, A-Z
	e.g. Carminum reliquiae (Erigone (Ἠριγόνη); Hermes (Ἑρμῆς); Hesiodos or Anterinys (Ἡσίοδος)); Catasterismi (Καταστερισμοί); Chronographiae (Χρονογραφίαι); De vetere comoedia (Περὶ τῆς ἀρχαίας κωμῳδίας) (Fragments); Geographica (Γεωγραφικά) (Fragments) - Cf. G87 Geography
3970.E5	Criticism
3970.E6	Erinna, 4th century B.C. Ἤριννα (Table P-PZ38)
3970.E65	Erotianus (grammarian) 1st century A.D. Glossarium in Hippocratem. Ἐρωτιανός. Παρ' Ἱπποκράτει λέξεων συναγωγή
3970.E68	Eryxias. Ἐρυξίας (Table P-PZ38)
(3970.E72-.E79)	Etymologica
	Compilations of the Byzantine period based upon the older works of Orion and Oros and upon other grammatical and lexicological works
	see PA5311+
	Cf. PA4257.O7 Orion
	Cf. PA4261.O7 Oros
3970.E85	Eubulus. Εὔβουλος (Table P-PZ38)

	Individual authors to 600 A.D. -- Continued
3971	Euclid. Εὐκλείδης
(3971.A2-.A38)	Editions
	see QA31
(3971.A39-.A69)	Translations
	see QA31
	Criticism, interpretation, etc.
(3971.A7A2)	Ancient. Commentaries. Scholia
(3971.A7A5-.A7Z3)	Arabic
(3971.A7Z5-.A7Z9)	Medieval
3971.A8-.Z3	Modern
3971.Z5	Language
3971.Z8	Glossaries, indices, etc. By date
3972	Euclides (Meg.) to Euripides
(3972.E82)	Euclides, of Megara, ca. 450-ca. 380 B.C. Εὐκλείδης
	see B305.E8
3972.E84	Eudemus of Rhodes, 4th to 3rd century B.C. Εὔδημος ὁ Ῥόδιος (Table P-PZ38)
	Cf. B577.E5+ Philosophy
	Cf. PA3893.E7 Aristoteles. Ethica Eudemia
3972.E86	Eudocia, Aelia, Augusta, consort of Theodosius II, emperor of the East, d. 460 A.D. Εὐδοκία (Table P-PZ38 modified)
3972.E86A61- .E86A78	Separate works. By title
	e.g. Epic poems; Centos (Homer)
3972.E88	Eudoxus, of Cnidus, fl. 365 B.C. Εὔδοξος (Table P-PZ38)
3972.E9	Euhemerus, fl. 311-288 B.C. Εὐήμερος (Table P-PZ38)
	Cf. PA6382 Ennius; fragments of translation preserved by Lactantius
3972.E93	Eunapius, of Sardes, fl. 367-414 A.D. Εὐνάπιος (Table P-PZ38 modified)
3972.E93A61- .E93A78	Separate works. By title
	e.g. Historiae (Chronikē historia hē meta Dexippon. Ἱστορικὰ ὑπομνήματα); Vitae sophistarum (Βίοι σοφιστῶν)
3972.E94	Euphorion, of Chalcis, ca. 276 B.C. Εὐφορίων (Table P-PZ38)
	Euphorion, of Chersonesus
	see Euphronius, of Chersonesus
	Euphronius, of Chersonesus (grammarian) 3rd century B.C. Εὐφρόνιος
	Eupolemus (historian) 2nd century B.C. Εὐπόλεμος
3972.E97	Eupolis (dramatist) fl. 429-411 B.C. Εὔπολις (Table P-PZ38)
	Euripides. Εὐριπίδης
3973	Editions
3973.A1	Papyri. Manuscripts (facsimile reproductions)

PA3050-4505

Individual authors to 600 A.D.
Euripides. Εὐριπίδης
Editions -- Continued

3973.A2	Collected plays. By date
3973.A3	Selected plays. School editions. By date
3973.A35	Cantica (Choral odes)
3973.A4	Selections. Quotations. Passages
	Separate works
3973.A5	Alcestis. Ἄλκηστις
(3973.A53)	Alcmeon. Ἀλκμέων
	see PA3973.Z5
3973.A6	Andromache. Ἀνδρομάχη
(3973.A7)	Andromeda. Ἀνδρομέδα
	see PA3973.Z5
(3973.A8)	Antigone. Ἀντιγόνη
	see PA3973.Z5
(3973.A9)	Antiope. Ἀντιόπη
	see PA3973.Z5
3973.B2	Bacchae. Βάκχαι
	Bellerophontes. Bellerophon. Βελλεροφόντης see PA3973.Z5
	Cresphontes. Κρεσφόντης see PA3973.Z5
3973.C9	Cyclops. Κύκλωψ
3973.E5	Electra. Ἠλέκτρα
	Erechtheus. Ἐρεχθεύς see PA3973.Z5
3973.H3	Hecuba. Ἑκάβη
3973.H4	Helena. Helen. Ἑλένη
3973.H5	Heracles (Hercules furens). Ἡρακλῆς μαινόμενος
3973.H6	Heraclidae. Children of Heracles. Ἡρακλεῖδαι
3973.H7	Hippolytus (H. Coronifer). Ἱππόλυτος στεφανηφόρος
(3973.H9)	Hypsipyle. Ὑψιπύλη
	see PA3973.Z5
3973.I6	Ion. Ἴων
3973.I7	Iphigenia in Aulide. Iphigenia in Aulis. Ἰφιγένεια ἡ ἐν Αὐλίδι
3973.I8	Iphigenia in Tauris. Ἰφιγένεια ἡ ἐν Ταύροις
3973.M4	Medea. Μήδεια
(3973.M6)	Melanippe. Μελανίππη
	see PA3973.Z5
(3973.O4)	Oedipus. Οἰδίπους
	see PA3973.Z5
3973.O7	Orestes. Ὀρέστης
(3973.P2)	Palamedes. Παλαμήδης
	see PA3973.Z5
(3973.P4)	Phaethon. Φαέθων
	see PA3973.Z5

	Individual authors to 600 A.D.
	Euripides. Εὑριπίδης
	Editions
	Separate works -- Continued
(3973.P5)	Philoctetes. Φιλοκτήτης
	see PA3973.Z5
3973.P6	Phoenissae. Phoenician women. Φοίνισσαι
(3973.P8)	Protesilaus. Πρωτεσίλαος
	see PA3973.Z5
3973.R5	Rhesus. Ῥῆσος
	Authorship doubtful
(3973.S8)	Stheneboea. Σθενέβοια
	see PA3973.Z5
3973.S9	Supplices. Ἱκέτιδες
(3973.T4)	Telephus. Τήλεφος
	see PA3973.Z5
3973.T8	Troades. Trojan women. Τρῳάδες
3973.Z5	Fragments. Lost plays. By date
	Class here collections and individual plays
	For treatises on these fragments whether general or restricted to a particular play see PA3977+
	Spurious works
	Rhesus see PA3973.R5
3973.Z9	Epistulae V
	By Sabidius Polio?
	Translations
3974.A1	Greek, Modern
	Latin
(3974.A18)	Ancient
	see PA6664 (Seneca); PA6382 (Ennius)
3974.A2	Modern
3975	English
3975.A1	Collected plays. By date
3975.A2	Selected plays. By date
3975.A25	Selections. Passages. Thoughts
3975.A5-.Z4	Separate plays
3975.Z5	Paraphrases, tales, etc.
3976.A-Z	Other. By language, A-Z
3976.7	Imitations. Adaptations. Parodies
3976.8	Illustrations
3976.9	Music
	For compositions of dramas see class M
	Interpretation and criticism
	Ancient and medieval
3977.A2A-.A2Z	Collections of criticisms and allusions. By editor, A-Z
3977.A3A-.A3Z	Biographies. By editor, A-Z

PA3050-4505

	Individual authors to 600 A.D.
	Euripides. Εὐριπίδης
	Interpretation and criticism
	Ancient and medieval -- Continued
3977.A4	Particular authors
	Including Aristophanes, Aristoteles, Quintilianus
	Scholia
3977.A5	Collections and selections. By date
(3977.A6A-.A6Z)	Particular plays
	see PA3973.A5+
3977.A7-.Z3	Particular authors, A-Z
3977.Z5	Arguments. By date
	Modern
3978.A2	Early to 1800/1850
3978.A5-.Z3	Later, 1800/1850-
3985	Representation on the stage
	Language. Style. Versification
3992.A-.Z3	General
	Including grammar and syntax
3992.Z6	Versification
3992.Z8	Glossaries. Indices. Concordances. By date
3994	Euro... to Gal...
3994.E77	Eusebius, of Caesarea, Bishop of Caesarea, ca. 260-ca. 340. Εὐσέβιος ὁ Παμφίλου (Table P-PZ38)
	Cf. BR65.E7+ Early Christian literature
3994.E8	Eutecnius (rhetor) date uncertain. Εὐτέκνιος (Table P-PZ38)
	For the paraphrase of the Ornithiaca (Ὀρνιθιακά), ascribed to Eutecnius see PA3968.D4Z9
	Cf. PA4250.N3 Nicander
3994.E9	Eutocius, of Ascalon, mathematician, b. ca. 480 A.D. Εὐτόκιος (Table P-PZ38)
3994.E97	Ezekiel, 2nd century B.C. Ἐζεκιῆλος (Table P-PZ38)
3994.F2	Fabius Pictor, Q., fl. ca. 225-216 B.C. Κόιντος Φάβιος (Table P-PZ38)
3994.F3	Faustus, of Byzantium, 4th century A.D. P'awstos, Buzandats'i (Table P-PZ38)
3994.F4	Favorinus (of Arelate in Gaul) 2nd century A.D. Φαβωρῖνος (Table P-PZ38)
	Epideictic speeches, etc. Fragments only
	Galen. Γαληνός
	Cf. R126.G2+ Medicine
3995	Editions
3995.A2	Comprehensive
3995.A5-Z	Treatises (not medical)
	Adhortatio ad artes addiscendas. Protrepticus. Προτρεπτικὸς ἐπὶ τὰς τέχνας

Individual authors to 600 A.D.
  Galen. Γαληνός
    Editions
      Treatises (not medical) -- Continued
        De captionibus quae per dictionem fiunt. Peri tōn para
          tēn lexin sophismatōn. Περὶ τῶν παρὰ τὴν λέξιν
          σοφισμάτων
        De optima doctrina. Περὶ τῆς ἀρίστης διδασκαλίας
        Institutio logica. Εἰσαγωγὴ διαλεκτική

3996	Translations
3997	Criticism
3998	Gall... to Her...
3998.G2	Gaudentius (date uncertain). Harmonica introductio. Γαυδέντιος. Ἁρμονικὴ εἰσαγωγή
3998.G3	Geminus, of Rhodus, fl. 70 B.C. Γεμῖνος (Table P-PZ38 modified)

Cf. QA31 Mathematics

3998.G3A61-.G3A78	Separate works. By title

e.g.

3998.G3A652	Elementa astronomiae. Introduction to astronomy. Εἰσαγωγὴ εἰς τὰ φαινόμενα

Cf. PA4400.S7 Pseudo-Proclus, Sphaera
Genethlius, of Patrae (rhetor) 3rd century A.D. Γενέθλιος
  Cf. PA4248.M13 Menander, of Laodicea
Georgius Choeroboscus see PA3948.C38

3998.G6	Gorgias, of Leontini, fl. 428 B.C. Γοργίας (Table P-PZ38)

Cf. PA4279.G7 Plato. Gorgias

3998.G62	Gorgias (the younger) rhetor, 1st century B.C. Schemata lexeos. Γοργίας. Περὶ σχημάτων
3998.G73	Gregory, of Nazianzus, Saint, fl. 362-380 A.D. Γρηγόριος Ναζιανζηνός (Table P-PZ38 modified)

For theological works see BR60+ ; BR1720

3998.G73A61-.G73A78	Separate works. By title

e.g. Carmina (Hymni); Homiliae. Epistulae; Orationes
Gregory, of Nyssa, Saint, fl. 371-380 A.D. Γρηγόριος
  Νύσσης
  For theological works see BR60+ ; BR1720
Gregory, Thaumaturgus, Saint, ca. 213-ca. 270 A.D.
  Γρηγόριος ὁ Θαυματουργός
  For theological works see BR60+ ; BR1720

3998.H13	Hadrian, Emperor of Rome, 76-138 A.D. Ἁδριανός (Table P-PZ38)

Hagias Troezenus, reputed author of the Nosti. Ἁγίας ὁ
  Τροιζήνιος. Νόστοι

3998.H135	Hanno, of Carthage, 5th (?) century B.C. Periplus. Ἅννων. Περίπλους

PA3050-4505

Individual authors to 600 A.D.

Gall... to Her... -- Continued

3998.H14	Harpocratio, of Alexandria, 2nd (?) century A.D. De facultatibus naturalibus animalium et herbarum et lapidum. Ἁρποκρατίων. Περὶ φυσικῶν δυνάμεων ζώων τε καὶ λίθων
3998.H15	Harpocration, Valerius, 1st or 2nd century A.D. Dictionarium decem oratorum. Lexicon of the ten orators. Ἁρποκρατίων ὁ Βαλέριος. Λέξεις τῶν δέκα ῥητόρων
3998.H16	Hecataeus, of Abdera (or Teos?) 4th to 3rd century B.C. Ἑκαταῖος ὁ Ἀβδηρίτης (Table P-PZ38 modified)
3998.H16A61- .H16A78	Separate works. By title e.g. Aegyptiaca (Fragments); De Hyperboreis (Fragments). Αἰγυπτιακά. Περὶ Ὑπερβορέων
3998.H161	Pseudo-Hecataeus, 2nd to 1st century B.C. (?) De Judaeis. Περὶ Ἰουδαίων
3998.H17	Hecataeus, of Miletus (logographer) fl. ca. 500 B.C. Ἑκαταῖος ὁ Μιλήσιος (Table P-PZ38 modified)
3998.H17A61- .H17A78	Separate works. By title e.g. Genealogiae (Historiae) (Fragments); Terrae circuitus (Fragments). Γενεαλογίαι. Περίοδος γῆς
	Hegemon, of Thasus, 5th century B.C. Ἡγήμων ὁ Θάσιος
	Hegesianax, of Alexandria Troas, fl. 193 B.C. Ἡγησιάναξ ὁ Ἀλεξανδρεὺς ἀπὸ Τρωάδος
3998.H181	Hegesippus (Egesippus). Ἡγήσιππος (Table P-PZ38 modified)
3998.H181A61- .H181A78	Separate works. By title
	De bello Judaico see PA4222.D3
3998.H182	Hegesippus, of Athens (Sunion) 4th century B.C. Ἡγήσιππος (Table P-PZ38 modified)
3998.H182A61- .H182A78	Separate works. By title
	De Halonneso see PA3950.H3
	Hegesippus ("comicus") 3rd century B.C. Ἡγήσιππος
	Hegesippus (ecclesiastical writer) fl. ca. 160-ca. 180 A.D. Ἡγήσιππος see BR60+ BR1720
	Hegesippus (epigrammatist) 4th century B.C. (?). Ἡγήσιππος
	Hegesippus, of Mecyberna (historian) 3rd century B.C. (?). Ἡγήσιππος
3998.H19	Heliodorus ("metricus") 1st century A.D. Heliodoros. Ἡλιόδωρος ὁ Μετρικός (Table P-PZ38) Cf. PA3879.A17 Aristophanes. Scholia

Individual authors to 600 A.D.
  Gall... to Her... -- Continued

3998.H193   Heliodorus (surgeon) 2nd century A.D. Ἡλιόδωρος (Table
               P-PZ38)

               Heliodorus (Bishop of Trikka) 4th (?) century A.D.
               Ἡλιόδωρος. Aethiopica see PA3998.H2

               Heliodorus, of Athens "periegeta" (date uncertain) De
               Acropoli Athenarum (fragments). Ἡλιόδωρος ὁ
               Περιηγητής. Περὶ ἀκροπόλεως

3998.H2   Heliodorus, of Emesa, 2nd century A.D. Aethiopica lib. X.
               Ἡλιόδωρος. Αἰθιοπικά

               Heliodorus, of Prusa. Ἡλιόδωρος see PA3868.A4

               Helladius, of Alexandria (grammarian) fl. ca. 389-425 A.D.
               Ἑλλάδιος Ἀλεξανδρεύς
                 Writings lost; by some authorities wrongly identified with
                    Helladius, of Antinoea

               Helladius, of Antinoea, son of Besantinous, 4th century
               A.D. Chrestomathia lib. IV. Ἑλλάδιος Βησαντινόου.
               Χρηστομαθεία

               Helladius, of Antinoupolis
                 see Helladius, of Antinoea

               Hellanicus, of Alexandria (grammarian), 3rd century B.C.
               (?). Ἑλλάνικος

3998.H22   Hellanicus, of Lesbos (Mytilene) 5th century B.C.
               Ἑλλάνικος Μιτυληναῖος

3998.H23   "Hellenica Oxyrhynchia."
                 Fragment of a Greek historical treatise containing events of
                    the year 396 B.C. The authorship has been variously
                    attributed to Theopompus of Chios, or to Cratippus, or to
                    Ephorus

3998.H26   Hephaestio (grammarian), 2nd century A.D. Hephaestion.
               Enchiridion de metris et poemate. Encheiridion.
               Ἡφαιστίων. Ἐγχειρίδιον περὶ μέτρων
                 Cf. PA3948.C38 Choeroboscus, Georgius.
                    Commentary on Hephaestio

3998.H263   Hephaestio Thebanus (astrologer), 4th century A.D.
               Ἡφαιστίων (Table P-PZ38)

3998.H267   Heraclean tablets

3998.H27   Heraclides. Ἡρακλείδης
                 Treatises on various authors of that name

3998.H28   Heraclides comicus (dramatist, Middle Comedy).
               Ἡρακλείδης (Table P-PZ38)

3998.H3   Heraclides criticus (Creticus), 3rd century B.C. (?).
               Ἡρακλείδης ὁ Κριτικός (Table P-PZ38)

PA3050-4505

Individual authors to 600 A.D.
Gall... to Her... -- Continued

3998.H32	Heraclides Cumanus (of Kyme), historian, 4th century B.C. (?). Heraclides, of Cyme. Persica. Ἡρακλείδης ὁ Κυμαῖος. Περσικά Fragments
3998.H33	Heraclides Lembus, 2nd century B.C. Ἡρακλείδης ὁ Λέμβος (Table P-PZ38) Works lost; presumably the author of the excerpts from the Politiae of Aristotle (De politiis. Περὶ πολιτειῶν), previously attributed to Heraclides Ponticus
3998.H34	Heraclides Lycius (sophist), fl. 194-214 A.D. Ἡρακλείδης ὁ Λύκιος (Table P-PZ38) Heraclides Milesius (grammarian), fl. ca. 100 A.D. Ἡρακλείδης
3998.H36	Heraclides Ponticus (of Heraclea on the Pontus Euxinus) ca. 390-ca. 310 B.C. Ἡρακλείδης ὁ Ποντικός (Table P-PZ38) Fragments only Allegoriae Homericae see PA4035.H4 De politiis libellus see PA3998.H33
3998.H37	Heraclides Ponticus, the Younger (grammarian), 1st century A.D. Ἡρακλείδης Ποντικὸς γραμματικός (Table P-PZ38 modified)
3998.H37A61- .H37A78	Separate works. By title e.g. Leschae (Didactic poem on grammatical questions, lost). Λέσχαι De politiis see PA3998.H33
3998.H375	Heraclides, of Tarentum (physician), fl. ca. 75 B.C. Ἡρακλείδης (Table P-PZ38)
(3998.H38)	Heraclitus, 1st century A.D. (?). Ἡράκλειτος Identity with the mythographical writer Heraclitus disputed Allegoriae Homericae see PA4035.H4
3998.H39	Heraclitus, mythographical writer (pseudonym?) De incredibilibus. Ἡράκλειτος. Περὶ ἀπίστων
3998.H4	Heraclitus, of Ephesus (the obscure), fl. ca. 500 B.C. Ἡράκλειτος ὁ Σκοτεινός (Table P-PZ38 modified) Cf. B220+ Philosophy
3998.H4A61-.H4A78	Separate works. By title e.g. De natura (Περὶ φύσεως) (Fragments only); Epistulae (Epistles of Heraclitus. Ἐπιστολαὶ Ἡρακλείτου) (Spurious)
3998.H42	Heraclitus, of Halicarnassus (lyric poet), 3rd century B.C. Ἡράκλειτος (Table P-PZ38)

Individual authors to 600 A.D.
Gall... to Her... -- Continued

3998.H45   Herennius (Herennios) disciple of Ammonios Sakkas, 3rd
            century A.D. Ἐρέννιος (Table P-PZ38)
                Writings lost; the Commentarius ad Metaphysica Aristotelis
                    (Ἐξήγησις εἰς τὰ Μετὰ τὰ φυσικά) ascribed to him is a
                    forgery, presumably by Andreas Darmarios
            Herennius Philo, of Byblos (Phoenicia) see PA4271.P2
(3998.H47) Herennius Modestinus, 3rd century A.D. Ἐρέννιος
                see class K
3998.H48   Hermagoras. Ἑρμαγόρας
                Treatises on various authors of this name
3998.H482   Hermagoras, of Amphipolis (Stoic philosopher) 3rd century
            B.C. Ἑρμαγόρας Ἀμφιπολίτης (Table P-PZ38)
3998.H483   Hermagoras, of Temnos, rhetor, 2nd century B.C.
            Ἑρμαγόρας (Table P-PZ38)
3998.H484   Hermagoras, of Temnos, rhetor (the younger) 1st century
            A.D. Hermagoras, Minor. Ἑρμαγόρας Καρίων (Table P-
            PZ38)
3998.H485   Hermagoras, rhetor, 2nd century A.D. Ἑρμαγόρας (Table
            P-PZ38)
            Hermas (author of "Pastor"). Ἑρμᾶς. Ποιμήν see
            BS2900.H4+
            Hermes, Trismegistus. Ἑρμῆς Τρισμέγιστος
                Class here editions of texts and translations (except English)
                    of the religious-philosophic treatises forming the "Corpus
                    Hermeticum" and of the treatises dealing with the occult
                    arts and sciences in so far as they are of Greek origin
                For English translations of the occult treatises, and studies on
                    these treatises see the subject
                For English translations of the "Corpus Hermeticum"
                    and studies of the "Corpus Hermeticum" written
                    from a philosophical or religious point of view see
                    B667.H3+
                Cf. BF1598.H6 Occult sciences
3998.H5   Poemander (Pimander; Pymander; De potestate et
            sapientia dei). Ποιμάνδρης. Editions. By date
                Class here also editions of the "Corpus Hermeticum"
                Poemander is a collection of 17 or 18 treatises by various
                    authors, although the title properly pertains to the first
                    treatise alone
            Separate works
            Ad Asclepium
                see Asclepius
                Cf. De animalium proprietatibus; De decanis; De plantis
                    XII zodiaci signorum; De plantis VII planetarum;
                    Poemander (treatises II (?), VI, IX, XIV, XV)

PA3050-4505

145

Individual authors to 600 A.D.
   Gall... to Her...
      Hermes, Trismegistus. Ἑρμῆς Τρισμέγιστος
         Separate works -- Continued
           Allegoriae
           Aphorismi Hermetis see PA3998.H5C4
           Ars Hermetis de transmutatione metallorum
             see Secreta

3998.H5A7
           Asclepius (De natura deorum; De verbo perfecto).
             Λόγος τέλειος
           Astrologiae secretorum flores see PA3998.H5C4

3998.H5B7
           Brontologion. Βροντολόγιον
           Canon. Κανόνιον
            Canon de decubitu infirmorum see PA3998.H5I2

3998.H5C4
           Centiloquium (Aphorismi Hermetis; Centum sententiae
             astrologicae; Liber propositionum; Liber florum;
             Astrologiae secretorum flores)
             Latin translation by Stephanus Messinensis (13th
                century) of an Arabic imitation of the Centiloquium of
                Claudius Ptolemaeus

3998.H5C6
           Chemia

3998.H5D2
           De animalium proprietatibus et remediis quae ex illis
             peti possunt ad Asclepium. Περὶ ζῴων δυνάμεων
             καὶ τῶν ἐξ αὐτῶν φαρμάκων πρὸς Ἀσκληπιόν
           De anulis liber (?)

3998.H5D4
           De castigatione animae (Epistola ad animam)
           De charactere liber (?)
           De compositione
           De confectionibus (an coniunctionibus) ad capiendum
             animalia silvestria
             see De quattuor confectionibus...
           De decanis ad Asclepium. Περὶ δεκανῶν πρὸς
             Ἀσκληπιόν
           De XII [duodecim] locorum nomenclatura et facultate.
             Περὶ τῆς τῶν ιβ΄ τόπων ὀνομασίης καὶ δυνάμεως
           De herbarum chylosi
             see De succis plantarum
           De imaginibus Jovis (?)
           De imaginibus Martis (?)
           De imaginibus Saturni (?)
           De iudiciis et significationibus stellarum beibeniarum et
             nativitatibus
           De lapide philosophico (De lapidis philosophici secreto)
           De lapidibus pretiosis

Individual authors to 600 A.D.
  Gall... to Her...
    Hermes, Trismegistus. Ἑρμῆς Τρισμέγιστος
      Separate works -- Continued
        De lunae mansionibus (Liber lunae de 28
            [duodetriginta] mansionibus lunae translatus ab
            Hermete; Liber ymaginum tr. ab Hermete qui latine
            praestigium Mercurii appellatur, Helyanin in lingua
            arabica)
        De mathesi libri II (?)
        De medicinis et coniunctionibus planetarum liber (?)
        De natura deorum see PA3998.H5A7
        De plantis XII [duodecim] zodiaci signorum ad
            Asclepium. Περὶ βοτανῶν τῶν ιβ' ζωδίων πρὸς
            Ἀσκληπιόν
        De plantis septem planetarum ad Asclepium. Περὶ
            βοτανῶν τῶν ζ' ἀστέρων πρὸς Ἀσκληπιόν
        De ponderibus. Περὶ σταθμῶν
        De potestate et sapientia dei see PA3998.H5
        De quattuor confectionibus ad omnia genera animalium
            capienda (Liber secundum Hermetem de quattuor
            [etc.]
        De XV [quindecim] stellis, XV herbis, XV lapidibus et
            XV figuris appropriatis
        De revolutionibus nativitatum libri II
        De septem anulis planetarum liber (?)
        De sigillis liber (?)
        De significationibus terrae motuum
            see Prognostica a terrae motibus
        De succis plantarum (De plantarum chylosi). Περὶ
            βοτανῶν χυλώσεως
        De tincturis physicis. Φυσικαὶ βαφαί
        De transmutatione metallorum
            see Secreta
        De verbo perfecto liber see PA3998.H5A7
        Definitiones Asclepii. Ὅροι Ἀσκληπιοῦ
            see Poemander (treatise XVI)
        Doctrina Hermetis de transmutatione metallorum
            see Secreta
        Epistola ad animam see PA3998.H5D4
        Expositiones rerum memorabilium et extractiones
            corporum mineralium
        Genikoi logoi. Γενικοὶ λόγοι
            Lost; Poemander X claims to be an epitome of that
                treatise
3998.H5I2   Iatromathematica (Canon de decubitu infirmorum).
            Ἰατρομαθηματικά

PA3050-4505

Individual authors to 600 A.D.
  Gall... to Her...
    Hermes, Trismegistus. Ἑρμῆς Τρισμέγιστος
      Separate works -- Continued
        Imaginum sive praestigiorum libri
          see De lunae mansionibus
        Kore kosmou. Κόρη κόσμου
          Fragments

3998.H5K8	Kyranides (Curanides). Κυρανίδες

        Liber de potestate et sapientia dei see PA3998.H5
        Liber florum see PA3998.H5C4
        Liber ymaginum translatus ab Hermete
          see De lunae mansionibus
        Liber lunae de XXVIII mansionibus
          see De lunae mansionibus
        Liber propositionum see PA3998.H5C4
        Liber secundum Hermetem de quattuor confectionibus
          see De quattuor confectionibus
        Liber trium verborum
        Methodus ad omne inceptum idonea. Μέθοδος εἰς
          πᾶσαν καταρχὴν ἐπιτήδειος
        Organum. Ὄργανον
        Prognostica a terrae motibus (De significationibus
          terrae motuum). Περὶ σεισμῶν
          Poem in 66 hexameters
        Prologus librorum Hermetis philosophi, regis Aegypti,
          super opere philosophico
        Secreta (Doctrina sive Ars Hermetis de transmutatione
          metallorum)
        Secreta secretorum (?)
        Statera Hermetis
          Not a title, but an astrological rule
        Tabula smaragdina
        Trutina Hermetis (Tabula dicto T.H.)

3998.H6	Translations
(3998.H6A1-.H6A19)	Syriac
(3998.H6A2-.H6A29)	Arabic
(3998.H6A3-.H6A39)	Hebrew
(3998.H6A4-.H6A59)	Latin
(3998.H6E3-.H6E9)	English
	French
3998.H6F3	Collected or selected works. By date
3998.H6F4	Poemander. By date
3998.H6F5-.H6F9	Other works
	Arrange alphabetically by title and subarrange by date
	German
3998.H6G3	Collected or selected works. By date

           Individual authors to 600 A.D.
             Gall... to Her...
               Hermes, Trismegistus. Ἑρμῆς Τρισμέγιστος
                 Translations
                   German -- Continued

3998.H6G4	Poemander. By date
3998.H6G5-.H6G9	Other works
	Arrange alphabetically by title and subarrange by date
	Italian
3998.H6I3	Collected or selected works. By date
3998.H6I4	Poemander. By date
3998.H6I5-.H6I9	Other works
	Arrange alphabetically by title and subarrange by date
	Spanish. Catalan
3998.H6S3	Collected or selected works. By date
3998.H6S4	Poemander. By date
3998.H6S5-.H6S9	Other works
	Arrange alphabetically by title and subarrange by date
3998.H6Z1-.H6Z49	Other European languages
	Arrange alphabetically by language and subarrange by date
(3998.H6Z5-.H6Z99)	Oriental languages
3998.H7A-.H7Z3	Criticism, interpretation, etc.
	Class here philological, textual and literary criticism
3998.H7Z5	Language. By date
3998.H7Z9	Glossaries, etc. By date
3998.H72	Hermesianax, of Colophon, 4th to 3rd century B.C. Elegi. Ἑρμησιάναξ. Ἐλεγεῖα
	Fragments
3998.H723	Hermias. Ἑρμείας (Ἑρμίας)
	Treatises on various authors known by this name
3998.H725	Hermias, of Alexandria, 5th century A.D. Commentary on Plato's Phaedrus. Ἑρμείας
3998.H727	Hermias (philosopher) 4th century B.C. Ἑρμείας (Table P-PZ38)
	Cf. PA3891.C2 Aristoteles. Scolion in Hermiam
3998.H729	Hermias philosophus, 5th or 6th (2nd or 3rd?) century A.D. Irrisio gentilium philosophorum. Ἑρμίας. Διασυρμὸς τῶν ἔξω φιλοσόφων
	Hermias Sozomenos. Ἑρμείας Σωζόμενος
	see BR60+ BR1720
3998.H73	Hermippus, of Athens (writer of comedies) 5th century B.C. Ἕρμιππος (Table P-PZ38)
3998.H732	Hermippus, of Berytus, 2nd century A.D. Ἕρμιππος Βηρύτιος (Table P-PZ38)

Individual authors to 600 A.D.
Gall... to Her... -- Continued

3998.H735	Hermippus, of Smyrna, "Callimacheus," fl. 200 B.C. (Hermippus peripateticus). Ἔρμιππος ὁ Καλλιμάχειος (Table P-PZ38)
3998.H74	Hermocrates, of Iasus, fl. ca. 300 B.C. Ἑρμοκράτης ὁ Ἰασεύς (Table P-PZ38)
3998.H75	Hermocrates, of Phocaea (sophist) fl. ca. 200 A.D. Ἑρμοκράτης (Table P-PZ38)
3998.H77	Hermogenes, historian (of Tarsus, 1st century A.D.?). Ἑρμογένης (Table P-PZ38)
	Hermogenes, of Tarsus (rhetor) 2nd century A.D. Ἑρμογένης
3998.H8	Editions (Ars rhetorica. Τέχνη ῥητορική). By date
3998.H8A3	De statibus. Περὶ τῶν στάσεων
3998.H8A4	De inventione. Περὶ εὑρέσεως
3998.H8A5	De formis oratoriis. Peri ideōn. Περὶ ἰδεῶν
3998.H8A53	Progymnasmata. Προγυμνάσματα
	Authorship disputed
3998.H8A55	Ratio tractandae gravitatis (De methodo gravitatis). Peri methodou deinotētos. Περὶ μεθόδου δεινότητος
	Authorship disputed
	Translations
3998.H8A6	Latin. By date
	Cf. PA6642.A63 Priscianus Caesariensis
3998.H8A7-.H8Z	Other. By language, A-Z, and date
	Criticism
3998.H9A1-.H9A6	Ancient and medieval (Byzantine)
3998.H9A7-.H9Z	Modern
3998.H95	Hermotimus, of Colophon (mathematician) 4th century B.C. Ἑρμότιμος (Table P-PZ38)
	Cf. QA31 Mathematics
	Hero, of Alexandria. Ἥρων ὁ Ἀλεξανδρεύς
3999.A2	Complete works. By date
3999.A3	Automata. Αὐτοματοποιικά
3999.A32	Barulcus. Βαρουλκός
3999.A34	Belopoeica. Βελοποιικά
3999.A36	Catoptrica. Κατοπτρικά
	Original lost; a Latin treatise with title Claudii Ptolomaei De speculis is most probably a translation of the Catoptrica
3999.A37	Chirobalistra. Χειροβαλίστρα
3999.A38	Commentarius in Euclidis Elementa
	Original lost; large portions in Arabic translation enclosed in the commentary of al-Narīzī (Anaritius ca. 900) and in a medieval Latin translation of the same
3999.A39	Definitiones (Vocabula quaedam geometrica). Ὅροι τῶν γεωμετρίας ὀνομάτων

Individual authors to 600 A.D.
    Hero, of Alexandria. Ἥρων ὁ Ἀλεξανδρεύς -- Continued

3999.A4	Dioptra. Περὶ διόπτρας
	For the Byzantine excerpts known as "Geodaesia" see PA5318
	Geodaesia
	see PA3999.A45; PA5318
3999.A45	Geometria (Geometrica; Geodaesia). Γεωμετρία
	Compilation revised by one Patricius (4th or 5th century, or Nicephorus patricius, 10th century?) based in part upon works of Hero (Metrica, etc.)
	For the Byzantine excerpts entitled "Geodaesia," see PA5318
3999.A46	Hodometron. Ὁδόμετρον
	Authorship disputed
3999.A48	Liber geeponicus. Γεηπονικὸν βιβλίον
	Compilation from Hero's Definitiones, Geometria, Mensurae, etc. It is the first treatise in a collection of geoponic writers, hence the inappropriate title
3999.A5	Mechanica. Μηχανικά
3999.A52	Mensurae. Μετρήσεις
	Compilation based in part upon Hero's works
3999.A54	Metrica lib. III (Rationes dimetiendi). Μετρικά
3999.A56	Pneumatica lib. II. Πνευματικά
3999.A58	Stereometrica. Στερεομετρικά
	Compilation revised by Patricius based in part upon Hero
3999.A6	Lost works
	Translations
3999.A7	Arabic
3999.A8	Latin
3999.A9-Z	Other. By language, A-Z
4000	Criticism
	Class here philological and textual criticism
4001	Hero, of Athens to Herod...
4001.H17	Hero, of Athens (rhetor) 1st century A.D. (?). Ἥρων (Table P-PZ38)
	Commentaries on Herodotus, Thucydides a.o., lost
(4001.H2)	"Hero, of Byzantium"
	see PA5318
	Herodas see PA4008.H2+
4001.H3	Herodes Atticus, 101-177 A.D. Ἡρώδης Ἀττικοῦ (Table P-PZ38)
	Only one oration De republica preserved, authorship of the oration wrongly disputed
	Herodianus (historian) 3rd century A.D. Herodian. Ἡρωδιανός

PA3050-4505

	Individual authors to 600 A.D.
	Hero, of Athens to Herod...
	Herodianus (historian) 3rd century A.D. Herodian.
	Ἡρωδιανός -- Continued
	Historiarum lib. VIII. History. Μετὰ Μάρκον βασιλείας
	ἱστορίαι
	Translations
4001.H4A4	Latin. By date
4001.H4A5-.H4Z	Other. By language, A-Z, and date
(4001.H4E5)	English
	see DG298
4001.H5	Criticism
	For historical treatises see Class DG
4001.H6	Herodianus, Aelius, "technicus," 2nd century A.D. Αἴλιος
	Ἡρωδιανός
	Cf. PA4445.T4 Theodosius, of Alexandria
4001.H73	Herodorus, of Heraclea (historian) ca. 400 B.C. Ἡρόδωρος
	ὁ Ἡρακλεώτης (Table P-PZ38)
	Herodotus. Ἡρόδοτος
4002.A2	Editions. By date
4002.A3	Selected books
4002.A4	Selections. Passages
4002.A8	Fragments (in papyri, etc.). By date
4002.A9	Spurious works
	Vita Homeri see PA4035.A4H4
4003	Translations
4004	Criticism
	For historical and geographical treatises see D78+ DE213+
	G84+
	For biography see D56.52.H45
4007	Language. Style. Technique. Glossaries. Indices
4007.A-.Z3	General
(4007.Z5)	Grammar
	Glossaries, indices, etc.
4007.Z7	Ancient. Lexicon Herodoteum. Ἡροδότου λέξεις
	Anonymous glossary, including glosses on Hippocrates.
	Authorship attributed to an otherwise unknown
	"Herodotus Lycius," also wrongly ascribed to
	Herodotus, the physician, disciple of Agathinus
4007.Z8	Modern. By date
4008	Herodotus (phys.) to Hes...
	Herodotus, physician, 1st century A.D. Ἡρόδοτος
	Cf. R126.A+ Medicine
	Cf. PA4007.Z7 Lexicon Herodoteum
	"Herodotus Lycius" see PA4007.Z7
	Herodotus, of Tarsus (skeptic philosopher) 2nd century
	A.D. Ἡρόδοτος Ταρσεύς

	Individual authors to 600 A.D.
	Herodotus. Ἡρόδοτος (phys.) to Hes...
	Herondas, 3rd century B.C. Herodas. Ἡρώνδας (Ἡρώδας)
4008.H2	Editions. By date
4008.H2A-.H2Z	Translations. By language, A-Z, and date
4008.H3	Adaptations, imitations, etc.
	For individual authors see classification under author in Classes PQ, PR, etc.
4008.H4	Criticism
	Herophilus (not Hierophilus) of Chalcedon, 3rd century B.C. Ἡρόφιλος
	Cf. R126.A+ Medicine
	Hesiod and his school. Ἡσίοδος
4009.A2	Editions. By date
4009.O7	Opera et dies. Works and days. Ἔργα καὶ ἡμέραι
4009.S3	Scutum Herculis. Ἀσπὶς Ἡρακλέους
	Spurious
4009.T5	Theogonia. Theogony. Θεογονία
4009.Z4	Fragments. By date
4009.Z5	Catalogus feminarum (Catalogi, Ehoeae). Ἠοῖαι
4009.Z52	Magnae ehoeae. Great catalogue. Ἠοῖαι μεγάλαι
4009.Z55	Other
4009.Z7	Hesiodi et Homeri certamen. Certamen Homeri et Hesiodi. Ἀγὼν Ἡσιόδου καὶ Ὁμήρου
4010	Translations. By language, title, and date
	Criticism and interpretation
	Ancient and medieval
4011.A1	Scholia and collections
4011.A15	Particular authors
4011.A2	Early to 1800 or 1850/70
4011.A5-Z	Later
4012.A-.Z3	Special topics, A-Z
(4012.Z4)	Illustrations
(4012.Z45)	History of study and appreciation of Hesiodus
(4012.Z48)	Textual criticism. Discussion of manuscripts, editions, etc.
4012.Z5	Technique. Language. Style
4012.Z6	Versification
4012.Z8	Glossaries, indices, etc., by date
4013	Heso... to Hippo...
4013.H2	Hesychius, of Alexandria, 5th century A.D. (?). Lexicon (Dictionarium). Ἡσύχιος. Λεξικόν
4013.H3	Hesychius Illustris, of Miletus, 6th century A.D. Hesychius, of Miletus. Ἡσύχιος ὁ Ἰλλούστριος (Table P-PZ38 modified)

PA3050-4505

Individual authors to 600 A.D.

Heso... to Hippo...

Hesychius Illustris, of Miletus, 6th century A.D. Hesychius,
of Miletus. Ἡσύχιος ὁ Ἰλλούστριος -- Continued

4013.H3A61-.H3A78   Separate works. By title
e.g. Historia Romana atque omnigena; Onomatologus
(Fragments (e.g. Vita Menagiana Aristotelis)); Origenes
Constantinopolitanae; Spurious works, including De
viris doctrina claris (A medieval compilation from
Diogenes Laertius and Suidas). Ἱστορία Ῥωμαϊκή τε καὶ
παντοδαπή. Ὀνοματολόγος. Πάτρια
Κωνσταντινουπόλεως. Περὶ τῶν ἐν παιδείᾳ
διαλαμψάντων

4013.H35   Hierocles (grammarian of uncertain date). Philogelos
(Facetiae). Ἱεροκλῆς. Φιλόγελως ἐκ τῶν Ἱεροκλέους καὶ
Φιλαγρίου γραμματικῶν (Ἀστεῖα)

4013.H4   Hierocles (grammarian) 6th century A.D. Synecdemus (List
of provinces and cities of the Byzantine Empire).
Ἱεροκλῆς. Συνέκδημος

4013.H42   Hierocles (paradoxographer?) 5th century A.D. Philistores.
Ἱεροκλῆς. Φιλίστορες
Fragments

4013.H44   Hierocles (stoic) 2nd century A.D. Ἱεροκλῆς (Table P-PZ38)

4013.H46   Hierocles, of Alexandria, Neoplatonist, 5th century A.D.
Ἱεροκλῆς (Table P-PZ38 modified)

4013.H46A61-   Separate works. By title
.H46A78   e.g. Commentarius in Aurea Pythagoreorum carmina
(Ὑπόμνημα εἰς τὰ τῶν Πυθαγορείων ἔπη τὰ χρυσᾶ),
including De providentia et fato (Περὶ προνοίας καὶ
εἱμαρμένης)
Facetiae see PA4013.H35

4013.H48   Hieronymus, of Cardia (historian) ca. 364-260 B.C.
Ἱερώνυμος Καρδιανός (Table P-PZ38)

4013.H49   Hieronymus, of Rhodes (peripatetic) ca. 290-230 B.C.
Ἱερώνυμος ὁ Ῥόδιος (Table P-PZ38)
Hierophilus
see Herophilus, of Chalcedon

4013.H5   Himerius (sophist) 4th century A.D. Ἱμέριος
Orations (twenty-four preserved entire)

4013.H65   Hipparchus (writer of comedies) fl. 263 B.C.? Ἵππαρχος
(Table P-PZ38)

4013.H68   Hipparchus (Pythagorean) 4th century B.C. Ἵππαρχος
(Table P-PZ38)

4013.H7   Hipparchus Bithynius (of Nicaea in Bithynia) fl. ca. 161-127
B.C. Ἵππαρχος (Table P-PZ38 modified)

Individual authors to 600 A.D.

Heso... to Hippo...

Hipparchus Bithynius (of Nicaea in Bithynia) fl. ca. 161-127 B.C. Ἵππαρχος -- Continued

4013.H7A61-.H7A78   Separate works. By title

e.g. In Arati et Eudoxi Phaenomena commentariorum libri III (Ἀράτου καὶ Εὐδόξου Φαινομένων ἐξηγήσεως βιβλία γ'); Liber asterismorum (De magnitudine et positione inerrantium stellarum) (Ἔκθεσις ἀστερισμῶν ἢ περὶ τῶν ἀπλανῶν ἀναγραφαί); Fragments

Hippasus (Pythagorean) 5th (?) century B.C. Ἵππασος

Hippias, of Elis (sophist) 5th century B.C. Ἱππίας ὁ Ἠλεῖος

    Cf. PA4279.H6+ Plato, Hippias

Hippocrates, of Chios (mathematician) 5th century B.C. Ἱπποκράτης

Hippocrates, of Cos, 5th century B.C. Ἱπποκράτης ὁ Κῷος

Editions

    see R126.H4+

Translations

    see R126.H5+

4016   Criticism (philological, textual criticism, etc.)
4016.Z5   Language
    Glossaries
4016.Z7   Ancient

    Cf. PA4007.Z7 Lexicon Herodoteum

4016.Z8   Modern. By date
4017   Hippocr... to Home...
4017.H3   Hipponax, of Ephesus, fl. ca. 540 B.C. Ἱππῶναξ (Table P-PZ38)

4017.H5   Hippys, of Rhegion, 3rd century B.C. (?). Ἵππυς (Table P-PZ38)

    Homer. Ὅμηρος

    Editions

(4018.A1)   Manuscripts and papyri

    For reproductions in facsimile see Z114; Z115Z

(4018.A13)   Editions of a particular manuscript

    see classification with printed editions

4018.A2   Comprehensive editions (Iliad, Odyssey, Carmina minora). By date

4018.A25   Selections from all the works

    Iliad and Odyssey. Ἰλιάς. Ὀδύσσεια

4018.A3   Editions. By date
4018.A35A-.A35Z   School editions. By editor, A-Z

    Selected books

4018.A4A-.A4Z   Critical editions. By editor, A-Z
4018.A5A-.A5Z   School editions. By editor, A-Z

    Portions

	Individual authors to 600 A.D.
	Homer. Ὅμηρος
	Editions
	Iliad and Odyssey. Ἰλιάς. Ὀδύσσεια
	Portions -- Continued
4018.A6	Continuous (from several books)
4018.A65	Miscellaneous
4018.A68	Summaries
	Selections. Quotations. Passages. Thoughts
4018.A7	Ancient (Collections of quotations)
	Centos
4018.A75	Collections and selections
4018.A78	Particular authors
4018.A8	Modern
4018.A9	Prospectus of editions, not published
4019-4020	Iliad. Ἰλιάς
4019.A1	Manuscript editions in facsimile
4019.A2	Complete editions. By date
	School editions
(4019.A3)	English and American
(4019.A4)	German
(4019.A5)	Other
	Editions of several (three or more) books
	Editions of books I and others in regular sequence
4020.A1	I-XIV (or I-XII; or I-VIII). By date
4020.A15	I-VI (or I-V; or I-IV). By date
4020.A17	I-III. By date
4020.A19	Editions of books I and others in irregular sequence. By date
4020.P1-.P24	Editions of particular books (one or two)
	Subarrange by selecting the Cutter number from the span .P1-.P9 that corresponds with the book of the Iliad being classified, e. g. Book IV = PA4020.P4; Book XXIV = PA4020.P24; etc.
	Including portions of a particular book, e.g., editions of the Catalogue of ships, Iliad II, v. 494-877, are classified with editions of book II
	Editions of two books are classified with the first
4020.Z5	Portions from several books. By date
4020.Z7	Selections. Anthologies. Chrestomathies. By date
4020.Z9	Epitomes. "Arguments"
	Odyssey. Ὀδύσσεια
(4021.A1)	Manuscript editions in facsimile
	see Z115Z.H75
4021.A2	Complete editions. By date
	School editions
(4021.A3)	English and American

	Individual authors to 600 A.D.
	Homer. Ὅμηρος
	Editions
	Odyssey. Ὀδύσσεια
	School editions -- Continued
(4021.A4)	German
(4021.A5)	Other
	Editions of several (three or more) books
	Editions of books I and others in regular sequence
4022.A1	I-XIV (or I-XII; or I-VIII). By date
4022.A15	I-VI (or I-V; or I-IV). By date
4022.A17	I-III. By date
4022.A19	Editions of books I and others in irregular sequence. By date
4022.P1-.P24	Editions of particular books (one or two)
	Subarrange by selecting the Cutter number from the span .P1-.P24 that corresponds with the book of the Odyssey being classified, e. g. Book IV = PA4020.P4; Book XXII = PA4020.P22; etc.
	Including portions of a particular book, e.g., editions of the Catalogue of ships, Iliad II, v. 494-877, are classified with editions of book II
	Editions of two books are classified with the first
4022.Z5	Portions from several books. By date
4022.Z7	Selections. Anthologies. Chrestomathies. By date
4022.Z9	Epitomes. "Arguments"
4023	Carmina minora
4023.A1	Collected or selected
	Separate works, A-Z
4023.B3	Batrachomyomachia. Battle of the frogs and mice. Βατραχομυομαχία. By date
4023.B3A-.B3Z	Criticism
4023.E7	Epigrammata. Ἐπιγράμματα. By date
4023.E7A-.E7Z	Criticism
4023.H8	Hymns (collected and selected). Homeric hymns. Ὁμηρικοὶ ὕμνοι
	Particular hymns
4023.H81	In Apollinem. Hymn to Apollo. Εἰς Ἀπόλλωνα. By date
	Authorship ascribed to Cynaethus, of Chios
4023.H81A-.H81Z	Criticism
4023.H83	In Cererem. Hymn to Demeter. Εἰς Δήμητραν. By date
4023.H83A-.H83Z	Criticism
4023.H84	Hymn to Dionysus. Εἰς Διόνυσον. By date
4023.H84A-.H84Z	Criticism
4023.H85	In Mercurium. Εἰς Ἑρμῆν. By date

Individual authors to 600 A.D.
    Homer. Ὅμηρος
      Editions
        Carmina minora
          Separate works, A-Z
            Hymns (collected and selected). Homeric hymns.
              Ὁμηρικοὶ ὕμνοι
            Particular hymns
              In Mercurium. Εἰς Ἑρμῆν. By date -- Continued

4023.H85A-.H85Z	Criticism
4023.H87	In Venerem. Hymn to Aphrodite. Εἰς Ἀφροδίτην. By date
4023.H87A-.H87Z	Criticism
4023.M3	Margites. Μαργίτης. By date
4023.M3A-.M3Z	Criticism

           Criticism, interpretation, etc.
              Class here criticism, etc., of all the minor works and of the Hymns
              For criticism confined to the Batrachomyomachia or to any other particular poem, see the poem

4023.Z5	General works
4023.Z6	Language, grammar, etc.
4023.Z7	Versification
4023.Z8	Glossaries. Concordances

        Translations
          Greek

(4024.A1)	Ancient and medieval paraphrases
	see PA4035

          Modern Greek

4024.A11	Comprehensive (or Iliad and Odyssey). By date
	Iliad. Ἰλιάς
4024.A12	Complete. By date
4024.A13	Selected books or portions. By date
	Odyssey. Ὀδύσσεια
4024.A14	Complete. By date
4024.A15	Selected books or portions. By date
4024.A16	Carmina minora. By date
4024.A17	Batrachomyomachia. By date
4024.A18	Hymni. By date

         Latin

(4024.A2)	Ancient
	see PA6202+ Roman literature

          Modern

4024.A25	Comprehensive (or Iliad and Odyssey). By date
	Iliad. Ἰλιάς
4024.A3	Complete. By date
4024.A33	Selected books. By date

	Individual authors to 600 A.D.
	Homer. Ὅμηρος
	Translations
	Latin
	Modern
	Iliad. Ἰλιάς -- Continued
4024.A35	Portions. Selections. By date
4024.A37	Particular books. By date
	Odyssey. Ὀδύσσεια
4024.A4	Complete. By date
4024.A43	Selected books. By date
4024.A45	Portions. Selections. By date
4024.A47	Particular books. By date
4024.A5	Carmina minora (Collected and selected). By date
4024.A53	Batrachomyomachia. By date
4024.A55	Hymni. By date
	Other languages
	A-Dutch
4024.B2	Basque (Table PA3)
4024.C2	Catalan (Table PA3)
	Celtic
4024.C3	Breton (Table PA3)
4024.C4	Cornish (Table PA3)
4024.C5	Gaelic (Table PA3)
4024.C6	Irish (Table PA3)
4024.C7	Manx (Table PA3)
4024.C8	Welsh (Table PA3)
	Danish see PA4030.S2
4024.D8	Dutch. Flemish. Frisian (Table PA3)
4025	English (Table PA9)
4026	E-French
4027	French (Table PA9)
4029	German (Table PA9)
	Including Low German
	H to S
4030.H8	Hungarian (Table PA3)
	Icelandic see PA4030.S4
4030.I8	Italian (Table PA3)
4030.P7	Portuguese (Table PA3)
4030.R8	Rumanian (Table PA3)
	Scandinavian
4030.S2	Danish. Dano-Norwegian (Table PA3)
4030.S4	Icelandic (Table PA3)
4030.S6	Swedish (Table PA3)
4030.S8	Spanish (Table PA3)
4031.A-Z	Slavic languages, A-Z
4031.B3	Bohemian (Table PA3)

PA3050-4505

	Individual authors to 600 A.D.
	Homer. Ὅμηρος
	Translations
	Other languages
	Slavic languages, A-Z -- Continued
4031.B6	Bulgarian (Table PA3)
4031.C7	Croatian (Table PA3)
4031.L3	Lettish (Table PA3)
4031.L6	Lithuanian (Table PA3)
4031.P7	Polish (Table PA3)
4031.R2	Russian (Table PA3)
4031.S2	Serbian (Table PA3)
4031.S6	Slovak (Table PA3)
4031.S8	Slovenian (Table PA3)
4031.U4	Ukrainian (Table PA3)
4031.W2	Wendic (Table PA3)
4032	Oriental, African, Artificial languages
(4032.1)	Popular and juvenile stories
	see subdivision "Paraphrases. Tales, etc." under translations of each language
(4032.3)	Dramatizations. Fiction based on Homer
	see the author
(4032.5)	Parodies. Travesties
	see the subdivision "Parodies" under translations of each language
	Art. Illustrations
	Ancient
4033.A2	Vases, sculptures, etc.
4033.A4	Illustrated manuscripts
4033.A5-Z	Modern. By artist, A-Z
4033.9	Music
	For compositions based on Homer's poems see Class M
	Criticism and interpretation
4035	Ancient and medieval
	Scholia
4035.A2	Editions. By date
	Including comprehensive and Iliad alone
4035.A3	Odyssey
(4035.A33)	Criticism
	see PA4037
4035.A35	Paraphrases
	Lives of Homer
	Class here texts only
	For criticism see PA4037
4035.A4	Collections. By date
4035.A4A-.A4Z	Particular, A-Z, by author or title
	Certamen Hesiodi et Homeri see PA4009.Z7

	Individual authors to 600 A.D.
	Homer. Ὅμηρος
	Criticism and interpretation
	Ancient and medieval
	Lives of Homer. Ὅμηρος
	Particular, A-Z, by author or title -- Continued
4035.A4H4	Herodotus (Pseudo-Herodotus). Vita Homeri
4035.A4P6	Plutarchus (Pseudo-Plutarchus). De vita et poesi Homeri
4035.A5	Treatises (Collections and selections)
4035.A6	Allusions (Collections and selections). By date
4035.A7-Z	Particular authors or works, A-Z
4035.A7	Apollonius Sophista. Lexicon homericum. Ἀπολλώνιος ὁ Σοφιστής
4035.A75	Aristarchus, of Samothrace (Alexandria), 2nd century B.C. Ἀρίσταρχος
	No writings left
	For literature about him see PA3874.A5
4035.A8	Aristonicus Alexandrinus. Ἀριστόνικος Ἀλεξανδρεύς
	Aristophanes Byzantius. Ἀριστοφάνης ὁ Βυζάντιος
	No writings left
	For literature about him see PA3889.A2
	Aristoteles. Poetica (cap.25) see PA3893.P5
	Certamen Hesiodi et Homeri see PA4009.Z7
	Crates Mallotes. Κράτης ὁ Μαλλώτης
4035.D4	Didymus Chalcenterus. Δίδυμος Χαλκέντερος
4035.E8	Eustathius, Archbishop of Thessalonica. Εὐστάθιος
4035.H4	Heraclitus. Allegoriae Homericae. Ἡράκλειτος. Ὁμηρικὰ προβλήματα
4035.H5	Herodianus, Aelius. Αἴλιος Ἡρωδιανός
4035.N5	Nicanor. Νικάνωρ
4035.P7	Porphyrius. Porphyry. Πορφύριος
	De Styge. Περὶ Στυγός
	Quaestiones Homericae. De antro nympharum. Peri tou en Odysseia tōn nymphōn antrou. Ὁμηρικὰ ζητήματα. Περὶ τοῦ ἐν Ὀδυσσείᾳ τῶν νυμφῶν ἄντρου
4035.P8	Proclus. Πρόκλος
	Apologia pro Homero (in his In libros Platonis De republica commentarius)
	Vita Homeri (in his Chrestomathia grammatica (Χρηστομάθεια γραμματική))
4035.T9	Tzetzes, John. Ἰωάννης Τζέτζης
	Allegoriae Homericae. Ὑπόθεσεις τοῦ Ὁμήρου ἀλληγορηθεῖσα
	In verse

PA3050-4505

Individual authors to 600 A.D.
Homer. Ὅμηρος
Criticism and interpretation
Ancient and medieval
Particular authors or works, A-Z
Tzetzes, John. Ἰωάννης Τζέτζης -- Continued
Exegesis in Iliadem (A1-102). Hypomnēma meta scholiōn eis tēn Iliada. Ἐξήγησις εἰς τὴν Ὁμήρου Ἰλιάδα
Theogonia. Θεογονία

4035.Z4	Zenodorus. Ζηνόδωρος
4035.Z5	Zenodotus, of Ephesus. Ζηνόδοτος
(4035.Z7)	Zoilus (Homeromastix). Ζωΐλος (Ὁμηρομάστιξ)
	see PA4500.Z57
4037	Modern
	Including treatises confined to the Iliad
4037.A2	Early: 1500-1800
	Later: 1800-
4037.A5	Collected papers, essays, studies, etc. (By several authors)
4037.A6-.Z3	Treatises (by individual authors, collected or single)
4037.Z5	Popular. Minor. (Single) Lectures, addresses, essays
4038.A-Z	Individual critics, historians, etc., A-Z
	Influence of Homer. History of study and appreciation
(4141)	General
(4142)	Ancient
(4149)	Medieval
	Modern
(4150)	General
4152.A-Z	By region or country, A-Z
4153	Translations (as subject)
	For translations in a particular language see PA4152.A+
(4154.A-Z)	Particular authors or persons, A-Z
	Interpretation, commentaries, etc.
	Iliad. Ἰλιάς
	see PA4035; PA4037
(4157.A2)	Commentaries without text, or with text subordinated to commentary
(4157.A5-Z)	Other
(4158)	Particular books
	Subdivide .A01-24A-Z by book and author
(4159)	Episodes. Portions from several books
(4161)	Detached passages. Variant readings

	Individual authors to 600 A.D.
	Homer. Ὅμηρος
	Criticism and interpretation
	Interpretation, commentaries, etc. -- Continued
	Odyssey. Ὀδύσσεια
	For editions of scholia and ancient and medieval commentaries see PA4035
	For treatises on the Odyssey in which the solution of the Homeric question is the chief object see PA4037
4167.A2	Commentaries without text, or with text subordinated to commentary
4167.A5-Z	Other
4168	Particular books
	Subdivide .A01-24A-Z by book and author
4169	Episodes. Portions from several books
4171	Detached passages. Variant readings
	Carmina minora see PA4023.Z5+
	Language. Style
4175	General
4176	General special
4177.A-Z	Special, A-Z
4177.A48	Alphabet
4177.C6	Compound words
4177.C64	Conversation. Speech
4177.D83	Duality (Logic)
4177.E6	Epic formulae
4177.E7	Epithets
	Metaphors
4177.N35	Names
	Orations
4177.R4	Reiterations. Tautology. Pleonasm
4177.S5	Similes
	Speech see PA4177.C64
4177.S94	Synonyms
4177.V6	Vocabulary
	Wit and humor
	Grammar
4179	General
	Special
	Dialects
4180	General
4181.A-Z	Special, by subject, A-Z
	Phonology
4182	General
4183.A-Z	Special, by subject, A-Z
	Morphology

PA3050-4505

	Individual authors to 600 A.D.
	Homer. Ὅμηρος
	Criticism and interpretation
	Language. Style
	Grammar
	Special
	Morphology -- Continued
4185	General
4186	Word formation (General)
	Special see PA4190+
	Syntax
4187	General
4188	Special
	Parts of speech (Morphology and syntax)
	Noun
4190	General
4191.A-Z	Special, A-Z
4191.C3	Case
4191.G4	Gender
4191.N8	Number
4192	Adjective
4193	Numerals
4194	Article
4195	Pronoun
	Verb
4197	General
4198	Special
4201	Particles
	Versification
4205	General
4206.A-Z	Special, A-Z
4206.H5	Hiatus
4207	Etymology
4209	Lexicography. Semantics
4209.A2	Treatises
4209.A5-.Z3	Concordances, indices, glossaries
	For ancient and medieval see PA4035
4209.Z5	School glossaries
4211	Homerus (of Byzantium) to Hyp...
4211.H55	Homerus, of Byzantium (dramatist) 3rd century B.C. Ὅμηρος (Table P-PZ38)
4211.H57	Horapollo, of Phainebythis (Phenebythis), 5th century A.D. Ὡραπόλλων (Table P-PZ38)
4211.H67	Horapollo Nilous, 4th (?) century A.D. Ὡραπόλλων Νειλῶος (Table P-PZ38 modified)

Individual authors to 600 A.D.
Homerus (of Byzantium) to Hyp...
Horapollo Nilous, 4th (?) century A.D. Ὡραπόλλων Νειλῶος
-- Continued

4211.H67A61- .H67A78	Separate works. By date
	e.g. Hieroglyphica (The original written in Coptic is lost; the translation into vulgar Greek is by Philippos). Ἱερογλυφικά. - Cf. PJ1091.A3+ Egyptian hieroglyphics
4211.H73	Hybreas (rhetor) 1st century B.C. Ὑβρέας (Table P-PZ38)
4211.H75	Hybrias Cretensis, 7th-6th century B.C. Ὑβρίας ὁ Κρής (Table P-PZ38)
	Hymns of Orpheus see PA4258.H8
4211.H9	Hypatia, d. 415 A.D. Ὑπατία (Table P-PZ38)
	Hyperides. Ὑπερείδης
4212.A2	Collections and selections. By date
	Particular orations
4212.A23	In (contra) Athenogenem. Κατὰ Ἀθηνογένους
4212.A24	In (contra) Demosthenem. Κατὰ Δημοσθένους ὑπὲρ τῶν Ἁρπαλείων
4212.A25	Pro Euxenippo. Hyper Euxenippou eisangelias apologia pros Polyeukton. Ὑπὲρ Εὐξενίππου ἀπολογία πρὸς Πολύευκτον
4212.A26	Oratio funebris. Epitaphios. Ἐπιτάφιος
4212.A27	Pro Lycophrone. Ὑπὲρ Λυκόφρονος ἀπολογία
4212.A28	Adversus Philippidem. Κατὰ Φιλιππίδου
	Translations
	English
4212.A3	Collections and selections. By date
4212.A31-.A39	Particular orations. By date
4212.A5-.A79	Other
4212.A8-.Z3	Criticism
4212.Z5-.Z8	Language, etc.
4213	Hyps... to Is...
4213.H9	Hypsicles, of Alexandria, mathematician, ca. 170 B.C. Ὑψικλῆς (Table P-PZ38)
	Iamblichus
	see Jamblichus
	Iason
	see Jason
4213.I2	Ibycus, of Rhegium, 6th century B.C. Ἴβυκος (Table P-PZ38)
4213.I4	Idomeneus, of Lampsacus, 3rd century B.C. Ἰδομενεύς (Table P-PZ38)
	Ilias parva see PA4225.L57
	Ilii persis see PA3873.A95
	Ioannes
	see Joannes

PA3050-4505

	Individual authors to 600 A.D.
	Hyps... to Is... -- Continued
4213.I6	Ion, of Chios (writer of tragedies, poems, etc.) 5th century B.C. Ἴων (Table P-PZ38)
4213.I65	Iophon (son of Sophocles, writer of tragedies) 5th century B.C. Ἰοφῶν (Table P-PZ38)
4213.I8	Irenaeus, Minucius Pacatus (lexicographer) 1st century A.D. Εἰρηναῖος (Table P-PZ38)
	Isaeus, fl. 390-350 B.C. Ἰσαῖος
4214.A2	Editions
4214.A31	De Apollodori hereditate. Περὶ τοῦ Ἀπολλοδώρου κλήρου
4214.A32	De Aristarchi hereditate. Περὶ τοῦ Ἀριστάρχου κλήρου
4214.A322	De Astyphili hereditate. Περὶ τοῦ Ἀστυφίλου κλήρου
4214.A324	De Cironis hereditate. Περὶ τοῦ Κίρωνος κλήρου
4214.A326	De Cleonymi hereditate. Περὶ τοῦ Κλεονύμου κλήρου
4214.A328	De Dicaeogenis hereditate. Περὶ τοῦ Δικαιογένους κλήρου
4214.A33	De Euphileto. Ὑπὲρ Εὐφιλήτου
4214.A34	De Hagniae hereditate. Περὶ τοῦ Ἁγνίου κλήρου
4214.A35	De Meneclis hereditate. Περὶ τοῦ Μενεκλέους κλήρου
4214.A36	De Nicostrati hereditate. Περὶ τοῦ Νικοστράτου κλήρου
4214.A37	De Philoctemonis hereditate. Περὶ τοῦ Φιλοκτήμονος κλήρου
4214.A38	De Pyrrhi hereditate. Περὶ τοῦ Πύρρου κλήρου
	Translations
4214.A39	Latin. By date
4214.A4	English. By date
4214.A41-.A79	Other. By language and date
4214.A8-.Z3	Criticism
4214.Z5	Language, etc.
4214.Z8	Glossaries, indices, etc. By date
4215	Isi... to Iso...
4215.I4	Isidore, of Charax (geographer, of uncertain date). Ἰσίδωρος ὁ Χαρακηνός (Table P-PZ38)
4215.I8	Isigonus, of Nicaea (paradoxographer of uncertain date). Ἰσίγονος (Table P-PZ38)
	Isocrates. Ἰσοκράτης
4216	Editions
4216.A2	Orations and letters (or Orations alone)
4216.A3	Selected orations
4216.A5-.Z3	Particular orations
	Aegineticus. Αἰγινητικός
	Archidamus. Ἀρχίδαμος
	Areopagiticus. Ἀρεοπαγιτικός
	De bigis. Περὶ του ζεύγους
	Busiris. Βούσειρις
	Adversus Callimachum. Πρὸς Καλλίμαχον

	Individual authors to 600 A.D.
	Isocrates. Ἰσοκράτης
	Editions
	Particular orations -- Continued
	Ad Demonicum (Paraenesis ad D.). To Demonicus. Πρὸς Δημόνικον
	Spurious
	Epistulae see PA4216.Z3+
	Euagoras. Εὐαγόρας
	Adversus Euthynum. Πρὸς Εὐθύνουν
	Helenae laudatio. Ἑλένης ἐγκώμιον
	Contra Lochitem. Κατὰ Λοχίτου
	Ad Nicoclem. To Nicocles. Πρὸς Νικοκλέα περὶ βασιλείας
	Nicocles. Νικοκλῆς ἢ Κύπριοι
4216.P2	De pace. Περὶ εἰρήνης
4216.P3	Panegyricus. Πανηγυρικός
4216.P4	Panathenaicus. Παναθηναϊκός
4216.P5	De permutatione. Περὶ ἀντιδόσεως
4216.P6	Ad Philippum. Philippus. Φίλιππος
4216.P7	Plataicus (Oratio Plataeensium). Πλαταϊκός
	Contra sophistas. Κατὰ τῶν σοφιστῶν
	Trapeziticus. Τραπεζιτικός
	Epistulae. Ἐπιστολαί
4216.Z3	Editions. By date
4216.Z4	Criticism
4217	Translations
4218	Criticism
4218.Z5	Language, style, etc.
4219	Isog... to Jam...
	Isogonus
	see Isigonus
	Ister (Istros) of Callatis. Ἴστρος
	Identical with Ister Callimacheus?
4219.I6	Ister Callimacheus (of Cyrene; slave and disciple of Callimachus) 3rd century B.C. Istrus, the Callimachean. Ἴστρος ὁ Καλλιμάχειος (Table P-PZ38)
	Identical with Ister of Callatis?
	Istros
	see Ister
4219.I7	Isyllus, of Epidaurus, fl. ca. 280 B.C. Ἴσυλλος (Table P-PZ38)
4220	Jamblichus, of Chalcis (in Syria), d. ca. 330 A.D. Iamblichus. Ἰάμβλιχος
	Cf. B669 Philosophy

PA3050-4505

Individual authors to 600 A.D.
   Jamblichus, of Chalcis (in Syria), d. ca. 330 A.D. Iamblichus.
   Ἰάμβλιχος Iamblichus. Ἰάμβλιχος -- Continued
     Commentariorum pythagoricorum lib. I-X. Συναγωγή τῶν
      Πυθαγορείων δογμάτων
        Books I-IV and VII preserved and published as independent
          treatises
      Adhortatio (Hortationes) ad philosophiam see
        PA4220.A47

4220.A38	De communi (generali) mathematum scientia. De communi mathematica scientia. Περὶ τῆς κοινῆς μαθηματικῆς ἐπιστήμης Commentariorum lib. III De fato see PA4220.A4
4220.A4	De mysteriis Aegyptiorum, Chaldaeorum, Assyriorum. Περὶ μυστηρίων Authorship disputed. Chapters 7-8 of section VIII have appeared as a separate work with title De fato
4220.A43	De vita Pythagorica. Περὶ τοῦ Πυθαγορικοῦ βίου Commentariorum lib. I

4220.A45	In Nicomachi Arithmeticam introductionem liber. Περὶ τῆς Νικομάχου Ἀριθμητικῆς εἰσαγωγῆς
	   Commentariorum lib. IV
	   Cf. PA4250.N6 Nicomachus, of Gerasa

4220.A47	Protrepticus (Adhortatio ad philosophiam; Protrepticae orationes ad philosophiam). Exhortation to philosophy. Λόγος προτρεπτικὸς εἰς φιλοσοφίαν Commentariorum lib. II
4220.A5	Theologumena arithmeticae (Theologia arithmetica). Theological principles of arithmetic. Θεολογούμενα τῆς ἀριθμητικῆς Commentariorum lib. VII; authorship disputed
4220.A6	Fragments and lost works
4220.A7-.Z3	Translations, by language, title (in Latin) and date
4220.Z5	Criticism, interpretation, etc. For philosophical treatises see B669
4221	Jamblichus, of Syria to Jos...
4221.J12	Jamblichus, of Syria, 2nd century A.D. Babyloniaca. Ἰάμβλιχος. Βαβυλωνιακά
4221.J2	Jason, of Cyrene, 2nd century B.C. (?). Ἰάσων ὁ Κυρηναῖος (Table P-PZ38)
4221.J3	Joannes, of Gaza (Joannes Gazes, J. Gazaeus) fl. ca. 536 A.D. Ἰωάννης (Table P-PZ38)
4221.J4	Joannes Lydus, b. 490 A.D. Lydus, Johannes Laurentius. Ἰωάννης Λαυρέντιος Φιλαδελφεὺς ὁ Λυδός (Table P-PZ38) Son of Laurentius in Philadelphia, Lydia

	Individual authors to 600 A.D.
	Jamblichus, of Syria to Jos... -- Continued
	Joannes Philoponus "grammaticus," bp. of Alexandria, fl.
	ca. 500-530 A.D. Philoponus, John. Ἰωάννης ὁ
	Φιλόπονος
	Cf. B673.J6+ Philosophy
4221.J5	Editions (Comprehensive). By date
4221.J5A4	De aeternitate mundi (Contra Proclum de mundi
	aeternitate). Κατὰ Πρόκλου περὶ ἀϊδιότητος κόσμου
4221.J5D3	De dialectis (De idiomatibus; De proprietatibus
	linguarum). Περὶ διαλέκτων
	Spurious
4221.J5D5	De dictionibus quae accentu variant significatum
	(Collectio vocum quae pro diversa significatione
	accentum diversum accipiunt). Περὶ τῶν διαφόρως
	τονουμένων καὶ διάφορα σημαινόντων
	Spurious; in some mss. wrongly ascribed to Cyrillus
4221.J5F4	De febribus. Περὶ πυρετῶν
4221.J5O6	De opificio (creatione) mundi lib. VII. Περὶ κοσμοποιίας
4221.J5P3	De paschate
4221.J5P8	De pulsibus. Περὶ σφυγμῶν
4221.J5T7	De tono. Τονικὰ παραγγέλματα
	Epitome of the Prosodia (Καθολικὴ προσῳδία) of
	Herodianus
	Cf. PA4001.H6 Herodianus
4221.J5U8	De usu astrolabii eiusque constructione. Περὶ τῆς τοῦ
	ἀστρολάβου χρήσεως καὶ κατασκευῆς
	Commentaries (Scholia). Σχόλια
(4221.J5Z2-.J5Z29)	Aristotle
	see PA3902
(4221.J5Z3)	Nicomachus, of Gerasa. Arithmetica
	see PA4250.N6+
(4221.J5Z5)	Porphyry. Isagoge
	see PA4396.Z4A2+
	Bible. Genesis chapter I see PA4221.J5O6
4221.J6	Translations
4221.J7	Criticism
	Joannes Stobaeus see PA4436
	Jon see PA4213.I6
	Jophon see PA4213.I65
	Josephus, Flavius, 1st century A.D. Φλάβιος Ἰώσηπος
	Cf. DS115.9.J6 Biography of Josephus
	Cf. DS116 History
4222	Editions
4222.A2	Comprehensive. By date
4222.A3	Selected works. By date

PA3050-4505

Individual authors to 600 A.D.
  Josephus, Flavius, 1st century A.D. Φλάβιος Ἰώσηπος
    Editions -- Continued

4222.A5   Antiquitates Judaicae lib. XX. Ἰουδαϊκὴ ἀρχαιολογία. By date

4222.C7   Contra Apionem sive De Judaeorum vetustate lib. II. Περὶ τῆς τῶν Ἰουδαίων ἀρχαιότητος. By date

4222.D3   De bello Judaico lib. VII. Περὶ τοῦ Ἰουδαϊκοῦ πολέμου. By date

4222.V5   Vita (Josephi vita). Ἰωσήπου βίος. By date
          Spurious works
            De Maccabaeis sive De imperio rationis. Περὶ αὐτοκράτορος λογισμοῦ
              see Bible. O.T. Apocryphal books. Maccabees IV
            Paraenesis ad Graecos, sive Sermo de causa universi praecipue adversus Platonem (Περὶ τοῦ παντός) see B667.H5+

4223   Translations
         Latin
          Ancient

4223.A13   Antiquitates Judaicae. By date
4223.A15   Contra Apionem. By date
           De bello Judaico
4223.A17   Rufinus (?). By date
4223.A19   "Hegesippus" (corrupt form of Josephus). By date
               Free translation transmitted among the works of Ambrose, Bishop of Milan, and in some manuscripts ascribed to him
4223.A19Z5-.A19Z9   Criticism. Authorship. Language
4223.A2A-.A2Z   Modern. By translator, A-Z
         Oriental
4223.A23   Syriac
4223.A25   Hebrew
            Including the history known under the name of Josippon or Joseph ben Gorion (Gorionides) derived in part from the Latin version of Hegesippus
4223.A27   Armenian
4223.A5-Z   Other
           For English translations see DS116
4224   Criticism
4225   Juba to Lib...
4225.J3   Juba II, King of Mauretania, ca. 50 B.C. to 23 A.D. Ἰόβας (Table P-PZ38)
4225.J37   Julianus Aegyptius (praefectus Aegypti) fl. between 520 and 565 A.D. Ἰουλιανὸς ἀπὸ ὑπάρχου Αἰγύπτιος (Table P-PZ38)
        Julianus Apostata see PA4225.J4+

	Individual authors to 600 A.D.
	Juba to Lib... -- Continued
4225.J38	Julianus, of Laodicea (astrologer) fl. ca. 497-500 A.D. Ἰουλιανός (Table P-PZ38)
	Fragments
	Cf. QB21 History of astronomy
	Cf. QB41 Early astronomical works
	Julianus, Flavius Claudius, Apostata, Emperor of Rome, 332-362 A.D. Julian, Emperor of Rome. Ἰουλιανός
4225.J4	Editions. By date
4225.J4A2	Selected works. By date
4225.J4A3-.J4A38	Orationes I-VIII
	Epistulae. Ἐπιστολαί
4225.J4A4	Collections and selections
4225.J4A5-.J4A69	Particular letters, A-Z
	Arrange by addressee or title
4225.J4A7	Adversus Christianos. Against the Galileans. Κατὰ Γαλιλαίων
4225.J4C3	Caesares (Convivium sive Caesares). Καίσαρες ἢ Συμπόσιον
4225.J4M5	Misopogon (Antiochicus sive Misopogon). Ἀντιοχικὸς ἢ Μισοπώγων
4225.J5	Translations
4225.J6	Criticism
	For historical treatises see DG317
4225.J63	Julianus the Theurgist. Ἰουλιανός (Table P-PZ38)
	Julius Africanus, Sextus see PA3860.A5
	Justus, of Tiberias, fl. 67 A.D. Ἰοῦστος ὁ Τιβεριεύς
	K
	see C
	"Lamprias." Λαμπρίας
4225.L36	Lasus, b. 548 B.C. Λάσος (Table P-PZ38)
	Laurentius Philadelphinus Lydus see PA4221.J4
	Leonidas, of Alexandria (physician) 1st century A.D. Λεωνίδας
	Leonidas, of Byzantium, 1st century B.C.(?). Λεωνίδας
	Leonidas, of Tarentum, fl. ca. 294-281 B.C. Epigrams. Λεωνίδας Ταραντίνος. Ἐπιγράμματα
	Leonidas, Julius, of Alexandria, 1st century A.D. Epigrams. Λεωνίδας Ἀλεξανδρεύς. Ἐπιγράμματα
4225.L54	Leontius, Scholasticus, fl. 540-555. Λεόντιος (Table P-PZ38)
	Lesbonax (grammarian) 1st century A.D.(?). De figuris grammaticis. Λεσβῶναξ. Περὶ σχημάτων
	Lesbonax (rhetor) 2nd century A.D. Λεσβῶναξ

PA3050-4505

	Individual authors to 600 A.D.
	Juba to Lib... -- Continued
4225.L57	Lesches (epic poet) 7th century B.C.(?). Λέσχης (Table P-PZ38)
	Supposed author of the Ilias parva (Ἰλιὰς μικρά)
	Leucippus. Λεύκιππος see B225+
	Lexica Segueriana see PA3499.L4
	Lexicon Messanense de iota adscripto
	Part of Orus, De orthographia, preserved in a Messina manuscript
	Libanius, 314-ca. 393 A.D. Λιβάνιος
4226	Editions
4226.A2	Comprehensive. By date
	Including editions of Orationes et declamationes
4226.A25	Selected miscellaneous orations. By date
4226.A3	Selected groups of orations. By date
	e.g. Panegyrici, Suasoriae, etc.
4226.A4	Declamationes. Μελέται. By date
4226.A5-.Z3	Particular orations or declamations. By Latin title, A-Z
4226.Z4	Progymnasmata. Προγυμνασμάτων παραδείγματα. By date
4226.Z65	Vita et argumenta orationum Demosthenis. Ὑποθέσεις τῶν λόγων Δημοσθένους. By date
	Epistulae. Ἐπιστολαί
4226.Z7	Comprehensive. By date
4226.Z8	Selected miscellaneous letters. By date
4226.Z9	Selected letters by group or addressee. By date
4226.Z97	Characters. Ἐπιστολιμαῖοι χαρακτῆρες
	Models for letter-writing, ascribed to Libanius or to Proclus, originally compiled in the age of Libanius and later enlarged
4227	Translations
4227.A2	Latin. By date
4227.A3-Z	Other, by language, A-Z, and date
4228	Criticism
4228.A-.Z3	General works
	Language, style, etc.
4228.Z5	General works
(4228.Z6)	Grammar, syntax
4228.Z8	Glossaries, indices, etc.
4229	Lic... to Luc...
	Licymnius, of Chios, 4th century B.C. Λικύμνιος
	Linus ("inventor" of song; personification of lamentation). Λίνος
4229.L14	Lobon of Argos. Λόβων (Table P-PZ38)
4229.L2	Lollianos. Λολλιανός (Table P-PZ38)

Individual authors to 600 A.D.
   Lic... to Luc... -- Continued
      Lollius Bassus, 1st century A.D. Λόλλιος Βάσσος
        To be distinguished from Bassus of Smyrna

4229.L3   Longinus, Cassius, ca. 213-272 A.D. Διονύσιος Κάσσιος
        Λογγῖνος
        Fragment of a commentary on Hephaestio. Σχόλια εἰς τὸ
          τοῦ Ἡφαιστίωνος Ἐγχειρίδιον
        Ars rhetorica. Τέχνη ῥητορική
          Fragments, and excerpts
        Spurious works

4229.L4-.L6   De sublimitate (De sublimi orationis genere). On the
          sublime. Περὶ ὕψους (Table P-PZ42a)
          By an unknown author of the 1st century A.D.
          Cf. PA3944.C5 Caecilius, of Calacte

4229.L7-.L9   Longus, 3rd (?) century A.D. Pastoralia de Daphnide et
        Chloe lib. IV. Daphnis and Chloe. Λόγγος. Κατὰ Δάφν···
        καὶ Χλόην (Table P-PZ42a)
      Lucian, of Samosata. Λουκιανός
        Editions

4230.A2   Comprehensive. By date
4230.A3   Selected works. School editions
4230.A4   Selected works (special groups)
          Including Menippean dialogues, Platonic (Lycinus)
            dialogues, Epistolary treatises

4230.A5-.Z7   Separate works
          Abdicatus. Ἀποκηρυττόμενος
          Adversus indoctum. Πρὸς τὸν ἀπαίδευτον καὶ πολλὰ
            βιβλία ὠνούμενον

4230.A6   Alexander. Alexandros. Ἀλέξανδρος ἢ Ψευδόμαντις
          Amores. Ἔρωτες
            Spurious
          Anacharsis. Ἀνάχαρσις ἢ Περὶ γυμνασίων
          Apologia pro mercede conductis see PA4230.D26
          Asinus see PA4230.L8
          Bacchus. Προλαλιὰ ὁ Διόνυσος

4230.B573   Bis accusatus. Δὶς κατηγορούμενος ἢ Δικαστήρια
          Calumniae non temere credendum. Περὶ τοῦ μὴ ῥᾳδίως
            πιστεύειν διαβολῇ
          Cataplus seu Tyrannus (De navigatione seu T.;
            Trajectus s.T.). Κατάπλους ἢ Τύραννος

4230.C5   Charidemus. Χαρίδημος ἢ Περὶ κάλλους
            Spurious
          Charon sive Contemplantes. Χάρων ἢ Ἐπισκοποῦντες
          Convivium seu Lapithae. Συμπόσιον ἢ Λαπίθαι

4230.C8   Cronosolon. Κρονοσόλων

PA3050-4505

Individual authors to 600 A.D.
Lucian, of Samosata. Λουκιανός
Editions
Separate works -- Continued

4230.C9	Cynicus. Κυνικός
	Spurious?
4230.D13	De astrologia. Περὶ τῆς ἀστρολογίης
4230.D15	De dipsadibus. Περὶ διψάδων
4230.D17	De domo (Oecus). Περὶ τοῦ οἴκου
4230.D2	De electro seu cygnis (Electrum). Περὶ τοῦ ἠλέκτρου ἢ τῶν κύκνων
4230.D23	De luctu. Περὶ πένθους
4230.D25	De mercede conductis. Περὶ τῶν ἐπὶ μισθῷ συνόντων
4230.D26	Apologia. Ἀπολογία
4230.D3	De morte Peregrini. Περὶ τῆς Περεγρίνου τελευτῆς
4230.D33	De sacrificiis. Περὶ θυσιῶν
4230.D35	De saltatione. Περὶ ὀρχήσεως
	Authorship disputed
	De somnio sive Vita Luciani
	see Somnium
4230.D37	De Syria dea. De dea Syria. Περὶ τῆς Συρίης θεοῦ
	Authorship disputed
	Dearum iudicium see PA4230.D45
4230.D39	Demonactis vita. Δημῶναξ
4230.D4	Demosthenis encomium. Δημοσθένους ἐγκώμιον
	Authorship disputed
4230.D43	Deorum concilium. Θεῶν ἐκκλησία
4230.D45	Deorum dialogi. Θεῶν διάλογοι
4230.D47	Dialogi marini (Dialogi deorum marinorum). Ἐνάλιοι διάλογοι
4230.D5	Dialogi meretricii. Dialogues of courtesans. Ἑταιρικοὶ διάλογοι
4230.D6	Dialogi mortuorum. Dialogues of the dead. Νεκρικοὶ διάλογοι
	Dionysos
	see Bacchus
4230.D7	Disputatio cum Hesiodo. Διάλεξις πρὸς Ἡσίοδον
	Authorship disputed
	Electrum see PA4230.D2
	Epigrammata. Ἐπιγράμματα
	Epistulae saturnales. Ἐπιστολαὶ κρονικαί
	Eunuchus. Εὐνοῦχος
	Fugitivi. Δραπέται
	Gallus (Somnium sive Gallus). Ὄνειρος ἢ Ἀλεκτρυών
	Halcyon. Ἀλκυών ἢ Περὶ μεταμορφώσεως
	Spurious (dialogue of the 2nd century B.C. transmitted also among the works of Plato)

Individual authors to 600 A.D.
    Lucian, of Samosata. Λουκιανός
      Editions
        Separate works -- Continued
          Harmonides. Ἁρμονίδης
          Hercules. Προλαλιὰ ὁ Ἡρακλῆς

4230.H453   Hermotimus. Hermotimos. Ἑρμότιμος
          Herodotus. Ἡρόδοτος ἢ Ἀετίων
          Hippias. Ἱππίας ἢ Βαλανεῖον
          Icaromenippus. Ἰκαρομένιππος
          Imagines. Εἰκόνες
            Pro imaginibus. Ὑπὲρ τῶν εἰκόνων
          Judicium vocalium. Δίκη φωνηέντων

4230.J843   Jupiter confutatus. Ζεὺς ἐλεγχόμενος
          Jupiter tragoedus. Ζεὺς τραγῳδός

4230.L493   Lexiphanes. Λεξιφάνης
          Longaevi
            see Macrobii

4230.L8   Lucius sive Asinus. Lucius, or, The ass. Λούκιος ἢ
            Ὄνος
            Authorship disputed
            Cf. PA4240.L3 Lucius of Patrae
            Cf. PA6207.M3+ Apuleius
          Macrobii (Longaevi). Μακρόβιοι
            Spurious

4230.M4   Menippus (M. seu Necyomantia). Μένιππος ἢ
            Νεκυομαντεία

4230.M87   Muscae encomium. Μυίας ἐγκόμιον
          Navigium seu Vota. Πλοῖον ἢ Εὐχαί
          Necyomantia see PA4230.M4
          Nero. Νέρων ἢ Περὶ τῆς ὀρυχῆς τοῦ Ἰσθμοῦ see
            PA4272.A55
          Nigrinus. Νιγρῖνος ἢ Περὶ φιλοσόφου ἤθους
          Ocypus. Ὠκύπους
          Oecus see PA4230.D17

4230.P133   Parasitus (De parasito). Περὶ παρασίτου ὅτι τέχνη ἡ
            παρασιτική

4230.P15   Patriae encomium. Πατρίδος ἐγκώμιον
            Authorship disputed

4230.P17   Phalaris prior, alter. Φάλαρις πρῶτος, δεύτερος

4230.P2   Philopatris. Φιλόπατρις
            Spurious (product of the 10th century)

4230.P3   Philopseudae. Φιλοψευδεῖς

4230.P4   Piscator (P. seu Reviviscentes). Halieus. Ἁλιεὺς ἢ
            Ἀναβιοῦντες
          Pro imaginibus
            see Imagines

PA3050-4505

Individual authors to 600 A.D.
Lucian, of Samosata. Λουκιανός
Editions
Separate works -- Continued

4230.P5	Pro lapsu in salutando. Ὑπὲρ τοῦ ἐν τῇ προσαγορεύσει πταίσματος
4230.P6	Prometheus es in verbis. Προμηθεὺς εἶ ἐν λόγοις
4230.P7	Prometheus seu Caucasus. Προμηθεὺς ἢ Καύκασος
4230.P8	Pseudologista seu De apophrade (P. seu De die nefasto). Ψευδολογιστὴς ἢ Περὶ τῆς ἀποφράδος
4230.P9	Pseudosophista sive Soloecista. Ψευδοσοφιστὴς ἢ Σολοικιστής
	A glossary of atticisms in form of a dialogue
	Spurious?
4230.Q6	Quo modo historia sit conscribenda. Πῶς δεῖ ἱστορίαν συγγράφειν
4230.R53	Rhetorum praeceptor. Ῥητόρων διδάσκαλος
	Saturnalia. Πρὸς Κρόνον
	Scytha sive Hospes. Σκύθης ἢ Πρόξενος
	Soloecista see PA4230.P9
	Somnium sive Gallus
	see Gallus
	Somnium sive Vita Luciani. Ἐνύπνιον (Περὶ τοῦ ἐνυπνίου ἤτοι Βίος Λουκιανοῦ
	Symposium
	see Convivium
	Timon. Τίμων ἢ Μισάνθρωπος
	Toxaris. Τόξαρις ἢ Φιλία
	Tragodopodagra. Τραγῳδοποδάγρα
	Trajectus
	see Cataplus
	Tyrannicida. Τυραννοκτόνος
	Tyrannus
	see Cataplus
4230.V483	Verae historiae I-II. Ἀληθὴς ἱστορία
	Vita Luciani
	see Somnium
4230.V5	Vitarum auctio. Biōn prasis. Βίων πρᾶσις
	Zeuxis sive Antiochus. Ζεῦξις ἢ Ἀντίοχος
	Spurious and doubtful works
4230.Z8	Collections and selections. By date
	Particular works see PA4230.A5+
	Criticism
	For particular works see PA4230.A5+
	For general works see PA4236
	Translations
4231.A15	Greek (Modern). By date

	Individual authors to 600 A.D.
	Lucian, of Samosata. Λουκιανός
	Translations -- Continued
4231.A2	Latin. By date
	English
4231.A5A-.A5Z	Collected and selected works. By translator, A-Z
4231.A58	Selections. By date
4231.A6-.Z3	Particular works, A-Z
	e.g.
4231.D5	Dialogi meretricii
	Imitations. Adaptations. Parodies
4231.Z9	Collections. By date
(4231.Z9A-.Z9Z)	Particular works
	see the author
4232.A-Z	Other languages, A-Z
	e.g.
	French
4232.F8A-.F8Z	Collected works, by translator, A-Z
4232.F81	Selected dialogues. By date
4232.F82-.F89	Particular dialogues and works
	Arrange by successive Cutter number and date
(4232.F89Z)	Imitations. Adaptations. Parodies
4236	Criticism
4236.A2	Scholia. By date
4236.A5-.Z3	Modern
4236.Z5	Language. Style
4236.Z8	Glossaries, indices, etc.
4240	Lucianus (Saint) to Lys...
(4240.L12)	Lucianus Samosatensis, Saint, presbyter of Antiochia.
	Lucian, of Antioch, Saint, d. 312. Λουκιανός
	see BR60+ BR1720
4240.L15	Lucillius (Lukillos?) epigrammatist, 1st century A.D.
	Λουκίλλιος (Table P-PZ38)
	Identical with Lucillus Tarrhaeus?
4240.L16	Lucillus Tarrhaeus (L., of Tarrha in Crete) 1st century A.D.
	Λούκιλλος (Table P-PZ38)
	Cf. PA4500.Z5 Zenobius. Compendium proverbiorum
	ex Tarrhaeo et Didymo
4240.L18	Lucius (disciple of Musonius) fl. ca. 110 A.D. Λούκιος.
	Apomnemoneumata Musonii philosophi (Fragments in
	Stobaeus)

PA3050-4505

Individual authors to 600 A.D.

Lucianus (Saint) to Lys... -- Continued

4240.L3   Lucius, of Patrae, 1st century A.D. Metamorphoses Lucii Patrensis. Λούκιος Πατρεύς. Μεταμορφώσεων λόγοι διάφοροι

A novel, presumably the source on which Lucian based his "Lucius sive Asinus" and Apuleius his "Metamorphoses"

Cf. PA4230.L8 Lucianus Samosatensis

Cf. PA6207.M3+ Apuleius

Lycophron (writer of tragedies) fl. ca. 273 B.C. Λυκόφρων

Alexandra (or Cassandra, poem in 1474 iambic trimeters) (Ἀλεξάνδρα); Tragedies, and a lexicographical work De comoedia (Περὶ κωμῳδίας), lost

4240.L4   Texts. By date

4240.L5   Criticism

Lycurgus, fl. 338-327 B.C. Λυκοῦργος

Fifteen orations, only one, "Oratio in Leocratem" (Κατὰ Λεοκράτους), preserved

4240.L6   Texts. By date

4240.L7   Criticism

Lyddus, Joannes see PA4221.J4

4240.L9   Lynceus, of Samos, fl. 300 B.C. Λυγκεύς (Table P-PZ38)

Lysias, ca. 445-ca. 380 B.C. Λυσίας

4241   Editions

4241.A2   Comprehensive. By date

4241.A3   Selected orations. By date

Particular orations

The orations are frequently referred to by their respective numbers

4241.A6   Contra Agoratum (or XIII). Κατ' Ἀγοράτου

4241.A7   Contra Alcibiadem I-II (or XIV-XV). Κατ' Ἀλκιβιάδου α' β'

Authorship of I disputed; II spurious

4241.A8   Contra Andocidem impietatis (or VI). Κατ' Ἀνδοκίδου

Spurious

4241.A9   Pro bonis Aristophanis (or XIX). Περὶ τῶν Ἀριστοφάνους χρημάτων

4241.C3   Pro Calliae sacrilegio (or V). Ὑπὲρ Καλλίου ἱεροσυλίας ἀπολογία

4241.D3   Contra dardanarios (frumentarios) (or XXII). Κατὰ τῶν σιτοπωλῶν

4241.D5   Contra Diogitonem (or XXXII). Κατὰ Διογείτονος

Fragments

4241.E2   Contra Epicratem (or XXVII). Κατὰ Ἐπικράτους

Epitaphius see PA4241.F8

4241.E4   Contra Eratosthenem (or XII). Κατ' Ἐρατοσθένους

Individual authors to 600 A.D.
  Lysias, ca. 445-ca. 380 B.C. Λυσίας
    Editions
      Particular orations -- Continued

4241.E5   Pro caede Eratosthenis (or I). On the murder of
            Eratosthenes. Ὑπὲρ τοῦ Ἐρατοσθένους φόνου
4241.E7   Eroticus. Ἐρωτικός
            Cf. PA4241.Z5 Epistulae
4241.E8   Contra Ergoclem (or XXVIII). Κατὰ Ἐργοκλέους
4241.E9   Contra Evandrum (or XXVI). Κατὰ Εὐάνδρου
4241.F3   Adversus familiares obtrectationis (Expostulatio cum
            familiaribus de maledictis) (or VIII). Κατηγορία πρὸς
            τοὺς συνουσιαστὰς κακολογιῶν
            Authorship disputed
           Adversus frumentarios see PA4241.D3
4241.F8   Oratio funebris (Funebris) (or II). Epitaphios. Ἐπιτάφιος
            Authorship disputed
4241.I6   Pro invalido (Pro impotente veterano) (or XXIV). For
            the invalid. Ὑπὲρ τοῦ ἀδυνάτου
4241.M3   Pro Mantitheo (or XVI). Ὑπὲρ Μαντιθέου
4241.M5   Pro milite (or IX). Ὑπὲρ τοῦ στρατιώτου
            Authorship disputed
4241.M8   Munerum acceptorum apologia (or XXI). Ἀπολογία
            δωροδοκίας
4241.N4   Pro bonis fratris Niciae (or XVIII). Ὑπὲρ τῶν τοῦ Νικίου
            ἀδελφοῦ (Περὶ τῆς δημεύσεως τῶν τοῦ Νικίου
            ἀδελφοῦ)
4241.N6   Contra Nicomachum (or XXX). Κατὰ Νικομάχου
4241.O4   Pro sacra oliva exscisa (or VII). Περὶ τοῦ σηκοῦ
4241.O6   Olympicus (or XXXIII). Ὀλυμπιακός
            Fragment
4241.P2   Contra Pancleonem (or XXIII). Κατὰ Παγκλέωνος
4241.P3   Contra Philocratem (or XXIX). Κατὰ Φιλοκράτους
4241.P4   Contra Philonem (or XXXI). Κατὰ Φίλωνος
4241.P6   Pro Polystrato (or XX). Ὑπὲρ Πολυστράτου
            Spurious
4241.P8   De publicis pecuniis (or XVII). Περὶ δημοσίων
            ἀδικημάτων
4241.R4   De republica (or XXXIV). Περὶ τῆς πολιτείας (Περὶ τοῦ
            μὴ καταλῦσαι τὴν πάτριον πολιτείαν Ἀθήνησι
4241.S5   Adversus Simonem (or III). Πρὸς Σίμωνα
4241.T5   Contra Theomnestum I-II (or X-XI). Κατὰ Θεομνήστου
            α′ β′
            Authorship of I disputed; II epitome of I
4241.T9   De affectata tyrannide (or XXV). Δήμου καταλύσεως
            ἀπολογία

Individual authors to 600 A.D.
Lysias, ca. 445-ca. 380 B.C. Λυσίας
Editions
Particular orations -- Continued

4241.V8   De vulnere praemeditato (or IV). Περὶ τραύματος ἐκ προνοίας

4241.Z5   Epistulae. Ἐπιστολαί
Fragments including the Eroticus (a speech in Plato's Phaedrus, delivered and also composed (?) by Lysias)

4242.A-Z   Translations. By language, A-Z
Subarrange by translator, if given, or date

4243   Criticism. Biography

4243.Z5   Language

4243.Z8   Glossaries, indices, etc. By date

4244   Lysic... to Menan...
Lysimachus (historian) 3rd century B.C. Λυσίμαχος
Lysimachus, of Alexandria, 2nd or 1st century B.C. Λυσίμαχος ὁ Ἀλεξανδρεύς

4244.M14   Macedonius (author of a paian, date uncertain). Μακεδόνιος (Table P-PZ38)

4244.M1413   Macedonius (author of epigrams) 6th century A.D. Μακεδόνιος Ὕπατος

4244.M142   Machon (writer of comedies) 3rd century B.C. Μάχων (Table P-PZ38)

4244.M146   Magnes (writer of comedies) 5th century B.C. Μάγνης (Table P-PZ38)

4244.M16   Magnus (physician) 2nd (?) century A.D. Μάγνος (Table P-PZ38)

4244.M162   Magnus, of Carrhae (historian) 4th century A.D. Μάγνος (Table P-PZ38)

4244.M164   Magnus, of Nisibis (physician) 4th century A.D. Μάγνος (Table P-PZ38)

4244.M17   Mago, of Carthage. Μάγων (Table P-PZ38)
Author of a work on agriculture, translated into Greek by Cassius Dionysius of Utica
Cf. PA3968.D45 Cassius Dionysius

4244.M174   Malchus, of Philadelphia (sophist) 5th century A.D. Μάλχος (Table P-PZ38)
Malchus, of Tyre see PA4396+

4244.M2   Manetho, of Sebennytos, 3rd century B.C. Μανεθών (Table P-PZ38)
Aegyptiaca. Αἰγυπτιακά
Fragments
Manethoniana (Apotelesmatica). Ἀποτελεσματικά
Spurious

Individual authors to 600 A.D.
Lysic... to Menan... -- Continued

4244.M217	Marcellinus (physician) 2nd (?) century A.D. Μαρκελλῖνος (Table P-PZ38)
4244.M22	Marcellinus (rhetor) 5th century A.D. Μαρκελλῖνος (Table P-PZ38 modified)
4244.M22A61- .M22A78	Separate works. By date

Vita Thucydidis. Peri tou Thoukydidou biou kai tēs ideas autou. Περὶ τοῦ Θουκυδίδου βίου καὶ τῆς ἰδέας αὐτοῦ (Original vita lost; a spurious vita in three parts contains in its first part remnants of the original vita); Commentary on Hermogenes, De statibus

4244.M23	Marcellus Sideta (of Sida, physician) 2nd century A.D. De re medica. Μάρκελλος Σιδήτης. Ἰατρικά

Poem in hexameters, 42 books lost.
Fragments: De viribus herbarum; De remediis ex piscibus (Περὶ ἰχθύων); De lycanthropia (Περὶ λυκανθρώπου)

4244.M24	Marcianus, of Heraclea Pontica, fl. ca. 400 A.D. Μαρκιανός (Table P-PZ38 modified)
4244.M24A61- .M24A78	Separate works. By title

e.g. Orbis descriptio see Pseudo-Scymnus; Periplus maris externi (Περίπλους τῆς ἔξω θαλάσσης); Epitome peripli maris interni Menippei (Ἐπιτομὴ τῶν τριῶν τοῦ ἐντὸς θαλάσσης περίπλου βιβλίων Μενίππου Περγαμηνοῦ) (Fragments) - Cf. PA4248.M173 Menippus, of Pergamon; Epitome geographiae Artemidori (Ἐπιτομὴ τῶν ἔνδεκα τῆς Ἀρτεμιδώρου τοῦ Ἐφεσίου γεωγραφίας βιβλίων) (Fragments) - Cf. PA3936.A23 Artemidorus, of Ephesus

Marcus Diaconus, fl. ca. 420 A.D. Μάρκος
see BR60+
Marcus Aurelius, Emperor of Rome, 121-180 see PA3938.9+
Margites see PA4023.M3

4244.M243	Marianus, fl. between 491-518 A.D. Μαριανός (Table P-PZ38)

Metrical paraphrases of Theocritus, Callimachus, a.o. (lost)

4244.M245	Marinus, of Neapolis (Samaria), neoplatonist, fl. 485 A.D. Μαρῖνος Νεαπολίτης (Table P-PZ38)
4244.M247	Marinus Tyrius (geographer), fl. ca. 100 A.D. Μαρῖνος ὁ Τύριος (Table P-PZ38)

Marmor Parium see PA4263.P2

4244.M25	Marsyas, of Pella, fl. 306 B.C. Macedonica. Μαρσύας. Μακεδονικά

Fragments
Not to be confused with Marsyas of Philippi who also wrote a history of Macedonia, likewise lost

Individual authors to 600 A.D.
Lysic... to Menan... -- Continued

4244.M253	Matris (rhetor), 2nd or 1st century B.C.? Μᾶτρις (Table P-PZ38)
4244.M255	Matron, of Pitana (parodist), 4th century B.C. Μάτρων (Table P-PZ38)
4244.M259	Maximus. Μάξιμος

Treatises on various authors known by this name

Maximus (astrologer), 1st (?) century B.C. De actionum auspiciis (Auspicia astrologica; De electionum auspiciis). Μάξιμος. Περί καταρχῶν

Didactic poem formerly ascribed to Maximus philosophus

4244.M262	Maximus (rhetor), 4th? century A.D. De objectionibus insolubilibus. Μάξιμος. Περί τῶν ἀλύτων ἀντιθέσεων
4244.M27	Maximus, of Tyre, 2nd century A.D. Μάξιμος (Table P-PZ38)

Maximus philosophus, d. 370 A.D. Μάξιμος
Teacher of Julian Apostata; works lost
De actionum auspiciis
see Maximus (astrologer)

4244.M29	Megara. Μεγάρα (Table P-PZ38)
4244.M3	Megasthenes, fl. 323-291 B.C. Indica. Μεγασθένης. Ἰνδικά
4244.M35	Melampodeia. Μελαμπόδεια (Table P-PZ38)

Melampus (Pseudo-Melampus). Malampus. De divinatione per palpitationes. Μελάμπους. Περί παλμῶν
Melampus, grammarian. Scholia on Dionysius Thrax. Μελάμπους
Authorship doubtful; by Diomedes?
Melanippides, of Melos (lyric poet) 5th century B.C. Μελανιππίδης
Melanthius (historian) 4th (?) century B.C. Μελάνθιος
Melanthius (lyric poet) 5th century B.C. Μελάνθιος
Melanthius (writer of tragedies) 5th century B.C. Μελάνθιος
Melanthius, of Rhodes (dramatist) 2nd century B.C. Μελάνθιος

4244.M4	Meleager, of Gadara, fl. ca. 80 B.C. Μελέαγρος (Table P-PZ38)

Compiler of a selection of epigrams, including about 130 epigrams of his own

Melissus, of Samos, fl. 444/1 B.C. Μέλισσος see B235.M3+

4244.M5	Memnon, of Heraclea Pontica (historian) fl. between 44 B.C. and 138 A.D. Historiae Heracleae Ponti. Μέμνων. Περί Ἡρακλείας

Lost

Menaechmus, of Sicyon, 4th century B.C. Μέναιχμος
Menander, of Athens. Μένανδρος

4245	Editions

	Individual authors to 600 A.D.
	Menander, of Athens. Μένανδρος
	Editions -- Continued
4245.A2	Collections and selections. By date
	Including editions of fragments
4245.A5-Z	Particular works
4245.S4	Sententiae. Menandrou gnōmai. Μενάνδρου γνῶμαι
4246	Translations
4246.A2	Latin
	Cf. PA6568 Plautus
	Cf. PA6755.A1+ Terence
4246.A5-Z	Other. By language, A-Z, and date
4247	Criticism
(4247.A2)	Ancient
4247.A5-.Z3	Modern
4247.Z5	Language. Grammar
4247.Z6	Versification
4247.Z8	Glossaries, indices, etc. By date
4248	Menander (Ephes.) to Mim...
4248.M12	Menander, of Ephesus, historian, 3rd (or 2nd) century B.C. Μένανδρος (Table P-PZ38)
4248.M13	Menander, of Laodicea (in Syria) rhetor, 3rd (?) century A.D. Μένανδρος (Table P-PZ38 modified)
4248.M13A61-.M13A78	Separate works. By title
	e.g. Divisio causarum genere demonstrativo (Διαίρεσις τῶν ἐπιδεικτικῶν) (Also ascribed to Genethlius, of Petra); De encomiis (Περὶ ἐπιδεικτικῶν) (Authorship disputed)
4248.M16	Menelaus, of Alexandria (mathematician) 1st century A.D. Sphaericorum libri III. Μενέλαος
4248.M17	Menippus, of Gadara (Syria) 3rd century B.C. Μένιππος (Table P-PZ38)
4248.M173	Menippus, of Pergamon (geographer) 1st century A.D. Μένιππος Περγαμηνός (Table P-PZ38)
	Fragments
	Cf. PA4244.M24 Marcianus, of Heraclea Pontica
4248.M175	Meno (disciple of Aristotle) 4th century B.C. Μένων (Table P-PZ38)
4248.M177	Menodotus, of Nicomedia (physician) 2nd century A.D. Μηνόδοτος (Table P-PZ38)
4248.M178	Menodotus, of Perinthus (historian) 3rd century B.C. Μενόδοτος ὁ Περίνθιος (Table P-PZ38)
4248.M179	Menodotus, of Samos (historian, of uncertain date). Μενόδοτος (Table P-PZ38)
	Not identical with Menodotus of Perinthus
4248.M182	Mesomedes, 2nd century A.D. Μεσομήδης (Table P-PZ38)
4248.M19	Metrodorus (epigrammatist) 4th century A.D. Μητρόδωρος (Table P-PZ38)

PA3050-4505

Individual authors to 600 A.D.
  Menander (Ephes.) to Mim... -- Continued

4248.M192   Metrodorus, of Lampsacus (Epicurean philosopher), 4th to
                3rd century B.C. Μητρόδωρος ὁ Λαμψακηνός (Table P-
                PZ38)
4248.M194   Metrodorus, of Skepsis (historian) d. 70 B.C. Μητρόδωρος
                ὁ Σκήψιος (Table P-PZ38)
              Milesia see PA3874.A54
4249   Mimnermus, of Colophon, 6th century B.C. Μίμνερμος (Table
                P-PZ37)
4250   Min... to Non...
4250.M13   Minucianus, rhetor (the older) 2nd to 3rd(?) century A.D.
                Μινουκιανός (Table P-PZ38)
4250.M131   Minucianus, rhetor (the younger) 3rd century A.D.
                Μινουκιανός (Table P-PZ38)
              Minucius Pacatus see PA4213.I8
4250.M14   Mnaseas, of Patrae or Patara 3rd century B.C. Μνασέας
                (Table P-PZ38)
4250.M2   Moeris, lexicographer (date unknown). Μοῖρις (Table P-
                PZ38)
              Moero
                see Myro
              Molo
                see Apollonius Molo
              Moschion [i.e. Muscio] (physician)
                see PA4435.S2+ Soranus, of Ephesus; PA6514.M9 Mustio
                  (Muscio), translator of Soranus
              Moschion (paradoxographer; date unknown). Μοσχίων
              Moschion (writer of tragedies) 4th century B.C. Μοσχίων
4250.M4   Moschus, fl. 150 B.C. Μόσχος (Table P-PZ38)
                For editions of Bion's and Moschus' poems see
                  PA3944.B4
                For editions of the poems of Bion, Moschus and
                  Theocritus see PA4442
              Musaeus (disciple of Orpheus, legendary poet). Μουσαῖος
                Cf. PA4253.O38 Onomacritus
              Musaeus (grammarian, epic poet) fl. between 491-527 A.D.
                (?) Hero et Leander. Hero and Leander. Μουσαῖος.
                Καθ' Ἡρὼ καὶ Λέανδρον
4250.M5   Texts. By date
4250.M6   Criticism
4250.M62   Musaeus, of Ephesus, 2nd century B.C. Μουσαῖος (Table
                P-PZ38)
              Myro (Moiro) of Byzantium, fl. ca. 300 B.C. Μοιρώ
              Myrtis, 5th century B.C. Μύρτις
4250.N13   Naumachius, 2nd century A.D. (?). Ναυμάχιος (Table P-
                PZ38)

Individual authors to 600 A.D.
Min... to Non... -- Continued

4250.N135	Neanthes, of Cyzicus, 3rd century B.C. Νεάνθης ὁ Κυζικηνός (Table P-PZ38)
4250.N136	Neanthes (the younger) 3rd to 2nd century B.C. Νεάνθης (Table P-PZ38)
4250.N14	Nearchus, of Crete, fl. 326 B.C. Νέαρχος (Table P-PZ38)
4250.N15	Nechepso-Petosiris. Astrologumena. Νεχεψῶ-Πετόσιρις. Ἀστρολογούμενα
4250.N153	Nemesius, Bishop of Emesa, 5th (?) century A.D. De natura hominis. Νεμέσιος. Περὶ φύσεως ἀνθρώπου Cf. BR65; BR1720
4250.N157	Neoptolemus, of Parion (Bithynia) 3rd century B.C. (?). Νεοπτόλεμος (Table P-PZ38)
4250.N16	Nepualius, 2nd or 3rd century A.D. (Table P-PZ38)
4250.N18	Nicander, of Colophon (epic poet) 3rd century B.C. Νίκανδρος (Table P-PZ38)

	Nicander, of Colophon (didactic poet) 2nd century B.C. Νίκανδρος
4250.N2	Editions. By date
4250.N2A5	Alexipharmaca. Alexipharmaka. Ἀλεξιφάρμακα
4250.N2T5	Theriaca. Θηριακά
4250.N2Z5	Lost works and fragments
	Heteroiumena. Ἑτεροιούμενα
	Georgica. Γεωργικά
	Translations
4250.N3	Greek paraphrases. By date
4250.N3A3	Latin. By date
4250.N3A5-.N3Z3	Other. By language, A-Z, and date
4250.N4	Criticism
4250.N4A2	Scholia
4250.N42	Nicanor, of Alexandria, 2nd century A.D. De interpunctione. Νικάνωρ ὁ Στιγματίας. Περὶ στιγμῆς Cf. PA4035.N5 Scholia on Homer
4250.N5	Nicolaus, of Damascus, b. ca. 64 B.C. Νικόλαος Δαμασκηνός (Table P-PZ38) Cf. PA3892.P5 Aristotles. De plantis
4250.N52	Nicolaus, of Myra (Nicolaus sophista) 5th century A.D. Νικόλαος (Table P-PZ38)
4250.N53	Nicomachus (son of Aristotle). Νικόμαχος (Table P-PZ38) For the Ethics of Aristotle, edited by Nicomachus see PA3893.E6
4250.N6	Nicomachus, of Gerasa (Arabia) ca. 150 A.D. Νικόμαχος Γερασηνός

Individual authors to 600 A.D.
    Min... to Non...
        Nicomachus, of Gerasa (Arabia) ca. 150 A.D. Νικόμαχος
            Γερασηνός -- Continued
            Arithmetica (Introductio arithmetica). Ἀριθμητική
                εἰσαγωγή
                Cf. PA4220.A45 Jamblichus
                Cf. PA6231.A7 Boethius
            Arithmetica theologumena. Θεολογούμενα ἀριθμητικῆς
                Excerpts
            Harmonices manuale. Encheiridion harmonikēs.
                Ἐγχειρίδιον ἁρμονικῆς
                Excerpts
        Nonnus, of Panopolis. Νόννος
            Editions

4251.A2	Comprehensive. By date
4251.A3	Dionysiaca. Διονυσιακά. By date
	Gigantomachia
	Lost; spurious?
4251.A4	Metaphrasis Evangelii Joannis. Paraphrase of St. John's Gospel. Μεταβολὴ τοῦ κατὰ Ἰωάννην ἁγίου Εὐαγγελίου. By date
4251.A5-Z	Translations. By language, A-Z, and date
4252	Criticism
4253	Nono... to Ori...
4253.N5	Nossis, ca. 300 B.C. Νοσσίς (Table P-PZ38)
	Nosti
	see Hagias Troezenus
4253.N55	Numenius (rhetor), 2nd century A.D. Νουμήνιος (Table P-PZ38)
	Cf. PA3864.A45 Alexander Numenii
4253.N6	Numenius, of Apamea, (philosopher) 2nd century A.D. Νουμήνιος (Table P-PZ38)
	Numenius, Alexander see PA3864.A45
	Nymphis, of Heracleia Pontica, fl. 280-240 B.C. Νύμφις
	Nymphodorus, of Syracuse (date uncertain). Νυμφόδωρος
4253.O2	Ocellus Lucanus (disciple of Pythagoras). De rerum natura. Peri tēs tou pantos physeōs. Ὄκελλος ὁ Λευκανός. Περὶ τῆς τοῦ παντὸς φύσεως
4253.O314	Oeconomica. Οἰκονομικά
4253.O32	Oenomaus, of Gadara, 2nd century A.D. Οἰνόμαος (Table P-PZ38)
4253.O33	Olympiodorus (alchemist). Commentary on Zosimus of Panopolis. Ὀλυμπιόδωρος
	Cf. PA4500.Z8 Zosimus
	Cf. QD25 Alchemy

Individual authors to 600 A.D.
    Nono... to Ori... -- Continued

4253.O335	Olympiodorus, of Alexandria (the elder) 5th century A.D. Ὀλυμπιόδωρος (Table P-PZ38)
4253.O34	Olympiodorus, of Alexandria (the younger) 6th century A.D. Ὀλυμπιόδωρος (Table P-PZ38 modified)

4253.O34A61-
.O34A78
	Separate works. By title
	    e.g. Vita Platonis; Commentary on Plato's Alcibiades I
	      (includes Vita Pl.) Gorgias, Philebus, Phaedo;
	      Commentary on the Meteorologica of Aristotle

	Olympiodorus, of Alexandria, diaconus, fl. ca. 510 A.D. Ὀλυμπιόδωρος see BR60+ BR1720
4253.O35	Olympiodorus, of Thebae (Egypt) historian, fl. 412-425 A.D. Ὀλυμπιόδωρος (Table P-PZ38)
	Onasander see PA4253.O4
4253.O36	Onesicritus, of Astypalaea, fl. 326 B.C. Ὀνησίκριτος (Table P-PZ38)

4253.O38	Onomacritus, 6th century B.C. Ὀνομάκριτος
	    Literary forger; "reviser" and author of the poems ascribed to
	      the legendary poets Orpheus and Musaeus

4253.O4	Onosander, fl. 49 A.D. Strategicus, sive De imperatoris institutione. Stratēgikos. Ὀνόσανδρος. Στρατηγικός
	Oppian, of Anazarbos (Cilicia) d. 211 or 212 A.D. Halieutica (De piscatione). Ὀππιανός. Ἁλιευτικά

4253.O5	Editions. By date
	    Including editions of the Halieutica followed by the
	      Cynegetica, formerly ascribed to Oppianus

4253.O6	Translations
4253.O6A2	Latin. By date
4253.O6A5-.O6Z	Other. By language, A-Z, and date
4253.O7	Criticism
4253.O72	Oppian, of Apamea (Syria) 3rd century A.D. Ὀππιανός (Table P-PZ40 modified)
4253.O72A61- .O72Z458	Separate works. By title

4253.O72C9	Cynegetica (De venatione). Κυνηγετικά
	    Cf. PA4253.O5 Editions of Halieutica and
	      Cynegetica

4253.O72D42	De aucupio. Ἰξευτικά Lost
	Oracula
4253.O8	Collections and selections
4253.O83	Oracula sibyllina
4253.O85	Oracula Chaldaica Ascribed to Zoroaster
4253.O87	Oracula deorum Hellenicorum

	Individual authors to 600 A.D.
	Nono... to Ori...
	Oracula -- Continued
4253.O9	Criticism (General and particular)
4253.O95	Orbicius (Urbicius) fl. between 491-518 A.D. De nominibus ordinum militarium. Ὀρβίκιος. Περὶ τῶν περὶ τὸ στράτευμα τάξεων
	Extract from the Tactica of Aelianus
	Oribasius. Ὀρειβάσιος
4254	Editions
4255	Translations
4256	Criticism
4257	Oric... to Orp...
	Origen (Origenes "Adamantius," Church father) 185/6-254/5 A.D. Ὠριγένης
	see BR60+ BR1720
	Origenes (Neoplatonist) 3rd century A.D. Ὠριγένης see B686.O8+
4257.O6	Orion, of Alexandria (grammarian) 4th century A.D. Ὠρίων (Table P-PZ38)
4257.O7	Orion, of Thebae (grammarian) 5th century A.D. Etymologicum. Ὠρίων
	Oros see PA4261.O7
	Orpheus (legendary poet). Ὀρφεύς
	Cf. PA4253.O38 Onomacritus
4258	Editions
4258.A2	Collections. By date
4258.A5-Z	Particular works
	Argonautica. Ἀργοναυτικά
4258.A6	Texts. By date
4258.A7	Criticism
	De lapidibus. Λιθικά
	Metrical version of a Greek treatise ascribed to "Damigeron magus"
	Cf. PA3948.D15 "Damigeron magus"
4258.D3	Texts. By date
4258.D4	Criticism
4258.H8	Hymni. Orphic hymns. Ὕμνοι. By date
4258.O7	Orphica. Ὀρφικά. By date
	Fragments
4259.A-Z	Translations. By language, A-Z, and date
4260	Criticism (General and Hymni)
4261	Ort... to Parm...
4261.O7	Orus (grammarian) 5th century A.D. (?). Ὦρος (Table P-PZ38 modified)

	Individual authors to 600 A.D.
	Ort... to Parm...
	Orus (grammarian) 5th century A.D. (?). Ὧρος -- Continued
4261.O7A61-.O7A78	Separate works. By title
	e.g. De orthographia (Περὶ ὀρθογραφίας) - For the Lexicon Messanense (part of De orthographia) considered as a separate work see that title; Ethnica (Ἐθνικά) (Lost)
	Ostanes (alchemist). Ὀστάνης
	Cf. QD25 Alchemy
	Pacatus see PA4213.I8
	Paeanius (Paeonius?) 4th century A.D. Paenius. Παιάνιος
	Metaphrasis in Eutropii Historiam Romanam see PA6384
4261.P36	Palaephatus (pseudonym (?); date uncertain: 4th to 3rd century B.C.?). De incredibilibus. Παλαίφατος. Περὶ ἀπίστων
4261.P38	Palladas, fl. ca. 400 A.D. Παλλάδας (Table P-PZ38)
4261.P39	Palladius (of Alexandria?) 6th century A.D. Palladios. Παλλάδιος (Table P-PZ38 modified)
4261.P39A61-.P39A78	Separate works. By title
	e.g. De cibo et potione (Περὶ βρώσεως καὶ πόσεως); De febribus concisa synopsis (Peri pyretōn syntomos synopsis. Περὶ πυρετῶν σύντομος σύνοψις); Scholia in Hippocratem
	Palladius, Bishop of Aspuna, d. ca. 430 A.D. Παλλάδιος
4261.P4	Collected works. Selected works. By date
4261.P4A-.P4Z	Separate works. By title, A-Z
4261.P4G35	De gentibus Indiae et de Bragmanibus. Περὶ τῶν τῆς Ἰνδίας ἐθνῶν καὶ τῶν Βραχμάνων
	Authorship disputed
	Historia Lausiaca. Lausiac history. Πρὸς Λαύσωνα τὸν πραιπόσιτον ἱστορία see BR190
	De vita et conversatione Joannis Chrysostomi. Dialogus de vita S. Joannis Chrysostomi. Διάλογος ἱστορικὸς περὶ βίου καὶ πολιτείας τοῦ μακαρίου Ἰωάννου Ἐπισκόπου Κωνσταντινοπόλεως τοῦ Χρυσοστόμου see BR1720.C5
4261.P5A-.P5Z	Translations. By language, A-Z
4261.P6	Criticism
4261.P63	Palladius, of Methone, sophist, 4th century A.D. Παλλάδιος (Table P-PZ38)
4261.P66	Pamphila, of Epidaurus, 1st century A.D. Παμφίλη (Table P-PZ38)
4261.P7	Pamphilus, of Alexandria (grammarian) 1st century A.D. Πάμφιλος (Table P-PZ38)
4261.P73	Pamprepios. Παμπρέπιος (Table P-PZ38)
	Panyassis, of Halicarnassus (epic poet) 5th century B.C. Πανύασσις

Individual authors to 600 A.D.
Ort... to Parm... -- Continued

4261.P8	Pappus, of Alexandria, 3rd century A.D. Πάππος (Table P-PZ38)
	Cf. QA31 Mathematics
4261.P88	Papyrus Lille 76, a-c
4262	Parmenides, of Elea, fl. ca. 500 B.C. Παρμενίδης (Table P-PZ37)
	Cf. B235.P2+ Philosophy
4263	Parm... to Paus...
4263.P17	Parmeniscus (grammarian of uncertain date). Παρμενίσκος (Table P-PZ38)
4263.P2	Paros chronicle (Marmor Parium)
	Parthenius, of Nicaea, 1st century B.C. Narrationes amatoriae. De amatoriis affectionibus. Παρθένιος. Ἐρωτικὰ παθήματα
4263.P3	Texts. By date
4263.P4	Criticism
	Pasicles, of Rhodes, 4th century B.C. Πασικλῆς
	Paulus, of Alexandria, 4th century A.D. Introductio in doctrinam de viribus et effectis astrorum. Elementa apotelesmatica. Παῦλος. Εἰσαγωγὴ εἰς τὴν ἀποτελεσματικήν
	Paulus Silentiarius, 6th century A.D. Paul, the Silentiary. Παῦλος Σιλεντιάριος
	Pausanias, 2nd century A.D. Descriptio Graeciae lib. X (De situ Graeciae). Παυσανίας. Περιήγησις τῆς Ἑλλάδος
4264.A2	Editions. By date
4264.A31-.A40	Particular books (complete)
4264.A6-Z	Particular regions, portions, or subjects (if not coextensive with a particular book)
	e.g.
4264.A8	Arx Athenarum a Pausania descripta
4264.O6	Description of Olympia
	For "The Attica of Pausanias" (book I of the Descriptio) see PA4264.A31
	Translations
4265	Latin. By date
	Other see DF27
4266	Criticism
4266.A-.Z3	General works
4266.Z5	Language, style
4266.Z8	Glossaries, indices, etc. By date
4267	Pausanias (Caes.) to Phil...
4267.P12	Pausanias, of Caesarea (sophist) fl. ca. 190-197 A.D. Παυσανίας (Table P-PZ38)

Individual authors to 600 A.D.
Pausanias (Caes.) to Phil... -- Continued

4267.P13   Pausanias, of Damascus? (historian) 4th century A.D.?
                  Παυσανίας ὁ Δαμασκηνός (Table P-PZ38)
4267.P14   Periplus Maris Erythraei. Περίπλους τῆς Ἐρυθρᾶς
                  Θαλάσσης
                  Wrongly ascribed to Arrianus
                  Periplus maris interni
                      see PA4244.M24 Marcianus, of Heraclea; PA4248.M173
                          Menippus, of Pergamon; PA4410.S14 Scylax
4267.P143   Periplus Ponti Euxini. Περίπλους Πόντου Εὐξείνου
                  Anonymous compilation from Arrianus, Menippus, Marcianus,
                      and Pseudo-Scymnus
                  Cf. PA4410.S18 Pseudo-Scymnus
                  Petosiris. Πετόσιρις see PA4250.N15
4267.P155   Phaedo, of Elis, 4th century B.C. Φαίδων (Table P-PZ38)
                  Writings lost
                  Cf. PA4279.P3 Plato. Phaedo
4267.P16   Phaedrus (Epicurean) fl. 90-70 B.C. De natura deorum.
                  Φαῖδρος. Περὶ θεῶν
                  Cf. PA4271.P3+ Philodemus, of Gadara. De pietate
                  Cf. PA6296.D4 Cicero. De natura deorum
                  Phalaris ("Pseudo-Phalaris"). Φάλαρις
                      148 letters purporting to be written by the tyrant of
                          Agrigentum (6th century B.C.), a product of the 4th
                          century A.D.
4267.P2   Texts. By date
4267.P25A-.P25Z   Translations. By language, A-Z, and date
4267.P3   Criticism
4267.P33   Phanocles. Φανοκλῆς (Table P-PZ38)
                  Phavorinus see PA3994.F4
4267.P35   Pherecrates (writer or comedies) fl. 420 B.C. Φερεκράτης
                  (Table P-PZ38)
4267.P4   Pherecydes, of Leros (P. Lerius) 5th century B.C.
                  Φερεκύδης (Table P-PZ38)
                      Identical (?) with Pherecydes of Athens, the genealoger. Not
                          to be confused with P. of Syros
                  Pherecydes, of Syros (P. Syrius) fl. 550 B.C. Φερεκύδης ὁ
                  Σύριος
                  Philagrius (grammarian of uncertain date) see PA4013.H35
                  Philagrius, of Epirus (physician) date uncertain. Φιλάγριος
4267.P5   Philemon (writer of comedies) 361-263 B.C. Φιλήμων
                  (Table P-PZ38)
                      The first of the three writers of comedies of this name
                  Philemon (lexicographers)
4267.P62   Philemon, of Athens, "glossographus," 3rd century B.C.
                      (?). Φιλήμων (Table P-PZ38)

PA3050-4505

191

Individual authors to 600 A.D.
Pausanias (Caes.) to Phil...
Philemon (lexicographers) -- Continued
4267.P63 Philemon (Atticist) fl. ca. 200 A.D. Φιλήμων
Spurious works ("Pseudo-Philemon")
Lexicon technologicum. Λεξικὸν τεχνολογικόν
A forgery of Jakob Diassorinos
4267.P67 Philetas (Philitas?) of Cos, 4th to 3rd century B.C. Φιλητᾶς
(Table P-PZ38)
4267.P69 Philippus, of Opus (Opuntinus), 4th century B.C. Φίλιππος
(Table P-PZ38)
4267.P7 Philippus, of Thessalonica, fl. ca. 37-40 A.D. Φίλιππος
Θεσσαλονικεύς (Table P-PZ38)
Compiler of an anthology of epigrams, author of ca. 80
epigrams
4267.P74 Philistion, of Nicaea (or Sardes, or Magnesia?) fl. 5 A.D.
Φιλιστίων (Table P-PZ38)
4267.P77 Philistus, of Naucratis (date uncertain). Φίλιστος (Table P-
PZ38)
4267.P78 Philistus, of Syracuse (historian) c. 356 B.C. Φίλιστος
(Table P-PZ38)
Philitas see PA4267.P67
Philo Alexandrinus see PA4268+
Philo Byblius see PA4271.P2
Philo Byzantius see PA4271.P13
Philo the elder see PA4271.P12
Philo Judaeus, of Alexandria, fl. 1-40 A.D. Φίλων
Cf. B689 Philosophy
4268 Editions
4268.A2 Comprehensive
4268.A25 Selected works (Miscellaneous)
Selected works (by group)
4268.A3 Philosophical works
4268.A4 Works on the Pentateuch
4268.A6 Historical and apologetical writings
Particular works
4268.A8 Alexander sive de eo quod rationem habeant bruta
animalia. De animalibus. Ἀλέξανδρος ἢ Περὶ τοῦ
λόγον ἔχειν ἄλογα ζῷα
Antiquitates biblicae see PA4268.Z7+
Apologia pro Judaeis see PA4268.D5
Breviarium temporum see PA4268.Z7+
4268.D13 De Abrahamo. Βίος σοφοῦ τοῦ κατὰ διδασκαλίαν
τελειωθέντος ἢ νόμων ἀγράφων (α′) ὅ ἐστι περὶ
Ἀβραάμ
4268.D15 De aeternitate mundi (De incorruptibilitate mundi). Περὶ
ἀφθαρσίας κόσμου

Individual authors to 600 A.D.
Philo Judaeus, of Alexandria, fl. 1-40 A.D. Φίλων
Editions
Particular works -- Continued

4268.D17   De agricultura [et] De plantatione. Περὶ γεωργίας α' β'
Commentary on Gen. IX: 20 (Part of Legum allegoriae)
De Alexandro see PA4268.A8
De animalibus see PA4268.A8
De animalibus [ad edendum concessis et prohibitis]
see PA4268.D24
De animalibus sacrificio idoneis see PA4268.D955
De [benedictionibus et] exsecrationibus see
PA4268.D37
De caritate see PA4268.D42

4268.D19   De cherubim et flammeo gladio. Περὶ τῶν χερουβὶμ καὶ
τῆς φλογίνης ῥομφαίας καὶ τοῦ κτισθέντος πρώτου
ἐξ ἀνθρώπου Κάιν
Part of Legum allegoriae, Gen. III: 24-IV: 1

4268.D2   De circumcisione. Περὶ περιτομῆς
De specialibus legibus I,1

4268.D22   De colendis parentibus. Περὶ γόνεων τιμῆς
De specialibus legibus II,3

4268.D24   De concupiscentia. Οὐκ ἐπιθυμήσεις
De specialibus legibus IV,3; includes chapter De
animalibus [ad edendum concessis et prohibitis]

4268.D26   De confusione linguarum. Περὶ συγχύσεως διαλέκτων
Part of Legum allegoriae; Gen. XI: 1-9

4268.D28   De congressu eruditionis gratia (De congressu
quaerendae erud. gr.). Περὶ τῆς πρὸς τὰ
προπαιδεύματα συνόδου
Part of Legum allegoriae; Gen. XVI: 1-6
De constitutione principum see PA4268.D285

4268.D283   De cophino (De festo cophini)
De creatione mundi see PA4268.D7

4268.D285   De creatione principum (De constitutione principum).
Περὶ καταστάσεως ἀρχόντων
De specialibus legibus IV,4

4268.D3   De Decalogo. Περὶ τῶν δέκα λογίων ἃ κεφάλαια νόμων
εἰσίν
De decem oraculis see PA4268.D3

4268.D33   De deo
Presumably fragment of the lost commentary on Genesis
XVIII-XIX preserved in an Armenian version (Gen.
XVIII: 2)

PA3050-4505

Individual authors to 600 A.D.
    Philo Judaeus, of Alexandria, fl. 1-40 A.D. Φίλων
      Editions
        Particular works -- Continued

4268.D35	De ebrietate. Περὶ μέθης
	Commentary on Gen. IX: 21 in two books, second book lost
	Part of Legum allegoriae: Gen. IX: 21
	De eo quod deterius potiori insidiatur see PA4268.Q6
4268.D37	De exsecrationibus. Περὶ ἀρῶν
	Part of a treatise with (presumed) title: De praemiis et poenis et benedictionibus et exsecrationibus
	Cf. PA4268.D73 De praemiis et poenis
4268.D372	De falso testimonio. Οὐ ψευδομαρτυρήσεις
	De specialibus legibus IV,2
	De festo cophini see PA4268.D283
4268.D374	De fortitudine. Περὶ ἀνδρείας
	Cf. PA4268.D96 De virtutibus
4268.D376	De fuga et inventione (De profugis). Περὶ φυγῆς καὶ εὑρέσεως (Περὶ φυγάδων)
	Part of Legum allegoriae: Gen. XVI: 6-14
4268.D378	De furto. Περὶ κλοπῆς
	De specialibus legibus IV,1
4268.D4	De gigantibus (De gigantibus sive Quod deus sit immutabilis). Περὶ γιγάντων ἢ Περὶ τοῦ μὴ τρέπεσθαι τὸ θεῖον
	Title of commentary on Gen. VI: 1-12; originally one continuous work; in the manuscripts and in the older editions, the commentary is divided into two treatises with respective titles De gigantibus. Quod deus sit immutabilis
	Part of Legum allegoriae: Gen. VI: 1-12
4268.D42	De humanitate (De caritate). Περὶ φιλανθρωπίας
	Cf. PA4268.D96 De virtutibus
	De incorruptibilitate mundi see PA4268.D15
	De Jona see PA4268.Z7+
4268.D44	De Josepho. De Iosepho. Βίος πολιτικοῦ ὅπερ ἐστὶ Περὶ Ἰωσήφ
4268.D5	De Judaeis (Apologia pro Judaeis). Περὶ Ἰουδαίων (Ἀπολογία ὑπὲρ Ἰουδαίων)
	Only a fragment preserved by Eusebius, Praep. evang. VIII,10. Presumably identical with the first book of the Hypothetica
4268.D52	De judice. Περὶ δικαστοῦ
	De specialibus legibus IV; part of chap. 2
4268.D54	De jure jurando. Περὶ εὐορκίας
	De specialibus legibus II,1

	Individual authors to 600 A.D.
	Philo Judaeus, of Alexandria, fl. 1-40 A.D. Φίλων
	Editions
	Particular works -- Continued
4268.D56	De justitia. Περὶ δικαιοσύνης
	De specialibus legibus IV,4
4268.D563	De mercede meretricis. Περὶ τοῦ μίσθωμα πόρνης εἰς τὸ ἱερὸν μὴ προσδέχεσθαι
	A title assigned in some manuscripts (and in the older editions) to a medieval combination of a portion of De sacrificiis Abelis et Caini with a portion of De victimas offerentibus
	Cf. PA4268.D758 De victimas offerentibus
	Cf. PA4268.D76 De sacrificiis Abelis et Caini
4268.D6	De migratione Abrahami. Περὶ ἀποικίας
	Part of Legum allegoriae: Gen. XII: 1-6
4268.D62	De monarchia. Περὶ μοναρχίας νόμοι
	De specialibus legibus I,2
	In some manuscripts and in the older editions, a separate treatise divided into two books, the second of which contains De templo (De mon. II,1-3) and De sacerdotibus (De mon. II,4-15)
	Cf. PA4268.D752 De sacerdotibus
	Cf. PA4268.D953 De templo
	De mundo see PA4268.Z7+
4268.D64	De mutatione nominum. Περὶ τῶν μετονομαζομένων καὶ ῶν ἕνεκα μετονομάζονται
	Part of Legum allegoriae: Gen. XVII: 1-22
4268.D66	De nobilitate. Περὶ εὐγενείας
	Part of the treatise De virtutibus, possibly only a portion of the very brief treatise De paenitentia
	De numeris see PA4268.Z5
4268.D7	De opificio mundi. Περὶ τῆς κατὰ Μωυσέα κοσμοποιίας
	Formerly held to be the first part of the Legum allegoriae and hence placed at the beginning of the commentary and of all the works
4268.D72	De paenitentia. Περὶ μετανοίας
	Part of the treatise De virtutibus
	Cf. PA4268.D66 De nobilitate
	De plantatione see PA4268.D17
4268.D722	De posteritate Caini. Περὶ τῶν τοῦ δοκησισόφου Κάιν ἐγγόνων καὶ ὡς μετανάστης γίνεται
	Part of Legum allegoriae: Gen. IV: 16-25

PA3050-4505

Individual authors to 600 A.D.
  Philo Judaeus, of Alexandria, fl. 1-40 A.D. Φίλων
    Editions
      Particular works -- Continued

4268.D73   De praemiis et poenis. Περὶ ἄθλων καὶ ἐπιτιμίων
                 Second appendix to the four books De specialibus
                    legibus. Part of a treatise with (presumed) title: De
                    praemiis et poenis et benedictionibus et
                    exsecrationibus
              De praemiis sacerdotum see PA4268.D754
              De profugis see PA4268.D376
4268.D75   De providentia I-II. Περὶ προνοίας α′ β′
4268.D752   De sacerdotibus. Περὶ ἱερέων
                 De specialibus legibus I,4
                 Cf. PA4268.D62 De monarchia
4268.D754   De sacerdotum honoribus (De praemiis sacerdotum).
                 Γέρα ἱερέων
                 De specialibus legibus I,5
4268.D758   De sacrificantibus (De victimas offerentibus). Περὶ
                 θυόντων
                 De specialibus legibus I,7
                 Cf. PA4268.D563 De mercede meretricis
4268.D76   De sacrificiis Abelis et Caini. Περὶ γενέσεως Ἄβελ καὶ
                 ὧν αὐτός τε καὶ ὁ ἀδελφὸς αὐτοῦ Κάιν ἱερουργοῦσιν
                 Part of Legum allegoriae: Gen. IV: 2-4
                 Cf. PA4268.D563 De mercede meretricis
              De Sampsone see PA4268.Z7+
4268.D77   De septenario et diebus festis. Περὶ ἑβδόμης
                 De specialibus legibus II,2
4268.D773   De sobrietate. Περὶ ὧν νήψας ὁ Νῶε εὔχεται καὶ
                 καταρᾶται
                 Part of Legum allegoriae: Gen. IX: 24-27
4268.D775   De somniis lib. II (Quod a deo mittantur somnia). Περὶ
                 τοῦ θεοπέμπτους εἶναι τοὺς ὀνείρους
                 Commentary on Gen. XXVIII: 12-22; XXXI: 11-13, and
                    XXXVII and XL f., dreams of Jacob and of Joseph.
                    The two books preserved are probably the fourth and
                    fifth of the five books of that work
                 Cf. Legum allegoriae
4268.D8   De specialibus legibus, libri I-IV. Περὶ τῶν ἐν μέρει
                 διαταγμάτων α′-δ′

Individual authors to 600 A.D>
  Philo Judaeus, of Alexandria, fl. 1-40 A.D. Φίλων
    Editions
    Particular works
      De specialibus legibus, libri I-IV. Περὶ τῶν ἐν μέρει
        διαταγμάτων α'-δ' -- Continued
        Liber I. Περὶ τῶν ἀναφερομένων ἐν εἴδει νόμων εἰς
          δύο κεφάλαια τῶν δέκα λογίων, τό τε μὴ νομίζειν
          ἔξω τοῦ ἑνὸς θεοὺς ἑτέρους αὐτοκρατεῖς καὶ τὸ μὴ
          χειρόκμητα θεοπλαστεῖν
          Contains seven chapters: 1. De circumcisione; 2. De
            monarchia; 3. De templo; 4. De sacerdotibus; 5. De
            sacerdotum honoribus; 6. De victimis; 7. De
            sacrificantibus
        Liber II: De specialibus legibus, quae referuntur ad
          tria decalogi capita, videlicet tertium, quartum,
          quintumque, De jure jurando religioneque, De
          sacro sabbato, De honore habendo parentibus.
          Περὶ τῶν ἀναφερομένων ἐν εἴδει νόμων εἰς τρία
          γένη τῶν δέκα λογίων, τὸ τρίτον, τὸ τέταρτον, τὸ
          πέμπτον, τὸ περὶ εὐορκίας καὶ σεβασμοῦ τῆς
          ἱερᾶς ἑβδόμης καὶ γονέων τιμῆς
          Contains three chapters: De iure jurando; De
            septenario et diebus festis; De colendis parentibus
        Liber III: De specialibus legibus quae referuntur ad
          duo decalogi capita, sextum septimumque:
          Contra moechos omnesque libidinosos, & contra
          homicidas omnemque violentiam. Περὶ τῶν
          ἀναφερομένων ἐν εἴδει νόμων εἰς δύο γένη τῶν
          δέκα λογίων, τὸ ἕκτον καὶ τὸ ἕβδομον, τὸ κατὰ
          μοιχῶν καὶ παντὸς ἀκολάστου καὶ τὸ κατὰ
          ἀνδροφόνων καὶ πάσης βίας
        Liber IV: De specialibus legibus, quae pertinent ad
          tria capita decalogi, nimirum octavum, nonum et
          decimum: De non committendis furti, falsi
          testimonii & concupiscentiae criminibus. Περὶ τῶν
          ἀναφερομένων ἐν εἴδει νόμων εἰς τρία γένη τῶν
          δέκα λογίων, τὸ ὄγδοον καὶ τὸ ἔνατον καὶ τὸ
          δέκατον, τὸ περὶ τοῦ μὴ κλέπτειν καὶ [μὴ]
          ψευδομαρτυρεῖν καὶ μὴ ἐπιθυμεῖν, καὶ περὶ τῶν εἰς
          ἕκαστον ἀναφερομένων καὶ περὶ δικαιοσύνης, ἣ
          πᾶσι τοῖς δέκα λογίοις ἐφαρμόζει, ὅ ἐστι τῆς ὅλης
          συντάξεως [τέλος]
          Contains the following four chapters: De furto; De falso
            testimonio (includes De iudice); De concupiscentia;
            De iustitia (includes De creatione principum)

PA3050-4505

Individual authors to 600 A.D.
Philo Judaeus, of Alexandria, fl. 1-40 A.D. Φίλων
Editions
Particular works
Legum allegoriae. Νόμων ἱερῶν ἀλληγορίαι τῶν μετὰ τὴν ἐξαήμερον -- Continued
1. Legum allegoriarum libri I. II. III. Νόμων ἱερῶν ἀλληγορίας α′ β′ γ′ (Gen. II: 1-17; II: 18-III: 1a; III: 8b-19)
In some manuscripts books I and II form one book; the original book II (Gen. III: 1b-8a) and book IV (Gen. III: 20-23) are lost
2. De cherubim et flammeo gladio (Gen. III: 24-IV: 1)
3. De sacrificiis Abelis et Cain (Gen. IV: 2-4)
4. Quod deterius potiori insidiari soleat (Gen. IV: 8-15)
5. De posteritate Caini (Gen. IV: 16-25)
6. De gigantibus. Quod deus sit immutabilis (Gen. VI: 1-12)
7. De agricultura [et] De plantatione (Gen. IX: 20)
8. De ebrietate (Gen. IX: 21)
9. De sobrietate (Gen. IX: 24-27)
10. De confusione linguarum (Gen. XI: 1-9)
11. De migratione Abrahami (Gen. XII: 1-6)
12. Quis rerum divinarum heres sit (Gen. XV: 2-18)
13. De congressu eruditionis gratia (Gen. XVI: 1-6)
14. De fuga et inventione (De profugis) (Gen. XVI: 6-14)
15. De mutatione nominum (Gen. XVII: 1-22)
16. De somniis (Gen. XXVIII: 12-22; XXXI: 11-13)
Liber antiquitatum biblicarum see PA4268.Z7+

4268.Q3 Quaestiones et solutiones in Genesim et Exodum. Ἐν Γενέσει καὶ τῶν ἐν Ἐξαγωγῇ ζητημάτων τε καὶ λύσεων βιβλία
Quaestiones in Genesim libri I-VI
Commentary on Gen. II: 4 to XXVIII: 9. Original lost; an Armenian translation contains nearly the whole work; an ancient Latin translation (previous to Hieronymus) comprises approximately the sixth book on Genesis
Quaestiones in Exodum libri I-V
Original lost; two books preserved in an Armenian translation
4268.Q5 Quis rerum divinarum heres sit. Περὶ τοῦ τίς ὁ τῶν θείων ἐστὶν κληρονόμος καὶ περὶ τῆς εἰς τὰ ἴσα καὶ ἐναντία τομῆς
Part of Legum allegoriae: Gen. XV: 2-18

PA3050-4505

Individual authors to 600 A.D.
  Philo Maior to Philos... -- Continued

4271.P2   Philo, Herennius, of Byblos, 1st to 2nd century A.D. Φίλων
                  Έρέννιος (Table P-PZ38 modified)

4271.P2A61-.P2A78   Separate works. By title
                  e.g. De differentia significationis (Περὶ τῶν διαφόρως
                      σημαινομένων (Περὶ διαφορᾶς σημασίας)) (Fragments
                      and an epitome preserved) - Cf. PA3864.A68
                      Ammonius; De urbibus et quos quaeque earum viros
                      illustres tulerit (Περὶ πόλεων καὶ οὓς ἑκάστη αὐτῶν
                      ἐνδόξους ἤνεγκεν) (Fragments); Phoenicum historia
                      (Φοινικικά) (Fragments)

           Philochorus, of Athens, 3rd century B.C. Φιλόχορος

           Philodemus, of Gadara, fl. 60 B.C. Φιλόδημος
              Cf. B598.P4+ Philosophy

4271.P3   Collected works. Selections. By date
4271.P3A-.P3Z   Individual works. By title, A-Z
4271.P4   Criticism

           Philogelos see PA4013.H35

           Philolaus, of Croton (Pythagorean) 5th century B.C.
              Φιλόλαος
              Cf. B235.P4+ Philosophy

           Philonides (writer of comedies) 5th century B.C. Φιλωνίδης

           Philonides, of Laodicea (Syria), Epicurean philosopher, fl.
              ca. 175-150 B.C. Φιλωνίδης

           Philoponus, Joannes see PA4221.J5+

           Philostephanus, of Cyrene (geographer and poet) 3rd
              century B.C. Φιλοστέφανος

           Philostorgius, fl. ca. 425 A.D. Φιλοστόργιος
              see BR60+ BR1720

           Philostrati see PA4272.Z5

4271.P79   Philostratus I, son of Verus, 1st century A.D.(?).
              Φιλόστρατος (Table P-PZ38)

4272   Philostratus, the Athenian, 2nd/3rd cent. (Philostratus II).
              Φιλόστρατος

4272.A2   Editions

4272.A3   Apollonii Tyanensis vita. Life of Apollonius of Tyana. Ἐς τὸν
              Τυανέα Ἀπολλώνιον
              Cf. PA3871.A6 Apollonius, of Tyana

4272.A35   Dissertationes. Διαλέξεις
              Two brief dissertations appended to the Epistulae; the first
                (entitled Epistula ad Aspasium) is by Philostratus III
              Cf. PA4273.P12 Philostratus III

4272.A4   Epistulae (Epistulae amatoriae). Ἐπιστολαί
              Authorship of letters 1-64 (Epistulae amatoriae (Ἐπιστολαί
                ἐρωτικαί)) disputed; letters 65-73, especially 70 and 73,
                considered genuine

Individual authors to 600 A.D.
    Philostratus, the Athenian, 2nd/3rd cent. (Philostratus II).
      Φιλόστρατος -- Continued

4272.A43	Gymnasticus. Γυμναστικός (Περὶ γυμναστικῆς)
4272.A45	Heroicus (dialogue). Ἡρωικός
4272.A5	Imagines (Icones). Εἰκόνες
(4272.A53)	Imagines posteriores (by Philostratus IV)
	see PA4273.P13
4272.A55	Nero (dialogue). Νέρων ἢ Περὶ τῆς ὀρυχῆς τοῦ Ἰσθμοῦ
	Transmitted among the works of Lucian
4272.A6	Vitae sophistarum. Lives of the sophists. Βίοι σοφιστῶν
4272.A7-.Z3	Translations. By language, A-Z, and date
4272.Z5	Criticism
	Including treatises on the various Philostrati
4273	Philostratus III to Pin...
4273.P12	Philostratus Lemnius (Philostratus III) b. ca. 191 A.D. Epistula ad Aspasium. Φιλόστρατος. Ἀσπασίῳ (Table P-PZ38)
	Cf. PA4272.A35 Philostratus II. Dissertationes
4273.P13	Philostratus IV (Philostratus minor, grandson of Philostratus II) fl. between 250 and 300 A.D. Imagines (called "Posteriores" in distinction from the Imagines of Philostratus II). Φιλόστρατος. Εἰκόνες (Table P-PZ38)
4273.P18	Philoxenos, of Alexandria, 1st century B.C. Φιλόξενος (Table P-PZ38)
	Philoxenus, of Cythera, 435-380 B.C. Φιλόξενος ὁ Κυθήριος
	Philoxenus, of Leucas, 4th century B.C. Φιλόξενος
4273.P2	"Philoxenus glossographus" (Pseudo-Philoxenus). Φιλόξενος
	Greek-Latin glossary, formerly ascribed to Flavius Theodorus Philoxenus (consul 525 A.D.)
	Philumenus (physician) 2nd century A.D. (?). Φιλούμενος
4273.P3	Phlegon, of Tralles (historian), 2nd century A.D. Φλέγων (Table P-PZ40)
4273.P4	Phocylides, of Miletus, fl. 544 B.C. Φωκυλίδης (Table P-PZ38 modified)
4273.P4A61-.P4A78	Separate works. By title
	e.g. Poems (Lost with the exception of a few fragments); Spurious works, including Poema admonitorium (Ποίημα νουθετικόν)
	Phoebammon, 5th-6th century A.D. Introduction to Hermogenes, De ideis. Φοιβάμμων
	Phoenix, of Colophon, fl. 292-289 B.C. Φοῖνιξ
	Photius (rhetor) 5th century A.D. Scholia in Hermogenem. Φώτιος
	Phrynichus (writer of comedies) fl. 429-414 B.C. Φρύνιχος

Individual authors to 600 A.D.
Philostratus III to Pin... -- Continued
Phrynichus (writer of tragedies) fl. 511-476 B.C. Φρύνιχος
4273.P6 Phrynichus Arabius, "atticista," 2nd century A.D. Φρύνιχος
Ἀράβιος (Table P-PZ38)
Phurnutus see PA3948.C8
Phylarchus, of Athens (Sicyon (?) Naucratis?) historian, 3rd
century B.C. Φύλαρχος
Physiologus. Φυσιολόγος
4273.P8 Editions. By date
Translations
For medieval translations see PQ,PT, etc.
4273.P9 Criticism
Pigres. Πίγρης
According to Suidas author of the Homeric poems "Margites"
and "Batrachomyomachia"
see PA4023.B3; PA4023.M3
Pindar. Πίνδαρος
4274.A2 Editions. By date
Selections
4274.A3 Miscellaneous
4274.A5 Special
Including Sicilian odes (Fourteen odes in praise of Sicilian
tyrants)
4274.I5 Isthmia. Isthmian odes. Ἴσθμια (Ἰσθμιονίκαις)
4274.N5 Nemea. Nemean odes. Νέμεα (Νεμεονίκαις)
4274.O5 Olympia. Olympian odes. Ὀλύμπια (Ὀλυμπιονίκαις)
4274.P5 Pythia. Pythian odes. Πύθια (Πύθιονίκαις)
4274.Z5 Fragments
4275.A-Z Translations. By language, A-Z
Subarrange each language by translator or editor, A-Z
4276 Criticism. Biography
4276.A1 Scholia. By date
4276.A2 Early works to 1800
4276.A5-.Z3 Treatises
4276.Z5 Language. Grammar
4276.Z6 Versification
4276.Z8 Glossaries, indices, etc. By date
4278 Pine... to Plas...
Plato. Πλάτων
4279.A2 Comprehensive editions. By date
4279.A24A-.A24Z Selections. Quotations. Thoughts. By editor, A-Z
Selected works
4279.A3 Miscellaneous
Class here collections of three or more works
For editions of two works classify with the first work

PA3050-4505

Individual authors to 600 A.D.
Plato. Πλάτων
Selected works -- Continued

(4279.A4)   By group
       e.g. Tetralogies or trilogies; Socratic dialogues; Dialectic dialogues

(4279.A5)   ' By subject

Separate works, A-Z

4279.A75   Alcibiades I (A. I De natura hominis). Ἀλκιβιάδης α' ἢ Περὶ φύσεως ἀνθρώπου
       Authorship disputed

4279.A77   Alcibiades II (A. II De voto). Ἀλκιβιάδης β' ἢ Περὶ προσευχῆς
       Spurious

     Amatores see PA4279.E7

     Anterastae see PA4279.E7

4279.A8   Apologia Socratis. Apology. Ἀπολογία Σωκράτους

     Axiochus see PA4279.Z5

4279.C2   Charmides (Charmides de temperantia). Χαρμίδης ἢ Περὶ σωφροσύνης

     Civilis de regno see PA4279.P6

     Civitas see PA4279.R4+

4279.C5   Clitophon (Clitophon exhortatorius). Κλειτοφῶν ἢ Προτρεπτικός
       Spurious

     Convivium see PA4279.S8

4279.C6   Cratylus (Cratylus de recta nominum ratione). Κρατύλος ἢ Περὶ ὀνομάτων ὀρθότητος

4279.C7   Critias (Critias de Atlantico bello). Κριτίας ἢ Ἀτλαντικός

4279.C8   Crito (Crito de eo quod est agendum). Κρίτων ἢ Περὶ πρακτέου

     De iusto see PA4279.Z5

     De lege see PA4279.M6

     De legibus
       see class K

     De republica see PA4279.R4+

     De virtute see PA4279.Z5

     Definitiones see PA4279.Z5

     Demodocus see PA4279.Z5

     Epinomis. Ἐπινομίς
       see class K

4279.E5   Epigrammata. Ἐπιγράμματα
       Thirty-two epigrams; authorship disputed

	Individual authors to 600 A.D.
	Plato. Πλάτων
	Separate works, A-Z -- Continued
4279.E6	Epistulae. Ἐπιστολαί

Eighteen letters; authorship of 2-13 disputed; the first letter purports to be written by Dio, Plato's friend; 14-18 spurious, belong to the collection of letters ascribed to Socrates and his school

Erasistratus see PA4279.Z5

| 4279.E7 | Erastae (Amatores seu de philosophia; Rivales; Anterastae). Ἐρασταὶ ἢ Περὶ φιλοσοφίας (Ἀντερασταί) |

Spurious

Eryxias see PA4279.Z5

4279.E8	Euthydemus (Euthydemus sive Litigiosus). Εὐθύδημος ἢ Ἐριστικός
4279.E9	Euthyphro (Euthyphro de sanctitate). Εὐθύφρων ἢ Περὶ ὁσίου
4279.G7	Gorgias (Gorgias de rhetorica). Γοργίας ἢ Περὶ ῥητορικῆς

PA3050-4505

Halcyon see PA4230.A2+

| 4279.H4 | Hermocrates. Ἑρμοκράτης |

Projected (?) to be the fourth dialogue in the tetralogy Respublica-Timaeus-Critas-Hermocrates

| 4279.H5 | Hipparchus (Hipparchus de lucri cupiditate). Ἵππαρχος ἢ Φιλοκερδής |

Spurious

4279.H6	Hippias maior (Hippias maior de pulchro). Ἱππίας μείζων ἢ Περὶ τοῦ καλοῦ
4279.H7	Hippias minor (Hippias minor de mendacio). Ἱππίας ἐλάττων ἢ Περὶ τοῦ ψεύδους
4279.I7	Io (Io de furore poetico). Ion. Ἴων ἢ Περὶ Ἰλιάδος (ἢ Περὶ ποιητικοῦ χαρακτῆρος ἢ Περὶ ποιητικῆς ἑρμηνείας)

Authenticity disputed

4279.L2	Laches (Laches de fortitudine). Λάχης ἢ Περὶ ἀνδρείας
	Leges (De legibus). Laws. Νόμοι ἢ Περὶ νομοθεσίας
	see class K
	Epinomis (Epinomis id est Legum appendix, vel Philosophus)
	see class K
4279.L8	Lysis (Lysis de amicitia). Λύσις ἢ Περὶ φιλίας
4279.M2	Menexenus (Menexenus, funebris oratio). Μενέξενος ἢ Ἐπιτάφιος λόγος
4279.M4	Meno (Meno de virtute). Μένων ἢ Περὶ ἀρετῆς
4279.M6	Minos (Minos de lege). Μίνως ἢ Περὶ νόμου

Spurious

| 4279.P2 | Parmenides (Parmenides de uno rerum principio). Παρμενίδης ἢ Περὶ ἰδεῶν |
| 4279.P3 | Phaedo (Phaedo de anima). Φαίδων ἢ Περὶ ψυχῆς |

	Individual authors to 600 A.D.
	Plato. Πλάτων
	Separate works, A-Z -- Continued
4279.P4	Phaedrus (Phaedrus de pulchro). Φαῖδρος ἢ Περὶ καλοῦ
	Cf. PA3998.H725 Hermias, of Alexandria
4279.P5	Philebus (Philebus de summo hominis bono). Φίληβος ἢ Περὶ ἡδονῆς
4279.P55	Philosophus. Φιλόσοφος
	Projected fourth dialogue of the tetralogy Theaetetus, Sophista, Politicus, Philosophus
	Philosophus (i.e. Epinomis vel Philosophus) see class K
	Politeia see PA4279.R4+
4279.P6	Politicus (Civilis de regno). Statesman. Πολιτικὸς ἢ Περὶ βασιλείας
4279.P8	Protagoras (Protagoras contra sophistas). Πρωταγόρας ἢ Σοφισταί
	Respublica (De republica lib. X). Republic. Πολιτεία (Πολιτειῶν ἢ Περὶ δικαίου βιβλία δέκα)
4279.R4	Editions
4279.R45	Selections
4279.R5	Selected books
	Particular books
4279.R51	Book I
4279.R52	Book II
4279.R53	Book III
4279.R54	Book IV
4279.R55	Book V
4279.R56	Book VI
4279.R57	Book VII
4279.R58	Book VIII
4279.R59	Book IX
4279.R6	Book X
4279.R7	Criticism
	Rivales see PA4279.E7
	Sisyphus see PA4279.Z5
4279.S6	Sophistes (Sophista de ente). Sophist. Σοφιστὴς ἢ Περὶ τοῦ ὄντος
4279.S8	Symposium (Convivium Platonis de amore). Συμπόσιον ἢ Περὶ ἔρωτος
4279.T3	Theaetetus (Theaetetus de scientia). Θεαίτητος ἢ Περὶ ἐπιστήμης
4279.T5	Theages (Theages de sapientia). Θεάγης ἢ Περὶ σοφίας
	Spurious
4279.T7	Timaeus (Timaeus de generatione mundi). Τίμαιος ἢ Περὶ φύσεως

Individual authors to 600 A.D.
Plato. Πλάτων
Separate works, A-Z -- Continued
4279.T9   Timaeus Locrus de anima mundi et naturae. Τιμαίω τῶ
Λοκρῶ περὶ ψυχᾶς κόσμω καὶ φύσιος
An extract from Plato's Timaeus, purporting to be the work
of Timaeus of Locri, a Pythagorean and principal
speaker in Plato's dialogue
Spurious and doubtful works
4279.Z5   Collections and selections. By date
Separate works (or treatises on such)
For dialogues of spurious, or doubtful origin, inserted in the
body of genuine writings see the geniune works
Alcibiades
see PA4279.A75+
Amatores see PA4279.E7
Anterastae see PA4279.E7
Axiochus (Axiochus de contemnenda morte). Ἀξίοχος ἤ
Περὶ θανάτου
In some of the earlier editions ascribed to Xenocrates, of
Chalcedon, and published with title "Liber de morte";
by other authorities it was attributed to Aeschines
Socraticus
Clitophon see PA4279.C5
De iusto. Περὶ δικαίου
De virtute. Περὶ ἀρετῆς
Definitiones. Ὅροι
Demodocus (Demodocus, vel De consultando).
Δημόδοκος ἤ Περὶ τοῦ συμβουλεύεσθαι
Epigrammata see PA4279.E5
Epinomis
see class K
Epistulae see PA4279.E6
Erasistratus
see Eryxias
Erastae see PA4279.E7
Eryxias (Eryxias, vel De divitiis). Ἐρυξίας ἤ Περὶ
πλούτου (Ἐρασίστρατος)
Halcyon see PA4230.A2+
Hipparchus see PA4279.H5
Hippias maior see PA4279.H6
Hippias minor see PA4279.H7
Io see PA4279.I7
Minos see PA4279.M6
Sisyphus (Sisyphus, vel De deliberando). Σίσυφος ἤ
Περὶ τοῦ βουλεύεσθαι (Ἀκέφαλος Σίσυφος)
Theages see PA4279.T5

PA3050-4505

	Individual authors to 600 A.D.
	Plato. Πλάτων
	Spurious and doubtful works
	Separate works (or treatises on such) -- Continued
	Timaeus Locrus de anima mundi et natura see PA4279.T9
(4279.Z8)	Criticism (General)
	see PA4291
	Translations
4280	Greek (Modern). Latin
4280.A1-.A299	Greek (Modern)
	Latin
(4280.A3)	Ancient
4280.A4	Medieval
4280.A5-Z	Modern
4280.A5A-.A5Z	Collected works. By translator, A-Z
4280.A53	Argumenta. By date
4280.A55A-.A55Z	Selections. Passages. Thoughts. By editor, A-Z
4280.A6A-.A6Z	Selected works. By translator, A-Z, or date
4280.A7-Z	Particular works. By (Latin) title and translator
(4281)	English
	see B358
(4282)	French
	see B359
(4283)	German
	see B360
(4284)	Italian
	see B361
(4285)	Other languages
	see B362+
(4287.9)	Adaptations (dramatizations, imitations, etc.), parodies
	Interpretation and criticism
	Ancient
	Greek
	Commentaries and treatises
4288.A2	Collections and selections from various authors. By date
(4288.A3)	Particular authors
	see the author
	For separate editions of commentaries on particular works, see the work, e.g. Proclus Lycius, Commentarius in Parmenidem, PA4279.P2
	Scholia
4288.A5	Collections and selections. By date
(4288.A6)	Scholia on particular works
	see the work
(4288.A7)	Criticism

PA3050-4505

	Individual authors to 600 A.D.
	Plotinus. Enneads I-VI. Πλωτῖνος. Ἐννεάδες
	Editions -- Continued
4363.A3	Selected Enneades
4363.A4	Selected treatises (three or more)
4363.A6-Z	Single treatises
	e.g.
	Ad Gnosticos (Enneas II, liber 9). Πρὸς τοὺς Γνωστικούς
	De animae descensu in corpora (Enneas IV, liber 8). Περὶ τῆς εἰς τὰ σώματα καθόδου τῆς ψυχῆς
	De contemplatione (De natura, et contemplatione, et uno) (Enneas III, liber 8). Περὶ θεωρίας (Περὶ φύσεως καὶ θεωρίας καὶ τοῦ ἑνός)
	De fato (Enneas III, liber 1). Περὶ εἱμαρμένης
	De pulchritudine (Enneas I, liber 6). Peri tou kalou. Περὶ τοῦ καλοῦ
	De triplici ad mundum intelligibilem ascensu (Enneas I, liber 3). Περὶ διαλεκτικῆς
	De virtutibus (Enneas I, liber 2). Περὶ ἀρετῶν
	Quod intelligibilia non sunt extra intellectum; item de ipso bono (Enneas V, liber 5). Ὅτι οὐκ ἔξω τοῦ νοῦ τὰ νοητὰ καὶ περὶ τἀγαθοῦ
4364	Translations
	Latin
	Medieval
4364.A2	Theologia sive mystica philosophia (De secretiori Aegyptiorum philosophia; "Theologia Aristotelis")
	Paraphrase of Enneades IV-VI, presumably composed in Syriac (by Johannan, of Euphemia?). The paraphrase purports to be a treatise of Aristotle commented by Porphyry. It is preserved in an Arabic and a medieval Latin translation
4364.A3	Modern. By date
4364.A5-Z	Other, A-Z
4365	Criticism
	Cf. B693 Philosophy
4366	Plot.. to Plutarch
4366.P6	Plutarchus (Neoplatonist) d. 432 A.D. Πλούταρχος ὁ Ἀθηναῖος
	Plutarch. Πλούταρχος ὁ Χαιρωνεύς
4367	Editions
4367.A2	Complete
4367.A25	Selected works from Parallelae vitae and Moralia
4367.A28	Selections. Passages. Thoughts
4368	Moralia. Ἠθικά
4368.A2	Complete editions

Individual authors to 600 A.D.
 Plutarch. Πλούταρχος ὁ Χαιρωνεύς
  Moralia. Ήθικά -- Continued
   Selected works
4368.A23   Miscellaneous
4368.A25   By group
                 Including Dialogues; Pedagogical or political treatises;
                    Treatises on ancient authors; etc.
4368.A28   Selections. Passages. Thoughts
             Separate editions
4368.A3   Ad principem ineruditum (De doctrina principum). Πρὸς
                 ἡγεμόνα ἀπαίδευτον
4368.A34   Adversus Coloten. Πρὸς Κωλώτην
4368.A35   Aetia Graeca (Quaestiones Graecae). Αἴτια Ἑλληνικά
4368.A36   Aetia physica (Quaestiones naturales). Αἴτια φυσικά
4368.A37   Aetia Romana (Quaestiones Romanae). Αἴτια Ῥωμαϊκά
4368.A38   Amatoriae narrationes (Eroticae narrationes). Ἐρωτικαὶ
                 διηγήσεις
                 Spurious
4368.A4   Amatorius (Eroticus). Ἐρωτικός
             An recte dictum sit latenter vivendum esse see
                 PA4368.D49
4368.A45   An seni respublica gerenda sit. Εἰ πρεσβυτέρῳ
                 πολιτευτέον
4368.A5   An virtus doceri possit (De virtute docenda). Εἰ
                 διδακτὸν ἡ ἀρετή
4368.A53   An vitiositas ad infelicitatem sufficiat. Εἰ αὐτάρκης ἡ
                 κακία πρὸς κακοδαιμονίαν
4368.A6   Animine an corporis affectiones sint peiores (Utrum
                 graviores sint animi morbi quam corporis). Πότερον
                 τὰ τῆς ψυχῆς ἢ τὰ τοῦ σώματος πάθη χείρονα
             Apophthegmata. Ἀποφθέγματα
4368.A63   Apophthegmata Lacaenarum. Ἀποφθέγματα
                 Λακαινῶν
                 Spurious
4368.A65   Apophthegmata Laconica. Ἀποφθέγματα Λακωνικά
                 Spurious
4368.A67   Apophthegmata regum et imperatorum.
                 Ἀποφθέγματα βασιλέων καὶ στρατηγῶν
                 Spurious
4368.A69   Criticism of Apophthegmata (general or particular)
4368.A7   Aquane an ignis sit utilior. Περὶ τοῦ πότερον ὕδωρ ἢ
                 πῦρ χρησιμώτερον
4368.B3   Bellone an pace clariores fuerint Athenienses (De
                 gloria Atheniensium). Πότερον Ἀθηναῖοι κατὰ
                 πόλεμον ἢ κατὰ σοφίαν ἐνδοξότεροι

PA3050-4505

Individual authors to 600 A.D.
Plutarch. Πλούταρχος ὁ Χαιρωνεύς
Moralia. Ἠθικά
Separate editions -- Continued

4368.B7	Bruta animalia (Bestias) ratione uti (Gryllus). Περὶ τοῦ τὰ ἄλογα λόγῳ χρῆσθαι
	Collecta parallela Graeca et Romana see PA4368.P3
4368.C6	Comparatio Aristophanis et Menandri (De comparatione Aristophanis et Menandri epitome). Συγκρίσεως Ἀριστοφάνους καὶ Μενάνδρου ἐπιτομή
	Compendium libri perditi cui argumentum fuit, Stoicos absurdiora poetis dicere see PA4368.S7
4368.C73	Conjugalia praecepta (Nuptialia praecepta). Γαμικὰ παραγγέλματα
4368.C75	Consolatio ad Apollonium. Παραμυθητικὸς πρὸς Ἀπολλώνιον
	Spurious
4368.C8	Consolatio ad uxorem (Consolatio ad Timoxenam). Παραμυθητικὸς εἰς τὴν γυναῖκα τὴν αὐτοῦ
	Convivalium disputationum (quaestionum) lib. IX see PA4368.Q2
	Convivium septem sapientum see PA4368.S4
	Cur Pythia nunc non reddat oracula carmine see PA4368.D56
	De adulatore et amico see PA4368.Q6
4368.D12	De Alexandri Magni fortuna aut virtute oratio I-II. Περὶ τῆς Ἀλεξάνδρου τύχης ἢ ἀρετῆς λόγος α′ β′
4368.D13	De amicorum multitudine. Περὶ πολυφιλίας
4368.D135	De amore fraterno. Περὶ φιλαδελφίας
4368.D14	De amore prolis (De amore paterno). Περὶ τῆς εἰς τὰ ἔκγονα φιλοστοργίας
4368.D15	De anima. Περὶ ψυχῆς
	Fragments
4368.D16	De animae procreatione in Timaeo Platonis. Περὶ τῆς ἐν Τιμαίῳ ψυχογονίας
4368.D17	Epitome libri de animae procreatione in Timaeo. Ἐπιτομὴ τοῦ Περὶ τῆς ἐν τῷ Τιμαίῳ ψυχογονίας
	De audiendis philosophis see PA4368.D57
	De audiendis poetis see PA4368.Q5
	De avaritia see PA4368.D23
4368.D18	De capienda ex inimicis utilitate (Quo pacto quis efficiat ut ex inimicis capiat utilitatem). Πῶς ἄν τις ἀπ' ἐχθρῶν ὠφελοῖτο
4368.D19	De cohibenda ira (De non irascendo). Περὶ ἀοργησίας
4368.D2	De communibus notitiis adversus Stoicos. Περὶ τῶν κοινῶν ἐννοιῶν πρὸς τοὺς Στωικούς

Individual authors to 600 A.D.
　Plutarch. Πλούταρχος ὁ Χαιρωνεύς
　　Moralia. Ἠθικά
　　　Separate editions -- Continued
　　　　De comparatione Aristophanis et Menandri epitome
　　　　　see PA4368.C6

4368.D23 　　　　De cupiditate divitiarum (De avaritia). Περὶ
　　　　　φιλοπλουτίας
4368.D24 　　　　De curiositate. Περὶ πολυπραγμοσύνης
　　　　　De daemonibus liber see PA4368.D64
　　　　　De defectu oraculorum see PA4368.D53
　　　　　De discernendo adulatore ab amico (De discrimine
　　　　　　amici et adulatoris) see PA4368.Q6
　　　　　De doctrina principum see PA4368.A3
4368.D27 　　　　De E apud Delphos. Περὶ τοῦ Ε (ΕΙ) τοῦ ἐν Δελφοῖς
　　　　　De educatione puerorum see PA4368.D5
4368.D28 　　　　De esu carnium oratio I-II. Περὶ σαρκοφαγίας λόγος α′
　　　　　β′
4368.D29 　　　　De exercitatione. Περὶ ἀσκήσεως
　　　　　　Spurious; preserved in a Syriac translation
4368.D3 　　　　De exilio. Περὶ φυγῆς
4368.D33 　　　　De facie quae in orbe lunae apparet. Περὶ τοῦ
　　　　　ἐμφαινομένου προσώπου τῷ κύκλῳ τῆς σελήνης
4368.D34 　　　　De fato. Περὶ εἱμαρμένης
　　　　　　Spurious
　　　　　De fluviis (De fluminibus) see PA4368.D35
4368.D35 　　　　De fluviorum et montium nominibus et de iis quae in illis
　　　　　inveniuntur. Περὶ ποταμῶν καὶ ὀρῶν ἐπωνυμίας καὶ
　　　　　τῶν ἐν αὐτοῖς εὑρισκομένων
　　　　　　Spurious
4368.D36 　　　　De formis dicendi. Περὶ χαρακτήρων
　　　　　　Lost
4368.D37 　　　　De fortuna. Περὶ τύχης
4368.D38 　　　　De fortuna Romanorum. Περὶ τῆς Ῥωμαίων τύχης
　　　　　De fortuna vel virtute Alexandri see PA4368.D12
　　　　　De fraterna amicitia see PA4368.D135
4368.D4 　　　　De garrulitate. Περὶ ἀδολεσχίας
4368.D42 　　　　De genio Socratis. Περὶ τοῦ Σωκράτους δαιμονίου
　　　　　De gloria Atheniensium see PA4368.B3
4368.D43 　　　　De Herodoti malignitate. Περὶ τῆς Ἡροδότου κακοηθείας
　　　　　De his qui tarde a numine corripiuntur (sero a numine
　　　　　　puniuntur) see PA4368.D6
　　　　　De immoderata verecundia see PA4368.D75
　　　　　De industria animalium see PA4368.T4
　　　　　De inimicorum utilitate see PA4368.D18
4368.D45 　　　　De invidia et odio. Περὶ φθόνου καὶ μίσους
　　　　　De ira cohibenda see PA4368.D19

Individual authors to 600 A.D.
Plutarch. Πλούταρχος ὁ Χαιρωνεύς
Moralia. Ἠθικά
Separate editions -- Continued

4368.D47　De Iside et Osiride. On Isis and Osiris. Περὶ Ἴσιδος καὶ Ὀσίριδος

De iustitia dei see PA4368.D6

4368.D49　De latenter vivendo (An recte dictum sit latenter vivendum esse). Εἰ καλῶς εἴρηται τὸ λάθε βιώσας

4368.D5　De liberis educandis (De educatione puerorum). Περὶ παίδων ἀγωγῆς

Spurious

4368.D51　De libidine et aegritudine (Utrum animae an corporis sit libido et aegritudo). Πότερον ψυχῆς ἢ σώματος ἐπιθυμία καὶ λύπη

Fragments

4368.D513　De metris. Περὶ μέτρων

Spurious

De mulierum virtutibus see PA4368.M7

4368.D52　De musica. Περὶ μουσικῆς

De nobilitate see PA4368.P7

De non irascendo see PA4368.D19

De odio et invidia see PA4368.D45

4368.D53　De oraculorum defectu. Περὶ τῶν ἐκλελοιπότων χρηστηρίων

4368.D54　De placitis philosophorum libri V. Περὶ τῶν ἀρεσκόντων τοῖς φιλοσόφοις

Spurious

4368.D55　De primo frigido. Περὶ τοῦ πρώτως (πρώτου) ψυχροῦ

De profectibus in virtute see PA4368.Q7

De puerorum educatione see PA4368.D5

4368.D56　De Pythiae oraculis (Cur Pythia nunc non reddat oracula carmine). Περὶ τοῦ μὴ χρᾶν ἔμμετρα νῦν τὴν Πυθίαν

De ratione audiendorum et legendorum poetarum see PA4368.Q5

4368.D57　De recta ratione audiendi. Περὶ τοῦ ἀκούειν

De sanitate tuenda see PA4368.D66

4368.D58　De se ipsum citra invidiam laudando (Qua quis ratione se ipse sine invidia laudet). Περὶ τοῦ ἑαυτὸν ἐπαινεῖν ἀνεπιφθόνως

4368.D6　De sera numinis vindicta (De his qui tarde a numine corripiuntur). Περὶ τῶν ὑπὸ τοῦ θείου βραδέως τιμωρουμένων

De sollertia animalium see PA4368.T4

4368.D63　De Stoicorum repugnantiis. Περὶ Στωικῶν ἐναντιωμάτων

Individual authors to 600 A.D.
  Plutarch. Πλούταρχος ὁ Χαιρωνεύς
    Moralia. Ἠθικά
      Separate editions -- Continued

4368.D64	De superstitione (De daemonibus). Περὶ δεισιδαιμονίας
4368.D65	De tranquillitate animi. Περὶ εὐθυμίας
4368.D66	De tuenda sanitate (valetudine) praecepta. Ὑγιεινὰ παραγγέλματα
4368.D67	De unius in republica dominatione, populari statu et paucorum imperio. Περὶ μοναρχίας καὶ δημοκρατίας καὶ ὀλιγαρχίας
	De utilitate ex inimicis capienda see PA4368.D18
	De virtute docenda see PA4368.A5
4368.D7	De virtute et vitio. Περὶ ἀρετῆς καὶ κακίας
4368.D72	De virtute morali. Περὶ τῆς ἠθικῆς ἀρετῆς
	De virtutibus mulierum see PA4368.M7
(4368.D73)	De vita et poesi Homeri lib. I-II. Περὶ τοῦ βίου καὶ τῆς ποιήσεως Ὁμήρου α' β'
	Spurious
	see PA4035.A4P6
4368.D74	De vitando acre alieno (usura). Περὶ τοῦ μὴ δεῖν δανείζεσθαι
4368.D75	De vitioso pudore (De immoderata verecundia; De vitiosa verecundia). Περὶ δυσωπίας
	Decem oratorum vitae see PA4368.V5
	Disputatio qua docetur ne suaviter quidem vivi posse secundum Epicuri decreta see PA4368.N7
	Epitome libri de animae procreatione in Timaeo see PA4368.D17
	Eroticae narrationes see PA4368.A38
	Eroticus see PA4368.A4
	Gryllus see PA4368.B7
4368.I5	Instituta Laconica. Παλαιὰ τῶν Λακεδαιμονίων ἐπιτηδεύματα
4368.I7	Institutio Traiani (De institutione principis epistola ad Traianum; De politica et imperatoria institutione)
	Spurious; a late Latin translation of a Greek compilation (lost) based upon the Apophthegmata, and other treatises of Plutarch
4368.M3	Maxime cum principibus philosopho esse disserendum. Περὶ τοῦ ὅτι μάλιστα τοῖς ἡγεμόσι δεῖ τὸν φιλόσοφον διαλέγεσθαι
4368.M7	Mulierum virtutes. De claris mulieribus. Γυναικῶν ἀρεταί
	Narrationes amatoriae see PA4368.A38

PA3050-4505

Individual authors to 600 A.D.
Plutarch. Πλούταρχος ὁ Χαιρωνεύς
Moralia. Ἠθικά
Separate editions -- Continued

4368.N7 Non posse suaviter vivi secundum Epicurum
(Disputatio qua docetur ne suaviter quidem vivi
posse secundum Epicuri decreta). Ὅτι οὐδ' ἡδέως
ζῆν ἔστι κατ' Ἐπίκουρον
Nuptialia praecepta see PA4368.C73

4368.P3 Parallela Graeca et Romana (Collecta parallela, etc.;
Parallela minora)
Spurious

4368.P5 Platonicae quaestiones. Πλατωνικὰ ζητήματα
Praecepta conjugalia see PA4368.C73
Praecepta de tuenda sanitate see PA4368.D66

4368.P6 Praecepta gerendae reipublicae. Πολιτικὰ
παραγγέλματα

4368.P7 Pro nobilitate. Ὑπὲρ εὐγενείας
Spurious; a medieval Greek retranslation of an ancient
Latin treatise, that was based upon the genuine work
of Plutarch (lost) and upon Aristotle's De nobilitate
Problemata see PA4368.Q2

4368.P9 Proverbia Alexandrinorum (quibus Alexandrini usi
sunt). Παροιμίαι αἷς Ἀλεξανδρεῖς ἐχρῶντο
Spurious
Qua quis ratione se ipse sine invidia laudet see
PA4368.D58

4368.Q2 Quaestiones convivales lib. IX (Symposiaca
problemata). Συμποσιακὰ προβλήματα

4368.Q3 Quaestiones de Arati signis. Αἰτίαι τῶν Ἀράτου
διοσημιῶν
Fragments
Quaestiones Graecae see PA4368.A35
Quaestione naturales see PA4368.A36
Quaestiones Platonicae see PA4368.P5
Quaestiones Romanae see PA4368.A37
Quo pacto quis efficiat ut ex inimicis capiat utilitatem
see PA4368.D18

4368.Q4 Quod in animo humano affectibus subjectum, parsne
sit eius an facultas. Εἰ μέρος τὸ παθητικὸν τῆς
ἀνθρώπου ψυχῆς ἢ δύναμις
Fragments

4368.Q5 Quomodo adolescens poetas (poemata) audire debeat
(De audiendis poetis; De ratione audiendorum et
legendorum poetarum). Πῶς δεῖ τὸν νέον
ποιημάτων ἀκούειν

Individual authors to 600 A.D.
    Plutarch. Πλούταρχος ὁ Χαιρωνεύς
        Moralia. Ήθικά
            Separate editions -- Continued

4368.Q6   Quomodo adulator ab amico internoscatur. Πῶς ἄν τις διακρίνειε τὸν κόλακα τοῦ φίλου

               Quomodo aliquis se laudare sine invidia possit see PA4368.D58

4368.Q7   Quomodo quis suos in virtute sentiat profectus. Πῶς ἄν τις αἴσθοιτο ἑαυτοῦ προκόπτοντος ἐπ' ἀρετῇ

               Regum et imperatorum apophthegmata see PA4368.A67

4368.S4   Septem sapientum convivium. Ἑπτὰ σοφῶν συμπόσιον

4368.S7   Stoicos absurdiora poetis dicere (quam poetis absurdiora dicere; Compendium libri cui argumentum fuit, Stoicos absurdiora [etc.]). Σύνοψις τοῦ ὅτι παραδοξότερα οἱ Στωικοὶ τῶν ποιητῶν λέγουσι

               Symposia problemata see PA4368.Q2

4368.T4   Terrestriane an aquatilia animalia sint callidiora (De sollertia animalium; De industria animalium). Πότερα τῶν ζῴων φρονιμώτερα, τὰ χερσαῖα ἢ τὰ ἔνυδρα

               Utrum animae an corporis sit libido et aegritudo see PA4368.D51

               Utrum graviores sint animi morbi quam corporis see PA4368.A6

               Virtutem doceri posse see PA4368.A5

4368.V5   Vitae decem oratorum. Βίοι τῶν δέκα ῥητόρων
                  Spurious
            Spurious and doubtful works

4368.Z5   Collections and selections. By date
               Separate editions see PA4368.A3+

        Vitae parallelae. Vitae. Βίοι παράλληλοι (Παράλληλα)
4369.A2   Complete editions
4369.A33   Selected biographies
4369.A35   Selected extracts, etc.
            Separate editions
               Separate editions of a Roman biography are listed under the name of the subject; separate editions of a Greek biography are arranged chronologically with those of the parallel biographies
4369.A38   Aemilius Paulus. Αἰμίλιος Παῦλος
               Cf. PA4369.T6 Timoleon. Aemilius Paulus
4369.A4   Agesilaus. Pompeius. Ἀγησίλαος. Πομπήϊος
               Cf. PA4369.P7 Pompeius

PA3050-4505

Individual authors to 600 A.D.
Plutarch. Πλούταρχος ὁ Χαιρωνεύς
Vitae parallelae. Vitae. Βίοι παράλληλοι (Παράλληλα)
Separate editions -- Continued

4369.A5	Agis et Cleomenes (Agis and Cleomenes). Tiberius et Gaius Gracchi. Ἄγις καὶ Κλεομένης. Τιβέριος καὶ Γάϊος Γράγχοι
	Cf. PA4369.C75 Cleomenes
	Cf. PA4369.G7 Gracchus, Gaius
	Cf. PA4369.G8 Gracchus, Tiberius
4369.A6	Alcibiades. Coriolanus. Ἀλκιβιάδης. Γάϊος Μάρκιος (Μάρκιος Κοριολανός)
	Cf. PA4369.C8 Coriolanus
4369.A7	Alexander. Caesar. Ἀλέξανδρος. Γ. Καῖσαρ
	Cf. PA4369.C2 Caesar
4369.A73	Antonius. Ἀντώνιος
	Cf. PA4369.D3 Demetrius Poliorcetes. Antonius
4369.A75	Aratus. Ἄρατος
	Without parallel life
4369.A8	Aristides. Cato Maior. Ἀριστείδης. Μάρκος Κάτων
	Cf. PA4369.C4 Cato Maior
4369.A9	Artaxerxes II (Artoxerxes). Ἀρτοξέρξης [ὁ δεύτερος]
	Without parallel life
4369.B8	Brutus. Βροῦτος
	Cf. PA4369.D7 Dio. Brutus
4369.C2	Caesar. Γ. Καῖσαρ
	Cf. PA4369.A7 Alexander. Caesar
4369.C3	Camillus. Κάμιλλος
	Cf. PA4369.T4 Themistocles. Camillus
4369.C4	Cato Maior. Μάρκος Κάτων
	Cf. PA4369.A8 Aristides. Cato Maior
4369.C5	Cato Minor. Κάτων (Uticensis)
	Cf. PA4369.P6 Phocion. Cato Minor
4369.C6	Cicero. Κικέρων
	Cf. PA4369.D5 Demosthenes. Cicero
4369.C7	Cimon. Lucullus. Κίμων. Λούκουλλος
	Cf. PA4369.L7 Lucullus
4369.C75	Cleomenes. Κλεομένης
	Cf. PA4369.A5 Agis et Cleomenes. Tiberius et Gaius Gracchi
4369.C8	Coriolanus. Γάϊος Μάρκιος (Μάρκιος Κοριολανός)
	Cf. PA4369.A6 Alcibiades. Coriolanus
4369.C9	Crassus, M. Κράσσος
	Cf. PA4369.N4 Nicias. Crassus
4369.D3	Demetrius Poliorcetes. Antonius. Δημήτριος [Πολιορκητής]. Ἀντώνιος
	Cf. PA4369.A73 Antonius

Individual authors to 600 A.D.
Plutarch. Πλούταρχος ὁ Χαιρωνεύς
Vitae parallelae. Vitae. Βίοι παράλληλοι (Παράλληλα)
Separate editions -- Continued

4369.D5	Demosthenes. Cicero. Δημοσθένης. Κικέρων
	Cf. PA4369.C6 Cicero
4369.D7	Dio (Dion). Brutus. Δίων. Βροῦτος
	Cf. PA4369.B8 Brutus
4369.E8	Eumenes. Εὐμένης
	Cf. PA4369.S4 Sertorius. Eumenes
4369.F2	Fabius Maximus. Φάβιος Μάξιμος
	Cf. PA4369.P4 Pericles. Fabius Maximus
4369.F5	Flamininus, T. Quinctius. Τίτος (Τ. Κοΐντιος Φλαμινῖνος)
	Cf. PA4369.P5 Philopoemen. Flamininus
4369.G2	Galba. Γάλβας
	No parallel life
4369.G7	Gracchus, Gaius. Γάϊος Γράγχος
	Cf. PA4369.A5 Agis et Cleomenes. Tiberius et
	Gaius Gracchi
4369.G8	Gracchus, Tiberius. Τιβέριος Γράγχος
	Cf. PA4369.A5 Agis et Cleomenes. Tiberius et
	Gaius Gracchi
4369.L7	Lucullus. Λούκουλλος
	Cf. PA4369.C7 Cimon. Lucullus
4369.L8	Lycurgus. Numa. Λυκοῦργος. Νομᾶς
	Cf. PA4369.N8 Numa
4369.L9	Lysander. Sulla. Λύσανδρος. Σύλλας
	Cf. PA4369.S8 Sulla
4369.M2	Marcellus. Μάρκελλος
	Cf. PA4369.P3 Pelopidas. Marcellus
4369.M5	Marius. Μάριος (Γάϊος Μάριος)
	Cf. PA4369.P9 Pyrrhus. Marius
4369.N4	Nicias. Crassus. Νικίας. Κράσσος
	Cf. PA4369.C9 Crassus
4369.N8	Numa. Νομᾶς
	Cf. PA4369.L8 Lycurgus. Numa
4369.O8	Otho. Ὄθων
	No parallel life
4369.P3	Pelopidas. Marcellus. Πελοπίδας. Μάρκελλος
	Cf. PA4369.M2 Marcellus
4369.P4	Pericles. Fabius Maximus. Περικλῆς. Φάβιος Μάξιμος
	Cf. PA4369.F2 Fabius Maximus
4369.P5	Philopoemen. Flamininus. Φιλοποίμην. Τίτος (Τ. Κοΐντιος Φλαμινῖνος)
	Cf. PA4369.F5 Flamininus
4369.P6	Phocion. Cato Minor (Uticensis). Φωκίων. Κάτων
	Cf. PA4369.C5 Cato Minor

PA3050-4505

Individual authors to 600 A.D.
Plutarch. Πλούταρχος ὁ Χαιρωνεύς
Vitae parallelae. Vitae. Βίοι παράλληλοι (Παράλληλα)
Separate editions -- Continued

4369.P7	Pompeius. Πομπήϊος
	Cf. PA4369.A4 Agesilaus. Pompeius
4369.P8	Publicola (Valerius Publicola). Ποπλικόλας (Οὐαλλέριος Ποπλικόλας)
	Cf. PA4369.S6 Solon. Publicola
4369.P9	Pyrrhus. Marius. Πύρρος. Μάριος (Γάϊος Μάριος)
	Cf. PA4369.M5 Marius
4369.R7	Romulus. Ῥωμύλος
	Cf. PA4369.T5 Theseus. Romulus
4369.S4	Sertorius. Eumenes. Σερτώριος. Εὐμένης
	Cf. PA4369.E8 Eumenes
4369.S6	Solon. Publicola (Poplicola. Valerius Publicola). Σόλων. Ποπλικόλας (Οὐαλλέριος Ποπλικόλας)
	Cf. PA4369.P8 Publicola
4369.S8	Sulla (Sylla). Σύλλας
	Cf. PA4369.L9 Lysander. Sulla
4369.T4	Themistocles. Camillus. Θεμιστοκλῆς. Κάμιλλος
	Cf. PA4369.C3 Camillus
4369.T5	Theseus. Romulus. Θησεύς. Ῥωμύλος
	Cf. PA4369.R7 Romulus
4369.T6	Timoleon. Aemilius Paulus. Τιμολέων. Αἰμίλιος Παῦλος
	Cf. PA4369.A38 Aemilius Paulus
	Valerius Publicola see PA4369.P8
	Translations
	Greek (Modern)
4372.A2	Complete works. By date
4372.A3	Selected works. By date
	Moralia
4372.M6	Collected and selected. By date
4372.M6A-.M6Z	Particular. By Latin title, A-Z, and date
4372.V6	Vitae parallelae. By date
4373	Latin (Table PA10)
	English
4374.A1	Complete works
4374.A2	Selected works from Moralia and Vitae
4374.A5A-.A5Z	Selections by editor (or date)
	Moralia
4374.M6	Complete. By date
4374.M7	Selected, and abridged. By date
4374.M8A-.M8Z	Separate treatises. By Latin title, A-Z, and date
	Vitae parallelae see DE7.P5
4375	French (Table PA10)
	For Amyot's translations see PQ1601.A5+

Individual authors to 600 A.D.
Plutarch. Πλούταρχος ὁ Χαιρωνεύς
Translations -- Continued

4376	German (Table PA10)
4377	Italian (Table PA10)
4378	Spanish and Portuguese (Table PA10)
	Other European languages
4379.D7-.D8	Dutch (Table PA11)
	Including Flemish and Frisian
	Scandinavian
4379.S2-.S3	Danish. Dano-Norwegian (Table PA11)
4379.S4-.S5	Icelandic (Table PA11)
4379.S6-.S7	Swedish (Table PA11)
4380	Slavic
4380.B6-.B7	Bohemian. Czech (Table PA11)
4380.P6-.P7	Polish (Table PA11)
4380.R8-.R9	Russian (Table PA11)
4381	Other languages
4381.H4-.H5	Hebrew (Table PA11)
	Criticism and interpretation
4382	General. Biography
4383	Textual criticism. History of text. Manuscripts. Editions, etc.
	Moralia
4384	General or miscellaneous
	Textual criticism see PA4383
	Particular works
	see the works
	Vitae parallelae
4385	General or miscellaneous
	For historial treatises see Class D
	Textual criticism see PA4383
	Particular Vitae
	see the Vitae
	History of appreciation and study
4387.A2	General
4387.A5-.Z3	By region or country, A-Z
4387.Z5A-.Z5Z	By individual, A-Z
4388	Translations (as subject)
4388.A2	General
4388.A5-Z	By individual translator and author
	e.g.
4388.N7A-.N7Z	North
4389	Language. Style. Technique
4389.A-.Z3	General
4389.Z5	Special (Grammar, etc.)
4389.Z8	Glossaries. Indices. Concordances. By date

PA3050-4505

	Individual authors to 600 A.D. -- Continued
4390	Plute... to Polyb...

Poemander see PA3998.H5

Polemo (physiognomist) see PA4390.P2

4390.P14   Polemo Iliensis, periegeta, fl. 177/6 B.C. Πολέμων ὁ Περιηγήτης (Table P-PZ38)

4390.P2   Polemo, Antoni(n)us, of Laodicea, sophist, ca. 88-145 A.D. Πολέμων ὁ Λαοδικεύς (Table P-PZ38 modified)

4390.P2A61-.P2A78   Separate works. By title

        e.g. Declamationes (Only two preserved); Physiognomica (Preserved in an Arabic translation and in a Greek paraphrase by Adamantius)

Polio, Sabidius see PA4407.S2

Pollio, Valerius, (lexicographer) 2nd century A.D. Πωλίων

4390.P3   Pollux, Julius, 180-238. Ἰούλιος Πολυδεύκης (Table P-PZ38 modified)

4390.P3A61-.P3A78   Separate works. By title

        e.g. Onomasticum (Onomastikon. Ὀνομαστικόν)

Hermeneumata--Colloquium see PA6381.D7

"Pollux, Julius, historian" ("Pseudo-Polydeuces"). Historia physica. Ἰούλιος Πολυδεύκης. Ἱστορία φυσική

    A forgery of Andreas Darmarios, 16th century

    see PA5310

Polus, of Acragas, sophist, b. ca. 440 B.C. Πῶλος

Polyaenus, of Lampsacus (disciple of Epicurus) 4th to 3rd century B.C. Πολύαινος see B512

4390.P5-.P7   Polyaenus (rhetor) 2nd century A.D. Strategemata. Πολύαινος. Στρατηγήματα (Table P-PZ42a)

Polyaenus, Julius (rhetor) 1st century B.C. Ἰούλιος Πολύαινος

Polybius. Historiarum lib. XL. Historiae. Πολύβιος. Ἱστορίαι

    Lib. I-V, preserved entire; large selections from I-XVI, XVIII, and fragments; lib. XVII, XIX, XXXVII and XL are lost

4391.A2   Editions

4391.A3   Selected books

4391.A4   Selected portions (with separate titles)

    Including De militia Romanorum; De diversitate civitatum; De legationibus

Translations

4392   Latin

Other languages see D58

4393   Criticism

    For historical criticism and commentaries see D58

4394   Polybius (Sard.) to Por...

4394.P5   Polybius, of Sardes, rhetor (date uncertain). Πολύβιος (Table P-PZ38)

	Individual authors to 600 A.D.
	Polybius (Sard.) to Por... -- Continued
4394.P7	Polycrates, of Athens, rhetor, fl. 390 B.C. Πολυκράτης (Table P-PZ38)
	Polydeuces
	see Pollux
	Porphyry, ca. 234-ca. 305. Πορφύριος
4396.A2	Editions. By date
4396.A3	Selected works
	Single works
4396.A35	Ad Boethum de anima. Πρὸς Βόηθον περὶ ψυχῆς
	Fragments
4396.A4	Ad Gaurum. Πρὸς Γαῦρον περὶ τοῦ πῶς ἐμψυχοῦνται τὰ ἔμβρυα
	In the manuscripts transmitted among the works of Galenus
4396.A5	Ad Marcellam (Epistula ad M. conjugem). Pros Markellan. Πρὸς Μαρκέλλαν
4396.A6	Adversus Christianos. Against the Christians. Κατὰ Χριστιανῶν
	Fragments
4396.D2	De abstinentia lib. IV (De abst. ab esu animalium; De abst. ab animalibus necandis; De non necandis ad epulandum animantibus). Περὶ ἀποχῆς ἐμψύχων
	Includes to a large extent Theophrastus De pictate
	Cf. PA4448.D5 Theophrastus De pietate
	De anima see PA4396.A35
(4396.D4)	De antro nympharum. Peri tou en Odysseia tōn nymphōn antrou. Περὶ τοῦ ἐν Ὀδυσσείᾳ τῶν νυμφῶν ἄντρου
	Allegoric interpretation of Odyssey XIII, 102-112
	see PA4035.P7
	De diis daemonibus see PA4396.E6
	De divinis et mysteriis see PA4396.E6
4396.D5	De philosophia ex oraculis haurienda. Περὶ τῆς ἐκ λογίων φιλοσοφίας
	Fragments
4396.D6	De regressu animae
	Original lost; fragments of a Latin translation (quoted by Augustinus De civ. Dei X)
4396.D8	De statuis (De statuis sive imaginibus deorum aut de cultu simulacrorum). Περὶ ἀγαλμάτων
	Fragments
(4396.D9)	De Styge. Περὶ Στυγός
	Fragments
	see PA4035.P7

PA3050-4505

Individual authors to 600 A.D.
Porphyry, ca. 234-ca. 305. Πορφύριος
Single works -- Continued

4396.E6 Epistula ad Anebonem, Aegyptium (De divinis atque daemonibus; De diis daemonibus; De divinis et daemonibus sententiae; De divinis et mysteriis). Pros Anebō. Πρὸς Ἀνεβὼ ἐπιστολή

Epistula ad Marcellam see PA4396.A5

Homericae quaestiones
see Commentaries below

In Aristotelem commentarii
see Commentaries below

In Ptolemaeum commentarii
see Commentaries below

Isagoge
see Commentaries below

4396.P4 Philologae historiae lib. V. Φιλόλογος ἱστορία (ἀκρόασις)
4396.P6 Philosophae historiae lib. IV. Φιλόσοφος ἱστορία
Fragments, and Vita Pythagorae (part of book I) preserved
Cf. PA4396.V6 Vita Pythagorae

Quinque voces
see Commentaries below

4396.S4 Sententiae ad intelligibilia ducentes. Ἀφορμαὶ πρὸς τὰ νοητά

4396.V54 Vita Plotini (De vita Plotini, et ordine scriptorum eius). Life of Plotinus. Περὶ Πλωτίνου βίου καὶ τῆς τάξεως τῶν βιβλίων αὐτοῦ

4396.V6 Vita Pythagorae. Pythagorou bios. Πυθαγόρου βίος
Part of first book of the author's Philosopha historia

Commentaries
Aristotle

4396.Z2 Isagoge (In Aristotelis Categorias introductio; Isagoge de quinque vocibus sive praedicabilibus; Quinque voces). Εἰσαγωγὴ εἰς τὰς Ἀριστοτέλους Κατηγορίας (Πέντε φωναί)

4396.Z3 In Aristotelis Categorias commentarius (In Aristotelis Categorias expositio [per interrogationem et responsum]). Ἐξήγησις εἰς τὰς Ἀριστοτέλους Κατηγορίας κατὰ πεῦσιν καὶ ἀπόκρισιν

Criticism
4396.Z4A2-.Z4A4 Ancient and medieval
Cf. PA3948.D17 David
Cf. PA3968.E3 Elias
Cf. PA6231.Z3+ Boethius

4396.Z4A5-.Z4Z Modern
(4396.Z5) Homer
see PA4035.P7

	Individual authors to 600 A.D.
	Porphyry, ca. 234-ca. 305. Πορφύριος
	Commentaries -- Continued
(4396.Z55)	Plato
	Plotinus see PA4363+
	Ptolemy
(4396.Z6)	In Ptolemaei Harmonica commentarius. Εἰς τὰ Ἀρμονικὰ Πτολεμαίου ὑπόμνημα see PA4406
(4396.Z7)	In Ptolemaei Quadripartitum introductio (Introductio in Ptolemaei opus de effectibus astrorum; Isagoge in Ptolemaei Tetrabiblon). Εἰσαγωγὴ εἰς τὴν Ἀποτελεσματικὴν τοῦ Πτολεμαίου see PA4406
	Spurious works
4396.Z9	De prosodia. Περὶ προσῳδίας
	Part of a commentary on the Ars of Dionysius Thrax; the other parts are lost
	Theologia see PA4364.A2
4397	Translations
4397.A2	Latin. By date
4397.A5-Z	Other. By language, title, and date
4398	Criticism. Biography
	For philosophical treatises see B697
4399	Port... to Pro...
4399.P13	Posidippus (dramatist) 4th century B.C. Ποσείδιππος (Table P-PZ38)
4399.P15	Posidippus, of Pella (epigrammatist) fl. ca. 270 B.C. Ποσείδιππος (Table P-PZ38)
4399.P16	Posidonius (Poseidonios). Ποσειδώνιος
	Treatises on various authors of this name
4399.P17	Posidonius (grammarian, disciple of Aristarchus) 2nd century B.C. Ποσειδώνιος (Table P-PZ38)
4399.P2	Posidonius, of Apamea (P. Rhodius) fl. 97-78 B.C. Ποσειδώνιος Ἀπαμεύς (Ῥόδιος) (Table P-PZ38)
4399.P35	Posidonius, of Corinth (date uncertain). Ποσειδώνιος Κορίνθιος (Table P-PZ38)
	Didactic poem on fishes, lost
4399.P37	Posidonius, of Olbia(?) historian, 2nd century B.C. Ποσειδώνιος Ὀλβιοπολίτης (Table P-PZ38)
	Posidonius, of Rhodus see PA4399.P2
	Potamon, of Alexandria (philosopher) 1st century B.C. Ποτάμων Ἀλεξανδρεύς
	Potamon, of Lesbos (Mytilene) historian and rhetor, 1st century B.C. Ποτάμων Μιτυληναῖος
	Pratinas, of Phleius (dramatist) 5th century B.C. Πρατίνας

PA3050-4505

Individual authors to 600 A.D.
  Port... to Pro... -- Continued
    Praxagoras, of Athens (historian) 4th century A.D.
      Πραξαγόρας
    Praxilla, of Sicyon, fl. ca. 455 B.C. Πράξιλλα
    Praxiphanes (Peripatetic philosopher and grammarian) 3rd
      century B.C. Πραξιφάνης

4399.P6	Priscianus, Lydus, 6th century A.D. Πρισκιανὸς ὁ Λυδός

                                      (Table P-PZ38 modified)

4399.P6A61-.P6A78   Separate works. By title
                                        e.g. Metaphrasis in Theophrasti De sensu; Solutiones
                                            eorum de quibus dubitavit Chosroes Persarum rex
                                            (Original lost)

4399.P8   Priscianus, Theodorus (physician) 4th century A.D.
                              Euporista
                                Preserved in the author's Latin translation

4399.P85   Priscus, of Panion (Panites), 5th century A.D. Πρίσκος
                              Πανίτης
                        Proclus (author of the Chrestomathia) 2nd century A.D. see
                              PA4400.C6
                  Proclus, 410-485. Πρόκλος Διάδοχος

4400.A2   Editions. By date
                    Separate works

4400.C4   Characteres epistolici (De epistulis conscribendis).
                            Ἐπιστολιμαῖοι χαρακτῆρες
                              Spurious; wrongly ascribed to either Proclus or Libanius

4400.C6   Chrestomathia (Electorum grammaticorum lib. IV).
                            Χρεστομάθεια γραμματική
                              Lost, with the exception of the extract in the Bibliotheca
                                    (Myriobiblon) of Photius. Authorship disputed
                  De conscribendis epistulis see PA4400.C4

4400.D3   De decem dubitationibus circa providentiam. Περὶ τῶν
                            δέκα πρὸς τὴν πρόνοιαν ἀπορημάτων
                            Original lost; Latin version by Guilelmus de Moerbeke, 13th
                                century

4400.D4   De malorum subsistentia. Περὶ τῆς τῶν κακῶν
                            ὑποστάσεως
                            Original lost; Latin version by Guilelmus de Moerbeke, 13th
                                century
                  De motu see PA4400.I5

4400.D5   De philosophia Chaldaica. On the Chaldean philosophy.
                            Εἰς τὰ λόγια
                            Extracts only

4400.D6   De providentia et fato et eo quod in nobis. Περὶ τῆς
                            προνοίας καὶ τῆς εἱμαρμένης καὶ τοῦ ἐφ' ἡμῖν
                            Original lost; Latin version by Guilelmus de Moerbeke, 13th
                                century

Individual authors to 600 A.D.
 Proclus, 410-485. Πρόκλος Διάδοχος
  Separate works -- Continued
4400.D7   De sacrificio et magia
    Original lost; Latin translation by Marsilius Ficinus
4400.D9   Duodeviginti argumenta adversus Christianos.
    Ἐπιχειρήματα ιη΄ κατὰ Χριστιανῶν
    Lost
4400.H7   Hymni. Ὕμνοι
4400.H9   Hypotyposis astronomicarum positionum. Ὑποτύπωσις
    τῶν ἀστρονομικῶν ὑποθέσεων
4400.I4   In Platonis theologiam lib. VI. Platonic theology. Περὶ τῆς
    κατὰ Πλάτωνα θεολογίας
4400.I5   Institutio physica (De motu lib. II). Στοιχείωσις φυσική
    (Περὶ κινήσεως)
4400.I6   Institutio theologica. Elements of theology. Στοιχείωσις
    θεολογική
4400.S7   Sphaera (De sphaera sive circulis coelestibus libellus).
    Σφαῖρα

PA3050-4505

    Spurious; an extract from the Isagoge in phaenomena of
    Geminus
  Commentaries
4400.Z1   Collections and selections. By date
   Particular authors
    see the author
(4400.Z17)   In primum Euclidis Elementorum librum IV. Eis prōton
    Eukleidou Stoicheiōn biblon. Εἰς πρῶτον Εὐκλείδου
    Στοιχείων βίβλον
(4400.Z19)   Commentarius in Hesiodi Opera et dies
    Extracts only
   In theologiam Platonis libri VI see PA4400.I4
(4400.Z22)   In Alcibiadem priorem Platonis. Alcibiades I
(4400.Z24)   In Cratylum Platonis. In Platonis Cratylum commentaria
    Extracts only
(4400.Z26)   In Parmenidem Platonis commentarii
    Seven books preserved; the remainder supplied by
    Damascius
(4400.Z28)   In Platonis Rem publicam
(4400.Z3)   Commentariorum in Platonis Timaeum lib. V. On the
    Timaeus
(4400.Z7)   Paraphrasis in Claudii Ptolemaei Quadripartitum
    (Paraphrasis in libros IV De siderum effectionibus)
    Spurious
4401   Translations
4402   Criticism
4403 Proc... to Pto...

	Individual authors to 600 A.D.
	Proc... to Pto... -- Continued
	Procopius, of Caesarea, fl. 527-562. Προκόπιος ὁ Καισαρεύς see PA5340
4403.P5	Procopius, of Gaza, fl. between 465-528 A.D. Προκόπιος (Table P-PZ38)
4403.P6	Prodicus, of Ceos, 5th century B.C. Horae. Πρόδικος ὁ Κεῖος. Ὧραι

4403.P5 Procopius, of Gaza, fl. between 465-528 A.D. Προκόπιος (Table P-PZ38)

4403.P6 Prodicus, of Ceos, 5th century B.C. Horae. Πρόδικος ὁ Κεῖος. Ὧραι
Lost
Cf. PA4494.H58 Xenophon. Hercules Prodiceus

4403.P7 Protagoras, of Abdera, 5th century B.C. Πρωταγόρας ὁ Ἀβδηρίτης (Table P-PZ38)
Cf. PA4279.P8 Plato. Protagoras

Pseudo-Callisthenes see PA3946.C3

Pseudo-Philoxenus see PA4273.P2

Pseudo-Polydeuces
see Pollux, Julius

Pseudo-Scymnus
see Scymnus

Ptolemaeus (Ptolemy, the Gnostic) 2nd century A.D.
Πτολεμαῖος see B638

Ptolemaeus, grammaticus see PA4403.P9

4403.P9 Ptolemaeus, of Ascalon (grammarian) 1st century A.D.(?). Πτολεμαῖος ὁ Ἀσκαλωνίτης (Table P-PZ38)
Works lost including his De differentia vocum (Περὶ διαφορᾶς λέξεων). The treatise published with this title by Fabricius (1798) and Heylbut (1887) is a spurious Byzantine extract from Herennius Philo
Cf. PA4271.P2 Herennius Philo

Ptolemy, 2nd cent. Πτολεμαῖος Κλαύδιος
Class here philological studies only. Class other works with the subjects in Classes G, QA, QB, etc.
For collected works see QB41
Editions

4404.A2 Comprehensive. By date

4404.A3 Three or more works. By date
Separate works
Almagestum. Almagest. Μαθηματικὴ σύνταξις

4404.A5 Editions. By date

4404.A6 Selected books or portions
Including Catalogus fixarum stellarum (in books 7 and 8)

4404.A8 Criticism

Apparitiones see PA4404.D4

Astrolabium see PA4404.P6

Astrologia aphoristica see PA4404.C4

Canon insignium urbium (Tabula urbium) see PA4404.G5

Individual authors to 600 A.D.
　Ptolemy, 2nd cent. Πτολεμαῖος Κλαύδιος
　　Separate works -- Continued
4404.C2　　　　　Canon regnorum. Table of reigns. Κανὼν βασιλειῶν
　　　　　　　　　A later addition is the so-called Hemerologium Florentinum,
　　　　　　　　　　a comparative list of months of seventeen peoples
　　　　　　　　　　including fasti consulares
　　　　　　　　　Cf. PA4404.T3 Tabulae manuales astronomicae
　　　　　　Canones expediti astronomici see PA4404.T3
　　　　　　Catalogus stellarum see PA4404.A5+
4404.C4　　　　　Centiloquium (Astrologia aphoristica; Fructus). Καρπός
　　　　　　　　　One hundred aphorisms, a spurious compilation chiefly
　　　　　　　　　　from the Quadripartitum
　　　　　　Cosmographia see PA4404.G3+
4404.D2　　　　　De analemmate. Περὶ ἀναλήμματος
　　　　　　　　　Fragments; the entire treatise preserved in the Latin
　　　　　　　　　　translation of Guilelmus de Moerbeke
　　　　　　De apparentiis et significationibus inerrantium see
　　　　　　　PA4404.D4
　　　　　　De criterio see PA4404.D6
4404.D4　　　　　De inerrantibus stellis (Apparitiones; De apparentiis et
　　　　　　　significationibus inerrantium). Φάσεις ἀπλανῶν
　　　　　　　ἀστέρων καὶ συναγωγὴ ἐπισημασιῶν
　　　　　　　Second part alone preserved
4404.D6　　　　　De iudicandi facultate [et animi principatu] (De criterio).
　　　　　　　Περὶ κριτηρίου καὶ ἡγεμονικοῦ
　　　　　　De speculis (spurious) see PA3999.A36
　　　　　　Fructus see PA4404.C4
　　　　　　Geographia (Cosmographia). Γεωγραφικὴ ὑφήγησις
4404.G3　　　　　　Editions (lib. I-VIII)
4404.G4　　　　　　Selected books (two or more)
　　　　　　　Single books (complete)
4404.G41　　　　　　Book I
4404.G42　　　　　　Book II
4404.G43　　　　　　Book III
4404.G44　　　　　　Book IV
4404.G45　　　　　　Book V
4404.G46　　　　　　Book VI
4404.G47　　　　　　Book VII
4404.G48　　　　　　Book VIII
4404.G5　　　　　　Selected portions
　　　　　　　　Including Arabia; Germania; Canon insignium urbium
(4404.G6)　　　　　Maps (ancient)
　　　　　　　　see G87
(4404.G7)　　　　　Criticism
　　　　　　　　see G87

PA3050-4505

	Individual authors to 600 A.D.
	Ptolemy, 2nd cent. Πτολεμαῖος Κλαύδιος
	Separate works -- Continued
4404.H3	Harmonica (Elementorum harmonicorum lib. III).
	Harmonics. Ἁρμονικά
	Derived mainly from Didymus, musician
4404.H9	Hypotheses (De hypothesibus planetarum liber).
	Planetary hypotheses. Ὑποθέσεις τῶν πλανωμένων
	Book II preserved in Arabic only
4404.I5	Inscriptio Canobi, 147 B.C.
	Magna constructio see PA4404.A5+
	Mathematica syntaxis
	see PA4404.A5+; PA4404.Q3
4404.O7	Optica. Optics. Ὀπτικὴ πραγματεία
	Books II-V preserved in the Latin translation by Eugenius,
	Admiral of Sicily (1150 A.D.) based on an Arabic
	version; book I lost
4404.P6	Planisphaerium (Astrolabium). Ἅπλωσις ἐπιφανείας
	σφαίρας
	Preserved only in the Latin translation of Hermannus
	Secundus (12th century) based upon an Arabic version
4404.Q3	Quadripartitum. Tetrabiblos. Μαθηματικὴ
	(Ἀποτελεσματικὴ) σύνταξις τετράβιβλος
	Authorship formerly disputed
4404.T3	Tabulae manuales astronomicae (Canones expediti
	astronomici). Πρόχειροι κανόνες (Προχείρων
	κανόνων διάταξις καὶ ψηφοφορία)
	Includes Canon regnorum
	Tetrabiblos see PA4404.Q3
4404.Z5	Spurious works
4405	Translations
4405.A2	Greek (Modern)
	Latin
4405.A4	Medieval
4405.A5	Modern
4405.A6-.Z3	Other. By language, A-Z, and Latin title
4405.Z5	Oriental
4406	Criticism and interpretation
4406.A2	Ancient
	Medieval
(4406.A3)	Arabic
4406.A4	Latin
	Modern
4406.A5	Early to 1800
4406.A6-Z	Recent, 1800+
4407	Ptole... to Sap...

	Individual authors to 600 A.D.
	Ptole... to Sap... -- Continued
4407.P2	Ptolemaeus Chennus fl. ca. 100 A.D. Πτολεμαῖος Χέννος (Table P-PZ38)
4407.P23	Ptolemaeus I Lagi (filius), King of Egypt, 367-283/2 B.C. (Ptolemy I Soter; Ptolemaeus Lagu; Ptolemaeus Soter). Πτολεμαῖος Σωτήρ (Table P-PZ38)
4407.P26	Ptolemaeus Epithetes, 2nd century B.C. Πτολεμαῖος Ἐπιθέτης (Table P-PZ38)
4407.P27	Ptolemaeus Pindarion, 2nd century B.C. Πτολεμαῖος Πινδαρίων (Table P-PZ38)

PA3050-4505

	Pyrrhon, of Elis, 4th to 3rd century B.C. Πύρρων see B610+
	Pythagoras, of Samos, fl. 530 B.C. Πυθαγόρας ὁ Σάμιος
	No genuine works
	Cf. B240+ Philosophy
	Spurious works
4407.P3	Collected works. Selected works. By date
4407.P3A-.P3Z	Separate works. By title, A-Z
	Carmen aureum. Golden verses. Χρυσᾶ ἔπη
	Cf. PA4013.H46 Hierocles, of Alexandria
	Epistulae Pythagorae et Pythagoreorum
	Pythagorica hypomnemata
	Lost
	Pythagorica praecepta
	A forgery of Giraldi, 1551
4407.P4A-.P4Z	Translations. By language, A-Z
4407.P5	Criticism
4407.P53	Pytheas, of Massalia, 4th century B.C. Πυθέας (Table P-PZ38)
	Quintus Smyrnaeus. Posthomerica lib. XIV. Κόϊντος Σμυρναῖος. Μεθ' Ὅμηρον
4407.Q4	Texts. By date
4407.Q5A-.Q5Z	Translations. By language, A-Z, and date
4407.Q6	Criticism
4407.R54	Rhianos of Crete. Ῥιανός (Table P-PZ38)
4407.R55	Rhinthon, of Tarentum (phlyacograph) 3rd century B.C. Ῥίνθων (Table P-PZ38)
4407.R6	Romanus Melodus, Saint, fl. 500. Ῥωμανὸς ὁ Μελωδός (Table P-PZ38)
4407.R8	Rufinus. Rufinos. Ῥουφῖνος (Table P-PZ38)
	Rufus, of Ephesus (physician) 2nd century A.D. Ῥοῦφος
4407.S2	Sabidius Pollio (Polio?) 1st century A.D. (Table P-PZ38)
	Supposed author of the five fictitious letters of Euripides, and of those of Aratus (lost)
	Cf. PA3973.Z9 Euripides. Epistulae V

	Individual authors to 600 A.D.
	Ptole... to Sap... -- Continued
4407.S3	Sallustius (Neo-Platonic writer). Σαλούστιος (Table P-PZ38)
	Author of a treatise entitled by its first editor Leo Allatius "De diis et mundo"
4407.S4	Salustius (Salustios or Salutios) 2nd century A.D. (?). Σαλούστιος (Table P-PZ38)
	Author of commentaries on Demosthenes, Herodotus a.o. (now lost)
4407.S5	Salustius (Salustios), Cynic philosopher, 5th century A.D. Σαλούστιος (Table P-PZ38)
	Salutius (Salutios)
	see Sallustius; Salustius
	Sappho. Σαπφώ
4408.A2	Editions. By date
	Including editions of fragments or particular odes
4408.A5-Z	Translations. By language, A-Z, and translator
4409	Criticism
4410	Sapr... to Sim...
4410.S13	Satyrus (Peripatetic biographer) fl. ca. 200 B.C. Σάτυρος (Table P-PZ38)
4410.S14	Scylax, of Caryanda (logographer) 6th century B.C. Σκύλαξ Καρυανδεύς (Table P-PZ38 modified)
	Works lost
4410.S14A61-.S14A78	Separate works. By title
	Spurious: Periplus maris interni (Periplus maris ad litora habitata Europae et Asiae et Libyae). Περίπλους τῆς θαλάσσης τῆς οἰκουμένης Εὐρώπης καὶ Ἀσίας καὶ Λιβύης
4410.S18	Scymnus, of Chios, fl. ca. 184/3 B.C. Σκύμνος
	Periegesis
	In prose; lost
	Pseudo-Scymnus. Orbis descriptio. Περιήγησις
	Poem in 742 verses followed by a metrical Periplus ponti euxini. In the older editions the poem is ascribed to Marcianus of Heraclea
	Secundus, Neo-Pythagorean see PA4410.S2
4410.S2	Secundus, of Athens, sophist, 2nd century A.D. Σεκοῦνδος
	No writings. The spurious nineteen "Sententiae" ascribed to him were at a later period appended to an anonymous "Vita Secundi philosophi taciturni." The various versions of this legend and its medieval derivations are classified according to the language of the version.
	Seleucus "Homericus" (grammarian) 1st century A.D. Σέλευκος ὁ Ὁμηρικός

Individual authors to 600 A.D.
Sapr... to Sim... -- Continued

4410.S4
Semonides, of Amorgos (7th or 6th century B.C.?).
Σημονίδης (Table P-PZ38)
Serenus, of Antinoe (mathematician) 4th century A.D.
Σερῆνος
Serenus, of Antissa
see Serenus, of Antinoe

4410.S47
Severus Iatrosophista, fl. betw. 30 B.C. and 14 A.D. De
clysteribus liber. Σεβῆρος (Σευῆρος). Περὶ ἐνετήρων
ἤτοι κλυστήρων πρὸς Τιμόθεον

(4410.S475)
Sextii (The Sextians: Quintus Sextius, father and son
(Sextius Niger?) Sotion, Celsus, a.o.)
see B514
For the Sententiae Sexti, by some authorities ascribed
to one of the Sextii see PA4410.S6

(4410.S476)
Sextius, Quintus (philosopher) fl. between 50 B.C. and 10
A.D. Σέξτιος Κόϊντος
Writings (in Greek) lost

(4410.S48)
Sextius Niger (Quintus Sextius, the son?) physician, fl.
between 10 and 40 A.D. (?). De materia medica.
Σέξτιος. Περὶ ὕλης
Lost

4410.S5
Sextus Empiricus, 2nd century A.D. Σέξτος Ἐμπειρικός
Cf. B620+ Philosophy

4410.S5A3
Pyrrhoniarum institutionum lib. III. Pyrrōneioi
hypotypōseis. Πυρρώνειοι ὑποτυπώσεις

4410.S5A4
Adversus dogmaticos lib. I-V. Πρὸς δογματικούς

4410.S5A5
Adversus mathematicos lib. I-VI. Pros mathēmatikous.
Πρὸς μαθηματικούς
In the manuscripts and in the older editions, the five books
of the earlier work Adversus dogmaticos follow
Adversus mathematicos and are designated as books
VII-XI of that work. The "Sceptica" (Σκεπτικά) in ten
books ascribed to Sextus Emp. by Suidas may
correspond to the eleven books comprised in the two
works, if books III and IV of Adv. math. formed one
book as presumably they did in some manuscripts

4410.S6
Sextus (Sextus Pythagoreus?). Sententiae. Sentences of
Sextus. Σέξτου γνῶμαι
Collection of aphorisms ascribed to one otherwise unknown
Sextus, called S. Pyth. by St. Jerome. Rufinus in the
preface to his translation states that according to tradition
Pope Sixtus II (Xystus) was their author. The text is
preserved in a christianized revision
Editions
Translations

PA3050-4505

	Individual authors to 600 A.D.
	Sapr... to Sim...
	Sextus (Sextus Pythagoreus?). Sententiae. Sentences of Sextus. Σέξτου γνῶμαι
	Translations -- Continued
4410.S6A2	Latin (Ancient by Rufinus, entitled "Enchiridion" or "Anulus")
4410.S6A21-.S6A69	Other
4410.S6A7-.S6Z	Criticism
	Sibyllina oracula see PA4253.O83
4410.S63	Silenus, of Caleacte (historian) 3rd century B.C. Σιληνός (Table P-PZ38)
	Silentiarius, Paulus
	see Paulus Silentiarius
4410.S65	Simias (Simmias) of Rhodes, 4th-3rd century B.C. Σιμίας (Σιμμίας) (Table P-PZ38)
4410.S66	Simocatta, Theophylactus. Θεοφυλάκτος ὁ Σιμοκάτης (Table P-PZ38)
4410.S67	Simon, of Athens, 5th (?) century B.C. De re equestri. Σίμων. Περὶ ἱππικῆς
	Fragment
4410.S69	Simon, of Athens (Simon Socraticus). Σίμων
	A fictitious person?
	For editions of the Dialexeis see PA3516
	For editions of the spurious dialogues ascribed to him and also to Aeschines Socraticus see PA3824.A4
	Simonides, of Amorgos see PA4410.S4
4411	Simonides, of Ceos, ca. 556-468 B.C. Σιμωνίδης (Table P-PZ37)
4412	Simos... to Soph...
4412.S3	Simplicius, of Cilicia, fl. 533 A.D. Σιμπλίκιος (Table P-PZ38)
	Socrates. Σωκράτης see B310+
4412.S8	Solon, ca. 639-559 B.C. Σόλων (Table P-PZ38)
	Sophocles. Σοφοκλῆς
	Editions
(4413.A1)	Papyri. Manuscripts (Facsimiles)
	see Z114; Z115Z
4413.A2	Collected plays. By date
4413.A3A-.A3Z	Selected plays. School editions. By editor, A-Z
4413.A4A-.A4Z	Selections. Quotations. Passages. By editor, A-Z
4413.A45	Cantica (choral songs)
	Separate plays
	Ajax. Αἴας (Αἴας μαστιγοφόρος)
4413.A5	Editions. By date
4413.A5A-.A5Z	Criticism
	Antigone. Ἀντιγόνη
4413.A7	Editions. By date

	Individual authors to 600 A.D.
	Sophocles. Σοφοκλῆς
	Editions
	Separate plays
	Antigone. Ἀντιγόνη -- Continued
4413.A7A-.A7Z	Criticism
	Electra. Ἠλέκτρα
4413.E5	Editions. By date
4413.E5A-.E5Z	Criticism
	Ichneutae. Ἰχνευταί
4413.I3	Editions. By date
4413.I3A-.I3Z	Criticism
	Inachos. Ἴναχος
4413.I52	Editions. By date
4413.I52A-.I52Z	Criticism
	Oedipus Coloneus. Oedipus at Colonus. Οἰδίπους ἐπὶ Κολωνῷ
4413.O5	Editions. By date
4413.O5A-.O5Z	Criticism
	Oedipus Tyrannus (Oedipus Rex). Οἰδίπους Τύραννος
4413.O7	Editions. By date
4413.O7A-.O7Z	Criticism
	Philoctetes. Φιλοκτήτης
4413.P5	Editions. By date
4413.P5A-.P5Z	Criticism
	Trachiniae. Τραχίνιαι
4413.T7	Editions. By date
4413.T7A-.T7Z	Criticism
4413.Y9	Fragments. By date
	Translations
4413.Z2	Greek, Modern
	Latin
4413.Z5	Ancient
4413.Z7	Modern
4414	English
4414.A1A-.A1Z	Collected plays. By translator, A-Z
4414.A2A-.A2Z	Selected plays. By translator or editor, A-Z
4414.A3	Selections. Passages. Thoughts
4414.A5-.T	Separate plays. By title, A-T
	Subarrange by translator, A-Z, if given, or by date
4414.Z5	Paraphrases, tales, etc.
	For juvenile literature see PZ8.1
4415.A-Z	Other. By language, A-Z
	Subarrange each language like PA4415.F8+
	e.g.
	France
4415.F8	Collected and selected works. By date

PA3050-4505

	Individual authors to 600 A.D.
	Sophocles. Σοφοκλῆς
	Translations
	Other. By language, A-Z
	France -- Continued
4415.F82.A-Z	Individual works, A-Z
	Subarrange by date
4415.7	Imitations. Adaptations. Parodies
4415.8	Illustrations
4415.9	Music
	Interpretation and criticism
4416	Ancient and medieval
4416.A2	Collections of criticisms and allusions
4416.A3	Vita Sophoclis. Σοφοκλέους βίος
(4416.A4A-.A4Z)	Particular authors, A-Z
	Scholia
4416.A5	Collections and selections
(4416.A6)	Particular plays
	see the plays PA4413
4416.A7-.Z3	Particular commentators
4416.Z5	Argumenta. Ὑποθέσεις. By date
	Class here texts only
	For treatises on the Argumenta see PA4417
(4416.Z9)	Criticism of scholia and ancient commentators
	see PA4417
4417	Modern
	General
(4417.A1)	Commentaries (without text)
4417.A2	Early to 1800/50
4417.A5-.Z3	Later, 1800/50-
	Special
(4417.Z5)	History of text. Discussions of manuscripts and editions
(4417.Z7)	Interpretation of detached passages. Variants.
4417.Z9	Minor: Popular addresses, etc.
	Language. Style. Versification
4432	General works
4433	Grammar. Syntax
4434.A-.Z3	Versification
4434.Z8	Glossaries. Indices. Concordances. By date
4435	Sopho... to Stob...
4435.S16	Sophron, 5th century B.C. Σώφρων (Table P-PZ38)
4435.S18	Sophronius, 4th century A.D. Σωφρόνιος (Table P-PZ38)
4435.S19	Sophronius, Saint, Patriarch of Jerusalem, ca. 560-ca. 638 A.D. Σωφρόνιος (Table P-PZ38)

Individual authors to 600 A.D.
　　Sopho... to Stob... -- Continued
　　　Soranus, of Ephesus (physician), 2nd century A.D.
　　　　Σωρανός ὁ Ἐφέσιος
　　　　Cf. PA6220.A9 Aurelianus
　　　　Cf. PA6514.M9 Mustio

4435.S2	Collected works. Selected works. By date
4435.S2A-.S2Z	Separate works. By title, A-Z
4435.S3A-.S3Z	Translations. By language, A-Z, and date
4435.S4	Criticism
4435.S413	Sortes Astrampsychi (Table P-PZ43)
4435.S415	Sosibius Laco (historian), 3rd century B.C. Σωσίβιος ὁ Λάκων (Table P-PZ38)
4435.S42	Sosylus (historian), 3rd century B.C. Σωσύλος (Table P-PZ38)
4435.S43	Sotades, of Maroneia, 3rd century B.C. Σωτάδης Μαρωνείτης (Table P-PZ38)
4435.S45	Soterichus Oasita (epic poet), 3rd century A.D. Σωτήριχος Ὀασίτης (Table P-PZ38)
4435.S47	Sotion, of Alexandria (peripatetic) fl. between 200 and 170 B.C. Σωτίων (Table P-PZ38)
4435.S472	Sotion, of Alexandria (peripatetic) 1st century A.D. Σωτίων (Table P-PZ38)
	Identical with Sotion, teacher of Seneca?
4435.S473	Sotion, of Alexandria (teacher of Seneca ca. 18-20 A.D.). Σωτίων (Table P-PZ38)
	Sozomen, 5th century A.D. Σαλαμάνης Ἑρμείας Σωζόμενος see BR60+ BR1720
(4435.S5)	Speusippus (philosopher), fl. 347-339 B.C. Σπεύσιππος see B626.S2
4435.S6	Stephanus, of Byzantium, 6th century A.D. Stephanos, ho Byzantios. De urbibus. Ethnica. Στέφανος Βυζάντιος. Ἐθνικά
	A geographical dictionary; epitome preserved
4435.S8	Stesichorus, of Himera, ca. 640-ca. 555 B.C. Στησίχορος (Table P-PZ38)
	Stesichorus, the younger, 4th century B.C. Στησίχορος
4436	Stobaeus, Joannes, 5th century A.D. Ἰωάννης ὁ Στοβαῖος
4436.A2	Editions (comprehensive)
	The anthology of Stobaeus (entitled Ἐκλογαὶ ἀποφθέγματα ὑποθῆκαι) was originally one work divided into four books comprising two volumes. In the course of the Middle Ages the two volumes were treated as two separate works entitled respectively: Eclogae physicae et ethicae, and Florilegium
4436.A3	Eclogae physicae et ethicae. Ἐκλογαὶ φυσικαὶ διαλεκτικαὶ καὶ ἠθικαί

	Individual authors to 600 A.D.
	Stobaeus, Joannes, 5th century A.D. Ἰωάννης ὁ Στοβαῖος -- Continued
4436.A4	Florilegium (Sermones; Sententiae). Ἀνθολόγιον (Ἐκλογαὶ ἀποφθεγμάτων (καὶ ὑποθηκῶν))
	Translations
4436.A5	Latin. By date
4436.A51-.A79	Other. By language and date
4436.A8-.Z5	Criticism and interpretation
(4438-4440)	Strabo (Strabo Amasensis) ca. 63 B.C. to ca. 19 A.D. Στράβων
	see G87.S86+
(4438)	Editions
	Geographia lib. XVII. Geography. Γεωγραφικά
(4438.A2)	Editions. By date
(4438.A3)	Selections
(4438.B1-.B17)	Particular books
(4438.P7)	Particular portions
	Including Armenia, Italia, etc.
(4438.Z5)	Fragments (Commentarii historici (Ἱστορικὰ ὑπομνήματα), etc.). By date
	For editions of fragments of a particular book see editions of that book
(4439)	Translations
(4440)	Criticism
4441	Strad.. to Theo...
4441.S5	Straton, of Lampsacus, fl. ca. 287-270 B.C. Στράτων Λαμψακηνός (ὁ Φυσικός) (Table P-PZ38)
	Cf. B626.S5+ Philosophy
	Cf. PA3892.A8 De audibilibus
	Cf. PA3892.C7 De coloribus
4441.S6	Straton, of Sardis, 2nd century A.D. Στράτων ὁ Σαρδιανός (Table P-PZ38)
4441.S68	Synesius (alchemist). Συνέσιος (Table P-PZ38)
	Synesius, of Cyrene, Bishop of Ptolemais, fl. 399-412 A.D. Συνέσιος Κυρηναῖος
4441.S7	Editions. By date
4441.S7A3	Selected works
	Single works
4441.S7A5	Aegyptiae narrationes (Aegyptius sive De providentia). Αἰγύπτιοι λόγοι ἢ Περὶ προνοίας
4441.S7C3	Calvitii encomium. Φαλάκρας ἐγκόμιον
4441.S7C5	Catastasis I-II
	Catastasis (I dicta in maximam barbarorum excursionem). Κατάστασις ῥηθεῖσα ἐπὶ τῇ μεγίστῃ τῶν βαρβάρων ἐφόδῳ

Individual authors to 600 A.D.
　Strad.. to Theo...
　　Synesius, of Cyrene, Bishop of Ptolemais, fl. 399-412 A.D.
　　　Συνέσιος Κυρηναῖος
　　　Single works
　　　　Catastasis I-II -- Continued
　　　　　Catastasis (II Constitutio sive Elogium Anysii).
　　　　　　Κατάστασις
　　　　Cynegetica. Κυνηγετικά
　　　　　Lost

4441.S7D3	De insomniis. Περὶ ἐνυπνίων
4441.S7D4	De dono astrolabii (Sermos ad Paeonium de d.a.). 　Λόγος ὑπὲρ τοῦ δώρου ἀστρολαβίου πρὸς Παιόνιον De providentia see PA4441.S7A5
4441.S7D5	De regno ad Arcadium, imperatorem. Περὶ βασιλείας
4441.S7D6	Dion sive De suo ipsius instituto. Δίων ἢ Περὶ τῆς κατ' 　αὐτὸν διαγωγῆς
4441.S7E6	Epistulae. Ἐπιστολαί 　159 in all; 157-159 considered spurious Homiliae. Ὁμιλίαι 　see class B Hymni. Hymns. Ὕμνοι 　see class B Spurious works see PA4441.S68
4441.S8A-.S8Z	Translations. By language, title (succesive Cutter 　number) and date
4441.S9	Criticism, interpretation, etc. 　For historical treatises see Class DG
4441.S95	Syrianus (Neo-Platonist) 5th century A.D. Συριανός (Table 　P-PZ38 modified)
4441.S95A61- 　.S95A78	Separate works. By title 　e.g. Commentaria in Hermogenem - Cf. PA3998.H9A+ 　　Hermogenes; Commentaria in Metaphysica [Aristotelis] 　　- Cf. PA3893.M5+ Aristoteles. Metaphysica, 　　PA3902.A6+ Commentaries on Aristotles
4441.T2	Teleclides (dramatist) 5th century B.C. Τηλεκλείδης (Table 　P-PZ38)
4441.T23	Telephus, of Pergamon (grammarian) 2nd century A.D. 　Τήλεφος Περγαμηνός (Table P-PZ38)
4441.T25	Teles (Cynic philosopher) fl. ca. 240 B.C. Τέλης (Table P- 　PZ38)
4441.T27	Telesilla (poet) fl. 510 B.C. (?). Τελέσιλλα (Table P-PZ38)
4441.T29	Telestes, of Selinus, 4th century B.C. Τελέστης ὁ 　Σελινούντιος (Table P-PZ38)
4441.T3	Terpander, of Antissa, (Lesbos) fl. 676/3 B.C. Τέρπανδρος 　(Table P-PZ38)

PA3050-4505

	Individual authors to 600 A.D.
	Strad.. to Theo... -- Continued
4441.T33	Teucer (Teukros) of Babylon, astrologer, fl. ca. 100 A.D. Τεῦκρος ὁ Βαβυλώνιος (Table P-PZ38) Identical with Teucer of Cyzicus?
4441.T34	Teucer (Teukros) of Cyzicus, historian, fl. ca. 50 B.C., or 100 A.D.(?). Τεῦκρος ὁ Κυζικηνός (Table P-PZ38) Identical with Teucer of Babylon?
(4441.T4)	Thales, of Miletus, fl. 585 B.C. Θαλῆς ὁ Μιλήσιος see B250
4441.T43	Thaletas, of Gortyn, fl. ca. 665 B.C. Θαλήτας (Table P-PZ38)
4441.T47	Theano (alleged wife of Pythagoras). Θεανώ. Spurious letters
4441.T5	Themistius (sophist) ca. 320-ca. 390 A.D. Orationes. Θεμίστιος. Λόγοι
4441.T53	Themistocles, 5th century B.C. Θεμιστοκλῆς. Spurious letters
	Theocritus. Θεόκριτος Συρακούσιος
4442	Editions
	Class here (1) editions of the Idylls (Εἰδύλλια) and Epigrams (Ἐπιγράμματα), or of the Idylls alone; (2) collections of the Greek bucolic poets: Theocritus, Bion, and Moschus Cf. PA3944.B4 Bion Cf. PA4250.M4 Moschus
(4442.A1)	Manuscripts. Papyri. Facsimiles see Z114; Z115Z
4442.A2	Other. By date
4442.A5	Selected poems (Idylls)
4442.C601-.C630	Particular poems (Idylls)
	Subarrange by idyll number, e.g. PA4442.C601 = Idyll 1; PA4442.C612 = Idyll 12; etc. For criticism of particular poems see PA4444.A2+
4442.E7	Epigrams
4442.Z5	Spurious poems
	Translations
4443.A1	Modern Greek
4443.A2	Latin
4443.A5-Z	Other. By language, A-Z, and translator
	Criticism and interpretation
	Ancient and medieval
4444.A2	Scholia
4444.A3	Scholia recentiora (Moschopulus (Μανουὴλ Μοσχόπουλος), Maximus Planudes (Μάξιμος Πλανούδης), Demetrius Triclinius (Δημήτριος Τρικλίνιος))
4444.A5-.Z3	Modern

	Individual authors to 600 A.D.
	Theocritus. Θεόκριτος Συρακούσιος
	Criticism and interpretation -- Continued
	Language
4444.Z5	General works
4444.Z6	Versification
4444.Z8	Glossaries, etc. By date
4445	Theod... to Theog...
4445.T2	Theodectes, of Phaselis (writer of tragedies and rhetor) fl. 365 B.C. Θεοδέκτης Φασηλίτης (Table P-PZ38)
4445.T21	Theodectes, of Phaselis (the younger) 4th century B.C. Θεοδέκτης Φασηλίτης (Table P-PZ38)
	Son of the preceding, editor of the Theodecteia (?)
4445.T3	Theodoretus, of Alexandria (grammarian, date uncertain). Θεοδώρητος (Table P-PZ38)
	Theodoretus (Theodoret), Bishop of Cyrrhus, ca. 393-457/8 A.D. Θεοδώρητος Κύρου
	see BR60+ BR1720
4445.T33	Theodorus (cyclograph, mythograph) 1st century B.C. Θεόδωρος (Table P-PZ38)
4445.T35	Theodorus, of Byzantium (rhetor) 5th century B.C. Θεόδωρος Βυζάντιος (Table P-PZ38)
4445.T37	Theodorus, of Gadara (grammarian and historian), fl. 1st century B.C. Θεόδωρος Γαδαρεύς (Table P-PZ38)
4445.T4	Theodosius, of Alexandria (grammarian), fl. ca. 400 A.D. Θεοδόσιος (Table P-PZ38 modified)
4445.T4A61-.T4A78	Separate works. By title
	e.g. Canones isagogici de flexione nominum et verborum(Peri grammatikēs. Περί γραμματικῆς (Κανόνες εἰσαγωγικοὶ περὶ κλίσεως ὀνομάτων καὶ ῥημάτων)); De accentibus (Περὶ τόνων (Ἐπιτομὴ τῆς Καθολικῆς προσῳδίας Ἡρωδιανοῦ) in 19 books (the 20th book added in the Paris manuscript, is a forgery by J.Diassorinos). The authorship is doubtful; wrongly ascribed to Arcadius)
4445.T5	Theodosius Tripolita (Theodosius, of Bithynia, astronomer and architect) 1st century B.C. Θεοδόσιος ὁ Τριπολίτης (Table P-PZ38 modified)
4445.T5A61-.T5A78	Separate works. By title
	e.g. De diebus et noctibus (Περὶ νυκτῶν καὶ ἡμερῶν); De habitationibus (Περὶ οἰκήσεων); Sphaericorum lib. III (Σφαιρικά)
4445.T7	Theodotus (Jewish epic poet) fl. ca. 200 B.C. De Judaeis (fragment). Θεόδοτος. Περὶ Ἰουδαίων
4446	Theognis, of Megara, 6th century B.C. Θέογνις Μεγαρεύς (Table P-PZ37)
4447	Theogno... to Theop...

PA3050-4505

Individual authors to 600 A.D.
Theogno... to Theop... -- Continued

4447.T27   Theon. Θέων
                  Treatises on the various authors of this name

4447.T3   Theon (grammarian) 1st century A.D. Θέων (Table P-
                  PZ38)
                  Commentaries on Theocritus, Apollonius, Callimachus, a.o.
                  (lost)

4447.T33   Theon, of Alexandria ("gymnastes") 2nd century A.D. Θέων
                  (Table P-PZ38)

4447.T4   Theon, of Alexandria (mathematician and astronomer) fl.
                  360-372 A.D. Θέων Ἀλεξανδρεύς (Table P-PZ38
                  modified)

4447.T4A61-.T4A78   Separate works. By title
                      e.g. Commentary on Aratus - Cf. PA3873.A7A1+ Aratus, of
                      Soli; Commentary on Euclides Optica; Commentaries
                      on Ptolemaeus, including Almagestum (Εἰς τὴν τοῦ
                      Πτολεμαίου Μεγάλην σύνταξιν ὑπομνήματα) and
                      Tabulae manuales astronomicae (Εἰς τὸν Πτολεμαίου
                      Πρόχειρον κανόνα) - Cf. PA4406.A2 Ptolemaeus,
                      Claudius

4447.T5   Theon, of Smyrna (mathematician and philosopher) 2nd
                  century A.D. Expositio eorum quae in arithmeticis ad
                  Platonis lecturam utilia sint. Expositio rerum
                  mathematicarum ad legendum Platonem utilium. Θέων
                  Σμυρναῖος. Περὶ τῶν κατὰ τὸ μαθηματικὸν χρησίμων εἰς
                  τὴν Πλάτωνος ἀνάγνωσιν

4447.T6   Theon, Aelius, of Alexandria, fl. ca. 100 A.D. (?).
                  Progymnasmata. Θέων Αἴλιος. Προγυμνάσματα

4447.T8   Theophanes, of Mytilene (historian and poet) 1st century
                  B.C. Θεοφάνης (Table P-PZ38)

                  Theophrastus. Θεόφραστος
                  Editions

(4448.A1)   Manuscripts. Papyri. Facsimiles
                      see Z114; Z115Z

4448.A2   Other. By date
                      Separate works

4448.A4   Characteres. Χαρακτῆρες (Ηθικοὶ χαρακτῆρες)

4448.A6   De causis plantarum lib. IX. Περὶ φυτῶν αἰτιῶν

4448.A8   Historia plantarum lib. VI. Inquiry into plants. Περὶ
                          φυτῶν ἱστορίας
                          Fragments and lost works

4448.D13   De amicitia. Περὶ φιλίας
                          Source of Cicero's Laelius de amicitia
                          Cf. PA6304.L2 Cicero

4448.D15   De animalibus. Περὶ ζώων

4448.D2   De dictione. Περὶ λέξεως

PA3050-4505

	Individual authors to 600 A.D.
	Thucydides. History of the Peloponnesian War. Θουκυδίδης. Ξυγγραφή (Ἱστορίαι. Περὶ τοῦ Πελοποννησιακοῦ Πολέμου)
	Editions -- Continued
(4452.A1)	Manuscripts. Papyri. Facsimiles
	see Z114; Z115Z
4452.A2	Other. By date
4452.A3	Selected books (three or more)
	Particular books (one or two)
4452.A31	Book I or I-II
4452.A32	Book II or II-III
4452.A33	Book III or III-IV
4452.A34	Book IV or IV-V
4452.A35	Book V or V-VI
4452.A36	Book VI or VI-VII
4452.A37	Book VII or VII-VIII
4452.A38	Book VIII
	Selected portions
4452.A5	Miscellaneous
4452.A6	Orations
4452.A7	Particular orations arranged alphabetically by orator
4452.A8-Z	Other
	e.g.
4452.P6	Description of the plague
4452.S7	Capture of Sphacteria
	Translations
4453.A1	Greek (Modern). By date
4453.A2	Latin. By date
	Other languages see DF229
	Criticism, interpretation, etc.
4460	Ancient (and medieval Byzantine) writers
4460.A1	Collections of allusions
(4460.A15)	Treatises
	Dionysius, of Halicarnassus
	De Thucydide ad Ae. Tuberonem see PA3966.D6
	Epistola ad Ammaeum II see PA3966.E7
	Scholia
4460.A2	Editions. By date
(4460.A2A-.A2Z)	Criticism
	see PA4461+
	Modern
	Commentaries (without text)
(4461.A1)	General
(4461.A11-.A18)	Particular books
	Treatises
4461.A2	Early (to 1800)

Individual authors to 600 A.D.

Thucydides. History of the Peloponnesian War. Θουκυδίδης.
Ξυγγραφή (Ἱστορίαι. Περὶ τοῦ Πελοποννησιακοῦ
Πολέμου)

Criticism, interpretation, etc.

Modern

Treatises -- Continued

4461.A5-.Z3	1800+
(4461.Z5)	History of text. Discussion of manuscripts and editions
4461.Z8	Interpretation of detached passages. Variants
	Language
4485	General works
4486	Grammar. Syntax
4486.Z8	Glossaries. Indices. By date
4487	Thud... to Timo...
4487.T35	Tiberius (rhetor, of uncertain date). De figuris apud Demosthenem. Τιβέριος. Περὶ τῶν παρὰ Δημοσθένει σχημάτων

PA3050-4505

4487.T38	Timachidas, of Lindos (grammarian) fl. 100 B.C. Τιμαχίδας (Table P-PZ38)
4487.T4	Timaeus, of Locri (Pythagorean). Timaeus Locrus. Τίμαιος ὁ Λοκρός
	No writings; existence of T., believed to be a contemporary of Socrates and Plato, doubted by some authorities
	Cf. B258.T4+ Philosophy
	Cf. PA4279.T9 Plato. Timaeus
4487.T5	Timaeus, of Tauromenium (historian) ca. 346-ca. 250 B.C. Τίμαιος ὁ Ταυρομενίτης (Table P-PZ38)
(4487.T6)	Timaeus, the Sophist, 4th century A.D. Lexicon vocum Platonicarum. Τίμαιος Σοφιστής. Λεξικὸν περὶ τῶν παρὰ Πλάτωνι λέξεων
	see PA4333.A1T5
4487.T63	Timagenes, of Alexandria, (historian) fl. 55-30 B.C. Τιμαγένης (Table P-PZ38)
4487.T7	Timon Phliasius (of Phlius) ca. 320-ca. 230 B.C. Silli. Τίμων ὁ Φλιάσιος. Σίλλοι
	Fragments
	Cf. B626.T5+ Philosophy
	Timotheus, of Gaza fl. ca. 500 A.D. Τιμόθεος Γαζαῖος
4488	Timotheus, of Miletus, fl. 400 B.C. Persae. Τιμόθεος ὁ Μιλήσιος. Πέρσαι
4489	Tin... to Tyr...
	Tryphiodorus (date uncertain). Ilii excidium. Iliou halōsis. Τρυφιόδωρος. Ἰλίου ἅλωσις
4489.T5	Text. By date
4489.T6	Criticism

Individual authors to 600 A.D.
　　Tin... to Tyr... -- Continued
　　　Tryphon, of Alexandria (grammarian) 1st century B.C.
　　　　Τρύφων
　　　Tyrannio (grammarian) fl. between 80 and 50 B.C.
　　　　Τυραννίων ὁ Πρεσβύτερος
　　　Tyrannio (the younger, grammarian), fl. between 50 and 20
　　　　B.C. Τυραννίων ὁ Νεώτερος

4490	Tyrtaeus, 7th century B.C. Τυρταῖος (Table P-PZ37)
4491	Tz... to X...
4491.U6	Ulpianus, of Ascalon (rhetor), 4th century A.D. Οὐλπιανός (Table P-PZ38)
	Urbicius see PA4253.O95
4491.V46	Vettius, Valens. Οὐέττιος Οὐάλης (Table P-PZ38)
	Vindonius, Anatolius see PA3866.A18
4491.X4	Xenocrates, of Aphrodisias, 1st century A.D. De alimento ex aquatilibus. Ξενοκράτης ὁ Ἀφροδισιεύς. Περὶ τῆς ἀπὸ τῶν ἐνύδρων τροφῆς
4491.X6	Xenocrates, of Chalcedon, 4th century B.C. Ξενοκράτης ὁ Χαλκηδόνιος (Table P-PZ38)
	For the spurious Liber de morte see Plato. Spurious works. Axiochus
	Cf. B626.X3+ Philosophy
4492	Xenophanes, of Colophon, 6th century B.C. Ξενοφάνης (Table P-PZ37)
	Cf. B258.X3+ Philosophy
	Xenophon. Ξενοφῶν
	Editions
(4494.A1)	Manuscripts. Papyri. Facsimiles
	see Z114; Z115Z
4494.A2	Other. By date
4494.A23	Selections, chrestomathies, etc.
	For text books see PA260
	Selected works
4494.A25	Three or more. By date
4494.A3	Scripta minor (Opuscula). By date
	Separate works
4494.A35	Agesilaus (De Agesilai Regis Lacedaemonii laudibus). Ἀγησίλαος
	Anabasis (De Cyri (minoris) expeditione lib. VII). Κύρου ἀνάβασις
4494.A4	Editions
4494.A5	School editions, by editor (or date)
(4494.A55)	Selections, chrestomathies
	see PA260
4494.A6	Selected books
	Particular books (one or two)

	Individual authors to 600 A.D.
	Xenophon. Ξενοφῶν
	Editions
	Separate works
	Anabasis (De Cyri (minoris) expeditione lib. VII). Κύρου ἀνάβασις
	Particular books (one or two) -- Continued
4494.A61	I (or I-II). By date
4494.A62	II (or II-III). By date
4494.A63	III (or III-IV). By date
4494.A64	IV (or IV-V). By date
4494.A65	V (or V-VI). By date
4494.A66	VI (or VI-VII). By date
4494.A67	VII. By date
4494.A7	Criticism
4494.A8	Apologia Socratis. Apology. Ἀπολογία Σωκράτους
	Authorship wrongly doubted
	Convivium see PA4494.S8
4494.C4	Cynegeticus (De venatione). On hunting. Κυνηγετικός
	Cyropaedia (De Cyri [maioris] institutione lib. VIII; De Cyri disciplina; Institutio C.). Κύρου παιδεία
4494.C5	Editions. By date
4494.C6	School editions. Selections. Chrestomathies
	Class here abridged text editions only
	For selections, etc. see PA260
	For school editions with complete text see PA4494.C5
4494.C7	Selected books
	Particular books
4494.C71	I (or I-II). By date
4494.C72	II (or II-III). By date
4494.C73	III (or III-IV). By date
4494.C74	IV (or IV-V). By date
4494.C75	V (or V-VI). By date
4494.C76	VI (or VI-VII). By date
4494.C77	VII (or VII-VIII). By date
4494.C78	VIII. By date
4494.C9	Criticism
4494.D3	De re equestri. On horsemanship. Περὶ ἱππικῆς
4494.D4	De re publica Atheniensium. Ἀθηναίων πολιτεία
	Spurious
4494.D5	De re publica Lacedaemoniorum. Constitution of the Lacedaimonians. Λακεδαιμονίων πολιτεία
4494.D8	De vectigalibus (De reditibus). On the revenues. Πόροι ἢ Περὶ προσόδων
	De venatione see PA4494.C4

PA3050-4505

	Individual authors to 600 A.D.
	Xenophon. Ξενοφῶν
	Editions
	Separate works -- Continued
4494.E7	Epistulae. Ἐπιστολαί
	Spurious
	Hellenica (Historia Graeca; De rebus Graecorum lib. VII). Ἑλληνικά
4494.H3	Editions. By date
4494.H5	Criticism
4494.H58	Hercules Prodiceus
	Myth of Hercules at the parting of ways; originally told by Prodicus of Ceus in his Horae, and retold by Xenophon in his Memorabilis II, 1:21-34
4494.H6	Hiero. Hieron. Ἱέρων ἢ Τυραννικός
4494.H8	Hipparchicus (De praefectura sive disciplina equestri). Ἱππαρχικός
	Historia Graeca see PA4494.H3+
	Institutio Cyri see PA4494.C5+
	Memorabilia (Commentariorum de dictis et factis Socratis lib. IV). Ἀπομνημονεύματα Σωκράτους
	Cf. PA4494.H58 Hercules Prodiceus
4494.M3	Editions. By date
4494.M4	School editions. By date
4494.M5	Selected books
4494.M6	Criticism
4494.O4	Oeconomicus. Οἰκονομικός
4494.S8	Symposium (Convivium). Συμπόσιον
	Translations
4495.A1-.A19	Greek (Modern)
4495.A2-.A29	Latin
	English
4495.A3	Collected works. By date
4495.A4A-.A4Z	Selected works ("Opuscula" and others). By translator, A-Z
4495.A5-Z	Particular works, A-Z. By Latin title
4496.A-Z	Other languages, A-Z
4497	Criticism and interpretation
	Language. Style
4499.A-.Z49	General works
4499.Z5	Grammar. Syntax
	Glossaries. Vocabularies. Indices
4499.Z8	General. By date
4499.Z8A-.Z8Z	Particular works, by title and date
4500	Xenophon (Ephes.) to end

	Individual authors to 600 A.D.
	Xenophon (Ephes.) to end -- Continued
	Xenophon, of Ephesus, 2nd (or 3rd?) century A.D.
	Ephesiacorum lib. V. Ephesiaca. Ξενοφῶν Ἐφέσιος.
	Ἐφεσιακά (Κατὰ Ἀνθίαν καὶ Ἀβροκόμην Ἐφεσιακά)
4500.X3	Editions. By date
4500.X4A-.X4Z	Translations. By language, A-Z, and date
4500.X5	Criticism
4500.Z3	Zeno Citiensis (Zeno, of Citium, Stoic) ca. 336-ca. 264 B.C.
	Ζήνων ὁ Κιτιεύς (Table P-PZ38)
	Cf. B626.Z2+ Philosophy
4500.Z41	Zeno Citiensis (the younger) rhetor, fl. 160 A.D. Ζήνων
	(Table P-PZ38)
4500.Z43	Zeno Eleates (Z., of Elea) fl. 464-460 B.C. Ζήνων ὁ
	Ἐλεάτης (Table P-PZ38)
	Cf. B196 Eleatics
	Cf. B258.Z3+ Greek philosophers
4500.Z45	Zeno, of Sidon (Epicurean) b. ca. 150 B.C. Ζήνων ὁ
	Σιδώνιος (Table P-PZ38)
4500.Z47	Zeno, of Tarsus (Stoic) fl. ca. 208 B.C. Ζήνων ὁ Ταρσεύς
	(Table P-PZ38)
	Cf. B626.Z4+ Philosophy
4500.Z5	Zenobius (sophist) 2nd century B.C. Compendium
	proverbiorum ex Tarrhaeo et Didymo. Ζηνόβιος.
	Ἐπιτομὴ τοῦ Ταρραίου καὶ Διδύμου παροιμιῶν
	Cf. PA3965.D17 Didymus Chalcenterus
	Cf. PA4240.L16 Lucillus Tarrhaeus
4500.Z53	Zenodorus (grammarian of uncertain date). Ζηνόδωρος
	(Table P-PZ38)
4500.Z54	Zenodorus (mathematician) fl. ca. 260 B.C. Ζηνόδωρος
	(Table P-PZ38)
4500.Z55	Zenodotus, of Ephesus, d. ca. 260 B.C. Ζηνόδοτος ὁ
	Ἐφέσιος (Table P-PZ38)
	For treatises on the Homeric studies of Zenodotus see
	PA4037
4500.Z56	Zenodotus Mallotes (Z., of Mallos) 2nd century B.C.
	Ζηνόδοτος ὁ Μαλλώτης (Table P-PZ38)
4500.Z57	Zoilus, of Amphipolis (sophist and historian) 5th to 4th
	century B.C. Ζωΐλος ὁ Ἀμφιπολίτης (Table P-PZ38
	modified)
4500.Z57A61- .Z57A78	Separate works. By title
	e.g. Homeromastix. Ὁμηρομάστιξ (Lost)
(4500.Z59)	Zoroaster. Ζωροάστρης
	see PA4253.O85

PA3050-4505

	Individual authors to 600 A.D.
	Xenophon (Ephes.) to end -- Continued
4500.Z6	Zosimus (historian, "comes, exadvocatus fisci") 5th century A.D. Historia nova. Ζώσιμος (κόμης καὶ ἀποφισκοσυνήγορος). Νέα ἱστορία
	Some authorities identify the historian with Zosimus, of Gaza
4500.Z63	Zosimus, of Ascalon (sophist) fl. between 491 and 518 A.D. Ζώσιμος Ἀσκαλωνίτης (Table P-PZ38)
4500.Z65	Zosimus, of Gaza (sophist) d. between 473 and 491 A.D. Ζώσιμος Γαζαῖος (Table P-PZ38)
	Cf. PA4500.Z6 Zosimus the historian
4500.Z8	Zosimus, of Panopolis (alchemist) 3rd or 4th century A.D. Ζώσιμος Πανοπολίτης
	Cf. PA4253.O33 Olympiodorus. Commentary on Zosimus of Panopolis
	Medieval and modern authors writing in Classical Greek
4505	Individual authors, A-Z
4505.G76	Groningen, Bernhard Abraham van (Table P-PZ40)

	Byzantine and modern Greek literature
	History and criticism
5000	Periodicals and societies
	Collections
5003	Several authors
5005	Individual authors
5010	General works
5015	General special
5020	Outlines, tables, etc.
5025	Addresses, essays, lectures
5030.A-Z	Special topics, A-Z
5030.C57	Christianity
5030.H44	Hell
5035.A-Z	Special countries, A-Z
5040	Biography (Collective)
	Collections
5050	Periodicals
	General, including vernacular literature
5070	Early to 1800
5075	1801-
	Special periods
	Medieval. Byzantine
	History and criticism
5101	Periodicals and societies
	Collections
5103	Several authors
5105	Individual authors
5107	Study and teaching
5109.A-Z	Biography of critics, historians, etc., A-Z
5110	General works
5115	General special
5120	Outlines, tables, etc.
5125	Addresses, essays, lectures
5130.A-Z	Special topics, A-Z
5130.L3	Labor
5130.M55	Mimesis
5130.M96	Mythology
5130.S65	Spirituality
5135.A-Z	Special regions or countries, A-Z
5140	Biography (Collective)
	Special forms
	Poetry
5150	General works
5151	Historical
5152	Political
5153	Religious
5154	Epic

PA5000-5660

251

	Special periods
	Medieval. Byzantine
	History and criticism
	Special forms
	Poetry -- Continued
5155	Popular. Folk literature
	Drama
5160	General works
5163	Religious
5165	Prose. Fiction. Romances
5166	Letters
5167	Wit. Humor. Satire
	Collections
	General
5170	Early to 1800
5171	1801-
5172	Minor
	Translations, by language
5173	English
5174.A-Z	Other, A-Z
	Special subjects
5175	Religion and magic
5176.A-Z	Other, A-Z
	Special countries or regions
5178	Crete
5179.A-Z	Other, A-Z
	Special forms, including translations
	Poetry
5180	General
5181	Anacreontic
5183	Religious
5185	Popular. Folk songs, ballads, etc.
5187	School and college verse
	Translations
5188.9	Polyglot
5189.A-Z	By language, A-Z
	Drama
5190	General
5193	Religious
5194.A-Z	Translations. By language, A-Z
	Prose. Romance. Fiction
5195	General
5196.A-Z	Translations. By language, A-Z
	Wit. Humor. Satire
5197	General
5198.A-Z	Translations. By language, A-Z

PA5000-5660

	Special periods
	Modern
	History and criticism
	Special forms
	Poetry -- Continued
5251	Historical
5252	Political
5253	Religious
5254	Epic
5255	Popular. Folk literature
	Drama
5260	General works
5263	Religious
5265	Prose. Fiction. Romances
5266	Letters
5267	Wit. Humor. Satire
5269	Juvenile literature (General)
	For special genres see the genre
	Collections
	General
5270	Early to 1800
5271	1801-
5272	Minor
	Translations, by language
5273	English
5274.A-Z	Other, A-Z
	Special subjects
5275	Religion and magic
5276.A-Z	Other, A-Z
	Special countries or regions
5278	Crete
5279.A-Z	Other, A-Z
	Special forms, including translations
	Poetry
5280	General
5281	Anacreontic
5283	Religious
5285	Popular. Folk songs, ballads, etc.
5287	School and college verse
	Translations
5288.9	Polyglot
5289.A-Z	By language, A-Z
	Drama
5290	General
5293	Religious
5294.A-Z	Translations. By language, A-Z
	Prose. Romance. Fiction

	Special periods
	Modern
	Special forms, including translations
	Prose. Romance. Fiction -- Continued
5295	General
5296.A-Z	Translations. By language, A-Z
	Wit. Humor. Satire
5297	General
5298.A-Z	Translations. By language, A-Z
	Individual authors or works
	Byzantine to 1600
	Subarrange each author or work by Tables P-PZ39, P-PZ40, or P-PZ43, unless otherwise specified
5301	A-Bar
5301.A363	Acominatus, Nicetas, Choniates, ca. 1140-1213. Νικήτας Ἀκομινᾶτος (Χωνιάτης) (Table P-PZ40)
5301.A45	Akropolitēs, Kōnstantinos, b. ca. 1250/55-ca. 1321. Κωνσταντῖνος Ἀκροπολίτης (Table P-PZ40)
(5301.A57-.A573)	Aphēgēsis Livistrou kai Rodamnēs. Αφήγησις Λιβίστρου καὶ Ροδάμνης
	see PA5319.L58+
5301.A6	Apostolios, Michaēl, ca. 1422-ca. 1480. Michael Apostolius. Μιχαὴλ Ἀποστόλης (Ἀποστόλιος) (Table P-PZ40)
5302	Barlaam and Joasaph. Βαρλαὰμ καὶ Ἰωάσαφ (Table P-PZ41)
5303	Bar-Cho
5303.B443	Belthandros kai Chrysantza. Βέλθανδρος καὶ Χρυσάντζα
5303.B45	Bembo, Pietro, 1740-1547. Πέτρος Μπέμπο
5303.B47	Bergadēs, 16th cent. Βεργαδῆς (Μπεργαδῆς)
5303.B5	Bidpai. Μπιντπάϋ
	Greek translation of the Arabic version, Kalilah wa-Dimnah
5303.C3	Canabutzes, Joannes. Ἰωάννης Καναβούτζης (Table P-PZ40)
5303.C35	Catonis disticha. Κάτωνος Ῥωμαίου γνῶμαι παραινετικαὶ δίστιχοι
5305	Choumnos, Geōrgios, ca. 1500. Γεώργιος Χοῦμνος (Table P-PZ37)
5310	Cho-Ety
	Choniates, Nicetas, ca. 1140-1213 see PA5301.A363
5310.C2	Christopherson, John, d. 1558. Ἰωάννης Χριστοφερσῶνος (Table P-PZ40)
5310.C3	Christus patiens (Christos paschōn). Χριστὸς πάσχων
5310.C35	Chronicle of Morea (Poem). Χρονικὸν τοῦ Μορέως
5310.C6	Cosmas, Saint (Legend). Βίος καὶ πολιτεία καὶ θαύματα τῶν ἁγίων ἀναργύρων Κοσμᾶ καὶ Δαμιανοῦ

PA5000-5660

Individual authors or works
Byzantine to 1600
Cho-Ety -- Continued

5310.D37	Dellaportas, Leonardos, 1330-1419 or 20. Λεονάρδος Ντελλαπόρτας (Table P-PZ40)
5310.D4	Demetrius Cydones, ca. 1324-ca. 1398. Δημήτριος ὁ Κυδώνης (Table P-PZ40)
5310.D45	Devarius, Matthaeus, b. 1505? Ματθαῖος Δεβαρῆς (Table P-PZ40)
5310.D46-.D463	Diēgēsis Alexandrou meta Semiramēs Vasilissas Syrias. Διήγησις Ἀλεξάνδρου μετὰ Σεμίραμης Βασίλισσας Συρίας (Table P-PZ43)
5310.D47	Diēgēsis paidiophrastos peri tōn tetrapodōn zōōn. Διήγησις παιδιόφραστος περὶ τῶν τετραπόδων ζώων (Table P-PZ43)
5310.D48	Diēgēsis tou Belisariou. Διήγησις τοῦ Βελισαρίου (Διήγησις ὡραιοτάτη τοῦ θαυμαστοῦ ἐκείνου ἀνδρὸς τοῦ λεγομένου Βελισαρίου)
5310.D5	Digenes Acritas (Epic poem). Digenis Akritas. Διγενὴς Ἀκρίτας
	Eadmer, d. 1124?
	see BX4705.E15
5310.E6	Ēmperiou historia. Ἠμπερίου ἱστορία (Ἰμπέριος καὶ Μαργαρώνα)
	Etymologica. Ἐτυμολογικά
5311	General. History and criticism
5312.E7	Etymologicum Gudianum. Γουδιανὸν ἐτυμολογικόν
5313	Etymologicum magnum. Ἐτυμολογικὸν μέγα
	Suda lexicon see PA5365
5314	Ety-Eus
5314.E8	Eustathius, Archbishop of Thessalonica, d. ca. 1194. Εὐστάθιος ὁ Θεσσαλονίκης (Table P-PZ40)
	Cf. PA4035.E8 Homer
5315	Eustathius Macrembolites, 12th cent. Εὐστάθιος Μακρεμβολίτης (Table P-PZ39)
5317	Eus-He
5317.F44	Filelfo, Francesco, 1398-1481. Φραγκῖσκος Φίλελφος
5317.F5	Floire and Blancheflor. Διήγησις ἐξαίρετος, ἐρωτικὴ καὶ ξένη Φλωρίου τοῦ πανευτυχοῦς καὶ κόρης Πλάτζια Φλώρης
5317.G27	Gabras, Michael, ca. 1290-ca. 1350. Μιχαὴλ Γαβρᾶς (Table P-PZ40)
5317.G3	Gazēs, Theodōros, ca. 1400-ca. 1475. Θεόδωρος Γαζῆς (Table P-PZ40)
5317.G4	Georgius Pisida, fl. 610-641. George the Pisidian. Γεώργιος ὁ Πισίδης (Table P-PZ40)

Individual authors or works
    Byzantine to 1600
        Eus-He -- Continued

5317.G43	Georgius, Trapezuntius, 1396-1486. George of Trebizond. Γεώργιος Τραπεζούντιος (Table P-PZ40)
5317.G56	Giorgio, di Gallipoli, 13th cent. Γεώργιος ὁ χαρτοφύλαξ Καλλιπόλεως (Table P-PZ40)
5317.G7	Gregoras, Nicephorus, 1295-1359 or 60. Νικηφόρος Γρηγορᾶς (Table P-PZ38)
5317.H35	Halōsis Kōnstantinoupoleōs. Ἄλωσις Κωνστανινουπόλεως (Table P-PZ43)
5318	Heron, of Byzantium. Ἥρων

          A writer of the 10th century who combined excerpts from poliorcetic writers with the "Geodaesia" (in the main an epitome of the Dioptera of Hero of Alexandria; 1-16 identical with Geometria 5-31)
          Cf. PA3999.A4 Dioptera
          Cf. PA3999.A45 Geometria

5319	He-Phe
5319.H57	Historia tou Ptōcholeontos. Ἱστορία τοῦ Πτωχολέοντος
5319.I25	Iakovos, Monachos. Ἰάκωβος, Μοναχός (Table P-PZ40)
5319.I6	Iōannēs Geōmetrēs. Ἰωάννης Γεωμέτρης (Table P-PZ40)
(5319.J6)	Joannes Lydus
	see PA4221.J4
5319.K26	Kalliklēs, Nikolaos. Νικόλαος ὁ Καλλικλῆς (Table P-PZ38)
5319.K27	Kallimachos kai Chrysorroē. Καλλίμαχος καὶ Χρυσορρόη (Table P-PZ40)
5319.K295	Kassianē, b. ca. 810. Κασσιανή (Table P-PZ40)
5319.K3	Katrares, Johannes, 14th cent. Ἰωάννης Κατράρης (Table P-PZ40)
5319.K64	Komnēnos, Alexios, 1106-1142. Ἀλέξιος Κομνηνός (Table P-PZ40)
5319.L46	Leo VI, Emperor of the East, 866-912. Λέων ΣΤ′ ὁ Σοφός, Αὐτοκράτωρ τοῦ Βυζαντίου (Table P-PZ40)
5319.L48	Leōn Choirosphaktēs, d. ca. 919. Λέων Χοιροσφάκτης (Table P-PZ40)
5319.L58-.L583	Libistros kai Rhodamnē. Λιβίστρος καὶ Ροδάμνη (Table P-PZ43)
5319.M3	Manasses, Constantine, d. 1187. Κωνσταντῖνος Μανασσῆς (Table P-PZ40)
5319.M36-.M363	Melissa (Byzantine prose work) (Table P-PZ43)
5319.M37	Melitēniōtēs, Theodōros, ca. 1320-1393. Θεόδωρος Μελιτηνιώτης (Table P-PZ40)
5319.M5	Michaēl, ho Italikos, Bishop of Philippopolis. Μιχαὴλ ὁ Ἰταλικός (Table P-PZ40)
5319.M67	Moschos, Dēmētrios. Δημήτριος Μόσχος (Table P-PZ40)
5319.N46	Nikēphoros ho Vasilakēs, 12th cent. Νικηφόρος ὁ Βασιλάκης (Table P-PZ40)

PA5000-5660

Individual authors or works
Byzantine to 1600
He-Phe -- Continued

5319.N5	Nikētas, ho Eugeneianos, 12th cent. Νικήτας ὁ Εὐγενειανός (Table P-PZ40)
5319.P28	Palaia kai Nea Diathēkē. Παλαιὰ καὶ Νέα Διαθήκη (Table P-PZ43)
5319.P3	Paulus Aegineta, 7th cent. Παῦλος ὁ Αἰγινήτης (Table P-PZ40)
5319.P38	Penthos thanatou, zōēs mataion kai pros Theon epistrophē. Πένθος θανάτου, ζωῆς μάταιον καὶ πρὸς Θεὸν ἐπιστροφή
5319.P5	Phalieros, Marinos. Μαρῖνος Φαλιέρος (Table P-PZ40)
5325	Phe-Pho
5325.P2	Philes, Manuel, ca. 1275-ca. 1345. Μανουὴλ Φιλῆς (Table P-PZ40)
5325.P5	Philippus Solitarius, fl. 1095. Φίλιππος ὁ Σολιτάριος (Table P-PZ40)
5330	Photius I, Saint, Patriarch of Constantinople, ca. 820-ca. 891. Φώτιος Α΄, Πατριάρχης Κωνσταντινουπόλεως (Table P-PZ39)
5333	Pho-Pic
5335	Pico della Mirandola, Giovanni, 1463-1494. Ἰωάννης Πίκο-ντέλα-Μιράντολα (Table P-PZ39)
5337	Pic-Pro
5337.P53	Pikatoros, Iōannēs, 16th cent. Ιωάννης Πικατόρος (Table P-PZ40)
5337.P54	Planudes, Maximus, ca. 1260-ca. 1310. Μάξιμος Πλανούδης (Table P-PZ40)
5337.P56	Plēthōn, Geōrgios Gemistos, 15th cent. George Gemistus Plethon. Γεώργιος Γεμιστὸς Πλήθων (Table P-PZ40)
5337.P64	Poliziano, Angelo, 1454-1494. Ἄγγελος Πολιτιανός (Table P-PZ40)
5340	Procopius, of Caesarea. Προκόπιος Καισαρεύς (Table P-PZ39) Byzantine historian Cf. DF505.7.P7 Byzantine historiography
5343	Proc-Prod
5345	Prodromus, Theodore, 12th cent. Θεόδωρος Πρόδρομος (Table P-PZ39)
5350	Prod-Pse
5355	Psellus, Michael, 11th cent. Μιχαὴλ Ψελλός (Table P-PZ39) Cf. B765.P8+ Philosophy
5360	Pse-Sui
5360.S72	Staphidakēs. Σταφιδάκης (Table P-PZ40)

Individual authors or works
　　Byzantine to 1600
　　　Pse-Sui -- Continued
　　　　Stephanitēs kai Ichnēlatēs. Στεφανίτης καὶ Ἰχνηλάτης
　　　　　(Greek version of Bidpai) see PA5303.B5
5360.S76　　　Stilbes, Constantine, 12th/13th cent. Κωνσταντῖνος
　　　　　Στιλβῆς (Table P-PZ40)
5365　　　Suda lexicon (Suidas). Σοῦδα (Σουΐδας) (Table P-PZ39)
5367　　　Sui-Theo
5367.S9　　　Symeon, 12th cent. Συμεών (Table P-PZ40)
5370　　　Theodorus Pediasimus, 14th cent. Θεόδωρος Πεδιάσιμος
　　　　　(Table P-PZ39)
5375　　　Theo-Tho
5375.T4　　　Theodorus Studita, Saint, 759?-826. Theodore Studites.
　　　　　Θεόδωρος ὁ Στουδίτης (Table P-PZ40)
5375.T43　　　Theodosius, Diaconus. Θεοδόσιος ὁ Διάκονος (Table P-
　　　　　PZ40)
5380　　　Thomas Magister, fl. 1310-1327. Thōmas Magistros.
　　　　　Θωμᾶς Μάγιστρος (Table P-PZ39)
5385　　　Tho-Tz
5385.T54　　　Timarion. Τιμάριον ἢ περὶ τῶν κατ' αὐτὸν παθημάτων
　　　　　(Table P-PZ43)
5385.T64　　　Tou Armourē. Τοῦ Ἀρμούρη (Table P-PZ43)
5390　　　Tzetzes, Joannes, 12th cent. Ἰωάννης Τζέτζης (Table P-
　　　　　PZ39)
　　　　　Cf. PA4035.T9 Homer
5395　　　Tz-Z
　　Modern, 1600-1960
　　　Subarrange by Table P-PZ40, unless otherwise specified
5609.A-Z　　Anonymous works. By title, A-Z
5609.D35　　　David. Δαβίδ (Table P-PZ43)
　　　　Erōtokritos (Ἐρωτόκριτος) see PA5610.K6
5609.N43　　　Nea historia Athesthē Kythēreou. Νέα ἱστορία Ἀθέσθη
　　　　　Κυθηρέου (Table P-PZ43)
5609.T69　　　Tragedia tou Hagiou Dēmētriou. Τραγέδια τοῦ Ἁγίου
　　　　　Δημητρίου (Table P-PZ43)
5609.T72　　　Tragoudi tēs Hagia Sophias. Τραγοῦδι τῆς Ἁγιᾶ Σοφιᾶς
　　　　　(Table P-PZ43)
5610.A-Z　　Individual authors, A-Z
5610.A3　　　Achelēs, Antōnios, 16th cent. Αντώνιος Αχέλης (Table P-
　　　　　PZ40)
　　　　Alepoudelēs, Odysseus, 1911-1996. Οδυσσέας
　　　　　Αλεπουδέλης see PA5610.E43
5610.A582　　　Alkaios, Theodōros, 1780-1833. Θεόδωρος Αλκαίος
　　　　　(Table P-PZ40)
5610.A624　　　Antōniadēs, Antōnios, 1836-1905. Αντώνιος Αντωνιάδης
　　　　　(Table P-PZ40)

PA5000-5660

Individual authors or works
Modern, 1600-1960
Individual authors, A-Z -- Continued

5610.A64	Aphthonidēs, Germanos, d. 1895. Γερμανός Αφθονίδης (Table P-PZ40)
	Apostolidēs, Petros, 1866-1937 see PA5610.N57
	Arcas, Pol. see PA5610.D4
	Augerēs, Markos, 1884-1973. Μάρκος Αυγέρης see PA5610.P3467
5610.B27	Balaōritēs, Aristotelēs, 1824-1879. Αριστοτέλης Βαλαωρίτης (Table P-PZ40)
	Barlas, Phaidros, 1925- see PA5610.M66
5610.B3	Barnalēs, Kōstas, 1884-1974. Κώστας Βάρναλης (Table P-PZ40)
	Bastias, Kōstēs, 1901-1972 see PA5610.M67
	Beratēs, Giannēs, 1904-1968 see PA5610.M7
5610.B4	Bernardakēs, Dēmētrios N. Dēmētrios N. Vernardakēs. Δημήτριος Νικολάου Βερναρδάκης (Table P-PZ40)
5610.B46	Bikelas, Dēmētrios, 1835-1908. Δημήτριος Βικέλας (Table P-PZ40)
5610.B49	Bizyēnos, Geōrgios, 1848-1896. Γεώργιος Βιζυηνός (Table P-PZ40)
	Boumē Papa, Rita, 1906-1984 see PA5610.M73
5610.B65	Bounialēs, Marinos Tzane. Μαρίνος Τζάνε Μπουνιαλής (Table P-PZ40)
5610.B7	Brettakos, Nikēphoros, 1911-1991. Νικηφόρος Βρεττάκος (Table P-PZ40)
	Cavafy, Constantine, 1863-1933 see PA5610.K2
5610.C438	Chatzopoulos, Kōnstantinos, 1868-1920. Kōstantinos Chatzopoulos. Κωσταντίνος (Κωνσταντίνος, Κώστας) Χατζόπουλος (Table P-PZ40)
5610.C45	Chortatzēs, Geōrgios, fl. 1600. Γεώργιος Χορτάτζης (Table P-PZ40)
5610.C4523	Chrēstovasilēs, Chrēstos, 1861-1937. Χρήστος Χρηστοβασίλης (Table P-PZ40)
5610.D27	Dapontes, Kōnstantinos, 1713 or 14-1784. Κωνσταντίνος Δαπόντες (Table P-PZ40)
5610.D36	Delēs, Geōrgios, 1870-1954. Γεώργιος Δελής (Table P-PZ40)
5610.D39	Demeter, Dimitrija, 1811-1872. Dimitrije Demeter (Table P-PZ40)
5610.D4	Dēmētrakopoulos, Polybios, 1864-1922. Polyvios Dēmētrakopoulos. Πολύβιος Δημητρακόπουλος (Table P-PZ40)
5610.D527	Diakrousēs, Anthimos, fl. 1645-1667. Άνθιμος Διακρούσης (Table P-PZ40)

Individual authors or works
Modern, 1600-1960
Individual authors, A-Z -- Continued

5610.D598   Doxas, Angelos, 1900-1985. Άγγελος Δόξας (Table P-
                 PZ40)
                 Drakoulidēs, N.N., (Nikolaos Nikolaou). Νικόλαος
                 Νικολάου Δρακουλίδης see PA5610.D598
5610.D68   Drakopoulou, Theōnē, 1881-1968. Θεώνη Δρακοπούλου
                 (Table P-PZ40)
5610.D69   Drimytikos, Nikolaos, 17th cent. Νικόλαος Δριμυτικός
                 (Table P-PZ40)
5610.D7   Drosinēs, Geōrgios, 1859-1951. Γεώργιος Δροσίνης
                 (Table P-PZ40)
5610.E43   Elytēs, Odysseas, 1911-1996. Οδυσσέας Ελύτης (Table
                 P-PZ40)
                 Epachtitēs, Giannos, 1867-1945. Γιάννος Επαχτίτης see
                 PA5610.V58
5610.E6   Ephtaliōtēs, Argyrēs, 1849-1923. Αργύρης Εφταλιώτης
                 (Table P-PZ40)
                 Erōtokritos. Ερωτόκριτος see PA5610.K6
5610.G38   Gazēs, Geōrgios, 1795-1855. Γεώργιος Γαζής (Table P-
                 PZ40)
5610.G77   Gryparēs, Iōannēs N., 1870-1942. Ιωάννης Γρυπάρης
                 (Table P-PZ40)
5610.H65   Horton, George, 1860-1942. Τζωρτζ Χόρτον (Γεώργιος
                 Χόρτων) (Table P-PZ40)
5610.I63   Iōannou, Manthos, 1665-1748. Μάνθος Ιωάννου (Table
                 P-PZ40)
5610.K2   Kabaphēs, Kōnstantinos Petrou, 1863-1933.
                 Kōnstantinos Petrou Kavaphēs. Κωνσταντίνος
                 Πέτρου Καβάφης (Table P-PZ40)
5610.K22   Kabbadias, Nikos, 1910-1975. Νίκος Καββαδίας (Table
                 P-PZ40)
5610.K226   Kairē, Euanthia N., 1799-1866. Ευανθία Ν. Καΐρη (Table
                 P-PZ40)
5610.K237   Kalligas, Paulos, 1814-1896. Παύλος Καλλιγάς (Table P-
                 PZ40)
5610.K24   Kalvos, Andreas, 1792-1867. Ανδρέας Κάλβος (Table P-
                 PZ40)
5610.K2515   Kampas, N.G. (Nikos G.), 1857-1932. Νίκος Γ. Καμπάς
                 (Table P-PZ40)
5610.K2517   Kampouroglous, Dēmētrios Grēgoriou, 1852-1942.
                 Δημήτριος Γρηγορίου Καμπούρογλους (Table P-
                 PZ40)
5610.K252   Kampysēs, Giannēs, 1872-1901. Γιάννης Καμπύσης
                 (Table P-PZ40)

Individual authors or works
Modern, 1600-1960
Individual authors, A-Z -- Continued

5610.K3	Karkavitsas, Andreas, 1866-1923. Ανδρέας Καρκαβίτσας (Table P-PZ40)
	Kavvadias, Nikos, 1910-1975 see PA5610.K22
5610.K39	Kazantzakēs, Nikos, 1883-1957. Νίκος Καζαντζάκης (Table P-PZ40)
5610.K523	Kondylakēs, Iōannēs, 1861-1920. Ιωάννης Κονδυλάκης (Table P-PZ40)
5610.K55	Koraēs, Adamantios, 1748-1833. Αδαμάντιος Κοραής (Table P-PZ40)
5610.K6	Kornaros, BitzentzosVitzentzos. Βιτσέντζος (Βιτζέντζος) Κορνάρος (Table P-PZ38) Supposed author of Erōtokritos (Ἐρωτόκριτος)
5610.K7	Koromēlas, Dēmētrios A., 1850-1898. Δημήτριος Ανδρέου Κορομηλάς (Table P-PZ40)
5610.K8	Koumanoudēs, Stephanos Ath., 1818-1899. Στέφανος Αθ. Κουμανούδης (Table P-PZ40)
5610.K89	Kyriakos, Aristeidēs N., 1864-1919. Αριστείδης Ν. Κυριάκος (Table P-PZ40)
5610.L23	Laganēs, Iōannēs, 19th cent. Ιωάννης Λαγάνης (Table P-PZ40)
5610.L36	Laskaratos, Andreas, 1811-1901. Ανδρέας Λασκαράτος (Table P-PZ40)
5610.L374	Lassanēs, Geōrgios, 1796-1870. Γεώργιος Λασσάνης (Table P-PZ40)
5610.L9	Lymperakē, Margarita. Μαργαριτα Λυμπερακη (Table P-PZ40)
	Lysanios, Gorgidas, 1796-1870. Γοργίδας Λυσάνιος see PA5610.L374
5610.M25	Mabilēs, Lorentsos, 1860-1912. Λορέντζος (Λορέντσος) Μαβίλης (Table P-PZ40)
5610.M2577	Malakasēs, Miltiadēs, 1869-1943. Μιλτιάδης Μαλακάσης (Table P-PZ40)
5610.M2838	Martinengou, Elisavet Moutza, 1801-1832. Ελισάβετ Μούτζα Μαρτινέγκου (Table P-PZ40)
5610.M285	Matesis, Antōnios, 1794-1874. Αντώνιος Μάτεσις (Table P-PZ40)
	Mavilēs, Lorentsos, 1860-1912 see PA5610.M25
	Melissanthē. Μελισσάνθη see PA5610.S54
5610.M35	Mellos, Élias, 1904-1973. Ηλίας Μέλλος (Table P-PZ40)
5610.M4	Ménage, Gilles, 1613-1692. Ζίλ Μενάζ (Table P-PZ40)
5610.M42	Mēnas, Minōïdēs, 1790-1860. C. Minoïde Mynas. Κωνσταντίνος Μινωΐδης Μηνάς (Table P-PZ40)
5610.M43	Mētsakēs, Michaēl, 1868-1916. Μητσακης, Μιχαηλ (Table P-PZ40)

Individual authors or works
Modern, 1600-1960
Individual authors, A-Z -- Continued

5610.M586	Montseleze, Theodōros. Θεόδωρος Μοντσελέζε (Table P-PZ40)
5610.M588	Mōraitidēs, Alexandros, 1850-1929. Αλέξανδρος Μωραΐτίδης (Table P-PZ38)
5610.M594	Moréas, Jean, 1856-1910. Ζαν Μορεάς (Table P-PZ40)
5610.M66	Mparlas, Phaidros, 1925- . Φαίδρος Μπαρλάς (Table P-PZ40)
5610.M67	Mpastias, Kōstēs Iōannou, 1901-1972. Κωστής Μπαστιάς (Table P-PZ40)
5610.M7	Mperatēs, Giannes, 1904-1968. Γιάννης Μπεράτης (Table P-PZ40)
5610.M73	Mpoumē Pappa, Rita, 1906-1984. Ρίτα Μπούμη Παππά (Table P-PZ40)
5610.M9	Myrivēlēs, Stratēs, 1892-1969. Στράτης Μυριβήλης (Table P-PZ40)
	Myrtiōtissa, 1881-1968. Μυρτιώτισσα see PA5610.D68
5610.N39	Nēphakēs, Nikētas, 1748-ca. 1818. Νικήτας Νηφάκης (Νηφάκος) (Table P-PZ40)
5610.N54	Nikolaidēs, V., d. 1903. Βασίλειος-Μιλτιάδης Νικολαΐδης (Table P-PZ40)
5610.N57	Nirvanas, Paulos. Παύλος Νιρβάνας (Table P-PZ40)
5610.O6	Orphanidēs, Theodōros Geōrgios, 1817-1886. Θεόδωρος Γεώργιος Ορφανίδης (Table P-PZ40)
5610.P27	Palaiologos, Grēgorios. Γρηγόριος Παλαιολόγος (Table P-PZ40)
5610.P3	Palamas, Kōstēs, 1859-1943. Κωστής Παλαμάς (Table P-PZ40)
5610.P3423	Panas, Panagiōtēs, 1832-1896. Παναγιώτης Πανάς (Table P-PZ40)
	Papadiamandopoulos, Ioannis, 1856-1910. Ιωάννης Παπαδιαμαντόπουλος see PA5610.M594
5610.P345	Papadiamantēs, Alexandros, 1851-1911. Αλέξανδρος Παπαδιαμάντης (Table P-PZ40)
5610.P3467	Papadopoulos, Geōrgios, 1884-1973. Γεώργιος Παπαδόπουλος (Table P-PZ40)
5610.P3468	Papadopoulou, Alexandra, 1867-1906. Αλεξάνδρα Παπαδοπούλου (Table P-PZ40)
5610.P35	Papastamou, Olga. Όλγα Παπαστάμου (Table P-PZ40)
5610.P417	Petimezas-Lauras, N. (Nikolaos), 1873-1952. Νικόλαος Πετιμεζάς-Λαύρας (Table P-PZ40)
5610.P5	Pieridēs, Th., 1908-1968. Θοδόσης Πιερίδης (Table P-PZ40)
5610.P513	Pikkolos, Nikolaos Savva, 1792-1866. Νικόλαος Σάββα Πίκκολος (Table P-PZ40)

PA5000-5660

Individual authors or works
Modern, 1600-1960
Individual authors, A-Z -- Continued

5610.P518	Pitzipios, Iakōvos Geōrgios, 1802-1876. Ιάκωβος Γεώργιος Πιτζίπιος (Πιτσίπιος) (Table P-PZ40)
	Politēs, Kosmas, 1893-1974. Κοσμάς Πολίτης see PA5610.T24
5610.P685	Provelengios, Aristomenēs, 1850-1936. Αριστομένης Προβελέγγιος (Table P-PZ40)
5610.P7	Psicharis, Ioannis, 1854-1929. Ιωάννης (Γιάννης) Ψυχάρης (Table P-PZ40)
5610.P8	Pŭrlichev, Grigor St., 1830-1893. Γκριγκόρ Παρλίτσεφ (Γρηγόριος Σταυρίδης)
	For general biography and criticism see PG1195.P8
5610.R35	Rankavēs, Alexandros Rizos, 1810-1892. Αλέξανδρος Ρίζος Ραγκαβής (Table P-PZ40)
5610.R45	Rēgas, Velestinlēs, 1757?-1798. Ρήγας Βελεστινλής (Table P-PZ40)
5610.R52	Rhoides, Emmanouēl, 1835-1923. Εμμανουήλ Ροΐδης (Table P-PZ40)
	Rodinos, Neophytos, ca. 1579-ca. 1659 see PA5649.R56
5610.R65	Rousmelēs, Savogias. Σαβόγιας Ρούσμελης (Table P-PZ40)
5610.S33	Sechretēs, Chatzēs, fl. 19th cent. Χατζής Σεχρέτης (Table P-PZ40)
	Seferis, George, 1900-1971. Γιώργος Σεφέρης see PA5610.S36
5610.S36	Sepheriadēs, Geōrgios, 1900-1971. Γεώργιος Σεφεριάδης (Table P-PZ40)
5610.S5	Sikelianos, Angelos, 1884-1951. Άγγελος Σικελιανός (Table P-PZ40)
5610.S54	Skandalakē, Hēbē Iōannou, 1910-1990. Ήβη Ιωάννου Σκανδαλάκη (Ήβη Κούγια-Σκανδαλάκη) (Table P-PZ40)
5610.S6	Solōmos, Dionysios, 1798-1857. Διονύσιος Σολωμός (Table P-PZ38)
5610.S612	Sourēs, Geōrgios, 1853-1919. Γεώργιος Σουρής (Table P-PZ40)
5610.S614	Soutsos, Panagiōtēs, 1806-1868. Παναγιώτης Σούτσος (Table P-PZ40)
5610.S62	Sperantsas, Stelios, 1888-1962. Στέλιος Σπεράντσας (Table P-PZ40)
5610.S67	Stam., Stam., 1865-1942. Σταμ. Σταμ. (Σταμάτιος Σταματίου) (Table P-PZ40)
5610.S74	Stathēs. Στάθης (Table P-PZ40)
5610.S75	Stavrinos. Σταυρινός (Table P-PZ40)

Individual authors or works
Modern, 1600-1960
Individual authors, A-Z -- Continued

5610.T24   Tadeloudēs, Paris, 1893-1974. Πάρις Ταδελούδης
                    (Ταβελούδης) (Table P-PZ40)
                  Taveloudēs, Paraskeuas. Παρασκευάς Ταβελούδης see
                    PA5610.T24
5610.T54   Theotokēs, Kōnstantinos, 1872-1923. Κωνσταντίνος
                    Θεοτόκης (Table P-PZ40)
5610.T64   Traulantōnēs, Antōnios, 1867-1943. Αντώνιος (Αντώνης)
                    Τραυλαντώνης (Table P-PZ40)
5610.T676   Tsakasianos, I.G. (Iōannēs G.),1853-1908. Ιωάννης
                    (Γιάννης) Γ. Τσακασιάνος (Table P-PZ40)
                  Valaōrites, Aristotelēs, 1824-1879 see PA5610.B27
                  Varnalēs, Kōstas, 1884-1974 see PA5610.B3
                  Venezēs, Elias, 1904-1973. Ηλίας Βενέζης see
                    PA5610.M35
5610.V52   Vestarchēs, Michaēl, d. 1662. Μιχαήλ Βεστάρχης (Table
                    P-PZ40)
                  Vikelas, Dēmētrēs, 1835-1908 see PA5610.B46
                  Vizyēnos, Geōrgios see PA5610.B49
5610.V58   Vlachogiannēs, Giannēs, 1867-1945. Γιάννης
                    Βλαχογιάννης (Table P-PZ40)
5610.V6   Vlachos, Angelos, 1838-1920. Άγγελος Βλάχος (Table P-
                    PZ40)
5610.V64   Vōtyras, Nikolaos V. Νικόλαος Β. Βωτυράς (Table P-
                    PZ40)
5610.V67   Voutyras, Dēmosthenēs, 1872-1958. Δημοσθένης
                    Βουτυράς (Table P-PZ40)
                  Vrettakos, Nikēphoros, 1911-1991 see PA5610.B7
5610.V98   Vyzantios, D.K. (Dēmētrios K.), 1790-1853. Δημήτριος Κ.
                    Βυζάντιος (Table P-PZ40)
5610.X49   Xenopoulos, Grēgorios, 1867-1951. Γρηγόριος
                    Ξενόπουλος (Table P-PZ40)
5610.X5   Xenos, Stephanos Theodōros, 1821-1894. Στέφανος
                    Θεόδωρος Ξένος (Table P-PZ40)
5610.Z35   Zampelios, Spyridōn, 1828-1881. Σπυρίδων Ζαμπέλιος
                    (Table P-PZ40)
                1961-2000
                  Subarrange each author by Table P-PZ40
                  Class here authors who started to publish about 1950 and
                    flourished after 1960. The author number is determined by
                    the second letter of the name
5611   Anonymous works (Table P-PZ28)
5612   A
5612.P6   Apostolidēs, Renos Hēraklē, 1924- . Ρένος Ηρακλή
                    Αποστολίδης (Table P-PZ40)

PA5000-5660

Individual authors or works
1961-2000 -- Continued

5613	B
5614	C
5615	D
5616	E
5617	F
5618	G
5619	H
5620	I
5621	J
5622	K
5623	L
5624	M
5625	N
5626	O
5627	P
5628	Q
5629	R

Renos, 1924- . Pένος see PA5612.P6

5630	S
5631	T
5632	U
5633	V
5634	W
5635	X
5636	Y
5637	Z
5638-5638.36	2001- (Table P-PZ29 modified)
5638.24	N
5638.24.O55	Nomisen, Giōrgos, 1940- (Table P-PZ40)
5638.29	S

Simenon, Zorz, 1940- see PA5638.24.O55

Local literature of Greece

5639.A-Z	By region, province, island, or island group, etc., A-Z
	Subarrange each by Table P-PZ26
5639.5.A-Z	By city, A-Z
	Subarrange each by Table P-PZ26

Modern Greek literature outside of Greece

5640-5649	Cyprus (Table P-PZ24 modified)
5649.A-Z	Individual authors or works, A-Z

Subarrange individual authors by Table P-PZ40 unless
otherwise specified
Subarrange individual works by Table P-PZ43 unless
otherwise specified
e.g.
For authors or works prior to 1600 see PA5301+

Modern Greek literature outside of Greece
  Cyprus
    Individual authors or works, A-Z -- Continued
      Kardianos, Dionysios. Διονύσιος Καρδιανός see
        PA5649.P365

5649.L37   Lara, Tzoulia. Τζούλια Λάρα (Table P-PZ40)
5649.M53   Michaelides, Vassilis, 1849-1917. Βασίλης Μιχαηλίδης
                  (Table P-PZ40)
                Papaioannou, Helenē. Ελένη Παπαϊωάννου see
                  PA5649.L37
5649.P365   Papageōrgiou, Spyros, 1940- . Σπύρος Παπαγεωργίου
                  (Table P-PZ40)
5649.R56   Rodinos, Neophytos, ca. 1579-ca. 1659. Νεόφυτος
                  Ροδινός (Table P-PZ40)
              United States. Canada
5649.5   History
5650   Collections
5655.A-Z   Individual authors, A-Z
                  Subarrange individual authors by Table P-PZ40
5660.A-Z   Other regions or countries, A-Z
                Under each country:
                .x   History and criticism
                .x2   Collections
                .x3   Individual authors

PA5000-5660

Roman literature
Generalities: Serial publications, etc.

(6000)	Generalities: Serial publications, etc.
	see PA1+ PA2001+
(6000.5)	Theory. Methodology
	see PA35+
	Literary history
	General works. Treatises. Compends
6001	Early to ca. 1800/1850
	English
6003	Treatises
6004	Compends
6005	French
6007	German
6008	Other
6009	Outlines. Quizzes. Tables. Charts
6011	Collected essays. Studies. Lectures
6012	Single lectures, addresses, pamphlets, etc.
	Biography of Roman authors
6013	Collected
	Individual authors see PA6202+
(6014)	Literary landmarks. Homes and haunts of authors
	see PA3006
(6015)	Iconography
	see class N
6017	Woman authors. Literary relations of women
6018.A-Z	Other classes of authors, A-Z
6018.E95	Exiled authors
6019	Relations to history, civilization, cultures, etc. (in general)
(6020)	Representation in art
	see class N
6021	Relations to Greek literature (and to ancient nations and countries)
	Cf. PA3010 Classical literature
	Cf. PA3070 Greek literature
	Relations to modern literature; Influence, etc.
	For influence on an individual author see the author
6023.A2	General
6023.A3	Latin, Medieval and modern
6023.A4-Z	By region or country, A-Z
6025	Translations (as subject)
6026	History of literary criticism, study and appreciation
	Cf. PA51+ Classical philology
	Cf. PA2041+ Latin philology
6027	Special topics
	For literary forgeries see PA3014.F6
	For plagiarism see PA3014.P6
6029.A-Z	Treatment and conception of special subjects, A-Z

Literary history
    Treatment and conception of special subjects, A-Z --
        Continued

6029.A57	Air
6029.A85	Astronomy
6029.B57	Birds
6029.B59	Birthplaces
6029.C35	Cato, Marcus Porcius, Uticensis
6029.C54	Clemency
6029.C57	Colors
6029.C65	Corsica
6029.D43	Dead
6029.E56	Emotions
6029.E87	Erotic literature. Sex
6029.F66	Food
6029.F75	Friendship
6029.F87	Future life
6029.H34	Hair
6029.H62	Honor
6029.H65	Horses
6029.I56	Interior decoration
6029.I57	Interpersonal relations
6029.I73	Italy
6029.L39	Law
6029.L6	Love
6029.L87	Luxury
6029.M3	Magic
6029.M4	Mental illness
6029.M44	Metamorphosis
6029.M65	Moderation
6029.M67	Moral conditions
	Nature
6029.N3	General
6029.N4	Special
	Including rivers, mountains, etc.
6029.P43	Peace
6029.P45	Philosophy
6029.P64	Political science
	Religion. Mythology. Hero legend
6029.R4	General
6029.R5	Special
	Including particular gods or heroes
6029.S25	Sadness
	Sex see PA6029.E87
6029.S5	Shame
6029.S62	Speech
6029.S95	Synesthesia

PA6000-6971

Literary history
  Treatment and conception of special subjects, A-Z --
    Continued

6029.T4	Technology
6029.T54	Time
6029.T7	Travel
6029.W37	War
6029.W48	Wine
6029.W5	Wisdom
6029.W52	Wit and humor
6030.A-Z	Treatment of special classes of people
6030.E95	Exiles
6030.F3	Fathers
6030.K55	Kings and rulers
6030.P5	Physicians
6030.S6	Slaves. Freedmen
6030.W7	Women
(6032)	Textual criticism, interpretation, etc.

    see PA6141+ PA3520+

By period
  For treatises confined to the earlier periods (including the
    "golden age" or part of it) see PA6001+

6035	Early Latin (Origins, etc. to 240 B.C. or 80 B.C.)
(6037)	Golden age (ca. 80 B.C. to 14 A.D.)

    see++

Literature of the empire
  For Christian literature see BR67

6041	Comprehensive, 14-600 (or 700)
6042	"Silver age," 14-177
6043	Later period and period of decline, 117-600 (700)

Poetry
  Including treatises on poetry and drama

6045	Congresses
6047	General

    For treatment and conception of special subjects see
     PA6029.A+

6047.5	Origins. Archaic period

    Cf. PA6035 Early Latin literature

Classic age see PA6047

6050	Silver age
6051	Later period
6053	Christian poetry
6054	Epic

Lyric see PA6047

6055	Didactic
6056	Satire ("Satura")

    Cf. PA6095 Prose

	Literary history
	Poetry -- Continued
6059.A-Z	Minor forms, A-Z
6059.E6	Elegy
6059.E65	Epigram
6059.E69	Epithalamium
6059.F3	Fable
6059.H95	Hymn
6063	Technique

Class here works on the theory of poetic art and history of development

For works on language, style, versification, etc., see PA6142

Cf. PA2329+ Latin philology

(6066)	Textual criticism, interpretation, etc.
	see PA6142
	Drama
6067	General
	Including technique
6068	Tragedy
6069	Comedy
6071	Minor
	Including atellani, mimi, etc.
(6072)	Textual criticism, interpretation, etc.
	see PA6143
	Theater and stage
6073	General works
6074	Special
6075.A-Z	Special theaters. By place, A-Z
	Prose
6081	General
	Including technique
6083	Oratory
6085	Rhetoric
6087	Dialogue
6089	Letters
6091	Fiction
6093	Biography. Autobiography
6095	Wit and humor. Satire. Parody
	Cf. PA6056 Treatises confined to the "satura"
6095.5	Prefaces
(6096)	By subject
	see the subject
(6097)	Textual criticism, interpretation, etc.
	see PA6144
6098.A-Z	Local, by region, province, place, etc., A-Z

PA6000-6971

	Collections
	Class here collections in which the Latin writers predominate
	For collections of both Greek and Latin authors see
	PA3401+
	General
	Papyri
(6100.A1-.A6)	Facsimiles and originals
	see PA3300.L1+
(6100.B1-.B6)	Typographical reproductions and editions
	see PA3335
(6100.M1-.M7)	Manuscripts (other than papyri)
	Printed editions
	Early to 1850
6101.A2	Delphin classics, 1674-1730
6101.A4	Delphin classics, Valpy editions, 1819-1830
6101.A5	Bibliotheca classica latina, 1819-1838
6101.A7-Z	Other collections. By editor, A-Z
(6102-6104)	Bibliotheca Teubneriana (Latin authors)
6105	Other
	School editions (Serial publications)
6111	American
6112	English
6113	French
6114	German
6115	Other
	Selections. Anthologies, etc.
	For textbooks see PA2095
(6116.A1)	Ancient and medieval
6116.A2	Early to 1800/1850
6116.A5-Z	Later, 1800/1850-
(6116.7)	Quotations
	see PN6080
6118.A-Z	Special, A-Z (by title, catchword title, or subject)
6118.A5	Anecdota
6118.F8	Fragments
6118.R4	Religion. Mythology
	By period
(6119.A1)	Early (Archaic to ca. 80 B.C.)
	see PA2510
(6119.A3)	Classic (ca. 80 B.C. to 14 A.D.)
	see PA6101+
6119.A5	"Silver age" (14-117) By date
6119.A7	Second to sixth (or seventh) century
	Christian literature
	see BR60+

Collections -- Continued
 Poetry
  For combined editions of Catullus, Tibullus and
   Propertius see PA6274.A2
(6121.A1) Ancient and medieval
   Cf. PA6128.A+ Anthologia latina
   Cf. PA6135.P8 Priapea
  Modern
6121.A2   General. By date
6121.A4   "Poetae latini minores." By date
6121.A6   Fragments. By date
6121.A7A-.A7Z   Selections. Anthologies. By editor
6121.A8   Quotations. Passages. Thoughts
    Cf. PN6080.5 Latin quotations
  By period
6123.A1   Early (Archaic) "Poetae antiquissimi." By date
    Cf. PA2510 Early Latin language
(6123.A22)   Classical
    see PA6121
6123.A3   Augustan age. By date
6123.A5   "Silver age," 14-117
6123.A7   Later period
6124   Christian poetry ("Poetae christiani")
    Cf. BR60+ Early Christian literature
    For miscellaneous religious poetry collections, and
     selections of hymns see BV468+
  Epic
6125.A1   Editions. By date
(6125.A5-Z)   Criticism, interpretation, etc.
    see PA6142
  Lyric
   General
    see PA6121
   Elegiac
6127.A1   Editions. By date
(6127.A5-Z)   Criticism, interpretation, etc.
     see PA6142
   Epigram. "Anthologia latina."
6128.A1   Editions. By date
(6128.A5-Z)   Criticism, interpretation, etc.
     see PA6142
   Didactic
6130.A1   Editions. By date
(6130.A5-Z)   Criticism, interpretation, etc.
     see PA6142
6131   "Poetae astronomici"
6132   "Poetae rei venaticae"

PA6000-6971

273

	Collections
	Poetry -- Continued
	Satura
6134.A1	Editions. By date
(6134.A5-Z)	Criticism, interpretation, etc.
	see PA6142
6135.A-Z	Minor, A-Z
6135.A3	Poetae aenigmatum
6135.B8	Bucolic. Poetae bucolici
6135.C3	Carmina consolatoria. Epicedia
6135.C4	Carmina familiae Caesareae
6135.C7	Carmina popularia
	Epitaphia see PA6128.A+
6135.F3	Fables. Poetae fabularum
6135.G6	Gnomic. Poetae sententiosi
	Hymni. Poetae christiani see PA6124
6135.L68	Love poetry
6135.P8	Priapea
	Cf. PA6519 Ovid. Priapea
	Drama
6137	General
6137.2	Tragedy
6137.3	Comedy
6137.5.A-Z	Various literary forms (in prose or verse), A-Z
6137.5.W5	Wit and humor
	Prose
6138.A1	General collections and selections. By date
	Special collections, A-Z
6138.L3	Laudationes funebres
6138.O8	Oratores. Panegyrici
6138.P3	Panegyrici
6138.R5	Rhetores
6139.A-Z	Scriptores
	Agrimensores see PA6139.G8
6139.A7	Astronomi
6139.B5	Biographi
6139.C7	Consolationum
(6139.E3)	Ecclesiastici
	see BR60+
6139.E7	Epistularum
6139.G3	Geographi
6139.G4	Itineraria
6139.G5	Regionarii
6139.G7	Grammatici
6139.G8	Gromatici (Agrimensores)
6139.H5	Historici
6139.H7	Historiae augustae

Collections
Prose
Special collections, A-Z
Scriptores -- Continued

6139.J7	Jurisprudentiae
6139.M2	Mathematici
(6139.M3)	Medici
	see R127.A1
6139.M4	Metrici et musici
6139.M5	rei Militaria
6139.M8	Mythographi
6139.M9	Mythographi Vaticani
6139.N3	rerum Naturalium
6139.P5	Philosophi
6139.P6	Physiognomici
6139.R8	rei Rusticae

Anonymous works
Class here works not otherwise provided for in PA6101+ or PA6202+

(6140.A2)	Collections
	see PA6101+
6140.A3-Z	Particular works, by title, A-Z
6140.A4	Aegritudo Perdiccae
(6140.A5)	Aetna
	see PA6202.A5
6140.A57	Alcestis Barcinonensis
6140.A6	Anonymus Valesii (Excerpta Valesiana)
6140.C3	Carmen de figuris
6140.C35	Carmina duodecim sapientum
6140.C58	Collatio Alexandri et Dindimi
	De rebus bellicis see PA6379.D23
	De viris illustribus see PA6379.D25
6140.D4	Declamatio in L. Sergium Catilinam

Wrongly ascribed to Porcius Latro; frequently published with editions of Sallustius
Historia Apollonii, regis Tyri see PA6206.A6
Origo gentis romanae see PA6518.O6
Peregrinatio Aetheriae see BR167
Pervigilium Veneris see PA6557.P3+
Querolus see PA6648.Q4+

6140.V47	Versus de Sodoma

Criticism, interpretation, etc.
Cf. PA25+ Classical philology
Cf. PA2025+ Latin philology
General; General special; Special topics
see PA6001+
Textual. Interpretation of detached passages

PA6000-6971

	Criticism, interpretation, etc.
	Textual. Interpretation of detached passages -- Continued
	General (Poets and prose writers)
6141.A2	Early to 1800
6141.A5-.Z3	Later, 1800-
6141.Z5	Language. Style
6141.Z6	Grammatical. Syntactical
	Cf. PA2071+ Latin grammar
6141.Z8	Lexicographical
	Cf. PA2351+ Latin philology
	Poetry
	General; General special; Special topics
	see PA6047+
	Textual. Interpretation of detached passages
6142.A2	Early, to 1800/1850
6142.A5-.Z3	1800/1850-
6142.Z5	Language. Style
6142.Z6	Grammatical. Syntactical
	Cf. PA2071+ Latin grammar
6142.Z7	Metrical and rhythmical

Class here works in which metrical questions are discussed
chiefly in the interest of interpretation or
characterization of a certain group of writers
For works written mainly for the elucidation of the system of
Roman metrics or of parts of it see PA2329+

6142.Z8	Lexicographical: Glossaries, indices; treatises, etc.
	Cf. PA2351+ Latin philology
	Drama
	General; General special; Special topics
	see PA6067+
	Textual. Interpretation of detached passages
6143.A2	Early, to ca. 1800/1850
6143.A5-.Z3	Later
6143.Z5	Language. Style
6143.Z6	Grammatical. Syntactical
6143.Z7	Metrical and rhythmical

Class here works in which metrical questions are discussed
chiefly in the interest of interpretation or
characterization of a certain group of writers
For works written mainly for the elucidation of the system of
Roman metrics or of parts of it see PA2329+

6143.Z8	Lexicographical: Glossaries, indices, treatises, etc.
	Cf. PA2351+ Latin philology
	Prose
	General; General special; Special topics
	see PA6081+
	Textual. Interpretation of detached passages

Criticism, interpretation, etc.
Textual. Interpretation of detached passages
Prose
Textual. Interpretation of detached passages --
Continued

6144.A2	Early, to 1800/1850
6144.A5-.Z3	Later, 1800/1850-
6144.Z5	Language. Style
	Cf. PA2311 General treatises
6144.Z6	Grammatical. Syntactical
	Cf. PA2071+ Latin grammar
6144.Z8	Lexicographical: Glossaries, indices, treatises, etc.
	Cf. PA2351+ Latin philology
	Translations
6155.A1	Polyglot. By date
	English
	General and miscellaneous
6155.A3-.L	By title of collection, A-L

Under each title:

.x	Collections and selections (Poetry and prose). By date
.xA1	Poetry
.xA2	Drama
.xA3	Prose
.xA7-.xZ	Individual authors

e. g.
Ancient classics for English readers

6155.A6 1878	Collections and selections
6155.A6A1	Selections from Roman poetry
6155.A6T3	Tacitus
	Loeb collection
(6156.A1)	Collections and selections (Poetry and prose). By date
(6156.A2)	Poetry. By date
(6156.A3)	Drama. By date
(6156.A4)	Prose. By date
(6156.A5-Z)	Individual authors
6157.L-Z	Other collections, L-Z

Under each title:

.x	Collections and selections (Poetry and prose). By date
.xA1	Poetry
.xA2	Drama
.xA3	Prose
.xA7-.xZ	Individual authors

6163	Anthologies. Selections
6164	Poetry
6165	Drama. Comedy

PA6000-6971

	Translations
	English -- Continued
6166	Prose
6169-6172	French (Table PA8)
6174-6177	German (Table PA8)
6179-6182	Italian (Table PA8)
6191.A-Z	Other. By language, A-Z
	Individual authors
	Subarrange by Tables P-PZ37 or P-PZ38 unless otherwise specified
	Unless otherwise specified, individual topical works by ancient Roman writers are classified in Class PA or in Classes B-Z according to language (for texts) or intent (for critical works)
	Class individual topical works in PA if included in the following categories: 1) Original Latin texts (without translations); 2) Philological or textual criticism and commentaries; 3) Commentaries specifically designed for use in conjunction with the original text
	Class individual topical works in B-Z if included in the following categories: 1) Translations with or without the original text; 2) Criticism and commentaries dealing primarily with the substance of the topic
6202	A to Ammianus
6202.A2	Accius, Lucius, 2nd century B.C. (Table P-PZ38)
6202.A25	Acro, Helenius, 2nd to 3rd century A.D. (Table P-PZ38)
	Cf. PA6766.A4 Terence
(6202.A26)	Pseudo-Acro
	see PA6408
	Acta fratrum Arvalium see PA2510+
(6202.A28)	Aegritudo Perdicae
	see PA6140.A4
	Aemilius Asper see PA6220.A4
	Aemilius Macer see PA6497.M2
	Aemilius Probus see PA6515+
	Aemilius Scaurus
	see Scaurus
	Aetheria see BR167
	Aethicus. Cosmographia ("Edicta Aethici philosophi cosmographi")
	A fictitious cosmography of the 7th century in six books professing to be St. Jerome's abridged translation of a Greek work
	Cf. PA6392.H93 Honorius

Individual authors
  A to Ammianus -- Continued
    Aetna (didactic poem)
      Author unknown; in the manuscripts transmitted as part of the Appendix to Virgil's poems, in the 15th century wrongly ascribed to Cornelius Severus, later with more probability to Lucilius Junior

6202.A5	Texts. By date
6202.A6	Criticism
	Afranius, Lucius
6202.A67	Texts. By date
6202.A68	Criticism
6202.A7	Africanus, Julius, 1st century A.D. (orator) (Table P-PZ38)

      Not to be confused with the chronicler Sextus Julius Africanus (fl. 195-240 A.D.) who wrote in Greek

    Albinovanus Pedo see PA6554.P6

6202.A73	Albucius Silus, C. (Table P-PZ38)

    Alcimus Ecdicius Avitus (St. Avitus) see PA6229.A9
    Alexandri itinerarium see PA6445.I7
  Ammianus Marcellinus, fl. 350-380 A.D.

6203.A2	Editions. By date

      Editions of A. ordinarily include the so-called "Anonymi Valesii" ("Excerpta Valesiana") fragments of two historical works dealing with the period of Constantinus, and Theoderich, respectively, and first pub. by Valesius in his edition of Ammianus, Paris, 1636
        Cf. PA6140.A6 Anonymi Valesii

6204.A-Z	Translations, by language, A-Z
6205.A-.Z3	Criticism
6205.Z5	Language
6205.Z8	Glossaries. Indices, etc. By date
6206	Amo... to Apu...
6206.A2	Ampelius, Lucius, 2nd (or 3rd?) century A.D. Liber memorialis

    Andronicus see PA6477.L2+
    Annaeus Cornutus see PA6375.C8
    Annaeus Seneca
      see Seneca

6206.A25	Annales maximi. (Annales pontificum)

    Annius Florus see PA6386+
    Anonymus (Anonymi) Valesii see PA6140.A6

6206.A3	Anthimus (Greek physician), fl. ca. 500 A.D. De observatione ciborum

    Anthologia latina see PA6128.A+
    Antias, Valerius
      see Valerius Antias
    Antipater see PA6375.C57

PA6000-6971

Individual authors

Amo... to Apu... -- Continued

Antistius Labeo, Marcus see PA6451.L17

Antistius Labeo, Pacuvius see PA6451.L18

Antonini itinerarium

see Itinerarium Antonini

6206.A35   Antoninus Pius, emperor of Rome, 86-161 A.D. (Table P-PZ38)

Cf. PA6389.F6+ Fronto

6206.A4   Antonius Musa (physician) fl. 23 B.C. (Table P-PZ38 modified)

6206.A4A61-.A4A78   Separate works. By title

e.g. Treatise on remedies in Greek (lost) (By some authorities ascribed to Petronius Musa); Spurious works: De herba betonica, De tuenda valetudine ad Maecenatem

6206.A5   Aphthonius (Apthonius), Aelius Festus, 3rd century A.D. (?). De metris omnibus lib. IV

Incorporated nearly word for word in the Ars grammatica of C. Marius Victorinus

Cf. PA6967.V5 Victorinus

6206.A55   Apicius, Caelius (De re coquinaria lib. X)

Probably compiled in the 3rd century A.D. by one Caelius, the title presumably reading Caelii Apicius de re coquinaria (similar to Ciceronis Cato de senectute)

Apollinaris see PA6694.S7+

Apollinaris, C. Sulpicius see PA6704.S5

6206.A6   Apollonius, of Tyrus (Historia Apollonii, regis Tyri, prose romance)

To the 6th century--betraying marked Christian influence-- belongs the oldest preserved revision of the fabulous account of "king" Apollonius, written by a Roman author of the 3rd or 4th century A.D.

For medieval derivations see the national literature in PA-PT

Appius Claudius Caecus, fl. 312-296 B.C.

Apthonius see PA6206.A5

Apuleius Barbarus see PA6208.H5

Apuleius

Editions

6207.A2   Complete works

6207.A3   Selected works

Particular works, A-Z

6207.A7   Apologia (Pro se de magia liber)

6207.D2   De deo Socratis

De magia see PA6207.A7

Individual authors
  Apuleius
    Editions
      Particular works, A-Z -- Continued

6207.D4   De mundo
          Free version of the pseudo-Aristotelian treatise De mundo
          Cf. PA3892.M7 Aristoteles
        De philosophia morali
          see De Platone lib. II

6207.D6   De Platone et eius dogmate
          In three books acc. to introduction; the 3rd book wanting in the principal mss. of bks. I-II. A treatise Peri[h]ermeniae Apulei (also with title De syllogismis categoricis) is by some authorities considered to be the 3rd book

6207.F6   Florida (Apulei Platonici Floridorum lib. I-IV)
          Selection of extracts from the public lectures of Apuleius. Of the original (in four books) an excerpt only is extant

        Metamorphoseon lib. XI (Asinus aureus)
          In the main the same story as Lucian's Lucius sive Asinus; both stories are derived from a Greek novel "Lucius Patrensis"
          Cf. PA4240.L3 Lucius, of Patrae

6207.M3   Editions
6207.M33   Selections
6207.M35   Tales. Episodes
          Psyche (Amor et Psyche; Cupido et Psyche)
6207.M4   Editions
(6207.M5)   Criticism. Interpretation
            see PA6217
6207.M51   Illustrations. Music
(6207.M7)   Criticism
          see PA6217
      Lost works and fragments
6207.Z5   Editions of fragments
         Carmen de virtutibus Orfiti
         Carmina amatoria
         De arboribus
         De arithmetica
         De musica
         De piscibus
         De re rustica
         Epitome historiarum
         Hermagoras (novel?)
         Hymni in Aesculapium

PA6000-6971

Individual authors
  Apuleius
    Editions
      Lost works and fragments
        Editions of fragments -- Continued
          Ludicra
            Including Carmina amatoria?
          Medicinalia
          Naturales quaestiones
          Orationes
            Cf. PA6207.F6 Florida
          Translations of Menander, and Plato's Phaedo
        Criticism see PA6217

6208	Spurious works
	Asclepius see PA3998.H5A7
	De syllogismis see PA6207.D6
	De remediis salutaribus (fragment)
6208.H5	Herbarium (De medicaminibus herbarum; De herbarum virtutibus)
	By an author of the 5th (ca.) century A.D., frequently called "Apuleius Barbarus" or "Pseudo-Apuleius"; wrongly attributed to Apuleius Celsus
6208.P4	Physiognomonia
	Translations
6209	English (Table PA12)
6210	French (Table PA12)
	Cf. PQ1810.A5 Lafontaine, Amour de Psyché et de Cupidon
6211	German (Table PA12)
6212	Italian (Table PA12)
6213	Spanish. Portuguese (Table PA12)
6214.A-Z	Other European, except Slavic, A-Z
6215.A-Z	Slavic, A-Z
6216.A-Z	Oriental and artificial, A-Z
	Criticism
6217	General, and Metamorphoses
	Language. Style
6219.A-.Z5	Grammar
6219.Z8	Glossaries. Indices, etc. By date
6220	Apuleius (minor) to Aus...
	Apuleius minor (Apuleius grammaticus) see PA8250
(6220.A14)	"Apuleius, L. Caecilius Minutianus". De orthographia (fragments)
	A modern forgery by Caelius Rhodiginus, professor at Ferrara 1508-12

	Individual authors
	Apuleius (minor) to Aus... -- Continued
6220.A15	Apuleius Celsus (physician) 1st century A.D. (Table P-PZ38)
	Cf. PA6208.H5 Herbarium
6220.A17	Aquila Romanus (rhetor) 3rd century A.D. (Table P-PZ38)
6220.A19	Arator, Subdiaconus, fl. 513-544. De actibus apostolorum (epic poem)
	Arruntius Stella, L.
	see Stella
6220.A25	Arusianus Messius, 4th century A.D. Exempla elocutionum ex Vergilio, Sallustio, Terentio, Cicerone digesta per literas
(6220.A27)	Arvalium fratrum acta
	see PA2510+
(6220.A28)	Arvalium fratrum carmen
	see PA2510+
(6220.A3)	Asconius Pedianus, Q., 1st century A.D.
	Commentarius in M. T. Ciceronis orationes (Orationum Ciceronis quinque enarratio) see PA6284.A3
	Contra obtrectatores Vergilii (lost)
	Spurious works ("Pseudo-Asconius") see PA6284.A4
	Asinius Pollio see PA6641.P7
6220.A4	Asper, Aemilius (grammarian) 2nd century A.D. (Table P-PZ38)
	Spurious work: Ars
	Cf. PA6823.A8 Vergilius
6220.A5	Atilius Fortunatianus, 4th century A.D. (Table P-PZ38)
6220.A55	Atticus, T. Pomponius, 109-32 B.C. (Table P-PZ38 modified)
6220.A55A61-.A55A78	Separate works. By title
	e.g. Liber annalis (Lost); De consulatu Ciceronis (In Greek; lost); Imagines (Lost) - Cf. PA6297.A5+
	Correspondence with Cicero
	Attius, L. see PA6202.A2
	Attius Labeo see PA6451.L15
	"Auctor ad Herennium" see PA6304.R7
6220.A6	Audax (grammarian; date and personality of A. unknown, first quoted at end of 7th century) (Table P-PZ38)
6220.A67	Aufidius, Cn. (historian) 1st century B.C. (Table P-PZ38)
6220.A7	Aufidius Bassus (historian) 1st century A.D. (Table P-PZ38)
	Aufidius Modestus see PA6514.M6
6220.A85	Augustus, Emperor of Rome (Table P-PZ38)
	Cf. DG279 History

	Individual authors
	Apuleius (minor) to Aus... -- Continued
6220.A9	Aurelianus, Caelius ("methodicus siccensis") 4th or 5th century A.D. (Table P-PZ38)
	Translator of Soranus
	Cf. PA4435.S2+ Soranus
	Aurelius Antoninus, Marcus, Emperor of Rome
	see PA3939; PA6389.F6+
	Aurelius Nemesianus see PA6514.N4
	Aurelius Prudentius see PA6648.P6+
	Aurelius Symmachus see PA6704.S7+
	Aurelius Victor see PA6966
	Ausonius, Decimus Magnus
6221.A2	Editions
6221.A25	Selections
	Some of the older editions combine under the arbitrary title "Idyllia" a selection of twenty poems including Bissula, Mosella, a.o.
	Particular works
	Cf. PA6955+ Appendix Vergiliana
6221.B5	Bissula
	Caesares
6221.C5	Cento nuptialis
6221.C7	Commemoratio professorum burdigalensium
	Eclogarum liber
	Ephemeris (id est totius diei negotium)
	Epicedium in patrem
	Epigrammata
6221.E7	Epistulae
6221.E8	Epitaphia
	i-xxvi based on a collection in the Pseudo-Aristotelian Peplos
	Gratiarum actio dicta domino Gratiano Augusto
	In prose
	Griphus ternarii numeri
	Idyllia see PA6221.A25
	Ludus septem sapientum
6221.M7	Mosella
	Ordo nobilium urbium
	Parentalia
	Periochae Homeri Iliadis et Odysseae
	In prose; authorship disputed
	Protrepticus
	Technopaegnion
6222	Translations
6223	Criticism. Biography, etc.

Individual authors -- Continued

6225	Avianus (Avianius?) 4th to 5th century A.D.
	Paraphrase in distichs of forty-two fables, based upon a prose paraphrase of Babrius in Latin (by Titianus?)
	Cf. PA3941 Babrius
6225.A2	Editions
	Paraphrases (Medieval)
(6225.A4)	Prose paraphrase (13th century)
(6225.A5)	Apologi Aviani
	Metrical
(6225.A6)	Novus Avianus (by a poet of Asti)
(6225.A7)	Novus Avianus vindobonensis [monacensis]
6225.A8-.Z3	Translations. By language, A-Z
6225.Z5	Criticism, interpretation, etc.
6227	Avienus, Rufius Festus, 4th century A.D.
6227.A2	Editions. By date
6227.A4	Aratus (Arati Phaenomena)
6227.A5	Ora maritima
	Fragment of 713 verses
6227.A6	Orbis terrae (Descriptio orbis terrae)
	Based on Dionysius Periegetes
	Cf. PA3968.D2+ Dionysius Periegetes
	Lost works
	"Fabulae Vergilianae." Extracts from Vergilius
	Metrical version of Livy's History
6227.A7-.Z3	Translations. By language, A-Z, and date
6227.Z5	Criticism (regardless of work)
6229	Avitus to Boet...
6229.A9	Avitus, Alcimus Ecdicius, Saint (Table P-PZ38)
	Cf. BR60+ Christian literature
	Baebius Italicus see PA6445.I2
	Balbus (gromatic writer) 1st century A.D.
	Spurious: De asse
	Written between 222 and 337 A.D.
	Balbus, Caecilius see PA6234.C3
	Bassus, Aufidius see PA6220.A7
	Bassus, Caesius see PA6271.C14
	Bassus, Saleius see PA6652.S4
	Boethius, d. 524
	Cf. B659 Philosophy
	Editions
6231.A2	Comprehensive
	Selected works
6231.A23	Miscellaneous
	By group
6231.A25	Philosophical
	Cf. PA6231.Z1 "Dialectica"

PA6000-6971

	Individual authors
	Boethius, d. 524
	Editions
	Selected works
	By group -- Continued
(6231.A27)	Opuscula sacra
	see BR60+
	Particular works
6231.A7	Arithmetica lib. II (De institutione arithmetica)
	Based upon Nicomachus, of Gerasa
	Ars geometriae see PA6231.Z7
6231.C3	Carmina
	Part of the Consolatio
(6231.C6)	Contra Eutychen et Nestorium (De persona et duabus naturis in Christo)
	see BT200
6231.C8	Consolatio lib. V (De consolatione philosophiae)
	De definitione see PA6967.V5
6231.D3	De differentiis topicis lib. IV
	Extracts from the 4th book appear in some mss. as independent treatises entitled respectively De rhetoricae cognatione, and Locorum rhetoricorum distinctio
	De disciplina scholarium
	see Spurious works
6231.D4	De divisione
(6231.D5)	De fide catholica
	Authorship disputed
	see BX1750
	De geometria
	see Spurious works
	De hebdomadibus see PA6231.Q7
	De institutione arithmetica see PA6231.A7
	De institutione musica see PA6231.M7
	De ordine peripateticae disciplinae
	Lost
	De persona et duabus naturis Christo contra Eutychen et Nestorium
	see Contra Eutychen et Nestorium
	De rhetoricae cognatione (communis speculatio de rhet. recog.) see PA6231.D3
6231.D6	De syllogismo categorico lib. II
6231.D7	Introductio ad categoricos syllogismos
6231.D8	De syllogismo hypothetico
(6231.D9)	De trinitate (Trinitas unus Deus ac non tres dii)
	see BT110

Individual authors
  Boethius, d. 524
    Editions
      Particular works -- Continued
        De unitate
          see Spurious works
        Dialectica see PA6231.Z1
        Geometria
          see PA6231.Z7 and PA6231.Z9
        Locorum rhetoricum distinctio see PA6231.D3

6231.M7   Musica lib. V (De institutione musica)
             Based on Nicomachus, of Gerasa, and Ptolemaeus
6231.Q7   Quomodo substantiae in eo quod sint bonae sint cum
             non sint substantialia bona
               In some of the older editions entitled: De hebdomadibus.
                 Not to be confused with the Liber regularum
                 theologiae of Alanus de Insulis which at a later period
                 was known as "Boetius de hebdomadibus."
           Trinitas unus Deus [etc.]
             see De trinitate
(6231.U8) Utrum Pater et Filius et Spiritus Sanctus de divinitate
             substantialiter praedicentur
             see BT110
      Works translated and interpreted by B.
6231.Z1   Collections and selections
              Including editions of "Dialectica," i.e., the treatises on logic
                and rhetoric translated or original
            Particular works
              Aristoteles. Organon
6231.Z2   Collections and selections
6231.Z21   In Categorias Aristotelis lib. IV
                In librum Aristotelis De interpretatione
6231.Z22   Prima editio (Commentaria minora) lib. II
6231.Z23   Secunda editio (Commentaria maiora) lib. VI
6231.Z24   Analytica priora Aristotelis
                  Original translation apparently lost. The translation
                    ascribed to him is believed to be the work of
                    Jacobus de Venetia (1128) revised by the editors
                    of Boethius
6231.Z25   Analytica posteriora Aristotelis
                  Original translation apparently lost. The translation
                    ascribed to him is believed to be the work of
                    Jacobus de Venetia (1128) revised by the editors
                    of Boethius

PA6000-6971

Individual authors
Boethius, d. 524
Works translated and interpreted by B.
Particular works
Aristoteles. Organon -- Continued

6231.Z26   Topica Aristotelis
                          Original translation apparently lost. The translation
                              ascribed to him is believed to be the work of
                              Jacobus de Venetia (1128) revised by the editors
                              of Boethius

6231.Z28   Elenchi sophistici Aristotelis
                          Original translation apparently lost. The translation
                              ascribed to him is believed to be the work of
                              Jacobus de Venetia (1128) revised by the editors
                              of Boethius

6231.Z29   Cicero. Topica
                          Part of lib. VI, and lib. VII lost
                      Porphyrius. Isagoge
6231.Z3   I In Porphyrium a Victorino translatum dialogi II (In
                          Isagogen Porphyrii commentorum editionis
                          primae lib. I-II)

6231.Z4   II In Porphyrium a se translatum libri V (In Isagogen
                          Porphyrii editionis secundae lib. V)

6231.Z5   Euclides. Elementa
                          Extracts preserved in Cassiodor's De artibus ac
                              disciplinis liberalium artium, and in a spurious
                              medieval compilation ascribed to Boethius, and
                              entitled: Ars geometriae et arithmeticae
                          Cf. PA6231.Z7 Ars geometriae et arithmeticae
                      Nicomachus, of Gerasa
                          see PA6231.A7; PA6231.M7
                  Spurious and doubtful works
6231.Z7   Ars geometriae et arithmeticae lib. V
                          A spurious medieval compilation; includes genuine extracts
                              from the Arithmetica of Boethius (in lib. II), and from his
                              version of the Elementa of Euclid (in lib. III-IV). Books I
                              and V contain a spurious gromatic treatise, in part
                              published by Lachmann with title Ex demonstratione
                              artis geometricae excerpta
                          Cf. PA6231.Z9 Geometria
                      De definitione (De definitionibus) see PA6967.V5
                      De fide catholica see PA6231.D5
                      De disciplina scholarium
                          Wrongly ascribed to Thomas Brabantinus Cantipratanus
                      De trinitate see BT110
                      De unitate et uno
                          By Dominicus Gundisalvi

	Individual authors
	Boethius, d. 524
	Spurious and doubtful works -- Continued
6231.Z9	Geometria lib. II
	A forgery of the 11th century based upon the Ars geometriae et arithmeticae. It includes extracts from Boethius, enlarged from other sources
6232	Translations
	Medieval
	see PQ, PR, PF, etc.
(6232.A2A6)	Anglo-Saxon
	see PR1549
(6232.A2F8)	Old French
	see PQ1533.S5
(6232.A2G5)	Old High German
	see PF3988
6232.A3-Z	Modern, by language and original title, A-Z
	Criticism, interpretation, etc.
6233.A2	Medieval
6233.A5-Z	Modern
6234	Bon... to Cae...
6234.B7	Brutus, M. Junius, d. 42 B.C. (Table P-PZ38)
	Cf. PA6297.B7 Cicero. Epistulae ad M.B.
6234.C3	"Caecilius Balbus" ("Caecilius Balbus De nugis philosophorum")
	In the main an anonymous, ancient Latin translation of a Greek collection of maxims, including interpolated sentences of Publilius Syrus
6234.C4	Caecilius Statius, 2nd century B.C. (Table P-PZ38)
	Comedies (fragments only)
6234.C45	Caecina, A., 1st century B.C. (Table P-PZ38)
	Caelius Antipater see PA6375.C57
	Caelius Aurelianus see PA6220.A9
6234.C7	Caelius Rufus, M., fl. 51-48 B.C. (Table P-PZ38)
	Cf. PA6279.C18 Cicero pro Caelio
	Cf. PA6297.A4 Cicero ad familiares, lib. VIII (letters of Caelius to Cicero)
	Caesar, Julius
	Editions
6235.A2	Comprehensive
	Including editions of the Bellum gallicum alone
6235.A5-Z	School editions. By editor, A-Z
	Selected books
6236.A-Z	Three or four books, by editor, A-Z
	For books I-V or I-VI see PA6235
	Two books or one book
6237.A1A-.A1Z	I (or I-II, or I, III, etc.). By editor, A-Z

PA6000-6971

	Individual authors
	Caesar, Julius
	Editions
	Selected books
	Two books or one book
6237.A2A-.A2Z	II (or II-III, or II, VI, etc.). By editor, A-Z
6237.A3A-.A3Z	III, etc. By editor, A-Z
6237.A4A-.A4Z	IV, etc. By editor, A-Z
6237.A5A-.A5Z	V, etc. By editor, A-Z
6237.A6A-.A6Z	VI, etc. By editor, A-Z
6237.A7A-.A7Z	VII (or VII-VIII). By editor, A-Z
6237.A8A-.A8Z	VIII. By editor, A-Z
(6237.Z5)	Chrestomathies, selections, etc.
	see PA2095
(6237.9)	Adaptations, dramatizations, etc.
	Particular works
	Bellum gallicum
	see PA6235+
6238.B2	De bello civili lib. III. By date
6238.B3	Criticism
	Supplementary works
6238.B35	Comprehensive editions
	Criticism
	see PA6246
	Particular works
	De bello gallico liber VIII (by A. Hirtius)
	see PA6235+
	Bellum africum (africanum)
	Author unknown (Asinius Pollio?)
6238.B4	Editions
6238.B45	Selected portions
6238.B5	Criticism
6238.B6	Bellum alexandrinum
	Authorship uncertain; ascribed to A. Hirtius and to C. Oppius
	Includes: Expeditio Domitii in Pharnacem, chapters 34-41; Bellum illyricum, 42-47; Risings in Spain, 48-64; Defeat of Pharnaces through Caesar, 65 to end
6238.B7	Criticism
6238.B9	Bellum hispaniense
	Author unknown
6238.F7	Lost works and fragments
	De analogia lib. II
	Anticatones
	Epistulae
	Iter (poem)
	Orationes

Individual authors
  Caesar, Julius
    Editions
      Lost works and fragments -- Continued

(6238.F8)   Criticism
      Spurious works
        Cosmographia Julii Caesaris see PA6392.H9
    Translations

(6239)   English
        see DC62; DG266
6240   French (Table PA13)
6241   German (Table PA13)
6242.A-Z   Other non-Slavic European, A-Z
6243   Slavic (Table PA13)
6244   Oriental, Artificial, etc.
6245   Illustrations
    Criticism, interpretation, etc.
      Class here only works intended for the interpretation of the
        text or pertaining to literary history
      For criticism of particular works (with the exception of Bellum
        gallicum) see the works
      For historical treatises see DG261+
      For technical military works see U35
6246   General treatises (and Bellum gallicum)
6246.A2   Early to 1800/50
6246.A5-.Z3   Later, 1800/50+
    Language. Style
6269.A-.Z3   General works
6269.Z5   Grammar. Syntax
6269.Z8   Glossaries. Indices, etc.
6269.Z9A-.Z9Z   Vocabularies for schools, by compiler, A-Z
        For textbooks, exercises, etc., based upon Caesar
         see PA2087
6271 Caesar Strabo to Cato
    Caesar Strabo, C. Julius, d. 87 B.C.
      Fragments of orations and tragedies
    Caesellius Vindex, L. (grammarian) 2nd century A.D.
6271.C14   Caesius Bassus, 1st century A.D. (Table P-PZ38)
6271.C18   Calpurnius Flaccus (rhetor) 2nd century A.D. (Table P-
      PZ38)
    Calpurnius Piso, C., d. 65 A.D. see PA6271.C2A3
    Calpurnius Piso Frugi, L., fl. 149 B.C. (annalist and orator)
    Calpurnius Siculus, T., fl. ca. 54 A.D.

PA6000-6971

	Individual authors
	Caesar Strabo to Cato
	Calpurnius Siculus, T., fl. ca. 54 A.D. -- Continued
6271.C2	Eclogae I-VII. By date

The seven Eclogae of C. were at an early period in the mss. combined with the four Eclogae of Nemesianus, and both for a long time passed as the poems of one and the same author, Calpurnius or Nemesianus

Cf. PA6514.N4 Nemesianus

Poems ascribed to Calpurnius

6271.C2A3	Panegyricus in Pisonem (De laude Pisonis)

Poem of 261 hexameters, presumably composed in honor of C. Calpurnius Piso (d. 65 A.D.). It has been ascribed to Calpurnius, Ovidius, Statius, and Saleius Bassus. In the mss. Vergilius, and Lucanus are named as authors respectively

6271.C2A4	Bucolica

Two poems apparently composed during the reign of Nero. By some authorities they have been identified with the lost poems Laudes Neronis, and Saturnalia of Lucanus

6271.C3	Criticism
6271.C33	Calvus, C. Licinius Macer, 82-ca. 46 B.C. (Table P-PZ38)
	Capella, Martianus see PA6511.M2+
6271.C35	Caper, Flavius (grammarian) 2nd century A.D. (Table P-PZ38)
6271.C37	Capitolinus, Julius, fl. ca. 330 A.D. (?) (Table P-PZ38)
6271.C374	Carmen adversus Marcionitas
6271.C376	Carmen contra paganos
	Carmen de Aetna see PA6202.A5+
	Carmen de bello actiaco see PA6652.R15
	Carmen de figuris see PA6140.C3
	Carmen de laude Pisonis see PA6271.C2A3
	Carmen de ponderibus et mensuris see PA6385.F8
	Carmen fratrum Arvalium
	see Arvalium fratrum carmen
6271.C38	Carmina Einsidlensia
6271.C4	Cassiodorus, Senator, ca. 487-ca. 580 (Table P-PZ40)
	Chronica
	De anima
	De orthographia
	Historia gothica (De origine actibusque Getarum)
	Lost

Cf. PA6445.J2 Abridged version of Jordanis

Institutiones divinarum lectionum (literarum)

Institutiones saecularium lectionum (De artibus ac disciplinis liberalium litterarum)

	Individual authors
	Caesar Strabo to Cato
	Cassiodorus, Senator, ca. 487-ca. 580 -- Continued
	Ordo generis Cassiodororum
6271.C4V3	Variae lib. XII (collection of letters and official documents composed by C.)
6271.C62	Cassius Felix, 5th century A.D. (Table P-PZ38)
6271.C63	Cassius Hemina, L. (historian) fl. 146 B.C. (Table P-PZ38)
	Cassius Longinus, C., d. 42 B.C.
	Cassius Parmensis, C., d. 30 B.C.
	Cassius Severus (orator) d. 32 A.D.
	Cato, philosophus see PA6272+
	Cato, Dionysius see PA6272+
	Cato, M. Porcius, Censorius, 234-149 B.C.
6271.C7	De agricultura (De re rustica)
	The only work preserved
6271.C7A3	Fragments. By date
	Cf. PA6955.D6 Appendix Vergiliana
6271.C8	Cato, Valerius (grammarian) 1st century B.C.
	Author of two poems (lost) Lydia, and Diana or Dictynna. According to some authorities the first poem "Lydia" is identical with the second part of the "Dirae" in the Appendix Vergiliana. The first part, too, which alone justifies the title "Dirae" has been ascribed to Val. Cato
	Cato, M. Porcius, Uticensis, 95-46 B.C.
	Catonis disticha (Dicta or Disticha Catonis)
	Collection of 56 brief sayings in prose followed by 164 (or more) distichs (2 hexameters each) in four books. In some manuscripts it is ascribed to Marcus Cato ("Dicta Marci Catonis ad filium suum"), in the older editions and literature to "Dionysius" Cato
6272.A2	Editions. By date
	Translations
	Medieval
(6272.1)	Greek
(6272.2)	Latin paraphrases and adaptations
(6272.3)	Latin continuations, supplements, etc.
(6272.4)	Germanic
(6272.4.E5)	English
	see class PR
(6272.4.G5)	German
	see class PT
(6272.4.G6)	Low German
	see class PT
(6272.4.G7)	Dutch
	see class PT

PA6000-6971

Individual authors
Catonis disticha (Dicta or Disticha Catonis)
Translations
Medieval
Germanic -- Continued

(6272.4.G8)	Icelandic
	see class PT
(6272.5)	Romance
	see class PQ
(6272.6)	Celtic
	see class PB
(6272.8)	Slavic
	see class PG
6273.A-.Z3	Modern, by language, A-Z
6273.Z5	Criticism

Catullus, C. Valerius, ca. 87-ca. 54 (or 82-52?) B.C.
        Class here also in their chronological order combined editions
            of Catullus, Tibullus and Propertius
        For separate editions of Propertius see PA6644
        For separate editions of Tibullus see PA6787.A2+

6274.A2	Editions. By date
6274.A25	Selections
6274.A4-Z	Single poems. By title
	If not known by name, arrange by first word of the poem
	For translations and criticism see PA6275+
6274.A8	Attis (carmen 63)
6274.C6	Coma Berenices (carmen 66)
6274.E7	Epithalamium Pelei et Thetidos (carmen 64)
6274.H9	Hymnos Klētikos
6275.A-.Z3	Translations. By language, A-Z, and translator
6275.Z5	Adaptations. Imitations. Parodies
	Criticism
6276.A-.Z3	General works
6276.Z5	Language
6276.Z6	Versification
6276.Z8	Glossaries. Indices, etc. By date
6277	Catulus to Cic...
	Catulus, Lutatius see PA6497.L5
	Celsus, Apuleius see PA6220.A15
6277.C3	Celsus, Aulus Cornelius, 1st century A.D.
	Author of a large encyclopedic work; De medicina lib. VIII, alone preserved
6277.C4	Censorinus, fl. 238 A.D.
6277.C6	Chalcidius, 4th century A.D. (Table P-PZ38)
	For his Latin translation of Plato's Timaeus, with commentary see PA4279.T7

	Individual authors
	Catulus to Cic... -- Continued
6277.C7	Charisius, Flavius Sosipater (grammarian) 4th century A.D. (Table P-PZ38 modified)
	Identical with a grammarian Flavianus, quoted in the grammatical literature?
6277.C7A61-.C7A78	Separate works. By title
	e.g. "Chronographer of 354 A.D." (A historical handbook of the city of Rome, apparently compiled in the year 354)
	"Chiro Centaurus" see PA6514.M8
	Cicero, Marcus Tullius
6278	Editions
6278.A2	Comprehensive. By date
6278.A3	Selections. Passages. Quotations. Thoughts
	Selected works
6278.A4	Miscellaneous, i.e., not forming a distinct group
	Particular groups
	Orationes see PA6279+
	Opera rhetorica see PA6294.A2+
	Opera philosophica see PA6295.A2+
	Epistulae see PA6297+
	Opera historica et geographica see PA6305.H5
	Poemata see PA6305.P5
	Translations by Cicero see PA6305.T8
	Fragments, lost works
	see PA6283; PA6305
	Spurious works see PA6306
	Orationes
	Editions
6279.A2	By date
(6279.A25)	Selections. Passages. Thoughts
	see PA6278.A3
	Selected orations (Miscellaneous: four or more regardless of title)
6279.A3A-.A3Z	To 1800/50. By editor, A-Z
6279.A4A-.A4Z	1800/50- By editor, A-Z
	Selected orations. By group
6279.A63	Causae (Forensic orations). By date
6279.A65	Orationes consulares. By date
	De lege agraria; Pro Rabirio perduellionis reo; In Catilinam I-IV; Pro L. Murena
6279.A67	Orationes caesareae. By date
	Pro Marcello; Pro Ligario; Pro rege Deiotaro
	Orationes in Catilinam see PA6279.C2+
	Orationes in Verrem see PA6282.A2+
	Orationes Philippicae see PA6280.A1+
	Orationes post reditum see PA6281.R4+

	Individual authors
	Cicero, Marcus Tullius
	Orationes
	Editions
	Selected orations. By group -- Continued
6279.A69	Other
	Single orations
	Titles are given in the shortest form, arranged by the most important word
	De aere alieno Milonis see PA6283.A5
6279.A8	De lege agraria [contra P. Servilium Rullum] I-III
	Fourth oration lost
	De rege Alexandrino see PA6283.A2+
	In C. Antonium et L. Catilinam see PA6281.T6
	In M. Antonium see PA6280.A1+
6279.A9	Pro Archia (Pro Archia poeta; Pro A. Licinio Archia)
	Cf. PA3873.A75 Archias
6279.B3	Pro Balbo (Pro Cornelio Balbo)
	In Q. Caecilium divinatio see PA6282.A4
6279.C15	Pro Caecina (Pro A. Caecina)
6279.C18	Pro Caelio (Pro M. Caelio Rufo)
	Cf. PA6234.C7 Caelius Rufus
	Cf. PA6297.A4 Cicero. Epistulae
	In Catilinam I-IV (In L. Catilinam)
6279.C2	Editions of I-IV, or I-III. By date
6279.C25	Selections
6279.C3	Editions of two orations. By date
	Editions of single orations
6279.C31	First. By date
6279.C32	Second. By date
6279.C33	Third. By date
6279.C34	Fourth. By date
6279.C5	Criticism
	In C. Antonium et L. Catilinam see PA6281.T6
	Invectiva in Catilinam (In Catilinam or. V) see PA6283.Z7I6
	In Clodium et Curionem see PA6283.C6
6279.C7	Pro Cluentio (Pro A. Cluentio Habito; Pro A. Cluentio Avito)
6279.C8	Pro Cornelio
	Cum populo gratias egit see PA6281.R42
	Cum senatui gratias egit see PA6281.R41
	In Curionem see PA6283.C6
6279.D3	Pro Deiotaro (Pro rege Deiotaro)
	Divinatio in Caecinam see PA6282.A4
(6279.D6)	Pro domo sua (De doma sua)
	see PA6281.R43

Individual authors
  Cicero, Marcus Tullius
    Orationes
      Editions
        Single orations -- Continued
          Antequam in exilium iret see PA6283.Z7P8

6279.F6	Pro Flacco (Pro L. Valerio Flacco)
6279.F8	Pro Fonteio (Pro M. Fonteio)
	Frumentaria oratio (De re frumentaria) see PA6282.A55
	De haruspicum responso see PA6281.R44
6279.I6	De imperio Cn. Pompei (Pro lege Manilia)
	De jurisdictione siciliensi see PA6282.A54
	Laudatio Caesaris see PA6283.A2+
	Laudatio Catonis see PA6283.A2+
	Laudatio Porciae see PA6283.A2+
	De lege agraria see PA6279.A8
	Pro lege Manilia see PA6279.I6
6279.L5	Pro Ligario (Pro Q. Ligario)
	Pro lege Manilia see PA6279.I6
6279.M3	Pro Marcello (Pro M. Marcello)
	De aere alieno Milonis see PA6283.A5
6279.M5	Pro Milone
6279.M8	Pro Murena (Pro L. Murena)
	De mutuo abolendis injuriis see PA6283.P3
	Pro pace see PA6283.P3
	Philippicae (In M. Antonium Phil. orationes XIV)
6280.A1	Comprehensive editions
6280.A3	Selected orations
	Single orations (or editions of two orations)
6280.A31	I-II (I, V)
6280.A32	II-III (II, XIV)
6280.A33	III-IV, etc.
6280.A34	IV-V
6280.A35	V-VI
6280.A36	VI-VII
6280.A37	VII-VIII
6280.A38	VIII-IX
6280.A39	IX-X
6280.A391	X-XI
6280.A41	XI-XII
6280.A42	XII-XIII
6280.A43	XIII-XIV
6280.A44	XIV
6280.A5-.Z3	Criticism
6281.P4	In Pisonem (In L. Pisonem)
6281.P6	Pro Plancio (Pro Cn. Plancio)

PA6000-6971

	Individual authors
	Cicero, Marcus Tullius
	Orationes
	Editions
	Single orations -- Continued
	Pro Postumo see PA6281.R3
	De praetura siciliensi see PA6282.A54
	De praetura urbana see PA6282.A53
	Pridie in exilium iret see PA6283.Z7P8
6281.P8	De provinciis consularibus
6281.Q4	Pro Quintio (Pro P. Quinctio)
	Ad Quirites see PA6281.R42
6281.R2	Pro Rabirio (Pro C. Rabirio perduellionis reo)
6281.R3	Pro Rabirio Postumo (Pro C. Rabirio Postumo)
	Post reditum orationes I-IV
6281.R4	Editions of I-IV, or I-III
	Single orations (or editions of two)
6281.R41	I Cum senatui gratias egit
6281.R42	II Cum populo gratias egit
6281.R43	III De domo sua ad pontifices
6281.R44	IV De haruspicum responso
6281.R5	Criticism
	De rege Alexandrino see PA6283.A2+
	Pro rege Deiotaro see PA6279.D3
6281.R7	Pro Roscio Amerino
6281.R8	Pro Roscio comoedo
	In Servilium Rullum see PA6279.A8
	Invectiva in Sallustium see PA6283.Z7R4
6281.S3	Pro Scauro (Pro Aemilio Scauro)
	In Senatu in toga candida see PA6281.T6
	Ad Senatum see PA6281.R41
	In Servilium Rullum see PA6279.A8
6281.S5	Pro Sestio (Pro P. Sestio)
	De signis see PA6282.A56
6281.S8	Pro Sulla (Pro C. Corn. Sulla)
	De suppliciis see PA6282.A57
6281.T6	In toga candida (In senatu in toga candida contra C. Antonium et L. Catilinam competitores)
6281.T7	Pro Tullio (Pro M. Tullio)
	In Valerium see PA6306
6281.V3	In Vatinium (In V. testem interrogatio)
	In Verrem I-VII
6282.A2	Comprehensive editions
6282.A3	Selected orations
	Single orations (or editions of two orations)
6282.A4	I Divinatio in Q. Caecilium

PA6000-6971

	Individual authors
	Cicero, Marcus Tullius
	Orationes
	Editions
	Spurious orations -- Continued
6283.Z7R4	Responsio ad orationem C. Sallustii Crispi (In C. Sallustium Crispum controversia; Declamatio in C. Sallustium; Invectiva in Sallustium)
	Ascribed to one Didius by the grammarian Diomedes
	Cf. PA6653.Z5 Sallustius. Invectiva in Ciceronem
	In Valerium see PA6306
	Criticism and interpretation
	Ancient. Scholia
6284.A2	Editions. Collections and selections
	Particular commentators
6284.A3	Q. Asconius Pedianus, 1st century A.D.
	Commentary lost with the exception of Orationum quinque enarratio (In L. Pisonem, pro Scauro, pro Milone, pro Cornelio, In toga candida)
6284.A4	Pseudo-Asconius (4th or 5th century A.D.)
	Commentarius in Div. in Caecilium, and In Verrem, Actio I, II, lib. 1, and 2, to 14 35
6284.A5	Scholia bobiensia
6284.A6	Scholiasta Gronovianus
6284.A7	Other
(6284.A8-Z)	Criticism (of scholia)
	see PA6285
6285	Modern
	Class here general works only
	For treatises on single orations see the oration
6285.A2	Early to 1800/50
6285.A5-Z	1800/50+
(6293)	Language, style, etc.
	see PA6350+
	Opera rhetorica
6294.A2	Editions
6294.A3	Selected works
	Particular works see PA6296+
(6294.A5-.Z3)	Criticism
	see PA6319+
(6294.Z5)	Language, style, etc.
	see PA6350+
	Opera philosophica
6295.A2	Editions
6295.A3	Selected works
	Particular works see PA6296+

Written originally in two books, named after [Q. Lutatius] Catulus, and [L. Licinius] Lucullus, subsequently in four books. Of the first edition "Academica priora" the second book (Lucullus) has been preserved, of the second "Academica posteriora," the first part of the first book and various fragments

PA6000-6971

Individual authors
  Cicero, Marcus Tullius
    Single works
      A to E -- Continued
        De consiliis suis see PA6305
        De consolatione see PA6296.C7
        De consulatu suo (epic) see PA6305
        De differentiis in rebus dubiis see PA6306
6296.D15   De divinatione lib. II
            Class here separate editions and editions combining De
              divinatione and De fato
        De essentia mundi see PA6304.T4
6296.D18   De fato
            Cf. PA6296.D15 De divinatione
6296.D2   De finibus bonorum et malorum lib. V
        De gloria see PA6305
        De inventione rhetorica see PA6304.R5+
        De iure civili in artem redigendo see PA6305
6296.D3   De legibus lib. III
        De memoria see PA6306
6296.D338   De natura deorum lib. I
6296.D4   De natura deorum lib. III ad M. Brutum
                  lib. IV see PA6306
6296.D5   De officiis lib. III
        De optimo genere dicendi see PA6304.O6
6296.D53   De optimo genere oratorum
6296.D6   De oratore lib. III
            Dedicated "Ad Quintum fratrem"
6296.D65   Selections, extracts, etc.
6296.D7   Criticism
        De perfecto oratore see PA6304.O6
        De petitione consulatus see PA6371.C4
        De proprietatibus terminorum see PA6306
        De provincia recte administranda see PA6297.Q9
        De ratione bene gerendae provinciae see PA6297.Q9
        De re militari see PA6306
        De republica lib. VI
            Cf. PA6304.S7 Somnium Scipionis
6296.D8   Texts. By date
6296.D9   Criticism
        De senectute see PA6296.C2
        De temporibus suis see PA6305
        De universitate see PA6304.T4
        De virtutibus see PA6305
        Differentiae similium orationis partium see PA6306
        Divinatio in Q. Caecilium see PA6282.A4
      Epistulae

	Individual authors
	Cicero, Marcus Tullius
	Single works
	Epistulae -- Continued
6297.A1	Comprehensive editions
6297.A2	Selected letters (from all or various groups)
6297.A23	Selected letters (School editions)
	By group
	"Ad familiares" lib. XVI (Epistulae familiares; Epistulae ad diversos)
6297.A3	Editions
6297.A33	Selected letters (Miscellaneous)
6297.A35	Selected books (Miscellaneous)
6297.A4	Single books
	e.g. lib. VIII, M. Caelii epistulae ad C.
6297.A49	Single letters
	e.g. "Ep. I (or IX) ad Lentulum"; "Aurea ad Lucceium epistula" (V, 12)
	Criticism see PA6298
	Ad Atticum libri XVI
	This collection includes letters of other persons to Atticus, e.g. L. Cornelius Balbus major, Cn. Pompeius Magnus, and letters of Cicero to other persons. It covers the period from 68 to 44 B.C.
	Class here also editions including the Epistulae ad Brutum and the Epistulae ad Quintum fratrem
6297.A5	Editions
6297.A53	Selected letters (Miscellaneous)
6297.A55	Selected books (Miscellaneous)
6297.A6	Single books
6297.A69	Single letters
	Criticism see PA6299
	Ad Marcum Brutum lib. II
	The original collection consisted of nine books, books 1-8 are lost. The eighteen letters of the so-called first book, and the five (or according to the older numeration seven) letters of the second book originally formed the 9th book of the collection. The letters of the second book chronologically precede those of the first. The authenticity of the correspondence of Cicero and Brutus has been disputed, but is now generally accepted. Only letters of the year 43 B.C. are preserved.
6297.B7	Editions
	Criticism see PA6301
	Ad Quintum fratrem libri III
	Cf. PA6371.C4 Quintus Tullius Cicero

PA6000-6971

	Individual authors
	Cicero, Marcus Tullius
	Single works
	Epistulae
	By group
	Ad Quintum fratrem libri III -- Continued
6297.Q6	Editions
6297.Q7	Selected letters (Miscellaneous)
6297.Q8	Selected books
6297.Q9	Single letters
	The first letter has been published under the title "De ratione bene gerendae provinciae (De provincia recte administranda; De boni provinciae praesidia officio)
	Criticism see PA6302
6297.Z3	Fragments
	Spurious letters
6297.Z4	Epistula ad Octavianum
	Criticism
6298	General; miscellaneous; Ep. ad familiares
6299	Ad Atticum
6301	Ad Brutum
6302	Ad Quintum fratrem
(6303)	Language, style, etc.
	see PA6350+
6304	G-Z
	Glaucus see PA6305
	Hortensius see PA6305
	Hypomnema see PA6305
	Invectiva in Catilinam see PA6283.Z7I6
6304.L2	Laelius de amicitia
	Laudationes see PA6283.A2+
	Lucullus see PA6296.A2
	Orationes see PA6279+
6304.O6	Orator ad M. Brutum (Orator, sive De optimo genere dicendi; De perfecto oratore)
	Orpheus see PA6306
6304.P2	Paradoxa stoicorum ad M. Brutum
6304.P4	Partitiones oratoriae (De partitione oratoria)
	Poemata see PA6305.P5
	Prognostica see PA6296.A6
	Responsio ad orationem C. Sallustii Crispi see PA6283.Z7R4

	Individual authors
	Cicero, Marcus Tullius
	Single works
	G-Z -- Continued
	Rhetorica (De inventione; Libri rhetorici; Rhetorica prima; Rhetorica vetus; Ars rhetorica)
	Two books written by Cicero in his youth, and in the editions usually combined with the anonymous work entitled "Rhetorica ad Herennium"
6304.R5	Editions (of De inventione, or of De inventione and Rhetorica ad Herennium)
6304.R7	Rhetorica ad Herennium (Rhetorica secunda; Rhetorica nova; "Auctor ad Herennium")
	A treatise in four books, written probably between 86 and 82 B.C., and quoted by St. Jerome as a work of Cicero's. The authorship has been variously attributed to L. Aelius Stilo, M. Antonius Gnipho, Ateius Praetextatus, and especially to Cornificius
6304.R8	Criticism
6304.S7	Somnium Scipionis
	Part of De republica, liber VI; at an early period separately circulated, and annotated, especially by Macrobius, also by Favonius Eulogius. It is frequently also published in the editions of Macrobius
	Cf. PA6498+ Macrobius
	Synonyma see PA6306
6304.T4	Timaeus (De universo; De universitate; De essentia mundi)
6304.T5	Topica ad C. Trebatium
	Cf. PA6231.Z29 Boethius
	Tusculanae disputationes
6304.T6	Editions
6304.T7	Selected books
	Single books
6304.T71	Book I
6304.T72	Book II
6304.T73	Book III
6304.T74	Book IV
6304.T75	Book V
6304.T8	Criticism
6305	Fragments and lost works
6305.A1	Editions (Collections)
	Single works
	Cf. PA6279+ for the larger fragments
	Admiranda
	Alcyones (poem)

PA6000-6971

Individual authors
  Cicero, Marcus Tullius
    Fragments and lost works
      Single works
        Translations of Greek authors
          Single authors -- Continued
            Aeschylus
            Aratus see PA6296.A6
            Aristophanes
            Euripides
            Homerus
            Plato
              Protagoras
              Timaeus see PA6304.T4
            Xenophon
              Cyropaedia
              Oeconomicus
        Uxorius (poem, lost)

6306   Spurious works
    Aenigmata Tullii
    Convivium Ciceronis (Sententiae sapientium qui fuerunt
      in convivio uno cum metullo [or Metullio, i.e. M.
      Tullius Cicero or Metellus?]
    Consolatio (Consolatio, vel de luctu minuendo; De
      consolatione) see PA6296.C7
    De memoria "quod non nulli crediderunt Tironis esse,
      liberti Cic. vel potius interpolatam particulam e libro IV
      Rhetoricorum"
    De mutuo abolendis injuriis
      see De pace
    De natura deorum liber IV
    De pace
      The oration published with title "De pace" or "De mutuo
        abolendis oblivione perpetua praeteritis injuriis," is a
        translation of Cassius Dio XLIV, 22-33
    De proprietatibus terminorum
      see Synonyma
    Differentiae similium orationis partium
    In C. Sallustium Crispum controversia see PA6283.Z7R4
    In Valerium oratio
    Invectiva in Catilinam see PA6283.Z7I6
    Invectiva in Sallustium see PA6283.Z7R4
    Orationes see PA6283.Z7A+
    Orpheus ad M. filium (O., sive De adolescente studioso
      ad M. f.)
      A forgery

PA6000-6971

Individual authors
 Cicero, Marcus Tullius
  Spurious works -- Continued
   Responsio ad orationem C. Sallustii Crispi see
    PA6283.Z7R4
   Synonyma (De proprietatibus terminorum; De dictionum
    proprietatibus; De verborum copia)
  Translations

6307-6308	English (Table PA14)
6309-6310	French (Table PA14)
6311-6312	German (Table PA14)
6313-6314	Italian (Table PA14)
6315.A-Z	Other European languages, except Slavic, A-Z

    Subarrange each language by Table PA14a
    e.g.

6315.S8	Spanish (Table PA14a)
6316.A-Z	Slavic languages, A-Z

    Subarrange each language by Table PA14a

6317.A-Z	Oriental languages, A-Z

    Subarrange each language by Table PA14a
  Criticism, interpretation, etc.

6318	Ancient

   Class here comprehensive criticism or criticism of particular
    groups of works
   For scholia in orationes see PA6284
   Cf. PA6220.A25 Arusianus Messius
   Cf. PA6231.Z29 Boethius. Commentary on Topica
   Cf. PA6385.F2 Favionus Eulogius. Commentary on
    Somnium Scipionis
   Cf. PA6392.G8 Grillius
   Cf. PA6498+ Macrobius. Commentary on Somnium
    Scipionis
   Cf. PA6967.V5 C. Marius Victorinus. Explanationis in
    Rhetoricam lib. II
  Modern
   For treatises on the history or politics of Rome in
    Cicero's age see DG260.C5+

6319	Early to 1800/50
6320	Later, 1800/50-
6322	Minor (Popular). Addresses, essays, lectures

  History of study and appreciation of Cicero
   (Ciceronianism)

6346	General
6347	Particular persons
6348	Translations (as subject)
6349	Study and teaching

   Including theory and method

	Individual authors
	Cicero, Marcus Tullius
	Criticism, interpretation, etc. -- Continued
	Language. Style. Technique
6350	General
	Including technique
6351	Special
	Grammar. Syntax
6352	General
6353	Special
	Style. Figures of speech, etc.
6357	General
6358	Special (Minor)
6361	Rhythm
6362	Collection of idioms
	Lexicography. Semantics
6363	Treatises
6366	Dictionaries. Concordances. Glossaries. Indices
	Class here general dictionaries and dictionaries confined to particular groups of works
6366.A2	Ancient
	Cf. PA6220.A25 Arusianus Messius
6367	Vocabularies (General for use in schools)
6369	Glossaries of particular orations
6370	Glossaries of particular works, A-Z
6371	Cicero (Q.) to Claud...
6371.C4	Cicero, Quintus Tullius, 102-43 B.C. (Table P-PZ38 modified)
6371.C4A61-.C4A78	Separate works. By title
	e.g. De petitione consulatus (Commentariolum petitionis) (A treatise in form of a letter, addressed to his brother Marcus, 64 B.C.); Four letters (three to Tiro, one to Marcus); Poems lost (fragment of Carmen de XII signis preserved)
6371.C5	Cincius Alimentus, L., fl. 210 B.C. (Table P-PZ38 modified)
6371.C5A61-.C5A78	Separate works. By title
	e.g. Annals (In Greek; fragments only); Fragments of seven antiquarian treatises in Latin, presumably by a writer of the same name, but of later date (Augustean age?)
6371.C7	Cinna Helvius, C., fl. 56 B.C. (Table P-PZ38)
	Claudianus, Claudius, fl. 395-404 A.D.
6372.A2	Editions
6372.A25	Selected works
	Carmina minora (Epistulae, idyllia, epigrammata)
	Single works
	De bello Gildonico (in part lost)
	De bello pollentino (gothico)

	Individual authors
	Claudianus, Claudius, fl. 395-404 A.D.
	Single works -- Continued
	De consulatu Stilichonis lib. III
6372.D6	De raptu Proserpinae lib. III
	Epithalamium de nuptiis Honori et Mariae
	Fescennina I-IV
	Four short poems
	In Eutropium lib. II
	In Rufinum lib. II
	Laus Serenae (Carm. min. XXX)
	Panegyricus de tertio consulatu Honorii Augusti
	Panegyricus de quarto consulatu Honorii Augusti
	Panegyricus de sexto consulatu Honorii Augusti
	Panegyricus Manlii Theodori
	Panegyricus Probini et Olybrii
	Phoenix, idyllium (Carm. min. XXVII)
	Greek poems
	Spurious and doubtful poems (Carm. min. Appendix)
6373.A-Z	Translations, by language, A-Z
6374	Criticism
6375	Claudianus Mam. to Cur...
6375.C4	Claudianus Mamertus, d. ca. 474 A.D. (Table P-PZ38 modified)
	Name "Ecdicius" not authentic
6375.C4A61-.C4A78	Separate works. By title
	e.g. Hymni (Spurious)
	De statu animae lib. III
	see class B
	Claudius, Servius
	see Clodius, Servius
6375.C43	Claudius Caesar, d. 54 A.D. (Table P-PZ38)
	Writings lost
	Claudius Mamertinus see PA6500.M28
6375.C45	Claudius Quadrigarius, Q., 1st century B.C. (Table P-PZ38)
	Claudius Rutilius Namatianus see PA6652.R7+
6375.C5	Cledonius (grammarian) 5th(?) century A.D. (Table P-PZ38)
	Clodius, Servius, or Claudius, Servius (grammarian) 1st century B.C.
	Clodius Tuscus, 1st century B.C.
	Cluvius Rufus, M., 1st century A.D.
6375.C57	Coelius Antipater, Lucius (Table P-PZ38)
	Coelius Rufus, M. see PA6234.C7
6375.C6	Columella, L. Junius Moderatus, 1st century A.D. (Table P-PZ38)

Individual authors
    Claudianus Mam. to Cur... -- Continued
6375.C65   Cominianus (grammarian) 4th(?) century A.D. (Table P-PZ38)
          Writings (lost) presumably the source of Charisius, Dositheus magister, and Excerpta Bobiensia
          Cf. PA6277.C7 Charisius
          Cf. PA6381.D6 Dositheus magister
          Cf. PA6385.E8 Excerpta Bobiensia
        Comminianus see PA6375.C65
(6375.C7)   Commodianus, 3rd(?) or 5th century A.D.
          see BR60+
        Congus, Junius, 1st century B.C. (M. Junius Congus "Gracchanus"?)
          Identical with M. Junius Gracchanus?
6375.C73   Consentius (grammarian) 5th century A.D. (Table P-PZ38)
        Consolatio ad Liviam (Epicedion Drusi) see PA6520.C7
        Corbulo, Cn. Domitius (historian) d. 67 A.D.
        Cordus, Aelius Junius (historian) 3rd century A.D.
        Cordus, Aulus Cremutius
          see Cremutius
6375.C76   Corippus, Flavius Cresconius, fl. ca. 549 A.D. (Table P-PZ38)
        Cornelius Fronto see PA6389.F6+
        Cornelius Gallus see PA6389.G3
        Cornelius Nepos see PA6515+
        Cornelius Severus see PA6694.S45
        Cornelius Sisenna see PA6696.S4
        Cornelius Tacitus see PA6705+
        Cornificius (rhetor)
          Rhetorica ad Herennium see PA6304.R5+
6375.C8   Cornutus, Lucius Anneaus, fl. 65 A.D. (Table P-PZ38 modified)
          For Greek works see PA3948.C8
6375.C8A61-.C8A78   Separate works. By title
          e.g. De enuntiatione vel orthographia (extract in Cassiodorus); Commentary on Vergilius (lost); Pseudo-Cornutus (Scholia in Persium; Scholia in Juvenalem)
        Corvinus, M. Val. Messala see PA6514.M2
        Cremutius Cordus, A., (historian) d. 25 A.D.
        Curiatus Maternus
          see Maternus, Curiatus

PA6000-6971

Individual authors

Claudianus Mam. to Cur... -- Continued

(6375.C9)   Curiosum urbis Romae regionum XIV cum breviaribus suis

    Transmitted in two redactions; the earlier one is entitled Notitia regionum. The two redactions combined and enlarged by Italian scholars of the 15th century, were published as the work of a newly discovered author "Publius Victor" with title "De regionibus urbis Romae." The Curiosum has also been published as the work of "Sextus Rufus."

    see class DG

Curtius Rufus, Q., fl. ca. 41 A.D. Historiae Alexandri Magni regis Macedonum (De rebus gestis Alex. M., lib. X)

    Books I-II lost; supplement by J. C. Freinsheim

6376.A2	Editions. By date
6376.A3A-.A3Z	Selections. By editor, A-Z
6376.A5	Selected books (three or more)
6376.B1-.B91	Particular books (one or two)
	e.g.
6376.B3	Book III (or III-IV)
6376.B9	Book IX
6376.B91	Book X
6377	Translations
6378	Criticism
6379	Curtius Val. to Don...
6379.C7	Curtius Valerianus (grammarian) 5th(?) century A.D. (Table P-PZ38)
(6379.C8)	Cyprianus (paraphrast of the Heptateuch)
	see BR60+ BR1720
(6379.C9)	Cyprianus, Thascius Caecilius, bp. of Carthage, ca. 200-258 A.D.
	see BR60+ BR1720
(6379.D15)	Damasus, pope, d. 384 A.D.
	Poems (chiefly epitaphs)
	see BR60+ Class CN
6379.D2	De excidio Troiae. "Dares Phrygius"

    A fictitious name borrowed from Ilias E9; the De excidio Troiae presumably is what the author claims for it, a free version of a Greek original composed early in the 6th century A.D. Editions of Dictys and Dares are frequently combined

    For the medieval literature based on this work see classes PQ, PR, PT, etc.

    Cf. PA6379.D3 Dictys Cretensis

De laude Pisonis see PA6271.C2A3

6379.D23   De rebus bellicis

	Individual authors
	Curtius Val. to Don... -- Continued
6379.D25	De viris illustribus urbis Romae ("Historia Liviana")
	In its single manuscripts frequently ascribed to the younger Plinius. In the earlier editions it has been ascribed successively to the younger Plinius, Suetonius, Cornelius Nepos and S. Aurelius Victor. The redactor of the "Historiae romanae compendium" calls it "Historia Liviana," although apparently not based directly upon Livius
	Cf. PA6966.A2 Victor, Sextus Aurelius
	Declamatio in L. Sergium Catilinam see PA6140.D4
	Dicta Catonis see PA6272+
6379.D3	"Dictys Cretensis." Ephemerides belli trojani lib. VI
	Fabulous history of the Trojan war purporting to be the diary of an eyewitness. The Greek original, of which only a fragment is thus far known, may have been composed at the time of its pretended discovery under Nero. The Latin version is by L. Septimius (presumably a grammarian of the fourth century)
	Cf. PA3965.D14 Greek literature
	Cf. PA6379.D2 Dares Phrygius
	Didius (rhetor of uncertain date) see PA6283.Z7R4
6379.D35	Diomedes (grammarian) 4th century A.D. Ars grammatica
	Dirae see PA6271.C8
	Domitius Corbulo
	see Corbulo
6379.D5	Domitius Marsus, 1st century B.C. (Table P-PZ38)
6379.D6	Donatianus (i.e.? Tiberius Claudius Maximus Donatianus, son of Ti. Claudius Donatus) (Table P-PZ38 modified)
6379.D6A61-.D6A78	Separate works. By title
	e.g. Fragments of "Ars grammatica accepta ex auditorio Donatiani" ("Donatiani fragmentum")
6380	Donatus, Aelius, 4th century A.D.
6380.A25	Ars minor (prima)
6380.A3	Ars maior (secunda)
(6380.A35)	Scholia in Terentium (including Vita)
	see PA6766
(6380.A38)	Scholia in Vergilium (including Vita)
	see PA6823
	Criticism
6380.A5	Ancient and medieval
6380.A6-Z	Modern
6381	Donatus (Ti.) to Enn...
6381.D5	Donatus, Tiberius Claudius, 4th to 5th century A.D. (Table P-PZ38 modified)
6381.D5A61-.D5A78	Separate works. By title

PA6000-6971

Individual authors
  Ennius, Q., 239-169 B.C. -- Continued
    Separate works

6382.A3   Annales (epic poem)
        About six hundred verses preserved
      Epicharmus
        Didactic poem on subjects of natural philosophy; based
          upon a spurious poem of Epicharmus
        Cf. PA3968.E8 Epicharmus
      Euhermerus (Sacra historia)
        Translation of the Hiera anagraphe of Euhemerus
      Heduphagetica
      Medea
      Praecepta (Protrepticus)
      Saturae
    Doubtful works
      De litteris syllabisque
      De metris
      De augurandi disciplina
6382.A8-Z   Criticism (regardless of works)
6383 Ennius (grammarian) to Eut...
6383.E12   Ennius (the younger, grammarian) (Table P-PZ38)
      Cf. PA6382 Ennius, Q. Doubtful works
    Ennodius, Magnus Felix, 473/4-521 A.D.
      Cf. BR60+ BR1720
    Epicedium Drusi (Consolatio ad Liviam) see PA6520.C7
6383.E7   Euanthius, of Constantinople (grammarian), 4th century
      A.D. (Table P-PZ38)
      Cf. PA6766.E7 Terentius
6383.E8   Eugraphius (grammarian) 6th (?) century A.D. (Table P-
      PZ38)
    Eulogius Favonius see PA6385.F2
6383.E9   Eumenius (panegyrist) 3rd century A.D. (Table P-PZ38)
6384 Eutropius, 4th century A.D. Breviarium ab urbe condita
    For the continuations of Paulus Diaconus and
      Landolphus Sagax see DG208
6385 Euty... to Florus
6385.E7   Eutyches (Eutychius or Euticius?) grammarian, 6th century
      A.D. (Table P-PZ38 modified)
6385.E7A61-.E7A78   Separate works. By title
      e.g. De aspiratione; De verbo (Ars de verbo)
6385.E8 Excerpta Bobiensia (Anonymus Bobiensis)
    A treatise "De nomine, de pronomine, de verbo," preserved in
      a manuscript formerly in Bobbio, now in Vienna
  Excerpta Valesia see PA6203+
6385.E85 Excidium Troiae

PA6000-6971

Individual authors

Euty... to Florus -- Continued

6385.E9   Expositio totius mundi et gentium (Expositio mundi)

         Latin translation in barbarous language of a Greek treatise; later much abridged and improved in style, it appears with title: Liber Junioris philosophi in quo continetur totius orbis descriptio

         For treatises on the language, see PA2673.E9

6385.E95   Exuperantius, Julius (historian), 4th or 5th century A.D. (Table P-PZ38)

         Fabius Maximus Servilianus, Q. (annalist) fl. 142 B.C.

         Fabius Pictor, Q., fl. ca. 225-216 B.C.

          Annales

            In Greek; later translated into Latin, presumably not by Fabius

         Faventinus, M. Cetius (date unknown) see PA6968.1

         Favinus Remmius see PA6385.F8

6385.F2   Favonius Eulogius, fl. ca. 385 A.D. Commentarius on Cicero's Somnium Scipionis

         Felix Ennodius

          see Ennodius

6385.F3   Fenestella, 52 B.C.-ca. 19 A.D. Annales

         Fragments only

6385.F4   Festus, Sextus Pompeius, 2nd century A.D. De verborum significatione lib. XX

         An abridgment (in part lost) of M. Verrius Flaccus, De verborum significatu

         For the epitome by Paulus Diaconus see PA8395.P3

6385.F6   Festus (Rufius or Rufus F.?) 4th century A.D. Breviarium historiae populi romani

         Figulus Nigidius see PA6518.N4

(6385.F65)   Filargirius, Junius (or Philargyrius) 5th(?) century A.D.

         see PA6823.P3

         Firmianus Lactantius see PA6451.L23

6385.F7   Firmicus Maternus, Julius, of Syracuse, fl. 336 A.D. (Table P-PZ38 modified)

6385.F7A61-.F7A78   Separate works. By title

         e.g. Matheseos libri VIII

         De errore profanarum religionum

          see BR60+ BR1720

         Flaccus

          see Calpurnius, Horace, Persius, Siculus, Valerius, Verrius

         Flavianus (grammarian) see PA6277.C7

6385.F8   Flavianus (Favinus?), Remmius (end of 4th or beginning of 5th century A.D.) Carmen de ponderibus et mensuris

         In the older editions frequently ascribed to Priscianus

         Flavius Caper see PA6271.C35

	Individual authors
	Euty... to Florus -- Continued
	Flavius Sosipater Charisius see PA6277.C7
	Flavius Vopiscus see PA6971.V7
	Florus, Julius see PA6386+
	Florus, Lucius Annaeus, 2nd century A.D.
6386	Editions
6386.A2	Epitomae libri II
6386.A3	Poems
6386.A35	Carmina
	Pervigilium Veneris see PA6557.P3+
6386.A4	Vergilius orator an poeta
	Autobiographical introduction alone preserved
6387	Translations
6388	Criticism
6389	Florus (P. A.) to Gell...
	Florus, P. Annius see PA6386+
6389.F18	Fortunatianus, C. Chirius (grammarian) 4th century A.D. (Table P-PZ38)
	Fortunatianus Atilius see PA6220.A5
	Fortunatus, Venantius Honorius Clementianus, bp., ca. 540-ca. 600 A.D. see PA8310.F7
	Frontinus, Sextus Julius
6389.F4	Collected works. By date
6389.F4A-.F4Z	Separate works. By title, A-Z
	De aquis urbis Romae lib. II (De aquaeductibus u.R.) see TD216
	Stratagematon lib. III
	A fourth book generally considered spurious
	Treatise on gromatics (fragments)
6389.F5	Criticism
	Fronto, Marcus Cornelius
	Correspondence with the emperors M. Aurelius; L. Verus, a.o.
6389.F6	Collected works. By date
6389.F7A4	Correspondence. By date
6389.F7A5-.F7Z	Criticism
	Fulgentius, Fabius Planciades
	Identity with F. the Bishop of Ruspe in Africa, 467-532, author of many theological treatises, disputed
6389.F8	Collected works. By date
6389.F8A-.F8Z	Separate works. By title, A-Z
	De aetatibus mundi et hominis
	Expositio sermonum antiquorum (De abstrusis sermonibus)
	Expositio Virgilianae continentiae see PA6823.F8
	Mythologiarum lib. III

PA6000-6971

	Individual authors
	Florus (P. A.) to Gell...
	Fulgentius, Fabius Planciades
	Separate works. By title, A-Z -- Continued
	Physiologus (lost)
	Super Thebaiden see PA6698
6389.F9	Criticism
	Gaius (jurist) 2nd century A.D.
	Class here philological works only
	For legal works see Class K
	Gallicanus, Vulcacius see PA6971.V8
6389.G3	Gallus, Gaius Cornelius, 69?-26 B.C. (Table P-PZ38)
	Cf. PA6955.C5 Verg. Appendix: Ciris
	Gallus, Titus, grammarian, 5th(?) century A.D. see PA6823.S2
	Gargilius (historian). Vita Alexandri Severi see PA6389.G5
6389.G5	Gargilius Martialis, Q., fl. ca. 240 A.D. (Table P-PZ38)
	Gaudentius, 5th (?) century A.D. see PA6823.S2
	Gellius, Aulus, 2nd century A.D. Noctes atticae
6390.A2	Editions. By date
6390.A25	Selections
6390.A5-Z	Translations. By language, A-Z
6391.A-.Z3	Criticism
6391.Z5	Language, etc.
6392	Gem... to Horatius
	Gennadius, presbyter of Marseille, 5th century see BR60+ BR1720
	Geographus Ravennas see PA6652.R18
6392.G3	Germanicus Caesar, 15 B.C.-19 A.D. Aratea
	Gildas Sapiens, ca. 500-569 see DA150
	Gracchanus, M. Junius see Congus, Junius
6392.G5	Gracchus, C. Sempronius, 154-121 B.C. (Table P-PZ38)
	Granius Licinianus see PA6451.L6
6392.G6	Grattius (Gratius Faliscus, of Falerii) fl. between 43 B.C. and 14 A.D. Cynegeticon
	Editions frequently include the Cynegetica of Nemesianus
(6392.G68)	Gregorius Turonensis (Saint, bp. of Tours, 538-594) see DC64
6392.G8	Grillius (grammarian) 5th (?) century A.D. Commentum in Ciceronis De inventione
6392.H15	Hadrianus, emperor of Rome, 76-138 A.D. (Table P-PZ38)
	Hegesippus see PA4223.A19
	Helvius Cinna see PA6371.C7
	Herennius ("Auctor ad Herennium," or Rhetorica ad H.) see PA6304.R7
	Hermerus, Claudius (veterinarian) see PA6514.M8

Individual authors
  Gem... to Horatius -- Continued
    Hilarianus, Q. Julius, bp. in Africa, fl. 397
      De ratione paschae numeroque annorum mundi see
        CE83
    Hirtius, Aulus see PA6235+
    Historia Apollonii see PA6206.A6
    Historia augusta see PA6139.H7
    Historia Liviana see PA6379.D25
    Homerus latinus see PA6445.I2
6392.H9   Honorius, Julius "orator" 5th (?) century A.D.
      Cosmographia
      "Recensio A" (Excerpta eivs sphaerae vel continentia;
        Excerpta cosmographiae)
      "Recensio B"
        A later redaction, preceded by the "Cosmographia Julii
          Caesaris" (a brief account of the survey of the Roman
          empire under Augustus beginning "Julio Caesare et
          Marco Antoni[n]o consulibus")
6392.H93   Cosmographia ("Aethici cosmographia")
        A compilation based upon Honorius (Recensio B) and
          Orosius, entitled in the older manuscripts
          "Cosmographia," or "Orthographa," or "Situs et
          descriptio orbis terrarum;" in later medieval
          manuscripts it is falsely ascribed to "Aethicus" (not to
          be confused with the fictitious cosmography in six
          books entitled "Edicta Aethici philosophi cosmographi")
        Cf. PA6202 "Aethicus Ister"
  Horace
    Editions
6393.A2   Opera (Carmina. Poemata). By date
6393.A3A-.A3Z School editions. By editor, A-Z (if anonymous, by date)
6393.A4   Selections (from Odes, Epistles, and Satires)
6393.A5   Selections. Quotations. Thoughts
    Separate works
      Ars poetica see PA6393.E6+
      Carmen saeculare see PA6393.C6
6393.C2   Carmina (Odae) lib. I-IV. By date
        Including editions of Carmina, Epodae and Carmen
          saeculare
6393.C3   Selected odes (from various books)
6393.C41-.C44 Selected books
        Divided by book, e.g. PA6393.C42 for Book II
6393.C51-.C54 Single odes
        Divided by book, ode number, and date; e.g.,
          PA6393.C53, no. 27, 1937 for Book III, Ode no. 27,
          published 1937

PA6000-6971

	Individual authors
	Horace
	Editions
	Separate works
	Carmina (Odae) lib. I-IV. By date
	Single odes -- Continued
6393.C6	Carmen saeculare
	Criticism
	see PA6410+
6393.C8	Epodae. By date
6393.C9	Criticism
6393.E2	Epistulae, lib. I-II
6393.E3	Liber I
6393.E4	Liber II
	Three epistles, known as the "literary epistles," including the "Ars poetica"
6393.E5	Single epistles
	Ars poetica (Epistula ad Pisones de arte poetica)
6393.E6	Editions
6393.E7	Criticism
6393.E75	Epistola ad Augustum
6393.E8	Criticism
	Class here criticism of all epistles, or of a single epistle, Ars poetica excepted
6393.S2	Satirae (Sermones) libri I-II
6393.S3	Liber I
6393.S4	Liber II
6393.S5	Single satires
6393.S8	Criticism
	Translations
	Polyglot. English
6394.A1	Polyglot. By date
	English
	Comprehensive (or selections from the Odes and the other works)
6394.A2	Various translators. By date
6394.A5-Z	Individual translators, A-Z
6395	Carmina
	Including translations of selected odes, or selected books, or translations of Odes and Epodes
6395.A2	Various translators. By date
6395.A5-.Z3	Individual translators, A-Z
6395.Z5A-.Z5Z	Particular odes, by translator, A-Z
6396	Other works
6396.A1	Epodes. Epistulae. Satirae. By date
	Epistulae and Satirae, or Satirae and Epistulae
6396.A2	Various translators. By date

	Individual authors
	Horace
	Translations
	Polyglot. English
	English
	Other works
	Epistulae and Satirae, or Satirae and Epistulae -- Continued
6396.A2A-.A2Z	Individual translators, A-Z
	Epistulae (collected or selected)
6396.E5	Various translators. By date
6396.E5A-.E5Z	Individual translators, A-Z
6396.E6A-.E6Z	Ars poetica. By translator, A-Z
6396.S3A-.S3Z	Satirae. By translator, A-Z
6397	French (Table PA15)
6398	German (Table PA15)
6399	Italian (Table PA15)
6400	Spanish (Table PA15)
6401.A-Z	Other European, except Slavic, A-Z
6402.A-Z	Slavic, A-Z
6403.A-Z	Oriental, A-Z
6404	Imitations. Adaptations. Parodies. Travesties
6406	Illustrations
6407	Music
6407.5	Anniversaries, celebrations, etc. Collections in prose or verse in honor of Horace
	Interpretation and criticism
	Ancient. Scholia
	Cf. PA6442.A2 Versification
	Editions
6408.A1A-.A1Z	Collections. By editor, A-Z
6408.A3	Pomponius Porphyrio, 3rd century A.D.
	Authenticity disputed
6408.A4	Pseudo-Acro
	Combination of scholia of various authors, largely based on Porphyrio
6408.A5	"Commentator Cruquianus"
	Collection of glosses, compiled and revised by J. Cruquius (Jacques de Crucque)
(6408.A8-.Z3)	Criticism
	see PA6410+
	Medieval
(6408.Z5)	Commentaries
	Glosses see PA6444
	Modern (General and Odes)
(6409)	Commentaries
	see PA6410+

	Individual authors
	Horace
	Interpretation and criticism
	Modern (General and Odes) -- Continued
6410	Early to 1800/50
6411	Later, 1800/50+
6411.Z5	Minor. Addresses, essays, lectures
6436	Technique
	Language. Style
6438	General
6439	Grammar. Syntax
6442	Versification
6442.A2	Ancient
6444	Glossaries. Indices. Concordances
6445	Hort... to Juv...
6445.H3	Hortensius Hortalus, Q., 114-50 B.C. (Table P-PZ38)
	Orations (fragments); poems; Annales, lost
6445.H35	Hosidius Geta, 2nd century A.D. (Table P-PZ38)
	Author (?) of Medea, tragoedia (a Vergilian cento)
	Cf. PA6801.A49 Vergilius
6445.H5	Hydatius (or Idacius) Lemicus, bp. of Aquae Flaviae (?) 5th century A.D. (Table P-PZ38 modified)
6445.H5A61-.H5A78	Separate works. By title
	e.g. Chronicon; Fasti ("Fasti Hydatii")
	Hyginus gromaticus, fl. between 98 and 117 A.D.
6445.H6	Editions. By date
6445.H6A3	Agrorum quae sit inspectio(?)
	Anonymous treatise ascribed to Hyginus
6445.H6A4	De limitibus. De condicionibus agrorum. De generibus controversiarum
6445.H6A5	De limitibus constituendis
	By a later gromatic writer of the same name (?)
6445.H6A6	De munitionibus castrorum
	A treatise of the 3rd (?) century, wrongly ascribed to Hyginus gromaticus
6445.H6A7-.H6Z3	Criticism
6445.H7	Hyginus, C. Julius, fl. ca. 60 B.C. to 10+ A.D.
	De agricultura (fragments)
	De apibus (fragments)
	De dis penatibus (lost)
	De familiis trojanis (lost)
	De origine et situ urbium italicarum (fragments)
	De proprietatibus deorum (lost)
	De viris claris
	De vita rebusque inlustrium virorum (fragments)
	Exempla (lost)
	Commentaries

	Individual authors
	Hort... to Juv...
	Hyginus, C. Julius, fl. ca. 60 B.C. to 10+ A.D.
	Commentaries -- Continued
	Helvius Cinna, Propempticon Pollionis (lost)
	Vergilius (fragments)
	Cf. PA6823.Z5 Vergilius
6445.H7A7-.H7Z3	Criticism
	Hyginus (mythographer)
	Presumably a writer of a later date (2nd century A.D.?) to be distinguished from Hyginus gromaticus, and also from C. Julius Hyginus, to whom the authorship of the Astronomiae, and of the Fabulae, was formerly ascribed
6445.H8	Editions. By date
6445.H8A3	De astronomia lib. IV (De astrologia. Poetica astronomica. Poeticon astronomicon)
6445.H8A4	Excerptum de astrologia Arati (Excerptio de astrologia)
	In the mss. also entitled: Yginus philosophus de imaginibus celi
6445.H8A6	Fabulae (Genealogiae. Fabulae)
	Originally two distinct works, now preserved in a mythological manual that consists of a meagre excerpt from the "Genealogiae," followed by the "Fabulae" (also an excerpt?), and the "Indices" (a later addition by an unknown compiler)
6445.H8A8-.H8Z3	Criticism
	Idacius see PA6445.H5
6445.I2	Ilias latina (Homerus latinus)
	1070 hexameters by Silius Italicus or Baebius Italicus? From the 12th century on, ascribed in mss. and in the older editions to "Pindarus" or "Pindarus Thebanus"
	Isidorus, bp. of Sevilla, ca. 570-636 A.D.
	Cf. BR60+
6445.I3	Collected works. Selected works. By date
6445.I3A-.I3Z	Separate works. By title, A-Z
	Chronica
	De natura rerum
	Epigrammata
	Etymologiarum libri XX (Origines) see AE2
	Historia Gothorum, Vandalorum et Suevorum
6445.I4A-.I4Z	Translations. By language, A-Z
6445.I5	Criticism
	Itala (Latin translation of the Bible) see BS72+
	Italicus see PA6445.I2
(6445.I6)	Itineraria
	see DG28+

	Individual authors
	Hort... to Juv...
	Itineraria -- Continued
6445.I7	Itinerarium Alexandri

Not an itinerary in the ordinary sense, i.e. a list of stations and roads of the Roman empire, but a narrative of the campaigns of Alexander the Great, based on Arrianus' Anabasis, and also on Pseudo-Callisthenes in the Latin translation of Julius Valerius to whom the authorship of the itinerary has been ascribed by some authorities. The last part, and the account of Trajan's war with Persia which formed part of the work are lost

Cf. PA3935.A3 Arrianus. Anabasis
Cf. PA3946.C3 Pseudo-Callisthenes
Cf. PA6791.V8+ Julius Valerius

	Itineraria Antonini
(6445.I75)	Itinerarium provinciarum Antoni[n]i Augusti
(6445.I77)	Imperatoris Antonini Augusti itinerarium maritimum
(6445.I8)	Itinerarium burdigalense (hierosolymitanum)

Journey from Burdigala (Bordeaux) to Jerusalem with description of sacred places

6445.J2	Jordanis, fl. 551 A.D. (Table P-PZ38 modified)
6445.J2A61-.J2A78	Separate works. By title

e.g. Getica (De origine actibusque Getarum) (An abridgment from the work of Cassiodorus) - Cf. PA6271.C4+ Cassiodorus; Romana (De summa temporum vel de origine actibusque gentis Romanorum; De regnorum ac temporum successione)

Jornandes see PA6445.J2

Josippus (Egesippus, Hegesippus) see PA4223.A19

6445.J3	Juba (writer on metrics) 2nd century A.D. (?) (Table P-PZ38)

Julius

see surnames Caesar, Hyginus, Paris, Valerius, etc.

Junior philosophus see PA6385.E9

Junius

see surnames Gallio, Filargirius, Juvenalis, etc.

Justinus, M. Junianius, 3rd(?) century A.D. Historiae philippicae ex Trogo Pompeio

6445.J6	Editions. By date
(6445.J7A-.J7Z)	Translations. By language, A-Z
	see D58
6445.J8	Criticism

Juvenal. Satirae I-XVI (lib. I-V)

Divided into five books: I-V, lib. I; VI, lib. II; VII-IX, lib. III; X-XII, lib. IV; XIII-XVI, lib. V

	Individual authors
	Juvenal. Satirae I-XVI (lib. I-V) -- Continued
6446	Editions
	Class here also editions of Juvenalis and Persius, or Juvenalis, Persius and Sulpicia
6446.A2	Comprehensive editions (or larger portion)
6446.A4	Selections. Quotations. Passages
6446.A5	Selected satires (three or more) or Selected books
6446.A61-.A76	Single satires (two or more)
	e.g.
6446.A61	Satira I (or I-II; or I,VI; etc.)
6446.A62	Satira II (or II-III; or II, V; etc.)
6446.A63	Satira III (or III-IV; or III, VIII; etc.)
6447	Translations
6448	Criticism, interpretation, etc.
6448.A1	Ancient. Scholia
	Medieval
6448.A15	Commentaries
	Glossae see PA6448.Z8
	Modern
6448.A2	Early to 1800/50
6448.A5-.Z3	Later, 1800/50+
	Language, style, technique
6448.Z5	General
6448.Z6	Grammar. Syntax
6448.Z7	Versification
6448.Z8	Glossaries. Indices. By date
6451	Juvenc... to Liv...
(6451.J7)	Juvencus, C. Attius, 4th century A.D. Evangeliorum lib. IV (Historia evangelica)
	see BS2552
6451.L15	Labeo, Attius, 1st century A.D. (Table P-PZ38 modified)
6451.L15A61-.L15A78	Separate works. By title
	e.g. Translation of Iliad and Odyssey (lost)
6451.L16	Labeo, Cornelius, 3rd (?) century A.D. (Table P-PZ38)
6451.L17	Labeo, M. Antistius (jurist, son of Pacuvius, A.L.), ca. 54 B.C.-ca. 17 A.D. (Table P-PZ38)
6451.L18	Labeo, Pacuvius Antistius (jurist, father of M. A. L.), d. 42 B.C. (Table P-PZ38)
6451.L2	Laberius, Decimus (writer of mimi), d. 43 B.C. (Table P-PZ38)
6451.L23	Lactantius Firmianus, Lucius Caecilius, 3rd century A.D. (Table P-PZ38)
	Cf. BR60+ BR1720

PA6000-6971

	Individual authors
	Juvenc... to Liv... -- Continued
6451.L25	Lactantius Placidus, 6th (?) century A.D. (Table P-PZ38)
	Under this name (otherwise unknown), manuscripts transmit scholia on the Thebais of Papinius Statius, presumably based upon an older commentary (5th century?), and in the 6th (?) century revised by one Lactantius Placidus, who was later confused with the ecclesiastical writer. A paraphrase in prose of Ovid's Metamorphoses entitled "Narrationes fabularum" also appears under the name of L.P.
	Cf. PA6531 Ovidius Naso. Paraphrases
	Cf. PA6698.A2 Statius. Scholia
6451.L27	Laevius (poet), 1st century B.C. Erotopaegnia
	Fragments
6451.L3	Lampridius, Aelius, 4th century A.D. (Table P-PZ38)
	Latinus Pacatus Drepanius see PA6554.P15
6451.L35	Latro, M. Porcius, fl. 4 B.C. (Table P-PZ38)
	Cf. PA6140.D4 Declamatio in Catilinam
6451.L39	Laudatio Turiae
6451.L4	Laudes Domini
6451.L53-.L533	Licentius, of Tagaste. Carmina ad Augustinum (Table P-PZ42)
6451.L6	Licianus, Granius (historian), 2nd (?) century A.D. (Table P-PZ38)
	Praenomen Gaius uncertain
	Licinius Macer Calvus, C. see PA6271.C33
	Licinus Porcius see PA6641.P83
	Livy. Ab urbe condita
	Of the 142 books of the history only books 1-10, 21-45, or Decades I, III, IV and part of V are preserved, apart from fragments, outlines ("periochae"), and epitomes
	Editions
6452.A2	By date
	Selected books. School editions
6452.A3A-.A3Z	Miscellaneous. By editor, A-Z
	First decade (Books 1-10)
6452.A4	Complete
6452.A5	Three or more
	Third decade (Books 21-30; 2nd Punic War)
6452.A6	Complete
6452.A7	Three or more
	Fourth (and fifth) decade (Books 31-40; 41-45)
6452.A8	Complete editions of 4th (or of 4th and 5th) decade
6452.A9	Three or more
	Including editions of 5th decade
	Single books (editions or one or two books)

	Individual authors
	Livy. Ab urbe condita
	Editions
	Single books (editions or one or two books) -- Continued
6452.B1-.B95	Books I-X
	e.g.
6452.B1	I (I-II or I, XXI; etc.)
6452.B2	II (II-III or II, VIII; etc.)
6452.B3	III (III-IV or III, V; etc.)
6452.B9	IX (IX-X or IX, XXI; etc.)
6452.B95	X (X, XXI; or X, XXV; etc.)
6452.C1-.C95	Books XXI-XXX
6452.D1-.D95	Books XXXI-XL
6452.E1-.E5	Books XLI-XLV
6452.F8	Fragments. By date
	Including editions of Fragmentum of book 91 in palimpsest vaticanus-palatinus 24 (on the Sertorian war)
	Summaries, outlines, etc.
	Ancient
6452.L5	Epitome Liviana
	Lost; existence disputed
6452.P4	Periochae
	For all the books with the exception of books 136-137; for the first book two periochae by different authors
	Julius Obsequens. Prodiga see PA6518.O2
(6452.Z2)	Cassiodorus. Chronica
	see PA6271.C4+
6452.Z3	Papyrus Oxyrhynchus
(6452.Z7)	Modern
	see PA6452.A3
6452.Z8	Supplements
(6452.Z9)	Lost works (Rhetorical and philosophical)
	see PA6459
	Translations
(6453)	English
	see DG207
6454	French
6455	German
6456	Italian
6457.A-Z	Other languages, A-Z
6458	Adaptations. Paraphrases. Tales. Dramatizations
	Interpretation, criticism, biography, etc.
(6459.A1)	Commentaries
6459.A2	Early to 1800
6459.A5-.Z3	Later, 1800+
6459.Z5	Minor. Addresses, essays, lectures
	Technique. Language. Style

PA6000-6971

	Individual authors
	Livy. Ab urbe condita
	Interpretation, criticism, biography, etc.
	Technique. Language. Style -- Continued
6472	General
	Grammar. Syntax
6474	General
6475	Special
6475.Z8	Glossaries, indices, etc. By date
6475.Z9	List of words. By date
6477	Livius (Andron.) to Luca...
	Livius Andronicus, fl. 240-207 B.C.
6477.L3A-.L3Z3	Criticism
6477.L3Z5	Grammar. Syntax
6477.L3Z6	Versification. By date
	Longus see PA6797.V7
	Lucan, 39-65
	Pharsalia (De bello civili)
6478.A2	Editions
6479.A-Z	Translations. By language, A-Z
	For medieval adaptations see the author in Class PQ, PT, etc.
6479.Z9	Prose paraphrases (Latin)
6480	Criticism
6480.Z9	Fragments (lost poems)
	Cf. PA6271.C2A3 Carmen de laude Pisonis (Panegyricus in Pisonem)
6481	Luci... to Lucr...
6481.L6	Lucilius, C., 2nd century B.C. Satirae lib. XXX
	Fragments
6481.L8	Lucilius Junior, 1st century A.D. (Table P-PZ38)
	Supposed author of the poem Aetna; addressee of Seneca's Epistulae morales
	For Aetna see PA6202.A5+
	Lucretius Carus, Titus. De rerum natura
6482	Editions
6482.A2	By date
6482.A3	Selected portions
6482.A4	Selections, thoughts, passages
6482.A5	Selected books
6482.A61-.A66	Single books
	Subarrange by book number, e.g. PA6482.A61, Book I; PA6482.A62, Book II; etc.
6483.A-Z	Translations. By language and translator, A-Z
	Criticism, interpretation, etc.
(6484.A1)	Commentaries
6484.A5-Z	General treatises

	Individual authors
	Lucretius Carus, Titus. De rerum natura
	Criticism, interpretation, etc. -- Continued
6485	Special. Minor
	Language. Technique
6495	General
6496	Grammar. Syntax
6496.Z6	Versification
6496.Z8	Glossaries, indices, etc., by date
6497	Luct... to Macr...
	Luctatius Placidus
	see Placidus, glossator
	Lusorius see PA6497.L7
6497.L5	Lutatius Catulus, Q., consul, 102 B.C. (Table P-PZ38)
6497.L7	Luxorius (Lusorius, Luxurius?) 6th century A.D. (Table P-PZ38)
	Epigrammatist, and supposed compiler of the Anthologia latina
	Cf. PA6128.A+ Anthologia latina
	Lygdamus
	Cf. PA6787.A43 Tibullus
6497.L8	Texts. By date
6497.L9	Criticism
6497.M2	Macer, Aemilius, d. 16 B.C. (Table P-PZ38 modified)
	The name of Macer Floridus or (Aemilius) Macer is erroneously given to the composition of a 10th century French physician Odo Magdunensis, De viribus herbarum
6497.M2A61-.M2A78	Separate works. By title
	e.g. De herbis; Ornithogonia; Theriaca
6497.M4	Macer, C. Licinius (annalist) d. 66 B.C. (Table P-PZ38)
	Macrobius, Ambrosius Aurelius Theodosius
	Presumably identical with Macrobius, the proconsul of Africa, who flourished from 399 to 422 A.D.
6498.A2	Editions. By date
	Saturnalia lib. VII
	Discussion on Virgil forms chief part of the work
	Commentarius in Ciceronis Somnium Scipionis
	De differentiis et societatibus graeci latinique verbi
	Excerpts only
6498.A5-Z	Translations, by language, A-Z
6499	Criticism
6500	Mae... to Mart...
6500.M2	Maecenas, C. Cilnius, d. 8 B.C. (Table P-PZ38)
	For works about Maecenas see DG291.7.M3
6500.M25	Maecianus, Lucius Volusius (jurist) 2nd century A.D. (Table P-PZ38 modified)

PA6000-6971

Individual authors
  Mae... to Mart...
    Maecianus, Lucius Volusius (jurist) 2nd century A.D. --
      Continued

6500.M25A61-
  .M25A78
	Separate works. By title
	  e.g. Assis distributio (Distributio partium)
	  Quaestionum de fidei commissis lib. XVI; Ex lege
	    rhodia; De publicis iudiciis lib. XIV
	      see class K

	Mallius Theodorus, Flavius see PA6786.T5
6500.M28	Mamertinus, Claudius, 4th century A.D. Panegyricus in Julianum Caesarem
	Mamertus, Claudianus see PA6375.C4
	Manilius, Marcus. Astronomicon
6500.M4	Editions
6500.M41-.M45	Single books
6500.M5	Translations
6500.M6	Criticism
	Manlius Theodorus, Flavius see PA6786.T5
6500.M65	Marcellinus comes, 6th century A.D. (Table P-PZ38 modified)

6500.M65A61-
  .M65A78
	Separate works. By title
	  e.g. Chronicon; Urbs Constantinopolitana nova Roma (Not
	    by Marcellinus)

6500.M68	Marcellus (Empiricus), Burdigalensis, fl. 395 A.D. De medicamentis
	Marcellus Nonius see PA6518.N6
	Marcianus Capella see PA6511.M2+

6500.M7	Marius Aventicensis (bp. of Avenches-Lausanne) d. 594
	  A.D. Chronicon
	    Continuation of the "Chronicon imperiale"
	    Cf. PA6648.P5A6 Chronicon imperiale

	Marius Fabius Victorinus see PA6967.V5

6500.M75	Marius Maximus, ca. 165-ca. 230 (Table P-PZ38)
	  Probably identical with the consul L. Marius Maximus
	    Perpetuus Aurelianus

	Marius Mercator see Mercator
	Marius Plotius Sacerdos see PA6652.S2
	Marius Victor see PA6965.V6
	Marius Victorinus see PA6967.V5
	Marsus, Domitius see PA6379.D5
	Martial
	Epigrammata (lib. XV)
6501.A2	Editions
6501.A3A-.A3Z	Selections. School editions. By editor, A-Z

	Individual authors
	Martial
	Epigrammata (lib. XV) -- Continued
(6501.A5)	Selected books (Three or more)
	see PA6501.A3
	Single books (one or two)
6501.A6	Epigrammaton liber (Liber Spectaculorum)
6501.B1	Liber I
6501.B2	Liber II
6501.B3	Liber III
6501.B4	Liber IV
6501.B5	Liber V
6501.B6	Liber VI
6501.B7	Liber VII
6501.B8	Liber VIII
6501.B9	Liber IX
6501.B93	Liber X
6501.B95	Liber XI
6501.B97	Liber XII
6501.C6	Xenia (Liber XIII)
6501.D6	Apophoreta (Liber XIV)
6501.E8	Single epigrams
6501.Z4	Spurious epigrams
	The medieval epigrams falsely ascribed to Martialis were composed by Godfrey of Cambrai, prior of St. Swithin's, Winchester
	Adaptations. Imitations
	For classification of adaptations and imitations see the author
(6501.Z5)	Ancient and medieval
(6501.Z7)	Modern
	Translations
6502	English
6503	French
6504	German
6505	Italian
6506.A-Z	Other languages, A-Z
	Criticism, interpretation, biography, etc.
6507	General
(6507.A1)	Commentaries
	Treatises
6507.A2	Early to 1800/50
6507.A5-.Z3	Later, 1800/50+
(6507.Z5)	Textual criticism. Interpretation of detached passages
6510	Language. Technique
6510.A-.Z3	General

PA6000-6971

	Individual authors
	Martial
	Criticism, interpretation, biography, etc.
	Language. Technique -- Continued
6510.Z4	Special
	Including characteristics of the epigram
6510.Z5	Grammar. Syntax
6510.Z6	Versification
6510.Z8	Glossaries, indices, etc. By date
	Martialis, Gargilius see PA6389.G5
6511	Martian... to Mela
	Martianus Capella. De nuptiis Philologiae et Mercurii
	Cf. PF3988.A7+ Old High German edition by Notker Labeo
6511.M2	Texts. By date
6511.M3	Criticism
6511.M4	Martinus Dumiensis or Bracarensis (abbot and bishop of Dumio, archbishop of Bracara) d. 580 A.D. (Table P-PZ38 modified)
6511.M4A61-.M4A78	Separate works. By title
	e.g. De ira (Excerpts from Seneca's De ira - Cf. PA6661.D5 Seneca. De ira); Formula honestae vitae (De quator virtutibus; De copia verborum; De forma et honestate vitae -Presumably based upon Seneca's De officiis. A combination of parts of the "Formula" with apothegms selected from the Epistulae morales of Seneca, is entitled Seneca de copia verborum)
	Doubtful works
	e.g. De moribus (Collection of apothegms selected in the 4th century (?) from Seneca, and from other writers; in the manuscripts ascribed to Seneca); De paupertate (Excerpts from Seneca's letters) see PA6663
	Theological works see BR65.A+
	Maternus, Curiatius (dramatist) 1st century A.D.
	Maternus, Julius Firmicus see PA6385.F7
6511.M45	Matius, C., 1st century B.C. (Table P-PZ38 modified)
6511.M45A61-.M45A78	Separate works. By title
	e.g. Work on gastronomy in three books (lost)
6511.M46	Matius, Cn., 1st century B.C. (Table P-PZ38 modified)
6511.M46A61-.M46A78	Separate works. By title
	e.g. Mimiambi (Fragments only); Translation of Iliad (Scanty fragments)
6511.M6	Maximianus Etruscus, fl. ca. 550 A.D. Elegiae VI
	Maximianus grammaticus see PA6967.V65
	Maximinus, "Metrorius" see PA6967.V65
	Maximus, Marius see PA6500.M75

	Individual authors
	Martian... to Mela -- Continued
	Maximus, Valerius see PA6791.V6+
	Medicina Plinii see PA6611.A3
6512	Mela, Pomponius, 1st century A.D. De chorographia libri III (De situ orbis)
6512.A2	Editions. By date
6512.A6-.Z3	Translations. By language, A-Z, and date
6512.Z5	Criticism
6512.Z6	Language
6512.Z8	Glossaries, indices, etc. By date
6514	Mele... to Nepos
6514.M12	Memnon, of Heraclea (Table P-PZ38)
(6514.M16)	Mercator, Marius, fl. 418 to 449 A.D.
	see BR60+
6514.M18	Merobaudes, Flavius, 5th century A.D. (Table P-PZ38)
	Meropius Pontius Anicius Paulinus see PA6554.P5
	Messala, M., augur
	Probably identical with M. Valerius Messala Rufus, author of De auspiciis
6514.M2	Messala Corvinus, M. Valerius, 64(?) B.C.-8 A.D. (or 13 A.D.?) (Table P-PZ38 modified)
6514.M2A61-.M2A78	Separate works. By title
	e.g. Orationes (fragments); Poems and memoirs (in Greek) lost; Spurious work: De progenie Augusti Caesaris (15th century)
6514.M3	Messala Rufus, M. Valerius, consul 53 B.C. (Table P-PZ38 modified)
	Probably identical with Messala augur
6514.M3A61- 6515.M3A78	Separate works. By title
	e.g. De auspiciis (Fragments); De familiis (Fragments)
	Messius, Arusianus see PA6220.A25
	"Modestus" (De vocabulis rei militaris ad Tacitum)
	Copied from Vegetius in the 15th century by Pomponius Laetus, or one of his pupils
6514.M6	Modestus (grammarian) (Table P-PZ38)
	Commentator of Horatius, probably different from Julius Modestus; identical (?) with Aufidius Modestus, mentioned by Plutarch, and with the grammarian M. mentioned by Martial
6514.M7	Modestus, Julius (grammarian) 1st century A.D. (Table P-PZ38)

	Individual authors
	Mele... to Nepos -- Continued
6514.M8	Mulomedicina Chironis
	Collection of prescriptions, compiled from the works of Chiro, Apsyrtus, a.o., translated from the Greek into vulgar Latin by Claudius Hermeros (?), and from vulgar into literary Latin by "Publius," i.e. Fl. Vegetius Renatus (Ars veterinaria)
	Musa, Antonius see PA6206.A4
6514.M9	Mustio (Muscio) 5th (?) century A.D. (Table P-PZ38 modified)
	Translator of Soranus
	Cf. PA4435.S2+ Soranus
6514.M9A61-.M9A78	Separate works. By title
	e.g. Cateperotiana. Gynaecia triacontados
6514.N2	Naevius, Cn. (dramatist) d. 201 B.C. (or 204?) (Table P-PZ38)
	Namatianus, Claudius Rutilius see PA6652.R7+
	Naso, P. Ovidius see PA6519+
	Nazarius (rhetor) fl. 322 A.D.
6514.N4	Nemesianus, M. Aurelius Olympius, fl. 283 A.D. (Table P-PZ38 modified)
6514.N4A61- 6515.N4A78	Separate works. By title
	e.g. Cynegetica (v. 1-325 preserved; editions frequently combined with those of the Cynegeticon of Grattius) - Cf. PA6392.G6 Grattius; Eclogae - Cf. PA6271.C2 Calpurnius Siculus; Halieutica (lost); Nautica (lost)
	Nepos, Cornelius. Vitae excellentium imperatorum
	Part of a lost work "De viris illustribus." Previously believed to be the work of Aemilius Probus, a grammarian of the time of Theodosius
6515.A2	Editions. By date
6515.A3A-.A3Z	School editions. By editor, A-Z
6515.A5-Z	Single Vitae
6516.A-.Z3	Translations. By language, A-Z
6516.Z5	Criticism, interpretation, etc.
6516.Z6	Language
6516.Z8	Glossaries, indices, etc. By date
6518	Nepot... to Ovi...
6518.N2	Nepotianus, Januarius, 3rd or 4th century A.D. (?). Epitome of Valerius Maximus, Factorum et dictorum memorabilium libri IX
	Nicanor Sevius
	see Sevius Nicanor
6518.N4	Nigidius Figulus, P., d. 45 B.C. (Table P-PZ38)
6518.N6	Nonius Marcellus (grammarian) 4th century A.D. De compendiosa doctrina

Individual authors
    Nepot... to Ovi... -- Continued
(6518.N63)   Notitia dignitatum omnium tam civilium quam militarium
             For this and the following works, "Notitia...", see Class DG or
               Class G
(6518.N64)   Notitia Galliarum
(6518.N65)   Notitia regionum Romae
            Cf. PA6375.C9 Curiosum urbis Romae regionum XIV
(6518.N66)   Notitia urbis Constantinopolitanae
6518.O2   Obsequens, Julius, 4th century A.D. De prodigiis
            Derived from an epitome (?) of Livius
            Cf. PA6452+ Livius
        Octavia (Praetexta) see PA6664.Z5+
        Octavianus see PA6220.A85
        Olympius see PA6514.N4
        Orestis tragoedia see PA6381.D8+
6518.O5   Orientus, 5th (?) century A.D. Commonitorium
            Two books in distichs, an exhortation to a Christian course of
              life; author probably identical with O., bishop of Auch.
        Origo Constantini imperatoris (first part of the "Excerpta
            Valesiana") see PA6203+
6518.O6   Origo gentis romanae
            Cf. PA6966 Victor, S. Aurelius
(6518.O8)   Orosius (Paulus?) 5th century A.D. Historiarum adversus
            paganos lib. VII
            see D17
    Ovid, 43 B.C.-17 or 18 A.D.
6519.A2   Editions. By date
6519.A3   Selected works (Miscellaneous)
          Selected groups
6519.A4   Carmina amatoria (erotica)
(6519.A5)   Fasti. Tristia. Epistulae ex Ponto
            see PA6519.F2
6519.A6   Selections. Chrestomathies. Passages
         Separate works
6519.A7   Amores lib. III
6519.A7A-.A7Z   Single poems. By title, A-Z
            e.g.
6519.A7D4   De anulo
6519.A8   Ars amatoria (Ars amandi; De arte amandi)
            Cf. PA6520.Z5A+ Medieval spurious works, De arte
              amandi
        Carmen de laudibus Augusti jam defuncti sermone getico
            see PA6519.Z5
        Carmen panegyricum in Pisonem see PA6271.C2A3
        Carmen triumphale see PA6519.Z5
        Consolatio ad Liviam (Epicedion Drusi) see PA6520.C7

PA6000-6971

	Individual authors
	Ovid, 43 B.C.-17 or 18 A.D.
	Separate works -- Continued
	De anulo (i.e. Amores II, 15) see PA6519.A7D4
6519.D4	De medicamine faciei
	De piscibus et feris see PA6519.H2
	Dirae in Ibin see PA6519.I2
	Elegia in Maecenatem see PA6520.E6
	Elegia in Messalam see PA6519.Z5
	Elegia in mortem Tibulli (Amores III, 9) see PA6519.A7A+
	Epicedion Drusi see PA6520.C7
	Epigrammata see PA6519.Z5
	Epigrammata scholastica de XII libris Aeneidos see PA6801.A65
	Epistulae see PA6519.H4+
6519.E6	Epistulae ex Ponto lib. IV (De Ponto lib. IV)
	Epithalamium see PA6519.Z5
	Fasti lib. VI
6519.F2	Editions. By date
6519.F3	School editions
6519.F4	Selected books
6519.F5	Selections. Chrestomathies
6519.F6A1-.F6A6	Single books (one or two)
	Arrange by book, e.g. PA6519.F6A1, Book I; PA6519.F6A2, Book II; etc. Subarrange by date
6519.F7	Single tales
6519.F9	Criticism
	Gigantomachia see PA6519.Z5
6519.H2	Halieutica (De piscibus et feris)
	Fragment
	Heroides (Heroidum epistulae; Epistulae)
	Fifteen fictitious love letters by women of the heroic age, with the addition of six letters in pairs (Paris-Helena; Leander-Hero; Acontius-Cydippe). The authenticity of these six letters, and of the letter Sappho to Phaon has been much disputed. The answers to the Heroidae composed by Sabinus (Ovid's friend) are lost. "A. Sabini Epistolae tres" printed in editions of Ovid were composed by Angelus Quirinus Sabinus, ca. 1467
6519.H4	Editions. By date
6519.H5	Selected letters
6519.H6A-.H6Z	Single letters
	e.g.
6519.H6S3	Sappho Phaoni
6519.H7	Criticism
6519.I2	Ibis

	Individual authors
	Ovid, 43 B.C.-17 or 18 A.D.
	Separate works -- Continued
	In malos poetas see PA6519.Z5
	Medea (tragedy) see PA6519.Z5
	Metamorphoses lib. XV
6519.M2	Editions. By date
6519.M3	School editions
6519.M4	Selected books
6519.M5	Selections. Chrestomathies
6519.M6A1-.M6A15	Single books (one or two)
	Arrange by book, e.g. PA6519.M6A1, Book I;
	PA6519.M6A13, Book XIII; etc. Subarrange by date
6519.M7	Single tales
6519.M9	Criticism
	Nux see PA6520.N8
	Phaenomena see PA6519.Z5
	Priapea (contributions by Ovid)
	Cf. PA6135.P8 Priapea
6519.R3	Remedia amoris
	Cf. PA6520.Z5A+ Medieval spurious works, De
	remedio amoris
	Somnium (Amores III, 5)
	see PA6519.A7
	Cf. PA6520.Z5A+ Medieval spurious works, De
	somno
	Tristia lib. V
6519.T5	Texts. By date
6519.T9	Criticism
6519.Z5	Lost works and fragments
	Carmen triumphale
	Elegia in Messalam
	Epigrammata
	Epithalamium
	Gigantomachia
	Halieutica see PA6519.H2
	In malos poetas
	Medea (tragedy)
	Phaenomena
	Poem in the Getic language (in honor of the family of
	Augustus)
	Criticism see PA6537
	Spurious works
	Carmen panegyricum in Pisonem see PA6271.C2A3

PA6000-6971

                     Individual authors
                       Ovid, 43 B.C.-17 or 18 A.D.
                         Spurious works -- Continued

6520.C7	Consolatio ad Liviam (Epicedion Drusi)
	237 distichs on the death of Drusus (9 B.C.), written soon after that event by an unknown poet who also wrote the two elegies on Maecenas
6520.E6	Elegia Vergilii Maronis in Maecenatem
	Two elegies by the same author who wrote the Consolatio ad Liviam
(6520.E8)	Epigrammata scholastica de XII libris Aeneidis
	see PA6801.A65
6520.N8	Nux (Liber nucis; De nuce)
	Spurious works, Medieval
6520.Z5	Collections and selections. By date
6520.Z5A-.Z5Z	Single works

                          Altercatio ventris et artuum (De ventre); Carmen de membris conspirantibus)
                            Also ascribed to Johannes Sarisberiensis
                          De anulo see PA6519.A7D4
                          De arte amandi (De amore)
                          De biria (Biria sive P. Ovidii Nasonis liber de procatione Jovis erga Alcmenam)
                          De cuculo (Cuculus sive Veris et hiemis conflictus; Contentio veris et hiemis in laudem cuculi)
                          De medicamine aurium
                          De morte cuculi
                          De nummo
                          De nuntio sagaci ("Ovidius puellarum")
                            Also entitled: "Liber trium puellarum;" it is a poem in leonine hexameters beginning: Summi victoris fierem cum victor amoris
                          De pediculo
                          De philomela (De vocibus avium et quadrupedum)
                          De pulice (by Ofilius Sergianus)
                          De remedio amoris ("Qui fuerit cupiens...")
                          De somno
                            Differs from Somnium
                          De tribus puellis (Liber trium puellarum)
                            Elegiac poem begins: Ibam forte viam
                          De ventre
                            see Altercatio ventris et artuum
                          De vetula lib. III
                            By Richard de Fournival (?)
                          Pamphilus (P. de amore; Carmen de arte amandi)
                       Translations

| 6521 | Polyglot |

	Individual authors
	Ovid, 43 B.C.-17 or 18 A.D.
	Translations -- Continued
6522	English
6522.A1	Collected works. By date
6522.A2	Selections
6522.A3	Selected works
6522.A7-.Z4	Single works (by original title)
6522.Z5	Adaptations. Imitations
6522.Z7	Parodies. Travesties
6523	French
6524	German
6525	Italian
6526	Spanish
6527.A-Z	Other European, except Slavic, A-Z
6528.A-Z	Slavic languages, A-Z
6530.A-Z	Oriental and artificial languages, A-Z
6531	Paraphrases. Tales. Adaptations

Class here Latin works only (e.g. Narrationes fabularum, ascribed to Lactantius Placidus)

For vernacular paraphrases, etc. see PA6521+

(6532)	Parodies, travesties, etc.

see PA6521+

6533	Illustrations
6534	Music
(6535.9)	Fiction, drama, etc., based on the life of Ovid

see the author

	Interpretation, criticism, biography, etc.
	General
(6536)	Commentaries
6537	Treatises
6537.A2	Early to 1800/1850
6537.A5-Z	Later, 1800/50+
	Language. Technique
6550	General
6551	Grammar. Syntax
6552	Versification
6553	Glossaries. Indices. By date
6554	Pa... to Pers...
6554.P15	Pacatus Drepanius, Latinius, fl. 388 A.D. (Table P-PZ38)
6554.P2	Pacuvius, M., ca. 220-ca. 132 B.C. (Table P-PZ38)
	Pacuvius Labeo see PA6451.L18
6554.P3	Palaemon, Q. Remmius (grammarian) 1st century A.D. Ars grammatica (lost)
6554.P4	Palladius Rutilius Taurus Aemilianus, 4th century A.D. De re rustica lib. XIV
	Lib. XIV (in verse) entitled: De insitione

PA6000-6971

Individual authors
　　Pa... to Pers... -- Continued
　　　　Panegyricus in Pisonem (poem) see PA6271.C2A3
　　　　Papinianus, Aemilius (jurist) d. 212 A.D.
　　　　　　see class K
6554.P45　　　Paris, Julius, 4th-5th century A.D. (Table P-PZ38)
　　　　　　Extract from Valerius Maximus
　　　　　　Cf. PA6791.V6+ Valerius Maximus
6554.P458　　Paulinus (S. Paulini Epigramma) ca. 408 A.D. (Table P-
　　　　　　PZ38)
6554.P5　　　Paulinus Nolanus (Pontius Meropius Anicius Paulinus,
　　　　　　bishop of Nola, Saint) 353(?)-431 A.D. (Table P-PZ38)
　　　　　　Letters and poems
6554.P52　　Paulinus Pellaeus (Paulinus, of Pella) ca. 376-ca.459
　　　　　Pedianus see PA6220.A3
6554.P6　　　Pedo, Albinovanus, fl. 16 A.D. (Table P-PZ38)
6554.P65　　Pelagonius Saloninus (veterinarian) 4th century A.D.
　　　　　　(Table P-PZ38)
(6554.P7-.P8)　Peregrinatio Aetheriae
　　　　　　see BR167
　　　　Persius. Satirae VI
　　　　　For editions combined with the Satires of Juvenalis see
　　　　　　PA6446
6555.A2　　　Editions
6555.A25　　Selections
6555.A5-Z　　Translations, by language, A-Z
6556　　　　Criticism
6557　　　Pert... to Pet...
　　　　Pervigilium Veneris
　　　　　By some authorities ascribed to Florus
6557.P3　　　Texts. By date
6557.P4　　　Criticism
　　　　Petronius Arbiter. Satirae (Satyricon)
　　　　　Fragments of books 15 and 16 only
6558.A2　　　Editions
　　　　Episodes, poems, etc.
6558.A3　　　Bellum civile (chapters 119-124)
6558.A5　　　Cena Trimalchionis (Trau fragment, "fragmentum Tragurii
　　　　　　Dalmatiae repertum," ch. 26-78)
6558.A55　　Trojae halosis (ch. 89)
　　　　　Other
6558.A58　　　Widow of Ephesus (ch. 111-112)
　　　　Forged fragments
6558.A6　　　Nodot
6558.A7　　　Lallemandus
6558.A73　　Epigrams (in the Anthologia latina)
　　　　　Authorship disputed

340

	Individual authors
	Petronius Arbiter. Satirae (Satyricon) -- Continued
6558.A75	"Glossae"
	The manuscripts of P. include a number of short Latin poems, and glosses collected by anonymous compilers from Gellius, Isidorus, and ecclesiastical writers, later wrongly attributed to Petronius
6558.A9-Z	Translations. By language, A-Z
	Subarrange by translator
6559	Criticism
(6560)	Special topics
6561	Language
6561.A-.Z3	General
6561.Z5A-.Z5Z	Special, A-Z
6561.Z5N3	Names
6561.Z6	Versification
6561.Z8	Glossaries, indices, etc. By date
6562	Petronius Musa to Phaedrus
	Petronius Musa, d. ca. 50 A.D.
	Cf. PA6206.A4 Antonius Musa
	Peutingeriana tabula
	see class G
	Phaedrus
6563.A2	Editions
6563.A4A-.A4Z	Selections. School editions. By editor or date
6563.A5	Appendix Perottina ("Fabulae ineditae XXXII repertae in codice Perottino Bibl. reg. neapolitanae")
6563.A6	"Novae fabulae"
	Fables preserved in prose paraphrases only
6564	Translations
6565	Paraphrases, adaptations, etc.
6565.A1	Romulus
(6565.A2)	Medieval
	see the authors
6565.A3-Z	Modern
6566	Criticism, interpretation, etc.
6567	Phi... to Plautus
	Philargyrius, Junius see PA6823.P3
6567.P2	Phocas ("grammaticus urbis Romae") 5th (?) century A.D. (Table P-PZ38 modified)
6567.P2A61-.P2A78	Separate works. By title
	e.g. Ars de nomine et verbo; Vita Vergilii (in verse and in prose); De aspiratione (Orthographia) (Spurious)
(6567.P3)	Physiognomonia
	see PA6208.P4
	Pictor
	see Fabius Pictor, Q.

PA6000-6971

	Individual authors
	Phi... to Plautus -- Continued
	Pindarus Thebanus see PA6445.I2
	Piso Frugi
	see Calpurnius Piso Frugi, L.
(6567.P4)	Placidus, glossator, 6th (?) century A.D.
	see PA2356
	Placitus Papyriensis, Sextus, 5th (?) century A.D. De medicina ex animalibus liber
	Plautus, Titus Maccius
6568	Editions
(6568.A1)	Manuscripts. Facsimiles
	see Z114; Z115Z
6568.A2	Comprehensive. By date
6568.A3	Selections. Quotations. Passages
6568.A4	Selected plays
6568.A5	School editions
	Single plays
6568.A6	Amphitruo
6568.A7	Asinaria
6568.A8	Aulularia
6568.B3	Bacchides
6568.C2	Captivi
6568.C4	Casina
	Sortientes possibly the original title
6568.C6	Cistellaria
6568.C8	Curculio
6568.E6	Epidicus
6568.M4	Menaechmi
6568.M5	Mercator
6568.M6	Miles gloriosus
6568.M7	Mostellaria (Phasma)
6568.P4	Persa
6568.P7	Poenulus
	For treatises on the Punic works and phrases see PJ4187
6568.P8	Pseudolus
6568.R7	Rudens
6568.S8	Stichus
6568.T6	Trinummus
6568.T8	Truculentus
6568.V5	Vidularia
	Lost plays and fragments
6568.Z5	Collections. By date
6568.Z5A-.Z5Z	Single plays
	Translations
6569-6570	English (Table PA16)

	Individual authors
	Plautus, Titus Maccius
	Translations -- Continued
6571-6572	French (Table PA16)
6573-6574	German (Table PA16)
6575-6576	Italian (Table PA16)
6577.A-Z	Other, except Slavic, A-Z
	Subarrange each language by Table PA16a
6577.S8	Spanish (Table PA16a)
6578.A-Z	Slavic languages, A-Z
	Subarrange each language by table PA16a
(6580)	Paraphrases. Tales
	For Latin works see the individual author
	For works in other languages see PA6569+
(6581)	Imitations. Adaptations
	For Latin works see the individual author
	For works in other languages see PA6569+
6582	Plautus in art
	Illustrations
	Music
	Criticism, interpretation, etc.
(6583)	Ancient
	Commentaries (lost)
	"Indices" (lists of genuine plays, lost)
(6583.A3)	"Argumenta" (metrical summaries)
(6583.A7-Z)	Criticism
	see PA6584+
	Modern
6584	General
(6584.A1)	Commentaries
6584.A5-Z	Early to ca. 1850
6585	Later, ca. 1850+
6585.Z9	Popular. Minor. Addresses. Essays. Lectures
	Language. Style. Technique
6601	General
6602	Special
	Including metaphor, puns, etc.
	Grammar. Syntax
6603	General
6604	Special
	Syntax
6605	General
6606	Special
	Versification
6607	General
6608	Special
6609	Lexicography

PA6000-6971

	Individual authors
	Plautus, Titus Maccius
	Criticism, interpretation, etc.
	Modern
	Language. Style. Technique
	Lexicography -- Continued
6609.A-.Z3	Treatises
6609.Z8	Glossaries. Concordances. Lists, etc. By date
6609.Z9	Lists of particular classes of words. By date
	Pliny, the Elder
	Naturalis historia, lib. XXXVII
6611.A2	Editions. By date
	Epitomes
	Ancient
	"Chorographia Pliniana"
	see Spurious works
6611.A3	Medicina Plinii (Breviarium Plinii; "Plinius Valerianus")
	Medieval
6611.A4	Chrestomathies. Selections. Passages
6611.A6	Selected books (Three or more)
6611.B01-.B37	Particular books
	Subarrange by book, e.g. PA6611.B01, Book I;
	PA6611.B15, Book XV; etc.
6611.Z5	Lost works and fragments
	A fine Aufidii Bassi lib. XXXI
	Fragments
	Bellorum Germaniae lib. XX
	De iaculatione equestri
	De vita Pomponi Secundi lib. II
	Dubii sermonis lib. VIII
	Fragments
	Studiosus lib. III
(6611.Z9)	Spurious works ("Pseudo-Plinius")
	"Chorographia Pliniana"
	Hypothetical work combining extracts from the Nat. hist.
	with selections from other authors
	Medicina Plinii see PA6611.A3
	Translations
(6612)	English
	see QH41
6613.A-Z	Other languages, A-Z
	Interpretation, criticism, etc.
	General
(6614.A1)	Commentaries
	Treatises
6614.A2	Early to 1800/50
6614.A5-Z	Later, 1800/50+

PA6000-6971

	Individual authors
	Plinius Val. to Priscianus -- Continued
	Pollio, Trebellius see PA6791.T6
6641.P75	Pompeius (grammarian), 5th (?) century A.D. Commentum artis Donati
	Pompeius Trogus see PA6791.T8
	Pompeius Festus, Sextus see PA6385.F4
	Pomponius Atticus, T. see PA6220.A55
6641.P77	Pomponius Bononiensis, L., fl. 89 B.C. Atellanae
	Titles only preserved
	Pomponius Mela see PA6512
	Pomponius Porphyrio see PA6641.P87
6641.P8	Pomponius Secundus, P. (dramatist), 1st century A.D. (Table P-PZ38)
	Cf. PA6611.Z5 Plinius. De vita Pomponi Secundi
	Porcius Cato
	see Cato
	Porcius Latro see PA6451.L35
6641.P83	Porcius Licinus, 2nd century B.C. (Table P-PZ38)
6641.P87	Porphyrio, Pomponius, 3rd century A.D. (Table P-PZ38 modified)
6641.P87A61- .P87A78	Separate works. By title
	Commentarii in Q. Horatium Flaccum see PA6408.A3
6641.P88	Porphyrius, Publilius Optatianus (Table P-PZ38)
6641.P89	Postumius Albinus, A., consul 151 B.C. Annales
	In Greek; lost
	Priapea see PA6135.P8
6642	Priscianus Caesariensis, 6th century A.D.
	Editions
6642.A2	Comprehensive (or Institutio and other works)
6642.A3	Institutio de arte grammatica lib. XVIII (Institutiones grammaticae; Ars)
6642.A4	Selected portions or sections or books
	Opera minora
6642.A5	Collections and selections
	Particular works
6642.A52	De accentibus
	Authorship doubtful
6642.A53	De figuris numerorum (in the older editions: De ponderibus et mensuris)
6642.A54	De laude Anastasii (poem)
	De nummis vel ponderibus (De ponderibus et mensuris) see PA6642.A53
6642.A57	De Terentii metris
6642.A58	Institutio de nomine et pronomine et verbo (in older editions: De declinatione nominum)

PA6000-6971

Individual authors
  Pros... to Quintilianus
    Prosper, Tiro, of Aquitania, Saint, 5th century A.D. (Prosper
      Aquintanus) -- Continued
    Theological works
      see BR60+
6648.P5A4   Poems
               De ingratis
                 Authorship disputed
               Ad conjugem
                 Authorship disputed
               De providentia divina
                 Authorship disputed
               Epigrams
6648.P5A5   Chronicon
               Three redactions: Chronicon "vulgatum," comprising the
                 period 378-445 only; Chronicon "integrum" or
                 "consulare," from Adam to 455 A.D. (based in part
                 upon the "Consularia Ravennatia"); Chronicon
                 "Augustanum" or "Canisianum," consisting of the
                 Chronicon "vulgatum" with two continuations to 451
                 and 457, respectively
               Cf. D17 World histories
6648.P5A6   "Chronicon imperiale" (Chronicon Pithoeanum)
               Arranged according to the years of the Emperor's reigns;
                 wrongly ascribed to Prosper
           Prudentius, b. 348 A.D.
             Cf. BR60+ BR1720
6648.P6   Collected works. By date
6648.P6A-.P6Z Individual works. By title, A-Z
               e.g. Apotheosis (Poem on the doctrine of the Trinity);
                 Cathemerinon; Contra Symmachum libri duo;
                 Dittochaeon; Hamartigenia; Peristephanon;
                 Psychomachia
6648.P7   Criticism
           Pseudo-Acro see PA6408.A4
           Pseudo-Asconius see PA6284.A4
           Pseudo-Dositheus see PA6381.D7
           Pseudo-Ovidius
             see PA6520
           Pseudo-Plinius see PA6611.Z9
           Pseudo-Victor see PA6966.A5
           Publilius Syrus, 1st cent. B.C.
             His plays are lost. Class here the "Sententiae," a collection of
               sentences derived from the plays of Publilius Syrus and
               enlarged from other sources, frequently published with
               title L.A. Senecae et P. Syri mimi Sententiae (Proverbia)

PA6000-6971

Individual authors
  Pros... to Quintilianus
    Publilius Syrus, 1st cent. B.C. -- Continued

6648.P8	Texts. By date
6648.P8A-.P8Z	Translations. By language, A-Z, and date
6648.P9	Criticism

    Quadrigarius, Q. Claudius see PA6375.C45
    Querolus
      Imitation of Plautus' Aulularia, author unknown, 4th century A.D.

6648.Q4	Texts. By date
6648.Q5	Criticism

    Quintilian
      Editions
        Institutionis oratoriae lib. XII
          Cf. PA6965.V5 Victor, C. Julius

6649.A2	Editions. By date
	Including editions of Institutiones oratoriae and Declamationes
6649.A4A-.A4Z	Selections, and selected books, by editor, A-Z
	Including textbooks
6649.B01-.B12	Particular books
	Subarrange by book, e.g. PA6649.B01, Book I; PA6649.B11, Book XI; etc.
6649.D3	De causis corruptae eloquentiae (lost)
6649.D5	Declamationes
	Spurious
6650.A-Z	Translations. By language, A-Z
	Subarrange by translator
6651	Criticism
6652	Quintilius to Sallustius
6652.R15	Rabirius, 1st century A.D. (Table P-PZ38)

      Wrote according to Seneca an epic poem on Marcus Antonius; by some authorities Rabirius is identified with the author of the fragment discovered in papyrus no. 817 of Herculaneum, published with title Carminis latini De bello actiaco sive alexandrino fragmenta ex volumine herculanensi nuper evulgata

6652.R18	Ravennas geographus, 7th century A.D. Cosmographia (Geographia)

      Translations of a Greek original?
    Remmius Flavianus (Favinus?) see PA6385.F8
    Remmius Palaemon, Q. see PA6554.P3
    Remus (Remius) Favinus see PA6385.F8
    Reposianus, 3rd (?) century A.D. De concubitu Martis et Veneris

Individual authors
　　Quintilius to Sallustius -- Continued

6652.R4 　　　Romanus, C. Julius (grammarian) 3rd century A.D. (Table
　　　　　　P-PZ38)

(6652.R43) 　　Romulus
　　　　　see PA3852.R6 Aesopus; PA6565 Phaedrus

6652.R45 　　Rufinianus, Julius, 4th century A.D. Liber de figuris
　　　　　sententiarum et elocutionis

6652.R47 　　Rufinus, of Antiochia (grammarian) 5th century A.D. (?)
　　　　　(Table P-PZ38 modified)

6652.R47A61-
.R47A78 　　　Separate works. By title
　　　　　　　e.g. Commentarium in metra Terentiana (Including Versus
　　　　　　　　de metris Terentii); De compositione et de metris
　　　　　　　　oratorum

(6652.R5) 　　Rufinus, Tyrannius (Turranius), of Aquileia, d. 410 A.D.
　　　　　　see BR60+ BR1720
　　　　　　Cf. PA4223.A17 Version of Josephus, De bello
　　　　　　　　Judaico, by Rufinus?
　　　　　　Cf. PA4410.S6A2 Sententiae of "Sextus Pythagoreus"
　　　Rufius Festus see PA6385.F6
　　　Rufius Festus Avienus see PA6227
　　　Rufus, M. Caelius see PA6234.C7
　　　Rufus, M. Cluvius
　　　　　see Cluvius
　　　Rufus Festus see PA6385.F6
　　　Rufus, Servius Sulpicius
　　　　　see Sulpicius
　　　Rufus, Valgius see PA6791.V95
　　　Rufus, L. Varius see PA6791.V97
　　　Rutilius Claudius Namatianus, fl. 416 A.D. De reditu suo
　　　　　lib. II
　　　　　Poem; second book for the greater part lost

6652.R7 　　　Texts. By date
6652.R8 　　　Criticism
6652.R9 　　Rutilius Lupus, P., 1st century A.D. Schemata lexeos lib. II
　　　　　(De figuris sententiarum et elocutionis
　　　　　Abridged translation of the treatise of the younger Gorgias
　　　Rutilius Rufus, P. (stoic philosopher, jurist, orator) fl. 105-
　　　　　92 B.C. De vita sua (fragments)
　　　Sabinus, (epic poet) d. before 15 A.D.
　　　　　Cf. PA6519.H4+ Ovidius. Heroides (Epistulae)
6652.S2 　　Sacerdos, Marius Plotius (grammarian) 3rd century A.D.
　　　　　Artis grammaticae libri III
　　　　　Cf. PA6643.P6C3 Catholica Probi
　　　Saevius Nicanor
　　　　　see Sevius Nicanor

	Individual authors
	Quintilius to Sallustius -- Continued
6652.S4	Saleius Bassus, 1st century A.D. (Table P-PZ38)
	Cf. PA6271.C2A3 Panegyricus in Pisonem
(6652.S5)	Saliorum carmina
(6652.S6)	Sallustius, Cn. fl. 67-45 B.C.
	Friend and correspondent of Cicero
	Empedoclea see PA6653.Z4
	Sallustius Crispus, C., ca. 86-35 B.C.
6653	Editions
6653.A2	Opera. By date
	Including editions of Catilina and Jugurtha together
(6653.A25)	Catilina and Jugurtha (together)
	see PA6653.A2
6653.A3A-.A3Z	School editions. By editor, A-Z
6653.A4	Catilina
6653.A6	Jugurtha
6653.A8	Historiae lib. V
	Fragments
6653.Z3	Doubtful works. By date
6653.Z4	Empedoclea
	Poem, lost; by Cn. Sallustius?
6653.Z5	Invectiva in Ciceronem
	Cf. PA6283.Z7R4 Cicero. Responsio ad orationem
	C. Sallustii Crispi
6653.Z6	Suaroriae (Incerti auctoris Epistulae duae ad C.
	Caesarem de republica ordinanda)
	Ad Caesarem senem de republica oratio
	Ad Caesarem senem de republica epistula
6654.A-Z	Translations. By language, A-Z
6656	Criticism
6656.Z5	Language. Grammar
6656.Z8	Glossaries. Indices, etc. By date
	Ancient
	Cf. PA6220.A25 Arusianus Messius
6658	Salo... to Seneca
	Sammonicus Serenus see PA6694.S34
6658.S2	Sasernae (father and son) fl. between 140 and 60 B.C. De
	agricultura (lost)
	Scaevola, P. Mucius, consul 133 B.C.
	see class K
	Scaevola, Q. Cervidius (jurist) 2nd century A.D.
	see class K
	Scaevola, Q. Mucius, augur, consul 117 B.C.
	see class K
	Scaevola, Q. Mucius, pont. max., d. 82 B.C.
	see class K

Individual authors
  Salo... to Seneca -- Continued
    Scaevus (Scaevius?) Memor (dramatist) 1st century A.D.
    Scaurus, Mamercus Aemilius, d. 34 A.D.
    Scaurus, Marcus Aemilius, consul 115 B.C.
6658.S3   Scaurus, Q. Terentius (grammarian), 2nd century A.D.
                        (Table P-PZ38 modified)
6658.S3A61-.S3A78   Separate works. By title
                         e.g. Ars grammatica (Fragments); De ordinatione partium
                             (Fragment); De orthographia; Commentary on Horace
                             (Lost)
6658.S4   Scribonius Largus, fl. 47 A.D. (Table P-PZ38)
                     Sedigitus, Volcacius see PA6971.V4
6658.S6   Sedulius (Caelius?) 5th century (Table P-PZ38)
                        Cf. BR60+ BR1720
6659   Seneca, Lucius Annaeus ("rhetor") ca. 54 B.C.-ca. 39 A.D.
                        Oratorum et rhetorum sententiae, divisiones, colores
                        Comprises "Suasoriae" (liber unus) and "Controversiae" (lib. I-
                            X). Books I, II, VII, IX, and X are preserved nearly entire;
                            books III-VI, and VIII in the epitome of the Controversiae. In
                            some of the earlier editions the Controversiae are wrongly
                            entitled "Declamationes." In the early period of humanism
                            the work of the elder Seneca was ascribed to the son
6659.A2-.A29   Editions
6659.A3-.A79   Translations
6659.A8-.Z3   Criticism
6659.Z5   Language
6659.Z8   Glossaries, etc. By date
                     Seneca, Lucius Annaeus, ca. 4 B.C.-65 A.D.
6661.A2   Comprehensive editions (prose works and tragedies or
                         prose works alone). By date
                       Selections. Chrestomathies. Passages. Thoughts
                          Cf. PA6664.A3 Tragoediae
                       Ancient and medieval see PA6663
                       Modern
6661.A4   General
6661.A5   By subject
                       Selected works
6661.A7   Miscellaneous. By date
6661.A7A-.A7Z   School editions. By editor, A-Z
                         Dialogi, lib. XII see PA6661.D8
                         Tragoediae see PA6664.A4
                       Single works
                          For individual tragedies see PA6664.A6+
                          Ad Polybium de consolatione see PA6661.D37
6661.A9   Apocolocyntosis (Ludus de morte Claudii Caesaris)
                         De aevi humani brevitate see PA6661.D25

PA6000-6971

	Individual authors
	Seneca, Lucius Annaeus, ca. 4 B.C.-65 A.D.
	Single works -- Continued
	De amicitia see PA6662.A5+
6661.D2	De beneficiis libri VII
6661.D25	De brevitate vitae (Ad Paulinum de brevitate vitae; De aevi humani brevitate; Dialogi, lib. X)
6661.D3	De clementia ad Neronem Caesarem lib. III
	lib. I, and beginning of II, preserved
6661.D33	De consolatione ad Helviam matrem (Dialogi, lib. XII)
6661.D35	De consolatione ad Marciam (Dialogi, lib. VI)
6661.D37	De consolatione ad Polybium (Dialogi, lib. XI)
	Authorship wrongly disputed
6661.D4	De constantia sapientis (Ad Serenum nec iniuriam nec contumeliam accipere sapientem, sive De constantia sapientis; Dialogi, lib. II)
	De copia verborum see PA6511.M4
	De forma et honestate vitae see PA6511.M4
6661.D5	De ira (Ad Novatum de ira lib. III; Dialogi, lib. III-V)
	Cf. PA6511.M4 Martinus, of Bracara, De ira
	De liberalibus studiis see PA6661.E7E001+
	De moribus see PA6663.A5+
	De mundi gubernatione see PA6661.D7
6661.D6	De otio (Ad Serenum de otio; Dialogi, lib. VIII)
	De paupertate see PA6663.A5+
6661.D7	De providentia (Ad Lucilium quare aliqua incommoda bonis viris accidant, cum providentia sit; Dialogi, lib. I)
	Published also with title De mundi gubernatione
	De quatuor virtutibus cardinalibus see PA6511.M4
	De remediis fortuitorum see PA6663.A5+
	De septem artibus liberalibus, sive De studiis liberalibus see PA6661.E7E001+
6661.D73	De tranquillitate animi (Ad Serenum de tr. animi; Dialogi, lib. IX)
6661.D75	De vita beata (Ad Gallionem de vita beata; Dialogi, lib. VII)
	De vita patris see PA6662.A5+
	De vivendi ratione see PA6661.E6+
6661.D8	Dialogi lib. XII
	Class here comprehensive editions or editions of various selected treatises of this group. For individual treatises see the separate titles
	Epigrammata
	Authorship doubtful
6661.E3	Editions. By date
6661.E4	Selected works. Selections. By date
6661.E5	Criticism

Individual authors
　　Seneca, Lucius Annaeus, ca. 4 B.C.-65 A.D.
　　　Single works -- Continued
　　　　Epistulae morales (Ad Lucilium epistularum moralium lib.
　　　　　XX)
　　　　　Consists of 124 letters (for the greater part treatises in form
　　　　　　of letters) divided into twenty books. The original
　　　　　　collection consisted of at least twenty-two books so that
　　　　　　two or more books are lost. The twenty-two books of
　　　　　　the older editions represent a different division of the
　　　　　　letters. In the earlier editions title reads also: Ad
　　　　　　Lucilium epistolarum liber de vivendi ratione

6661.E6	Editions. By date
6661.E7	Selections. Passages. Thoughts. By date
	Cf. PA6663.A5+ De paupertate
6661.E7A2	Selected letters (Miscellaneous)
6661.E7A3	Selected books (three or more)
6661.E7B01-.E7B20	Single books
	Subarrange by book, e.g. PA6661.E7B15, Book XV
6661.E7E001- 　.E7E124	Single letters
	Subarrange by Epistula, e.g. PA6661.E7E088, Epistula 　　88 (entitled in some separate editions from the initial 　　words "De liberalibus studiis"); subarrange further by 　　date
6661.E8	Criticism
	Epistulae ad Paulum see PA6663.E7
	Monita see PA6663.M7
6661.N3	Naturales quaestiones (Ad Lucilium naturalium 　quaestionum lib. VII [VIII])
	Liber IV (incomplete) comprises portions of an originally 　　independent book, now lost
	Orationes see PA6662.A5+
	Proverbia see PA6663.P8
	Quare aliqua incommoda bonis viris accidant cum 　providentia sit see PA6661.D7
	Quo modo amicitia continenda sit see PA6662.A5+
	Quo modo in sapientem no cadat iniuria see PA6661.D4
6662	Fragments and lost works
6662.A2	Collections
6662.A5-Z	Single works, A-Z
	De amicitia (correct title: Quo modo amicitia continenda 　　sit)
	De forma mundi
	Part of the Naturales quaestiones?
	De fortuitis
	No fragments
	Cf. PA6663.A5+ De remediis fortuitorum

	Individual authors
	Seneca, Lucius Annaeus, ca. 4 B.C.-65 A.D.
	Tragoediae ("Seneca tragicus") -- Continued
6664.A4	Selected tragedies
	Single tragedies
6664.A6	Agamemnon
6664.H4	Hercules furens
6664.H6	Hercules Oetaeus
	Authorship much disputed
6664.M4	Medea
6664.O5	Oedipus
6664.P5	Phaedra (Hippolytus)
6664.P7	Phoenissae (Thebais)
	Two fragments
6664.T5	Thyestes
6664.T8	Troades (Hecuba)
6664.Z5-.Z6	Octavia
	Not by Seneca, composed after Seneca's death
	Criticism see PA6685+
	Translations
	For philosophical works see B615+
6665-6666	English (Table PA17)
6667-6668	French (Table PA17)
6669-6670	German (Table PA17)
6671-6672	Italian (Table PA17)
6673.A-Z	Other. By language, A-Z
	Subarrange each language by Table PA17a
(6674)	Imitations. Adaptations. Parodies
	see PA6665+
6674.8	Seneca in poetry, fiction, etc.
6674.9	Illustrations
	Criticism. Biography. Interpretation
	For historical treatises see class DG
(6675.A1)	Commentaries
	Treatises
6675.A2	Early to 1800/50
6675.A5-.Z3	1800/50+
6675.Z9	Minor. Addresses, essays, etc.
6676	History of text. Discussion of mss. and editions
(6676.A2)	General
	see PA6675
6676.A5-Z	Textual criticism. Interpretation of detached passages, etc.
	Criticism of tragedies
6685	General
	Particular plays
	see the plays

PA6000-6971

Individual authors
  Seneca, Lucius Annaeus, ca. 4 B.C.-65 A.D.
    Criticism. Biography. Interpretation
      Criticism of tragedies -- Continued

6686	Special topics
	Including technique
	For language see PA6689+
(6688)	History of study and appreciation. Influence. Translations
	(as subject)
	Language. Style. Technique
	Cf. PA6686 Tragedies
6689	General
6690	Special. Minor
	Grammar. Syntax
6691	General
6692	Special
6693.A-.Z3	Versification
	Glossaries, indices, etc.
6693.Z8	General (and prose works). By date
6693.Z9	Special (Tragedies). By date
6694	Seni... to Silius
	Sententiae Publilii Syri see PA6648.P8+
	Sententiae Rufi see PA6663.M7
	Sententiae Senecae see PA6663.P8
	Sententiae Sexti see PA4410.S6A2
	Sententiae Varronis see PA6792.Z9
	Septimius, Lucius see PA6379.D3
	Septimius Serenus see PA6694.S3
	Sequester, Vibius see PA6965.V35
(6694.S28)	Seren[i]us (?) Q. (date uncertain)
	Q. Sereni Liber medicinalis (poem) see PA6694.S34
6694.S3	Serenus, Septimius (date uncertain: 2nd-3rd century A.D.)
	(Table P-PZ38 modified)
6694.S3A61-.S3A78	Separate works. By title
	e.g. Opuscula ruralia (fragments)
6694.S33	Serenus Sammonicus, d. 212 A.D. Rerum reconditarum
	libri (lost)
6694.S34	Serenus Sammonicus, fl. 200 A.D. (Son of the preceding)
	(Table P-PZ38)
	Identical (?) with the author of the poem entitled "Liber
	medicinalis Quinti Sereni"
	Sergius (grammarian) see PA6694.S4+
	Servius (grammarian) fl. ca. 400 A.D.
6694.S4	Comprehensive editions. By date
(6694.S4A2)	Commentaries on Donatus
	see PA6380
(6694.S4A23)	Commentarius in Artem Donati

Individual authors
Seni... to Silius
Servius (grammarian) fl. ca. 400 A.D.
Commentaries on Donatus -- Continued
(6694.S4A25)   Sergii De litera, de syllaba, de pedibus, de accentibus,
de distinctione commentarius (Sergii in Donati
artem primam commentaria)
(6694.S4A27)   Sergii Explanationum in artem Donati lib. II
(6694.S4A29)   Pompeii Commentum artis Donati
Cf. PA6641.P75 Pompeius
(6694.S4A3)   Commentarii in Vergilii Carmina
see PA6823.S5
Minor works (Authorship disputed)
6694.S4A33   Centimetrum (De centum metris)
6694.S4A35   De finalibus
(6694.S4A37)   De metris Horatii
(6694.S4A39)   "Glossae Servii grammatici" (Spurious Latin-Greek
glossary)
see PA2356
6694.S4A7-.S4Z   Criticism (regardless of work)
For criticism of Commentarii in Vergilii Carmina see
PA6824+
6694.S43   Severianus, Julius, 5th century A.D. Praecepta artis
rhetoricae (De arte dicendi)
(6694.S435)   Severus, bishop of Minorca, fl. 418 A.D. De virtutibus ad
Judaeorum conversionem in Minoricensi insula factis
see DP302
Severus Maioricensis
see Severus, bishop of Minorca
6694.S45   Severus, Cornelius, fl. between 43 B.C. and 14 A.D. (Table
P-PZ38)
Cf. PA6202.A5+ Aetna (poem)
6694.S46   Severus, Julius (date unknown). Expositio de pedibus
(6694.S47)   Severus, Sulpicius, fl. 389-403 A.D.
6694.S48   Severus Sanctus Endelechius
6694.S5   De mortibus boum
Author identical (?) with the orator Endelechius, fl. ca. 395
A.D.
Sevius Nicanor, fl. ca. 100 B.C.
6694.S6   Siculus Flaccus, 2nd (?) century A.D. De condicionibus
agrorum
Sidonius, C. Sollius Modestus Apollinaris, ca. 430-ca. 480
A.D.
6694.S7   Editions. By date
6694.S7A5-.S7Z   Translations. By language, A-Z, and date
6694.S8   Criticism
Silius Italicus, Tiberius Catius

PA6000-6971

	Individual authors
	Seni... to Silius
	Silius Italicus, Tiberius Catius -- Continued
	Punica
6695.A2	Editions. By date
6695.A3-.A69	Translations. By language (alphabetically)
	Criticism
6695.A7-.Z3	General works
6695.Z5	Language. Grammar
6695.Z6	Versification
6695.Z8	Glossaries. By date
(6695.Z9)	Ilias latina
	see PA6445.I2
6696	Silo... to Statius
	Silvia Aquitana
	see Peregrinatio Aetheriae
	Simfosius see PA6704.S95
6696.S3	Sinnius Capito (grammarian) fl. between 43 B.C. and 14 A.D. (Table P-PZ38)
6696.S35	Sisebuto, King of the Visigoths, d. 621 A.D. (Table P-PZ38)
6696.S38	Sisenna (grammarian) 2nd (?) century A.D. (Table P-PZ38 modified)
6696.S38A61-.S38A78	Separate works. By title
	e.g. Commentaries on Plautus (lost)
6696.S4	Sisenna, L. Cornelius, d. 67 B.C. (Table P-PZ38 modified)
6696.S4A61-.S4A78	Separate works. By title
	e.g. Historiae (Fragments preserved through Nonius); Translation of the Milesiaca of Aristides (Fragments)
	Sixtus II, pope see PA4410.S6
	Solinus, C. Julius, 3rd cent.? Collectanea rerum memorabilium (Polyhistor)
6696.S5	Texts. By date
6696.S6	Criticism
	Sollius Apollinaris Sidonius see PA6694.S7+
	Soranus see PA6791.V93
6696.S7	Spartianus, Aelius, 3rd century A.D. (Table P-PZ38)
	Spurinna, Vestricius see PA6965.V34
	Statius, Caecilius see PA6234.C4
	Statius, P. Papinius (Publius Papinius)
6697.A2	Editions. By date
6697.A3	Silvae lib. V
6697.A4-.A43	Thebais (Table P-PZ43)
	Carmen panegyricum in Pisonem see PA6271.C2A3
6697.A5	Fragments (Achilleis, etc.)
6697.A6-Z	Translations, by language, title, and date
6698	Criticism, interpretation, etc.
6698.A2	Scholia, by Lactantius Placidus

	Individual Statius, P. Papinius (Publius Papinius)
	Criticism, interpretation, etc.
6698.A5-.Z3	Modern
6698.Z5	Language. Grammar
6698.Z6	Versification
6698.Z8	Glossaries. By date
6699	Statius Urs. to Suetonius
	Statius Ursulus Tolosensis, rhetor, fl. 57 A.D.
	Stella, L. Arruntius, 1st century A.D.
	Stilo Praeconinus, L. Aelius, 1st century B.C.
	Sueius
	Fragments of two poems (Moretum; Pulli)
	Suetonius, ca. 69-ca. 122
	De vita Caesarum lib. VIII
6700.A2	Editions. By date
	Including editions comprising the Caesares and the
	fragments together
6700.A25	Selections. Passages. Thoughts
6700.A3	Selected books (three or more)
	Particular books (one or two)
6700.A31	Lib. I Julius Caesar
6700.A32	Lib. II Augustus
6700.A33	Lib. III Tiberius
6700.A34	Lib. IV Caligula
6700.A35	Lib. V Claudius
6700.A36	Lib. VI Nero
6700.A37	Lib. VII Galba. Otho. Vitellius
6700.A38	Lib. VIII Vespasianus. Titus. Domitianus
6700.A6	Lost works and fragments
	De viris illustribus
	see PA6700.D3+
6700.D3	De grammaticis et rhetoribus
6700.D32	De historicis: Vita C. Plinii Secundi
6700.D34	De oratoribus: Vita Passieni Crispi
	De poetis
6700.D5	Vita Horatii
6700.D6	Vita Terentii
6700.D63	Vita Lucani
6700.D65	Vita Persii
6700.D7	Vita Tibulii
6700.D8	Vita Vergilii
6700.D9	Criticism
	Confined to De viris illustribus or parts of it
6700.Z5A-.Z5Z	Other lost works
6701.A-Z	Translations. By language, A-Z
	For translations of the Caesars see DG277
	For historical treatises see DG278

PA6000-6971

Individual authors
    Suetonius, ca. 69-ca. 122 -- Continued
      Criticism
        Class here general works and works confined to criticism of
          the Caesares

6702.A2	Early to 1800/50
6702.A5-.Z3	1800/50+
6702.Z5	Language
6702.Z8	Glossaries. By date
6703	Suetonius Paulinus, C. (historian) 1st century A.D. (Table P-PZ37)
6704	Sul... to Tacitus

    Sulla, L. Cornelius, 138-78 B.C. Res gestae L. Cornelii
      Sullae
      Fragments

6704.S4	Sulpicia, fl. between 43 B.C. and 14 A.D. (Table P-PZ38)
	Cf. PA6787.A43 Tibullus
6704.S41	Sulpicia ("Caleni uxor") fl. between 81 and 96 A.D. (Table P-PZ38)
	Poems (fragments)
6704.S42	"Sulpiciae satira"
	70 hexameter of a much later period, by some authorities ascribed to Sulpicia Caleni
6704.S5	Sulpicius Apollinaris, C., of Carthago, 2nd century A.D. (Table P-PZ38)

    Sulpicius Rufus, Servius (jurist) d. 43 B.C.
      see class K
    Sulpicius Severus
      see Severus, Sulpicius
    Sulpicius Victor
      see Victor, Sulpicius
    Symmachus, Quintus Aurelius, d. 405

6704.S7	Collected works. Selected works. By date
6704.S7A-.S7Z	Separate works. By title, A-Z
6704.S7A4	Epistulae
6704.S7A6	Orationes
6704.S7R2	Relationes
6704.S8A-.S8Z	Translations. By language, A-Z
6704.S9	Criticism
6704.S95	Symphosius

        One hundred riddles in verse of the 4th or 5th century A.D.,
          ascribed to an otherwise unknown S., and wrongly to
          Lactantius
    Syrus, Publius see PA6648.P8+
  Tacitus, Cornelius
    Editions

	Individual authors
	Tacitus, Cornelius
	Editions -- Continued
(6705.A1)	Manuscripts. Facsimiles
	see Z114; Z115Z
6705.A2	By date
6705.A3	Selections. Passages. Thoughts
6705.A4	Selected works, or portions from all his works
	Historical works
	Annales, lib. I-VI, XI-XVI
	Including Annales and Historiae together
6705.A5	Editions. By date
6705.A55	Selections
6705.A6	Selected books (three or more)
6705.A6B1-.A6B16	Particular books (one or two)
	Subarrange by book, e.g. PA6705.A6B14, Book XIV
6705.A9	Criticism
	Historiae, lib. I-V
6705.H5	Editions. By date
6705.H55	Selections
6705.H6	Selected books (three or more)
6705.H6B1-.H6B5	Particular books (one or two)
	Subarrange by book, e.g. PA6705.H6B2, Book II
6705.H7	Criticism
	Historiae (and Opera minora)
6705.H8	Texts. By date
6705.H9	Criticism
	Opera minora
6706.A2	Editions
	Single works
	Agricola (De vita Julii Agricolae liber; De vita et moribus Julii Agricolae)
6706.A3	Texts. By date
6706.A3A-.A3Z	Criticism
	Dialogus de oratoribus
	Authorship formerly much disputed. By some authorities ascribed to Quintilianus or C. Caecilius Plinius Secundus
6706.D5	Texts. By date
6706.D5A-.D5Z	Criticism
	Germania (De origine et situ Germanorum; De origine, situ, moribus ac populis Germanorum; De situ Germaniae)
6706.G4	Texts. By date
6706.G4A-.G4Z	Criticism
	Translations

PA6000-6971

	Individual authors
	Tacitus, Cornelius
	Translations -- Continued
6707	English (Table PA18)
	For historical works see DG207
6708	French (Table PA18)
6709	German (Table PA18)
6710	Italian (Table PA18)
6712.A-Z	Other languages, A-Z
	Subarrange each language by Table PA18a
6713	Adaptations. Imitations
(6714)	Dramatizations
	see the author
	Criticism and interpretation; biography
	General
(6716.A1)	Commentaries
	Treatises
6716.A2	Early to 1800/50
6716.A5-.Z3	1800/50+
6716.Z5	Minor. Addresses, essays, etc.
6747	Technique
	Language. Grammar. Style
6749	General
	Including style
	Grammar. Syntax
6750	General
6752	Special
6753	Glossaries, indices, etc.
6754	Tad... to Terentius
6754.T2	Tanusius Geminus (annalist) 1st century B.C. (Table P-PZ38)
	Wrongly identified with the epic poet Volusius by some authorities
	Tarquitius Priscus, 1st century B.C.
	Terence see PA6755+
6754.T47	Terentianus, Claudius (Table P-PZ38)
6754.T6	Terentianus Maurus (grammarian) 2nd century A.D. De litteris, syllabis, metris
	Terentius Apher, Publius (Terence)
	Editions
(6755.A1)	Manuscripts. Facsimiles
	see Z114; Z115Z
6755.A2	Other editions. By date
6755.A25	Argumenta
6755.A3	Selections. Passages. Thoughts
6755.A4	Selected plays
	Single plays

	Individual authors
	Terentius Apher, Publius (Terence)
	Editions
	Single plays -- Continued
6755.A5	Adelphi
6755.A6	Andria
6755.E8	Eunuchus
6755.H4	Heauton timorumenos
6755.H6	Hecyra
6755.P5	Phormio
	Translations
6756	English (Table PA19)
6757	French (Table PA19)
6758	German (Table PA19)
6759	Italian (Table PA19)
6760	Spanish (Table PA19)
6761.A-Z	Other. By language, A-Z
	Subarrange by translator or date
(6762)	Paraphrases. Tales
(6763)	Imitations. Adaptations
6764	Illustrations
	Criticism and interpretation; biography
	Ancient
6766.A4	Acro, Helenius
	Commentaries on Adelphi and Eunuchus (lost)
6766.A5	Arusianus Messius
	Cf. PA6220.A25 Arusianus Messius
	Donatus, Aelius
6766.D7	Editions. By date
(6766.D7A-.D7Z)	Criticism
	see PA6380
6766.E7	Euanthius
	Portion preserved by Donatus?
(6766.E8)	Eugraphius
(6766.P8)	Priscianus Caesariensis
(6766.R8)	Rufinus
	Scholia
	Bembina
	Other
	Glossae Terentianae see PA6785.A2
6767	Medieval
	Modern
(6768.A1)	Commentaries
6768.A2	Early to 1800/50
6768.A5-.Z3	1800/50+
6769	Minor. Addresses, essays, etc.
	Language. Style

PA6000-6971

	Individual authors
	Terentius Apher, Publius (Terence)
	Criticism and interpretation; biography
	Language. Style -- Continued
6782	General
6783	Grammar. Syntax
6784	Versification
6784.A2	Ancient authors
6785	Glossaries, indices, concordances, etc.
6785.A2	Ancient and medieval; "Glossae Terentianae"
	Modern
6785.A3	Lexicographical treatises
6785.A5-.Z3	Dictionaries, concordances
6785.Z5	Glossaries for schools
6785.Z8	Special lists, phrasebooks, etc.
6786	Terentius Cl. to Tibullus
	Terentius Clemens (jurist) 2nd century A.D.
	see class K
	Terentius Scaurus see PA6658.S3
	Terentius Varro see PA6792+
6786.T5	Theodorus, Flavius Manlius (Mallius) consul 399 A.D.
	(Table P-PZ38 modified)
6786.T5A61-.T5A78	Separate works. By title
	e.g. De metris; De natura rerum (lost)
	Theodorus Priscianus see PA6643.P18
6786.T6	Theodosius (?) fl. ca. 530 A.D. De terra sancta (De situ
	terrae sanctae)
	Name of author uncertain; Theodorus? Theodoricus?
6786.T7	Tiberianus (Table P-PZ38)
	Writer of poems; identical with T., 332 A.D. "comes
	Hispaniarum"?
	Tiberius (Tib. Claudius Nero), emperor, 42 B.C.-37 A.D.
	De vita sua (lost)
	Orationes (fragments)
	Tibullus
	Editions
	For combined editions of Catullus, Tibullus, and Propertius,
	see PA6274

Individual authors

Tibullus

Editions -- Continued

6787.A2	Comprehensive editions ("Corpus Tibullianum"). By date

The "Corpus Tibullianum" comprises books I and II, elegies by Tibullus; book III, six elegies by a poet with (assumed?) name "Lygdamus"; book IV: 1, Panegyricus, by an unknown poet; 2-12, elegies on the love of Sulpicia for Cerinthus; 13-14, a short elegy and an epigram (both in all probability composed by Tibullus). The elegies 2-12 consist of two groups; in the first Sulpicia is the subject, the second contains six poetical letters composed by Sulpicia herself. In the mss. the poems are divided into three books; in many editions book III is divided into two (III and IV)

6787.A3	Selected elegies (miscellaneous)
	Selected books
6787.A31	I (or I-II) "Delia." "Nemesis"
6787.A32	II ("Nemesis")
6787.A33	III (or III-IV)
6787.A34	III, 1-6 ("Neaera") elegies by "Lygdamus"
	Cf. PA6497.L8+ Lygdamus
6787.A35	III, 7 (or IV, 1) "Panegyricus"; "Laudes Messalae" (author unknown)
6787.A4	III, 8-18 (or IV, 2-12) "Sulpicia"
6787.A42	III, 8-12 (or IV, 2-6) Elegies on Sulpicia (by Tibullus?)
6787.A43	III, 13-18 (or IV, 7-12) Elegies composed by Sulpicia
6787.A44	III, 19-20 (or IV, 13-14)
6787.A5	Selections. Quotations
6787.A6	Single elegies
6787.Z5	Priapea
	Spurious
6788	Translations
6789	Criticism
6791	Tic... to Varro
6791.T25	Tiro, M. Tullius, 1st century B.C. (Table P-PZ38)
	Cf. Z81 Tironian notes
6791.T29	Titianus (senior) Julius, 2nd century A.D. (Table P-PZ38)
6791.T3	Titianus (junior) Julius, 2nd-3rd century A.D. (Table P-PZ38)
	Presumably the translator of Aesopian fables (from Babrius?)
	Cf. PA3941 Babrius
6791.T38	Titinius (Table P-PZ38)
6791.T5	Trajanus, Emperor of Rome, 53-117 A.D. (Table P-PZ38)
	Cf. PA6638.A5 Correspondence of Pliny the Younger with Trajanus
	Tranquillus see PA6700+

PA6000-6971

	Individual authors
	Tic... to Varro -- Continued
6791.T6	Trebellius Pollio, 3rd century A.D. (Table P-PZ38)
	Cf. PA6445.J6+ Justinus
6791.T8	Trogus, Pompeius
	Tullius Cicero see PA6278+
	Turanius
	see Rufinus, Tyrannius
	Turpilius, Sextus (dramatist) d. 103 B.C.
	Tyrannius
	see Rufinus, Tyrannius
	Ulpianus, Domitius (jurist) d. 228 A.D.
	see class K
	Valerianus, Curtius see PA6379.C7
	Valerius Antias (annalist) 1st century B.C.
	Valerius Cato see PA6271.C8
	Valerius Flaccus, Gaius, 1st cent. Argonautica
	Cf. PA3872 Apollonius Rhodius
6791.V4	Texts. By date
6791.V4A-.V4Z	Translations. By language, A-Z
6791.V5	Criticism
	Valerius Maximus. Factorum et dictorum memorabilium libri IX
	Cf. PA6518.N2 Nepotianus
	Cf. PA6554.P45 Julius Paris
6791.V6	Texts. By date
6791.V6A-.V6Z	Translations. By language, A-Z
6791.V7	Criticism
	Valerius Polemius, Julius, 3rd or 4th century A.D. Res gestae Alexandri Magni translatae ex Aesopo graeco
	Latin version of Pseudo-Callisthenes, the earliest version preserved; author identical (?) with Polemius, consul 338 A.D.
	Cf. PA6445.I7 Itinerarium Alexandri
6791.V8	Texts. By date
6791.V9	Criticism
	Valerius Probus see PA6643.P6+
6791.V93	Valerius Soranus, Q. (Valerius, Q., of Sora) d. 82 B.C. (Table P-PZ38)
6791.V95	Valgius Rufus, C., consul 12 B.C. (Table P-PZ38)
	Elegies and epigrams (fragments)
6791.V97	Varius Rufus, L., fl. 41-20 B.C. (Table P-PZ38)
	Varro, Marcus Terentius
	Editions
6792.A2	Comprehensive. By date
6792.A3	De lingua latina (lib. XXV)
	Books V-X preserved

PA6000-6971

Individual authors -- Continued
Vergilius Maro, Publius (Virgil)
Editions
(6801.A1)	Manuscripts. Facsimiles
	see Z114; Z115Z
6801.A2	Other. By date
6801.A3A-.A3Z	School editions. By editor, A-Z
	Including selected works
6801.A45	Selections, passages, thoughts, etc.
	Outlines, summaries
(6801.A47)	Ancient ("Argumenta")
	see PA6801.A65
6801.A48	Other
6801.A49	Centos
	Aeneis
6801.A5	Editions. By date
6801.A6A-.A6Z	School editions. By editor, A-Z
6801.A65	Argumenta
(6801.A68)	Selections, passages, thoughts, etc.
	see PA6801.A45
6801.A7	Selections: episodes, large continuous portions
	Selected books (three or more)
6802.A1	I-VI (or I-III, VI; or I, IV-VI; etc.)
6802.A2	II, etc.
6802.A3	III, etc.
6802.A9	IX-XII, or X-XII
6803.B21-.B32	Single books (one or two)
	e.g.
6803.B21	I (I-II; or I, VI; etc.)
6803.B22	II (II-III; or II, VIII; etc.)
6803.B23	III (III-IV; or III, IX; etc.)
(6803.Z9)	Postaeneidea
	see the author
	Criticism see PA6823+
6804	Bucolica and Georgica
6804.A2	Editions. By date
(6804.A25)	Selections, passages, thoughts
	see PA6801.A45
	Bucolica (Eclogae)
6804.A3	Editions. By date
6804.A4	Selected eclogues (three or more)
	Single eclogues (one or two)
6804.A41	Ecloga I (or I-II; or I, IV; etc.)
6804.A42	Ecloga II (etc.)
6804.A43	Ecloga III (etc.)
6804.A44	Ecloga IV (etc.)
6804.A45	Ecloga V (etc.)

PA6000-6971

	Individual authors
	Vergilius Maro, Publius (Virgil)
	Translations
	Modern
	A-English
	Celtic -- Continued
6806.C45	Manx (Table PA4)
6806.C46	Welsh (Table PA4)
	Danish see PA6814.S2
6806.D8	Dutch. Flemish. Friesian. Afrikaans (Table PA4)
6807	English (Table PA5)
6809	French (Table PA5)
6811	German (Table PA5)
6812	Hungarian (Table PA5)
6813	Italian (Table PA5)
	Other Western European languages
6814.P7	Portuguese (Table PA4)
6814.R7	Rumanian (Table PA4)
	Scandinavian
6814.S2	Danish. Dano-Norwegian (Table PA4)
6814.S4	Icelandic (Table PA4)
6814.S6	Swedish (Table PA4)
6815	Spanish (Table PA5)
	Slavic languages
6816.B6	Bohemian (Table PA4)
6816.B8	Bulgarian (Table PA4)
6816.C7	Croatian (Table PA4)
6816.L3	Lettish (Table PA4)
6816.L5	Lithuanian (Table PA4)
6816.P7	Polish (Table PA4)
6816.R7	Russian (Table PA4)
6816.R9	Ruthenian (Ukrainian) (Table PA4)
6816.S4	Serbian (Table PA4)
6816.W4	Wendic (Table PA4)
	Oriental languages
6817	Indo-European (Table PA5)
	Semitic
6817.2	Hebrew (Table PA5)
6817.3	Turkic (Table PA5)
6817.4	Japanese (Table PA5)
6817.5	Mongolian (Table PA5)
6817.6	Austronesian (Table PA5)
6817.8	African languages (Table PA5)
	Artificial languages see PM8060+

                    Individual authors
                      Vergilius Maro, Publius (Virgil) -- Continued
                        Paraphrases, etc.
                          Class here Latin paraphrases only
                          For children's books see PZ8.1; PZ25; PZ35; etc.
                          For vernacular paraphrases, parodies, dramatizations,
                              etc. see PA6806+

6818	Paraphrases, tales
6818.3	Dramatization, fiction, etc.
6818.5	Parodies. Travesties
(6818.7)	Imitations
	see the author
	Illustrations. Art
	Ancient
	Illustrated manuscripts
(6819.A2)	Facsimiles
	see Z115Z
(6819.A5-Z)	Treatises
	see PA6824+
(6819.5)	Paintings. Mosaic work
6820	Modern
(6820.9)	Music
	see class M; ML
	Anniversaries. Celebrations, etc.
	Writings in prose or verse in honor of Vergilius
6821.A1	Collections
6821.A2-Z	Other
(6821.5)	Iconography. Monuments, etc.
	see PA6824+
(6821.9)	Fiction, drama, etc. based on life of Vergilius
	see the author
	Criticism and interpretation
	Class here general works and works restricted to Aeneis
6823	Ancient
	Commentaries and scholia
6823.A2	Collections and selections. By date
	Single authors
6823.A8	Asper, Aemilius
	Commentarius
	Fragments
	"Vergilius Aspri" (Quaestiones Vergilianae)
	Authorship doubtful
6823.B7	Brevis expositio Vergilii Georgicorum
6823.D6	Donatus, Aelius. Commentarius Vergilii
	Praefatio, Vita, and introduction to Bucolica
	preserved

                       Individual authors
                          Vergilius Maro, Publius (Virgil)
                            Criticism and interpretation
                               Ancient
                                 Commentaries and scholia
                                 Single authors -- Continued

6823.D8	Donatus, Tiberius Claudius. Interpretationum Vergilianarum Aeneidos lib. I-XII
(6823.F6)	Florus, L. Annaeus. Vergilius orator an poeta see PA6386
6823.F8	Fulgentius, Fabius Planciades. Expositio Vergilianae continentiae
	Glossae see PA6950.A2
(6823.M3)	Macrobius, Theodosius see PA6498+
6823.P3	Philargyrius, Junius. Explanatio in Bucolica Vergilii
6823.P6	Priscianus Caesariensis. Partitiones XII versuum Aeneidos Cf. PA6642.A59 Priscianus Caesariensis
6823.P8	"Pseudo-Probus" ("M. Valerii Probi in Vergilii Bucolica et Georgica commentarius,") Falsely ascribed to Probus
6823.S2	Scholia bernensia (Codex bernensis 172 sec. IX/X) On Bucolica and Georgica; compiled from Junius Philargyrius, Gaudentius, T. Gallus, a. o.
6823.S3	Scholia Danielis (Servius auctus) Cf. PA6823.S5 Servius. In Vergilii carmina commentarius
6823.S4	Scholia veronensia (Palimpsest manuscript in Verona) Compiled chiefly from the commentaries of Asper, Cornutus, Velius Longus, and Haterianus

6823.S5	Servius. In Vergilii carmina commentarius
	    Transmitted in a shorter and a larger version, the former by Servius, the latter (known as "Scholia Danielis," "Servius auctus") is an anonymous compilation from Servius and other sources; the main source of both versions is the commentary of Ae. Donatus
	    For criticism see PA6824+
	    Cf. PA6823.S3 Scholia Danielis

(6823.S8)	Sulpicius Apollinaris. Argumenta see PA6801.A65
6823.Z5	Lost commentaries, fragments, etc.
	Vitae Vergilianae
6823.Z7	Collections. By date

Individual authors
  Vergilius Maro, Publius (Virgil)
    Criticism and interpretation
      Ancient
        Vitae Vergilianae -- Continued
          Single vitae
            see the authors
      Modern

6824	Early to 1800
	1800-
6825.A2	Periodicals. Societies. Serials
6825.A3	Collected studies (by various authors). By date
(6825.A4)	Commentaries
6825.A5-Z	Treatises
6826	Minor. Addresses. Essays. Lectures
6929	Study and teaching

           Including theory and method
    Style. Language. Technique

6931	General
6932	Special (Rhetorical)

        Including allegory, similes, figures of speech, epithets, etc.
      Grammar

6935	General
6939	Special
6941	Syntax
6945	Versification

      Lexicography

6949	Treatises

        Glossaries. Indices. Concordances

6950	Ancient ("Glossae")
6950.A2	Editions. By date
(6950.A5-Z)	Criticism

           see PA6824+

6951	Medieval
6952	Modern
6952.Z5	List of names. By date
6953	School glossaries. By date

  Appendix Vergiliana
    Collection of poems alleged to have been composed by
      Vergilius in his youth, and for the greater part already
      known to Suetonius. The earlier collection comprised:
      Culex, Dirae, Copa, Aetna, Ciris, Catalepton, Priapea,
      Epigrammata (presumably those in the Catalepton). The
      other poems are later additions
      Cf. PA6958 Spurious poems

6955.A2	Editions (Comprehensive or miscellaneous). By date

    Single works

	Individual authors
	Vergilius Maro, Publius (Virgil)
	Appendix Vergiliana
	Single works -- Continued
	Aetna see PA6202.A5+
6955.C3	Catalepton (Catalecta)
	Includes three priapea, and fourteen small poems (epigrammata) some of which were in all probability composed by Virgil
6955.C5	Ciris
	Not by Virgil, though ascribed to him by some authorities; possibly composed by Cornelius Gallus
6955.C7	Copa
6955.C8	Culex
	De rosis nascentibus (by Ausonius?)
	De viro bono (by Ausonius)
6955.D6	Dirae
	Elegia in Maecenatem see PA6520.E6
	Epigrammata see PA6955.C3
	Est et non (poem by Ausonius)
	Moretum
	Priapea see PA6955.C3
6956.A-Z	Translations, by language, A-Z, and date
	For translations of a particular poem, see the poem
6957	Criticism (General)
6958	Spurious poems (not included in the Appendix Vergiliana)
	Vergilius. Legend (Vergilius in the Middle Ages)
6959	Legends. Biographies
6959.A15	Undated editions
6959.A2	Collections. By date
6959.A5-Z	Particular legends
6961	Treatises
6965	Vergilius to Victor
	Vergilius Maro (grammarian) see PA8443
6965.V3	Verrius Flaccus, M., fl. ca. 10 B.C. De verborum significatu (lost)
	For the extract of Sextus Pompeius Festus see PA6385.F4
	For the extract of Paulus Diaconus see PA8395.P3
6965.V32	Versus Agresti episcopi de fide ad Avitum episcopum
6965.V33	Verus, L., emperor, d. 169 A.D. (Table P-PZ38)
	Cf. PA6389.F6+ Fronto
6965.V34	Vestricius Spurinna, fl. 69 A.D. (Table P-PZ38)
	Poems lost; the four poems published with title "De contemtu seculi" are a forgery of C. Barth

Individual authors
Vergilius to Victor -- Continued

6965.V35   Vibius Sequester (4th or 5th century A.D.). De fluminibus, fontibus, lacubus, nemoribus, paludibus, montibus, gentibus per litteras

Victor I (pope, 189-199 A.D.)
    see BR60+

Victor (bishop of Capua) d. 554
    see BR60+

Victor (bishop of Cartenna) 5th century
    see BR60+

Victor (bishop of Tunnuna) fl. 544-565 A.D.
    Chronicon
       see BR60+

6965.V46   Victor (bishop of Vita) 5th century (Table P-PZ38 modified)
6965.V46A61-
.V46A78   Separate works. By title

      Historia persecutionis Africanae provinciae see BR65.A+

Victor, Aurelius see PA6966

6965.V5   Victor, C. Julius, 4th century A.D. Ars rhetorica
Hermagorae, Ciceronis, Quintiliani, Aquili, Marcomanni, Taciani [or Titiani?]
    Mainly based upon Quintilianus

6965.V6   Victor, Claudius Marius "orator massiliensis," 5th century A.D. (Table P-PZ38 modified)
    Probably identical with the rhetor Victorinus mentioned by Gennadius

6965.V6A61-.V6A78   Separate works. By title
      Aletheia, seu Commentationes in Genesin (Meterical paraphrase of Genesis 1-19 in three books see BR65.A+

"Victor, Publius"
    see Curiosum urbis Romae regionum

6965.V85   Victor, Saint, Bp. of Vita, fl. 484 (Table P-PZ38)
6966   Victor, Sextus Aurelius (Victor, Aurelius; Victor Afer) fl. 360-389 A.D.

PA6000-6971

	Individual authors
	Victor, Sextus Aurelius (Victor, Aurelius; Victor Afer) fl. 360-389 A.D. -- Continued
6966.A2	Historia romana (Historiae romanae breviarium; Historiae romanae compendium; "Historia tripertita")
	A combination of the author's "Caesares" with two anonymous works "Origo gentis romanae" and "De viris illustribus urbis Romae." The "Origo" and the "Caesares" have not been transmitted outside of the Corpus. "De viris illustribus" exists in separate manuscripts most of which ascribe the authorship to the younger Plinius; the redactor of the Corpus calls it "Historia Liviana." In many earlier editions, the authorship of the three works is ascribed to S. Aurelius Victor. Most of the printed editions include the so-called Epitome. The two anonymous works and the "Epitome" are sometimes referred to as the works of "Pseudo-Victor."
6966.A4	Caesares (Historiae abbreviatae ab Augusto Octaviano, id est a fine Titi Livii, usque ad consulatum decimum Constantii Augusti et Iuliani Caesaris tertium)
6966.A5	"Epitome" (Libellus de vita et moribus imperatorum breviatus ex libris Sexti Aurelii Victoris a Caesare Augusto usque ad Theodosium
	Not an abstract from the Caesares, but a compilation from various authors
(6966.A53)	Origo gentis romanae
	For separate editions and treatises restricted to the Origo, see PA6518.O6
(6966.A55)	De viris illustribus
	see PA6379.D25
6966.A8-.Z3	Translations. By language, A-Z, and date
6966.Z5	Criticism
6967	Victor, Sulp. to Vitruvius
	Victor, Sulpicius (Sulpitius) 4th century A.D. Institutiones oratoriae
6967.V4	Victorinus "grammaticus," 4th century A.D. (Table P-PZ38 modified)
	Two treatises apparently written by the same author. In the manuscripts the Ars is ascribed to "Victorinus (Victurinus) grammaticus," or to Palaemon, the metrical treatise to Palaemon, in the earlier editions the two works appear under the name of Maximus Victorinus
6967.V4A61-.V4A78	Separate works. By title
	e.g. Ars Victorini grammatici de analogia ac de questionibus aliis (De arte grammatica); De hexametro versu sive heroico (De metrica institutione)

Individual authors

Victor, Sulp. to Vitruvius -- Continued

Victorinus, petabionensis episcopus (bishop of Pettau) 3rd century

see BR60+

6967.V5   Victorinus, C. Marius (Victorinus Afer) 4th century A.D. (Table P-PZ38 modified)

6967.V5A61-.V5A78   Separate works. By title

e.g. Ars grammatica (De enunciatione litterarum, orthographia et metris) (The substance of this work is the prosody of Aphthonius (De metris omnibus libri IV) to which V. prefixed a dissertation on orthography, and added an appendix "De metris horatianis." In the earlier editions the "Ars" is ascribed to Maximus Victorinus); De definitionibus (Wrongly ascribed to Boethius); Explanationum in Ciceronis Rhetoricam lib. II (Commentum in C. Rhetoricam) (In the manuscripts, the commentary is ascribed to Q. Fabius Laurentius, or to Marius Fabius Victorinus, or to Fabius Laurentius Marius Victorinus (fusion of names of author and editor?). In the earlier editions, the author's name is frequently given as Marius Fabius Victorinus); Lost works: Translation of Porphyrius, Isagoge; Doubtful works: De attributis personae et negotio

Theological treatises and poems

see BR60+

Ars de analogia (Doubtful) see PA6967.V4

De hexametro versu (Doubtful) see PA6967.V4

Victorinus, Claudius Marius see PA6965.V6

Victorinus, Marius Fabius

see Victorinus, C. Marius, Explanationes in Ciceronis Rhetoricam

6967.V65   Victorinus, Maximus (Maximinus? Maximianus? Date unknown). De ratione metrorum

In the manuscripts followed by a short treatise "De finalibus metrorum," in some of them ascribed to one "Metrorius" Maximinus

Cf. PA6967.V4 Victorinus "grammaticus"

Cf. PA6967.V5 Victorinus, C. Marius

Victorius Aquitanus (of Limoges?) fl. 457 A.D.

Canon paschalis see CE83

Victorius, Claudius Marius see PA6965.V6

Vindex, L. Caesellius

see Caesellius Vindex, L.

Vindicianus (physician) 4th century A.D.

Virgil see PA6801+

Virgilius. Itinera hierosolymitana

Individual authors
Victor, Sulp. to Vitruvius -- Continued
Virgilius Maro "grammaticus," 7th century A.D see PA8443
Virgilius Maro, Publius see PA6801+
Viri illustres see PA6379.D25
Vitruvius Pollio
Cf. NA340.V5 Architecture

6968	Editions
6968.1	Epitome (by M. Cetius Faventinus)
6969	Translations
6970	Criticism
6971	Viv... to Z
6971.V4	Volcacius Sedigitus, 1st century B.C. De poetis
	Fragment of a didactic poem
6971.V5	Voltacilius Pilutus, L. (or Plotus? historian) fl. 81 B.C. (Table P-PZ38)
	Identical with M. Voltacilius Pitholaus, partisan of Pompeius?
6971.V6	Volusius (Q.) epic poet, 1st century B.C. (Table P-PZ38)
	Cf. PA6754.T2 Tanusius
	Volusius Maecianus, L. see PA6500.M25
6971.V7	Vopiscus, Flavius, 3rd to 4th century A.D. (Table P-PZ38)
6971.V8	Vulcacius Gallicanus, 3rd to 4th century A.D. (Table P-PZ38)

	Medieval and modern Latin literature
	History and criticism
8001	Periodicals and societies
8002	Congresses
8003	Collections
8004.A-Z	Studies in honor of a particular person or institution. Festschriften. By honoree, A-Z
8015	General works
8020	Outlines, tables, etc.
8023	Addresses, essays, lectures
8025	Biography (Collective)
	Cf. PA83+ Classical scholars
8027	General special. Miscellaneous
8030.A-Z	Special topics, A-Z
8030.C44	Celtic authors
8030.C45	Censorship
8030.C47	Christian literature
8030.D47	Desire
8030.D53	Didactic literature
8030.E76	Erotic literature
8030.F45	Feminism
8030.J6	Joseph, the patriarch
8030.L33	Labor and laboring classes
8030.P35	Parodies
8030.P36	Pastoral literature
8030.W65	Women authors
	Special periods
8035	Medieval to 1350
8040	Modern, 1350-
8043	Recent, 19th-20th centuries
8045.A-Z	Special countries, A-Z
	Special forms
	Poetry
8050	General works
8051	Medieval
8052	Modern
	Epic
8053	General works
8054	Animal epics
	Lyric
	see PA8050+
8055	Epigrams
8056	Religious
	Including Christian poetry
8057	Didactic
8060	Satire
8063.A-Z	Other special forms, A-Z

PA8001-8595

	History and criticism
	Special forms
	Poetry
	Other special forms, A-Z -- Continued
8063.V57	Visual poetry
8065.A-Z	Special subjects, A-Z
8065.A54	Animals
8065.A77	Art
	Christian poetry see PA8056
8065.C5	Church
8065.C56	Cities and towns
8065.C65	College verse
8065.D4	Death
8065.D73	Dreams
8065.E43	Elegiac poetry
8065.E76	Erotic poetry
8065.F75	Friendship
8065.H65	Homer
8065.H85	Humanism
8065.L6	Love poetry
8065.P45	Philosophy
8065.P64	Political poetry
8065.S8	Student songs (Vagantenpoesie, chants des Goliards, etc.)
8065.T7	Travel
	Drama
8073	General
8075	Tragedy
8076	Comedy
8077	Religious drama
8079	Other special
	Prose
8081	General works
8085	Oratory. Rhetoric
8089	Letters
8091	Fiction
8095	Wit. Humor. Satire
8096	Other
	Collections
	General
8101	Early to 1800
8105	1801-
8110	Selections. Anthologies
	Special periods
8112	Medieval
	Modern
8114	General

	Collections
	Special periods
	Modern -- Continued
8115	14th-16th centuries
8116	17th-18th centuries
8117	19th-20th centuries
8118.A-Z	Special countries, A-Z
	Special forms
	Poetry
8119	Periodicals
8120	General
8122	Medieval, to 1350
8123	Modern
8125.A-Z	Special countries, A-Z
	e.g.
8125.G7	Great Britain
	Including college verse
	Special kinds
8126	Epic
8127	Lyric
8128	Epigrams
8129	Religious
8131	Didactic
8133.A-Z	Other, A-Z
	College verse see PA8133.S3
8133.J47	Jesuit poetry
8133.P37	Pastoral poetry
8133.P6	Political poetry
8133.P76	Prose poetry
8133.S3	School and college verse
8133.S65	Sonnets
8133.S8	Student songs. Songs of the Vaganten or Goliards. Carmina Burana
	Cf. PA8125.G7 Great Britain
	Drama
8135	General
8137	Medieval, to 1350
8138	Modern
8140.A-Z	Special countries, A-Z
	e.g.
8140.G7	Great Britain
8142	Religious drama
8145	Prose. Prose fiction
8146	Orations
8147	Letters
8148	Wit and humor. Parodies. Satires
8149	Miscellaneous. Essays, dialogues, etc.

PA8001-8595

	Collections -- Continued
	Translations from Latin into other languages
8160	Polyglot
	English
8161	General
8163	Selections. Anthologies
8164	Poetry
8165	Drama
8166	Prose
(8167)	Individual authors
	see PA8200+
	French
8171	General
8173	Selections. Anthologies
8174	Poetry
8175	Drama
8176	Prose
(8177)	Individual authors
	see PA8200+
	German
8181	General
8183	Selections. Anthologies
8184	Poetry
8185	Drama
8186	Prose
(8187)	Individual authors
	see PA8200+
	Italian
8191	General
8193	Selections. Anthologies
8194	Poetry
8195	Drama
8196	Prose
(8197)	Individual authors
	see PA8200+
8199.A-Z	Other languages, A-Z
	Individual authors or works
	Medieval to 1350
8200	A-Ab
8201	Abailard, Pierre, 1079-1142
	Cf. B765.A2+ Philosophy
	Cf. BX890 Collected works
	Cf. BX4705.A2 Biography
	Letters of Abailard and Héloise
8201.A3	Latin
8201.A4	English
8201.A41	Metrical versions

	Individual authors or works
	Medieval to 1350
	Abailard, Pierre, 1079-1142
	Letters of Abailard and Héloise -- Continued
8201.A5	French
8201.A6	German
8201.A7	Italian
8201.A8	Spanish
8201.A81-.A89	Other languages (alphabetically)
	e.g.
8201.A87	Russian
8201.A9	Criticism
	Historia calamitatum
	Often printed as the first letter in letters of Abailard and Héloise
8201.H3	Latin
8201.H4	English
8201.H41	Metrical versions
8201.H5	French
8201.H6	German
8201.H7	Italian
8201.H8	Spanish
8201.H81-.H89	Other languages (alphabetically)
	e.g.
8201.H87	Russian
8201.H9	Criticism
8212.A2	Abbo, abbot of Fleury, d. 1004 (Table P-PZ40)
8212.A25	Abbo, Monk of St. Germain, ca. 805-ca. 923 (Table P-PZ40)
8212.A3	Adalbéron, Bp. of Laon, d. 1030 (Table P-PZ40)
8215	Adam de Saint Victor, d. 1192 (Table P-PZ39)
	Cf. PQ1412.A2 Early French translations
8217	Ad-Ae
8217.A28	Adamus Bremensis, 11th century (Table P-PZ40)
8217.A29	Ademarus Cabannensis, ca. 988-1034 (Table P-PZ40)
8217.A295	Adolfus, von Wien, 14th cent. (Table P-PZ40)
8217.A3	Aedilvulfus, abbot, fl. 803 (Table P-PZ40)
8217.A34	Aequivoca
8230	Aesopus
	Medieval Latin versions
8240.A3	Alan, of Tewkesbury, 12th century (Table P-PZ40)
8240.A5	Alanus de Insulis, d. 1202 (Table P-PZ40)
8240.A6	Albertanus Brixiensis, 13th century (Table P-PZ40)
	For medieval translations see Classes PQ, PR, PT
8240.A7	Albertus Stadensis, 13th century (Table P-PZ40)
8245	Alcuin, 735-804 (Table P-PZ37)
	Cf. LB125.A4+ Education

PA8001-8595

Individual authors or works
Medieval to 1350 -- Continued

8246	Alc-Ale
8246.A43	Aldhelm, Saint, Bp. of Sherborne, 640?-709 (Table P-PZ40)
8246.A44	Alexander, of Ashby, 12th/13th cent. (Table P-PZ40)
	Alexander the Great (Romances, etc.)
8247	Historia de preliis
	Latin translation by Leo, Archipresbyter, from the work of Pseudo-Callisthenes
8248	Other medieval Latin versions
8249	Ale-Am
8249.A62	Alphabetum narrationum
8249.A63	Alphanus I, Abp. of Salermod, 1085 (Table P-PZ40)
8250.A2	Amarcius, 11th century (Table P-PZ40)
8250.A23	Anastasio, 14th century (Table P-PZ40)
8250.A236	André le chapelain (Table P-PZ40)
8250.A24	Andreas de Rode, 13th century (Table P-PZ40)
	Antichrist (Drama) see PA8360.L8
8250.A3	Archipoeta, fl. 1140-1165 (Table P-PZ40)
8250.A45	Arnold, of Lübeck, d. 1212 (Table P-PZ40)
8250.A46	Arnulf, of Lisieux, d. 1184 (Table P-PZ40)
8250.A5	Arrigo da Settimello, fl. ca. 1192 (Table P-PZ40)
8250.A9	Auctoritates Aristotelis
8255	Aungerville, Richard, known as Richard de Bury, bp. of Durham, 1287-1345 (Table P-PZ39)
	Cf. Z992 Philobiblion
8256.A87	Aurelius, Cornelius, ca. 1460-1531 (Table P-PZ40)
8257.B3	Baldricus, abp. of Dol, 1046-1130 (Table P-PZ40)
8257.B35	Balduinus Iuvenis, 13th century (Table P-PZ40)
8257.B38	Barlaam and Joasaph (Table P-PZ40)
	Bartholomaeus Anglicus, 13th century see AE2
8260	Beda Venerabilis, 673-735 (Table P-PZ37)
	Cf. BR746 Ecclesiastical history
	Cf. PR1578 Anglo-Saxon literature
8265	Bed-Ber
	Bernard de Morlaix or Morlas see PA8270
8270	Bernard, of Cluny, 12th century (Table P-PZ39)
8275	Ber-Bid
8275.B25	Bernard Silvestris, fl. 1136 (Table P-PZ40)
8275.B27	Berno von Reichenau, d. 1048 (Table P-PZ40)
8275.B3	Bersuire, Pierre, ca. 1290-1362 (Table P-PZ40)
8275.B4	Bestiary
	For versions based exclusively on the Greek Physiologus see PA4273.P8+
8280	Bīdpāī
	Latin translations of the Arabic version, Kalilah wa-Dimnah

Individual authors or works

Medieval to 1350 -- Continued

8285	Bid-Bo
8290	Bonaventura, Saint, cardinal, 1220-1274 (Table P-PZ39)
	Cf. BX4700.B68 Biography
8295.B5	Boncompagno da Signa, 13th century (Table P-PZ40)
8295.B57	Bonvesin, da la Riva, ca. 1250-1314? (Table P-PZ40)
8295.B6	Bramis, John, 14th century (Table P-PZ40)
8295.B7	Brendan, Saint. Legend
8295.B85	Burgundius, Joannes, d. 1194 (Table P-PZ40)
8295.C3	Caesarius, of Heisterbach, ca. 1180-ca. 1240 (Table P-PZ40)
8295.C4	Carmen ad Flavium Felicem de resurrectione mortuorum
8295.C43	Carmen in victoriam Pisanorum
8295.C46	Carmina fingo
8300	Catonis disticha
	Medieval Latin versions
	Cf. PA6272+ Roman literature
8303	Cat-Char
8303.C45	Cena Cipriani
8305	Charlemagne. Gesta Karoli Magni
8306.C45	Chronica Adefonsi Imperatoris
8310.C6	Colonne, Guido delle, 13th century (Table P-PZ40)
	For early Italian translations see PQ4299.C7
8310.C67	Columban, 543-615 (Table P-PZ40)
8310.C69	Composita verborum
8310.C7	Conradus Hersaugiensis, ca. 1070-ca. 1150 (Table P-PZ40)
8310.C72	Convenole, da Prato, d. ca. 1340 (Table P-PZ40)
8310.C75	Conventum (Table P-PZ43)
8310.D27	Danielis ludus (Table P-PZ43)
	Dante see PQ4311
8310.D35	De Babione
8310.D352	De coniuge non ducenda
8310.D353	De excidio Troiae
8310.D37	De nuncio sagaci
8310.D38	De ortu Waluuanii
8310.D39	De rebus in Oriente mirabilibus
8310.D4	Debate of the body and the soul
8310.D5	Dialogus creaturarum (Table P-PZ43)
8310.D53	Dionysius, de Burgo Sancti Sepulchri, Bishop, d. 1342 (Table P-PZ40)
8310.D58	Dolopathos
8310.D6	Donizo (Table P-PZ40)
8310.D74	Drogo de Altovillari, 1196 or 1197-1271 or 1272 (Table P-PZ40)
	Duns, Johannes, Scotus see B765.D7+

PA8001-8595

Individual authors or works

Medieval to 1350 -- Continued

8310.E33	Ecbasis cujusdam captivi
8310.E4	Egbert von Lüttich, fl. ca. 1026 (Table P-PZ40)
8310.E45	Einhard, ca. 770-840 (Table P-PZ40)
8310.E5	Ekkehard I, Dean of St. Gall, d. 973 (Table P-PZ40)
8310.E52	Ekkehard IV, ca. 980-ca. 1060 (Table P-PZ40)
8310.E54	Elias, of Thriplow, 13th century (Table P-PZ40)
8310.E55	Ellinger, Abbot of Tegernsee (Table P-PZ40)
8310.E7	Ermoldus Nigellus, 9th century (Table P-PZ40)
8310.E8	Etienne de Rouen, moine au Bec, d. 1149 (Table P-PZ40)
8310.E873	Etymachia
8310.E9	Eupolemius (Table P-PZ40)
8310.F35	Fasciculus morum
8310.F48	Florilegium Gallicum
8310.F5	Florilegium prosodiacum
8310.F7	Fortunatus, Venantius Honorius Clementianus, bp., ca. 540-ca. 600 (Table P-PZ40)
8310.F74	Frechulf, Bishop of Lisieux, fl. 825-852 (Table P-PZ40)
8310.G25	Garsias (Table P-PZ40)
8310.G28	Gauterus de Wymburnia, 13th century (Table P-PZ40)
8310.G3	Gautier de Châtillon, fl. 1170-1180 (Table P-PZ40)
8310.G4	Geoffrey of Monmouth, bp. of St. Asaph, 1100?-1154 (Table P-PZ38)
	Supposed author of Vita Merlini
8310.G425	Gervase of Tilbury, ca. 1160-ca. 1211
8318	Gesta Friderici I. metrice
	Gesta Romanorum
8320	Editions. By date
8323	Translations. By language, A-Z
	For early texts see Classes PQ, PR, PT
8325	Criticism
8326	Gesta Theoderici
8330.G5	Gilles de Corbeil, fl. 1200 (Table P-PZ40)
8330.G53	Gilo, of Paris, d. ca. 1142 (Table P-PZ40)
8330.G54	Giovanni, da Capua, 13th cent. (Table P-PZ40)
8330.G55	Giovanni del Virgilio, fl. 1319 (Table P-PZ40)
8330.G57	Giraldus Cambrensis, 1146?-1200? (Table P-PZ40)
8330.G59	Gottfried von Reims, b. 1095 (Table P-PZ40)
8330.G6	Gottfried von Viterbo, d. 1191? (Table P-PZ40)
8330.G62	Gottschalk, of Orbais, ca. 803-ca. 867 (Table P-PZ40)
8330.G64	Gregorius, Abbot of Monte Sacro, ca. 1187-ca. 1248 (Table P-PZ40)
8330.G65	Grosseteste, Robert, 1175?-1253 (Table P-PZ40)
8330.G67	Guglielmo da Pastrengo, ca. 1290?-1362 (Table P-PZ40)
8330.G7	Guicennas, 13th century (Table P-PZ40)
8330.G73	Guido de Basochis, d. 1203 (Table P-PZ40)

	Individual authors or works
	Medieval to 1350 -- Continued
8330.G8	Guilelmus, Blessensis, 12th century (Table P-PZ40)
8330.G82	Guilelmus Apuliensis, 12th century (Table P-PZ40)
8330.G83	Guillelmus, Paduanus, 13th cent. (Table P-PZ40)
8330.G85	Gunther, of Pairis, fl. 1200 (Table P-PZ40)
8330.H3	Henry of Avranches, 13th century (Table P-PZ40)
8330.H34	Herbordus, d. 1168 (Table P-PZ40)
	Hermann von Reichenau see PA8330.H35
8330.H35	Hermannus Contractus, 1013-1054 (Table P-PZ40)
8330.H37	Herzog, Ernst (Table P-PZ40)
8330.H4	Hilarius, 12th century (Table P-PZ40)
8330.H5	Hildebertus, Abp. of Tours, 1056?-1133 (Table P-PZ40)
8330.H6	Hildegard, Saint, 1098?-1178 (Table P-PZ40)
	Cf. BR65.A+ Early Christian literature
	Cf. BX4700.H5 Biography
8330.H7	Hisperica famina
	Historia de preliis see PA8247
8330.H75	Historia Meriadoci
8330.H78	Hoveden, John, d. 1275 (Table P-PZ40)
8330.H8	Hrabanus Maurus, abp., 784?-856 (Table P-PZ40)
8340	Hrotsvit, of Gandersheim. Roswitha (Table P-PZ37)
8347.H75	Hugo, von Mâcon, 13th century (Table P-PZ40)
8347.H77	Hugo Primas Aurelianensis, ca. 1093-ca. 1160 (Table P-PZ40)
8347.H79	Hugo von Lüttich, 14th century (Table P-PZ40)
8347.H8	Hugo von Trimberg, fl. 1260-1309 (Table P-PZ40)
8347.I8	Isengrimus, ca. 1148 (Table P-PZ40)
(8350)	Isidorus, Saint, bp. of Seville, d. 636
	see PA6445.I3+
8360.J2	Jacopone da Todi, 1230-1306 (Table P-PZ40)
8360.J49	Jezebel (Norman Latin poem)
(8360.J5)	Joannes de Garlandia, ca. 1195-ca. 1272
	see PA8360.J66
8360.J6	Joannes, of Hildesheim, d. 1375 (Table P-PZ38 modified)
8360.J6A61-.J6A78	Separate works. By title
	e.g. Historia trium regum
8360.J63	Johannes, de Alta Silva, fl. 1184-1212 (Table P-PZ40)
8360.J65	Johannes de Hauvilla (Table P-PZ40)
8360.J66	John of Garland, ca. 1195-ca. 1272 (Table P-PZ40)
8360.J67	John, of Salisbury, Bishop of Chartres, d. 1180 (Table P-PZ40)
8360.J7	Joseph of Exeter, fl. 1190 (Table P-PZ40)
	De bello troiano
	Josephus Exoniensis see PA8360.J7
	Josephus Iscanus see PA8360.J7
8360.J8	Julian, Saint, bp. of Toledo, d. 690 (Table P-PZ40)

PA8001-8595

Individual authors or works

Medieval to 1350 -- Continued

8360.K3	Karolus Magnus et Leo papa
8360.K65	Konrad, von Mure, 1210-1281 (Table P-PZ40)
8360.L3	Lambert, of Saint-Omer (Table P-PZ40)
8360.L354	Laurentius, Veronensis, 12th cent. (Table P-PZ40)
8360.L36	Lawrence of Durham, ca. 1114-1154 (Table P-PZ40)
8360.L38	Ledrede, Richard, bp. of Ossovy, d. 1360 (Table P-PZ40)
8360.L4	Leges Langobardorum
	Leo, archipresbyter, 10th century see PA8247
8360.L46	Leo, of Vercelli, Bishop of Vercelli, d. 1026 (Table P-PZ40)
8360.L47	Letaldus, 10th cent.
8360.L515	Libellus de Constantino Magno eiusque matre Helena
8360.L52	Liber Floretus
8360.L58	Liudprandus, Bp. of Cremona, d. ca. 972 (Table P-PZ40)
8360.L8	Ludus de Antichristo (Drama)
8360.L9	Ludus paschalis sive de passione Domini
8360.L93	Lull, Ramón, d. 1315 (Table P-PZ40)
8360.L95	Lumen anime
8370	Lupus, Servatus, abbot of Ferrières, 9th century (Table P-PZ37)
8375	Lup-Map
8380	Map, Walter, fl. 1200 (Table P-PZ39)
8385	Map-Ne
8385.M3	Marbode, Bishop of Rennes, 1035?-1123 (Table P-PZ40)
8385.M32	Matthaeus Vindocinensis (Table P-PZ40)
8385.M35	Mattias, d. 1350 (Table P-PZ40)
8385.M4	Metellus, von Tegernsee, fl. 1167 (Table P-PZ40)
8385.M5	Miracula Beatae Mariae Virginis
8385.M64	Montecassino Passion play
8385.M8	Mussato, Albertino, 1261-1329 (Table P-PZ40)
8390	Neckham, Alexander, 1157-1217 (Table P-PZ39)
8395	Ne-Pi
	Nivardus see PA8347.I8
8395.N6	Notker Balbulus, ca. 840-912 (Table P-PZ40)
8395.O28	Odo, of Cheriton, d. 1247 (Table P-PZ40)
8395.O29	Odo, of Magdeburg, 13th century (Table P-PZ40)
8395.O3	Odo, Saint, abbot of Cluny, 879-942 (Table P-PZ40)
8395.O4	Officium sepulchri seu resurrectionis (Liturgical drama)
8395.O5	Officium stellae (Bilsen)
8395.P23	Pamphilus de amore
8395.P24	Passio Pelagii (Table P-PZ40)
8395.P28	Paulinus II, Saint, d. 802 (Table P-PZ40)
8395.P3	Paulus Diaconus, ca. 720-797 (Table P-PZ40)
	For his Roman history see DG208
8395.P32	Peckham, John, Abp. of Canterbury, d. 1292 (Table P-PZ40)

	Individual authors or works
	Medieval to 1350
	Ne-Pi -- Continued
8395.P34	Peter, the Venerable, ca. 1092-1156 (Table P-PZ40)
8395.P35	Petrus, Presbyter, 13th century (Table P-PZ40)
8395.P36	Petrus Alfonsi, 1062-1110? (Table P-PZ40)
8395.P4	Petrus de Ebulo, fl. 1196 (Table P-PZ40)
8395.P43	Petrus Pictor (Table P-PZ40)
	Physiologus see PA8440.T3
	Pierre, la Vénérable, ca. 1092-1156 see PA8395.P34
8400	Pietro Damiani, Saint, 1007?-1072 (Table P-PZ39)
	Cf. BV469.P5+ Latin hymns
	Cf. BX4700.P77 Lives of the saints
8405	Pio-Ps
8405.P57	Planctus Mariae
8405.P58	Polythecon
8405.P6	Pseudo-Turpin (Table P-PZ40)
	Cf. PQ1501.P87+ Early French translations
8420	Q-Se
8420.Q53	Quid suum virtutis
8420.Q55	Quilichinus de Spoleto, fl. 1236 (Table P-PZ40)
8420.R175	Ratherius, of Verona, ca. 890-974 (Table P-PZ40)
8420.R177	Raymundus, de Rocosello, b. ca. 1220 (Table P-PZ40)
8420.R18	Red book of Ossory
8420.R2	Reginald, of Canterbury, fl. 1112 (Table P-PZ40)
8420.R24	Riccardo, da Venosa, b. 1302? (Table P-PZ40)
	Richard de Bury see PA8255
8420.R25	Richardus Pictavienis, 12th century (Table P-PZ40)
8420.R3	Ridevallus, Joannes, fl. 1330 (Table P-PZ40)
	Commentary of Fulgentius see BL720
8420.R6	Roger, of Waltham, d. 1336 (Table P-PZ40)
8420.R63	Rogerius, Archbishop of Split, ca. 1201-1266 (Table P-PZ40)
	Roswitha see PA8340
8420.R75	Rudolf, von Liebegg, d. 1332 (Table P-PZ40)
8420.R78	Rudolf von Schlettstadt (Table P-PZ40)
8420.R8	Rudolphus Tortarius, monk of Fleury, b. 1063 (Table P-PZ40)
8420.R9	Ruodlieb (Romance)
8420.S15	Salutati, Caluccio, 1331-1406 (Table P-PZ40)
8420.S16	Samson, d. 890 (Table P-PZ40)
8420.S18	Saxo Grammaticus, d. ca. 1204 (Table P-PZ40)
8420.S2	Sedulius Scotus, 9th century (Table P-PZ40)
	Servatus Lupus see PA8370
8420.S35	Severus, of Malaga, Bishop of Malaga (Table P-PZ40)
8430	Seven Sages

	Individual authors or works
	Medieval to 1350
	Seven Sages -- Continued
8430.A1	Medieval Latin versions. By date
	For versions in other languages see Classes PC, PQ, PR, PT, etc.
	Cf. PN687.S43 Special topics in medieval literature
8435	Se-Ta
8435.S47	Speculum hominis
8435.S5	Speculum sapientiae
8440.T3	Theobaldus Episcopus. Physiologus
	A metrical bestiary
8440.T33	Theodulf, Bishop of Orléans, ca. 760-821 (Table P-PZ38)
8440.T35	Theodulus, 9th century (Table P-PZ38)
8440.T37	Thiofridus, abbot of Echternach, d. 1110 (Table P-PZ40)
8440.T4	Thomas of Celano, fl. 1257 (Table P-PZ40)
	Dies Irae see BV469.D5+
	Thomas Aquinas, Saint
	see B765.T5; BX890; BX1749; BX4700.T6; etc.
8442	Ti-Vir
8442.T73	Tragoedia Mauritius
8442.V3	Valerius, Marcus, 12th century (Table P-PZ40)
	Veronese riddle see PQ4556.V53
8442.V45	Versus de Unibove (Table P-PZ43)
8442.V5	Vinsauf, Geoffrey de, fl. 1200 (Table P-PZ40)
8443	Virgilius Maro, the grammarian, 7th century (Table P-PZ39)
8445	Vir-Z
8445.V48	Vita et transitus Sancti Hieronymi
8445.V52	Vita Sancti Albani
8445.V53	Vitalis Blesensis, fl. 1160-1175 (Table P-PZ40)
8445.W34	Walahfrid Strabo, 807?-849 (Table P-PZ40)
8445.W35	Walter, of England, Archbishop of Palermo, fl. 1177 (Table P-PZ40)
8445.W37	Warner, of Rouen, fl. 996-1026 (Table P-PZ40)
	Walter, of Chatillon, fl. 1170-1180 see PA8310.G3
8445.W48	Wido, Bp. of Amiens, d. 1075? (Table P-PZ40)
8445.W49	Willibald, Presbyter, 8th century (Table P-PZ40)
8445.W5	Wireker, Nigellus, ca. 1130-ca. 1200 (Table P-PZ40)
	Modern, 1350-
	Subarrange each author by Table P-PZ40 unless otherwise specified
8450.A2	Abad, Diego José, 1727-1779 (Table P-PZ40)
8450.A23	Acevedo, Pedro Pablo de, 1522-1572 (Table P-PZ40)
8450.A26	Acquaviva, Belisario (Table P-PZ40)
8450.A27	Acquaviva, Rodolfo, 1658-1729 (Table P-PZ40)
8450.A32	Addison, Joseph, 1672-1719 (Table P-PZ40)
	Aeneas Sylvius Bartholomaeus Piccolomini see PA8556

Individual authors or works

Modern, 1350- -- Continued

8450.A34	Agosti, Girolano Oliviero, 1509-1558 (Table P-PZ40)
8450.A35	Agricola, Rudolf, 1443-1485 (Table P-PZ40)
8450.A4	Alabaster, William, 1567-1640 (Table P-PZ40)
8450.A5	Alberti, Leone Battista, 1404-1472 (Table P-PZ40)
8450.A52	Albinus, Petrus, 1534-1598 (Table P-PZ40)
8450.A6	Alcionio, Pietro, fl. 1520 (Table P-PZ40)
8450.A64	Alegrete, Manuel Telles da Silva, marquez de, 1682-1736 (Table P-PZ40)
8450.A645	Alexander VII, Pope, 1599-1667 (Table P-PZ40)
8450.A65	Allegreti, Giacomo, ca. 1326-1393 (Table P-PZ40)
8450.A654	Alsop, Anthony, 1671 or 2-1726 (Table P-PZ40)
	Ammonio, 1478-1517 see PA8485.D637
8450.A6555	Amoedo Carballo, Hermenexildo, 1747-1811 (Table P-PZ40)
8450.A66	Anchieta, José de, 1534-1597 (Table P-PZ40)
8450.A7	Andreä, Johann Valentin, 1586-1654 (Table P-PZ40)
8450.A8	Andrelinus, Publius Faustus, d. 1518? (Table P-PZ40)
8450.A82	Andrés, Domingo, 16th century (Table P-PZ40)
8450.A824	Angéli, Pietro, 1517-1596 (Table P-PZ40)
8450.A83	Anghiera, Pietro Martire d', 1457-1526 (Table P-PZ40)
8450.A87	Antoninus Bassianus Caracalla (Table P-PZ40)
8450.A88	Antonio da Rho, 15th cent. (Table P-PZ40)
8450.A89	Appendini, Urban, 1777-1834 (Table P-PZ40)
8455	Aquino, Tommaso Niccolò d', 1665-1721 (Table P-PZ39)
8457.A45	Arlier, Antoine, ca. 1502-1545? (Table P-PZ40)
8457.A5	Arnolletus, Ioannes (Table P-PZ40)
8460	Ascham, Roger, 1515-1568 (Table P-PZ39)
	Cf. LB475.A7+ Education
8461.A78	Audebert, Germain, 1518-1598 (Table P-PZ40)
8461.A8	Audiberti, Camillo Maria, fl. 1711 (Table P-PZ40)
8461.A9	Augurello, Giovanni Aurelio, 1454?-1537? (Table P-PZ40)
8461.A94	Aureli, Ludovico, 1592-1637 (Table P-PZ40)
8461.A975	Avancini, Nicolaus von, 1611-1686 (Table P-PZ40)
8462.B14	Bachmann, Christian, fl. 1607-1611 (Table P-PZ40)
8462.B15	Badius Ascensius, Jodocus, 1462-1535 (Table P-PZ40)
8462.B17	Baerland, Adrian van, 1486?-1538 (Table P-PZ40)
8462.B2	Baerle, Kaspar van, 1584-1648 (Table P-PZ40)
8462.B23	Baerle, Melchior van, b. ca. 1540 (Table P-PZ40)
8462.B25	Balbi, Girolamo, ca. 1460-ca. 1535 (Table P-PZ40)
8463.B2	Balde, Jakob, 1604-1668 (Table P-PZ40)
8463.B25	Baltimore, Frederick Calvert, 7th baron, 1731-1771 (Table P-PZ40)
8463.B3	Balzac, Jean Louis Guez, sieur de, d. 1654 (Table P-PZ40)
	Cf. PQ1713 French literature
8463.B7	Baptista Mantuanus, 1448-1516 (Table P-PZ40)

Individual authors or works

Modern, 1350- -- Continued

8463.B76	Barbara, Ermolao, 1454-1493 (Table P-PZ40)
8463.B8	Barbosa, José, 1674-1750 (Table P-PZ40)
8465	Barclay, John, 1582-1621 (Table P-PZ39)
8470.B27	Bartholomaeus, Coloniensis, ca. 1460 - ca. 1516 (Table P-PZ40)
8470.B3	Bartholomaeus Macharii van Tongeren, d. ca. 1482 (Table P-PZ40)
8471	Barzizza, Gasparino, ca. 1360-ca. 1431 (Table P-PZ39)
8475.B253	Bartolini, Riccardo, ca. 1470-1528 or 1529 (Table P-PZ40)
8475.B3	Basini, Basinio, 1425-1457 (Table P-PZ40)
8475.B33	Bastard, Thomas, 1566-1618 (Table P-PZ40)
8475.B335	Baudelaire, Charles, 1821-1867 (Table P-PZ40)
8475.B34	Baudius, Dominique, 1561-1613 (Table P-PZ40)
8475.B38	Bebel, Heinrich, 1472-ca. 1516 (Table P-PZ40)
8475.B4	Beccadelli, Antonio, called Panormita, 1394-1471 (Table P-PZ40)
8475.B45	Bél, Mátyás, 1684-1749 (Table P-PZ40)
8475.B5	Bembo, Pietro, cardinal, 1470-1547 (Table P-PZ40)

> Cf. BX4705.A+ Biography
> Cf. DG677.A2 History of Venice
> Cf. PQ4608 Italian literature

8475.B53	Benci, Francesco, 1542-1594 (Table P-PZ40)
8475.B56	Bernardo, Paolo de, d. 1393 (Table P-PZ40)
8475.B58	Berni, Francesco, 1497 or 1498-1535 (Table P-PZ40)
8475.B6	Beroaldo, Filippo, 1453-1505 (Table P-PZ40)
8475.B7	Beveridge, John, fl. 1765 (Table P-PZ40)
8475.B8	Bèze, Théodore de, 1519-1605 (Table P-PZ40)

> Class here Poemata, etc.
> Cf. BX9419.B4 Biography

8477.B3	Bidermann, Jakob, 1577 (or 1578)-1639 (Table P-PZ40)
8477.B33	Bieżanowski, Stanisław, Józef, 1628-1693 (Table P-PZ40)
8477.B35	Bignicourt, Simon de, 1709-1775 (Table P-PZ40)
8477.B4	Biondo, Flavio, 1388-1463 (Table P-PZ40)
8477.B46	Birck, Sixt, 1500-1554 (Table P-PZ40)
8477.B5	Bisschop, Jan de, fl. 1700 (Table P-PZ40)
8477.B52	Bizzarri, Pietro, 16th century (Table P-PZ40)
8477.B526	Bloccius, Petrus, ca. 1530-ca. 1585 (Table P-PZ40)
8477.B53	Blyenburg, Damas van, b. 1558 (Table P-PZ40)
8477.B534	Boaistuau, Pierre, d. 1566 (Table P-PZ40)
8477.B535	Bocatius, Ioannes, 1569-1621 (Table P-PZ40)
	Boccaccio, Giovanni see PQ4274.A2+
8477.B5354	Bocer, Johannes, 1526-1565 (Table P-PZ40)
8477.B536	Boissard, Jean Jacques, 1528-1602 (Table P-PZ40)
8477.B54	Bojardo, Matteo Maria, conte di Scandiano, 1440 (or 1441)-1494

Individual authors or works
Modern, 1350- -- Continued

8477.B543	Bojeris, Laurencijus, 1563-1619
8477.B548	Bond, Samuel, d. 1885 (Table P-PZ40)
8477.B55	Bonet, Honoré, fl. 1378-1398 (Table P-PZ40)
8477.B56	Bonfini, Antonio, 1427-1502 (Table P-PZ40)
8477.B58	Bonifacio, Dragonetto, d. ca. 1526 (Table P-PZ40)
8477.B59	Bonincontri, Lorenzo, 1410-1491 (Table P-PZ40)
8477.B6	Bonnefons, Jean, 1554-1614 (Table P-PZ40)
8477.B67	Bouček Venkovánek, Šimon (Table P-PZ40)
8477.B7	Bourne, Vincent, 1695-1747 (Table P-PZ40)
8477.B73	Boutard, François, 1664-1729 (Table P-PZ40)
8477.B76	Bracciolini, Poggio, 1380-1459 (Table P-PZ40)
8477.B79	Brant, Sebastian, 1458-1521 (Table P-PZ40)
	Cf. PT1509 German literature
8477.B8	Brathwaite, Richard, 1588?-1673 (Table P-PZ40)
8477.B85	Brizard, Nicolas, ca. 1520-1565 (Table P-PZ40)
8477.B86	Brooke, Samuel, d. 1632 (Table P-PZ40)
8477.B877	Bruni, Leonardo, 1369-1444 (Table P-PZ40)
8477.B88	Brunius, Carl Georg, 1792-1869 (Table P-PZ40)
8477.B9	Bruschius, Caspar, 1518-1557 (Table P-PZ40)
8480	Buchanan, George, 1506-1582 (Table P-PZ39)
8481.B83	Buchner, Ulrich, 1560-1602 (Table P-PZ40)
8482.B25	Budé, Guillaume, 1468-1540 (Table P-PZ40)
8482.B26	Bugnot, Gabriel, d. 1673 (Table P-PZ40)
8483.B8	Bulteel, Gislain, seigneur de la Clyte, 1555-1611 (Table P-PZ40)
8483.B85	Bunić, Dubrovčanin, Jakov, 1469-1534 (Table P-PZ40)
(8485.B65)	Buonaccorsi, Filippo
	see PA8485.C215
8485.B69	Burtius, Nicolaus, b. ca. 1450 (Table P-PZ40)
8485.B7	Burton, John, 1710-1771 (Table P-PZ40)
8485.B8	Burton, Robert, 1577-1640 (Table P-PZ40)
	Cf. PR2223+ English literature
8485.B84	Busche, Hermann van dem, ca. 1468-1534 (Table P-PZ40)
8485.C17	Calaminus, Georg, 1549-1595 (Table P-PZ40)
8485.C2	Calcagnini, Celio, d. 1541 (Table P-PZ40)
8485.C212	Caldo, Matteo, 15th-16th centuries (Table P-PZ40)
8485.C213	Caldogno, Francesco Bernardino, b. ca. 1497 (Table P-PZ40)
8485.C215	Callimachus, Philippus, 1437-1496 (Table P-PZ40)
8485.C22	Calvete de Estrella, Juan Cristóbal, d. 1593 (Table P-PZ40)
8485.C225	Calvin, Jean, 1509-1564 (Table P-PZ40)
8485.C23	Camberlyn, Jean Baptiste Guillaume, 1772-1833 (Table P-PZ40)
8485.C26	Campanella, Tommaso, 1568-1639 (Table P-PZ40)

Individual authors or works

Modern, 1350- -- Continued

8485.C265	Campano, Giannantonio, Bishop, 1429-1477 (Table P-PZ40)
8485.C3	Cancer, comoedia
8485.C315	Cantalicio, Giovanni Battista, d. 1515 (Table P-PZ40)
8485.C32	Canter, Jacobus, ca. 1471-ca. 1539 (Table P-PZ40)
8485.C33	Canterus, Theodorus, 1545-1617 (Table P-PZ40)
8485.C35	Capece, Scipione, d. 1551 (Table P-PZ40)
8485.C37	Cappella, Giovanni Antonio, fl. 1649 (Table P-PZ40)
8485.C373	Caramanaeus, Antonius Matthiasaevius, 17th century (Table P-PZ40)
8485.C375	Caro, Miguel Antonio, 1843-1909 (Table P-PZ40)
8485.C377	Carrara, Giovanni Michele Alberto, 1438-1490 (Table P-PZ40)
8485.C379	Carvalho, Thomaz de, 1819-1897 (Table P-PZ40)
8485.C3795	Casa, Giovanni della, abp., 1503-1556 (Table P-PZ40)
	Cf. PQ4617.C6 Italian literature
8485.C3796	Castiglione, Baldassare, conte, 1478-1529 (Table P-PZ40)
	Cf. PQ4617.C65 Italian literature
8485.C39	Catherine, of Bologna, Saint, 1413-1463 (Table P-PZ40)
8485.C45	Cayado (or Caiado), Henrique, d. 1508 (Table P-PZ38)
8485.C48	Celtes, Conradus, 1459-1508 (Table P-PZ40)
8485.C485	Cerva, Elio Lampridio, 1462 or 1463-1520 (Table P-PZ40)
	Cervinus, Aelius Iampridius see PA8485.C485
8485.C496	Chartier, Alain, 15th century (Table P-PZ40)
8485.C497	Chaundler, Thomas, 1418-1490 (Table P-PZ40)
8485.C5	Chorier, Nicolas, 1612-1692 (Table P-PZ40)
8485.C514	Chytraeus, David, 1531-1600 (Table P-PZ40)
8485.C517	Cichinus, Georgius, 1514-1599 (Table P-PZ40)
8485.C519	Ciołek, Jakób, 1587-1648 (Table P-PZ40)
8485.C5197	Cirapa lingonus
8485.C53	Ciriaco de' Pizzicolli, of Ancona, 1391-1459 (Table P-PZ40)
8485.C58	Clénard, Nicolas, 1493 or 1494-1542 (Table P-PZ40)
8485.C6	Clüver, Philipp, 1580-1622 (Table P-PZ40)
	Cf. G120 Geography
	Cluverius, Philippus see PA8485.C6
8485.C64	Collatius, Petrus Apollonius, 15th century (Table P-PZ40)
8485.C7	Collotes de Jantillet, Aleixo, fl. 1679 (Table P-PZ40)
8485.C73	Commire, Jean, 1625-1702 (Table P-PZ40)
8485.C74	Comoedia sine nomine
8485.C75	Copernicus, Nicolaus, 1473-1543 (Table P-PZ40)
	Supposed authors of Septem sidera
8485.C77	Cordus, Euricius, 1486-1535 (Table P-PZ40)
8485.C7715	Coricius, Janus, 1457?-1527 (Table P-PZ40)
8485.C772	Cornazzano, Antonio, 1429-1484 (Table P-PZ40)

Individual authors or works
Modern, 1350- -- Continued

8485.C7723	Coronini, Rodolfo, 1731-1791 (Table P-PZ40)
8485.C7725	Corraro, Gregorio, 1411-1464 (Table P-PZ40)
8485.C773	Cortese, Alessandro, ca. 1465-1491 (Table P-PZ40)
8485.C774	Cortesi, Paolo, 1465-1510 (Table P-PZ40)
8485.C775	Corvinus, Elias, 1537-1602 (Table P-PZ40)
8485.C78	Cotta, Giovanni, 1480-1510 (Table P-PZ40)
8485.C792	Courtois, Hilaire, fl. 1533-1545 (Table P-PZ40)
8485.C793	Coustau, Pierre (Table P-PZ40)
8485.C8	Cowley, Abraham, 1618-1667 (Table P-PZ40)
	Cf. PR3370+ English literature
8485.C82	Crabeels, Judocus J.C.A. (Judocus Johannes Carolus Antonius), 1743-1812 (Table P-PZ40)
8485.C83	Crashaw, Richard, 1613?-1649 (Table P-PZ40)
	Crijević, Ilija see PA8485.C485
8485.C843	Crinito, Pietro, 1465-ca. 1504 (Table P-PZ40)
8485.C847	Crucius, Jacobus, 1579-ca. 1653 (Table P-PZ40)
8485.C848	Crucius, Levinus (Table P-PZ40)
8485.C85	Crusius, Thomas Theodor, 1648-1728 (Table P-PZ40)
8485.C86	Cruz, Luís da, 1543-1604 (Table P-PZ40)
8485.C88	Cunaeus, Petrus, 1586-1638 (Table P-PZ40)
8485.C9	Cunich, Raimondo, 1719-1794 (Table P-PZ40)
8485.C92	Cybeleius, Valentinus, b. ca. 1490 (Table P-PZ40)
8485.D25	Dall'Isola, Matteo, fl. 15th/16th cent. (Table P-PZ40)
8485.D28	Darcio, Giovanni, da Venosa, 16th cent. (Table P-PZ40)
8485.D3	Dartis, Jean, 1572-1651 (Table P-PZ40)
8485.D48	Dati, Agostino, 1420-1478 (Table P-PZ40)
8485.D5	Dati, Leonardo, bp. of Massa, 1408-1472 (Table P-PZ40)
8485.D6	Dedekind, Friedrich, d. 1598 (Table P-PZ40)
8485.D63	De la Pryme, Charles, 1817-1899 (Table P-PZ40)
8485.D635	De Ludzisko, Joannes, ca. 1400-ca. 1447 (Table P-PZ40)
8485.D6354	De Thomeis, Antonio, 15th century (Table P-PZ40)
8485.D636	Della Casa, Giovanni, 1503-1556 (Table P-PZ40)
8485.D637	Della Rena, Andrea, 1478-1517 (Table P-PZ40)
8485.D644	Destito, Giulio Cesare, 1594-1648 (Table P-PZ40)
8485.D65	Dicta de arbore quae dicitur Imago hominis
8485.D67	Dinckel, Johannes, 1545-1601 (Table P-PZ40)
8485.D683	Disputatio nova contra mulieres
8485.D684	Disputatio physiolegistiea de ivre et natvra pennalivm
8485.D685	Dispvtatio de cornelio et eivsdem natvra ac proprietate
8485.D688	Does, Johan van der, 1545-1604 (Table P-PZ40)
8485.D7	Dolet, Etienne, 1508-1546 (Table P-PZ40)
8485.D715	Domitius, Petrus, 1446-1518 (Table P-PZ40)
8485.D72	Donati, Andreas Angelo (Table P-PZ40)
8485.D723	Donisius (Table P-PZ40)
8485.D725	Dorat, Jean, 1508-1588 (Table P-PZ40)

PA8001-8595

Individual authors or works
Modern, 1350- -- Continued

8485.D73	Dorlandus, Petrus, 1454-1507 (Table P-PZ40)
8485.D736	Dorpius, Martinus, 1485-1525 (Table P-PZ40)
8485.D75	Drury, William, d. ca. 1641 (Table P-PZ40)
8485.D8	Du Bellay, Joachim ca. 1525-1560 (Table P-PZ40)
	Cf. PQ1668+ French literature
8485.D9	Du Cerceau, Jean Antoine, 1670-1730 (Table P-PZ40)
8485.D93	Dubravius, Jan, ca. 1486-1533 (Table P-PZ40)
8485.D98	Dybinus, Nicolaus (Table P-PZ40)
8485.E32	Eck, Johann, 1486-1543 (Table P-PZ40)
8485.E5	Elegia de originali peccato
	Enea Sylvio Piccolomini see PA8556
	Epistolae obscurorum virorum
8490	Editions. By date
8492	Selections
8493.A-Z	Translations. By language, A-Z
8495	Criticism
8497.E67	Equicola, Mario, 1470-1525 (Table P-PZ40)
8497.E7	Erasmius, Janus, d. 1658 (Table P-PZ40)
	Erasmus, Desiderius, d. 1536
	Cf. BR350.E7 Reformation
8500	Collected works. By date
8501	Selections
	For Colloquies see PA8507
8502.A-Z	Translations. By language, A-Z
	Adagia see PN6410
	Apophthegmata
	see PN6299+
	Colloquia
8506	Editions. By date
8507	Selections
8508.A-Z	Translations. By language, A-Z
	e.g.
	For special colloquies see PA8509.A+
8508.E5	English
8508.F8	French
8509.A-Z	Special. By name, A-Z (Latin or Greek titles)
8510	Criticism
8511	Epistolae. Letters
	Moria encomium (Praise of folly)
8512	Editions. By date
8513	Selections
8514.A-Z	Translations. By language, A-Z
8515	Criticism
8517.A-Z	Other works, A-Z

	Individual authors or works
	Modern, 1350-
	Erasmus, Desiderius, d. 1536 -- Continued
8517.Z9	Doubtful or spurious works
	e.g.
8517.Z9J8	Julius Secundus
8518	Biography and criticism
8518.A1	Periodicals. Societies. Collections
8518.A15	Autobiography, journals, etc.
	Correspondence (General)
	Cf. PA8511 Epistolae
8518.A2	Collected. By date
8518.A3A-.A3Z	By correspondent, A-Z
8518.A4	Collected letters to Erasmus. By date
8518.A5-Z	General works
8520.E87	Estienne, Henri, 1531-1598 (Table P-PZ40)
8520.E93	Eufrenius, Albertus, 1581-1626 (Table P-PZ40)
8520.F27	Facio, Bartolomeo, d. 1457 (Table P-PZ40)
8520.F3	Faerno, Gabriello, d. 1561 (Table P-PZ40)
8520.F35	Falcón, Jaime Juan, b. 1522 (Table P-PZ40)
8520.F36	Fascitelli, Onorato,1502-1564 (Table P-PZ40)
8520.F392	Fedele, Cassandra, 1465-1558 (Table P-PZ40)
8520.F393	Fénelon, François de Salignac de la Mothe-, 1651-1715 (Table P-PZ40)
8520.F395	Fernández de Santaella, Rodrigo, 1444-1509 (Table P-PZ40)
8520.F4	Ferrari, Antonio de, Galateo, 1444-1519 (Table P-PZ40)
8520.F45	Fiera, Battista, 1469-1538 (Table P-PZ40)
8520.F5	Filelfo, Francesco, 1398-1481 (Table P-PZ40)
8520.F52	Filelfo, Giovanni Mario, 1426-1480 (Table P-PZ40)
8520.F55	Filetico, Martino, ca. 1430-ca. 1490 (Table P-PZ40)
8520.F6	Flaminio, Marco Antonio, d. 1550 (Table P-PZ40)
8520.F62	Flayder, Friedrich Hermann, 1596-1640 (Table P-PZ40)
8520.F6314	Fletcher, Phineas, 1582-1650
8520.F632	Flores poetarum de virtutibus et vitiis
8520.F633	Florio, Francesco, 15th century (Table P-PZ40)
8520.F64	Folengo, Teofilo, 1496-1544 (Table P-PZ40)
8520.F645	Fontius, Bartholomaeus, 1445-1513 (Table P-PZ40)
8520.F647	Foreest, Jan van, 1586-1651 (Table P-PZ40)
8520.F65	Fortescue, George, 1578?-1659 (Table P-PZ40)
8520.F7	Fracastoro, Girolamo, 1483-1553 (Table P-PZ40)
	For English translations of poem "Syphilis," see RC201
8520.F74	Francesco, di Tommaso, ca. 1445-1514 (Table P-PZ40)
8520.F75	Francius, Petrus, 1645-1704 (Table P-PZ40)
8520.F76	Frankfurter, Bartholomeus, b. 1490? (Table P-PZ40)
8520.F8	Fraunce, Abraham, fl. 1587-1633 (Table P-PZ40)

Individual authors or works

Modern, 1350- -- Continued

8520.F83	Fredo, Andrzej Maksymilian, ca. 1620-1679 (Table P-PZ40)
8520.F84	Freitag, Arnold (Table P-PZ40)
8520.F845	Frexius, Bartholomaeus (Table P-PZ40)
8520.F85	Frischlin, Nicodemus, 1547-1590 (Table P-PZ40)
8520.F9	Frulovisi, Tito Livio dei, fl. 1429-1456 (Table P-PZ40)
8520.F92	Frycz Modrzewski, Andrzej, ca. 1503-ca. 1572 (Table P-PZ40)
	Cf. DK4284.F7 Frycz as a political and social theorist
	Fullonius, Gulielmus see PA8520.G62
8520.G115	Gaeomemphio Cantaliensis, pseud. (Table P-PZ40)
8520.G127	Gager, William, fl. 1580-1619 (Table P-PZ40)
8520.G13	Gaguin, Robert, 1433-1501 (Table P-PZ40)
8520.G15	Gambara, Lorenzo, 1506-1596 (Table P-PZ40)
8520.G2	García Matamoros, Alonso, d. 1572 (Table P-PZ40)
8520.G25	Garzoni, Giovanni, 1419-1505 (Table P-PZ40)
8520.G3	Gast, Johann, d. 1572 (Table P-PZ40)
8520.G33	Gazet, Angelin, 1568-1653 (Table P-PZ40)
8520.G36	Genovesi, Vittorio, 1887- (Table P-PZ40)
8520.G4	Geraldini, Antonio, 1449?-1489 (Table P-PZ40)
8520.G5	Gesner, Johann Mattias, 1691-1761 (Table P-PZ40)
8520.G53	Gevaerts, Jean Gaspard, 1593-1666 (Table P-PZ40)
8520.G55	Giannettasio, Niccolò Partenio, 1648-1715 (Table P-PZ40)
8520.G58	Giraldi, Lilio Gregorio, 1479-1552 (Table P-PZ40)
8520.G59	Giustolo, Pierfrancesco, d. 1510 (Table P-PZ40)
8520.G6	Glareanus, Henricus, 1488-1563 (Table P-PZ40)
8520.G62	Gnaphaeus, Gulielmus, 1493-1568 (Table P-PZ40)
8520.G625	Goclenius, Rudolph, 1547-1628 (Table P-PZ40)
8520.G63	Gómez Ortega, Casimiro, 1740-1818 (Table P-PZ40)
8520.G637	Gonzalez, Joan Angel, ca. 1480-1548 (Table P-PZ40)
8520.G638	Gonzalez, Thomas, 1592 or 1593-1659 (Table P-PZ40)
8520.G64	Goodwin, George, fl. 1620 (Table P-PZ40)
8520.G65	Gosky, Martin, fl. 1650 (Table P-PZ40)
8520.G7	Goveanus, Antonius, ca. 1505-1565? (Table P-PZ40)
8520.G74	Gower, John, 1325?-1408 (Table P-PZ40)
8520.G77	Gray, Thomas, 1716-1771 (Table P-PZ40)
8520.G8	Grenville, William Wyndham Grenville, baron, 1759-1834 (Table P-PZ40)
8520.G84	Gretser, Jakob, 1562-1625 (Table P-PZ40)
8520.G9	Grosso, Stefano, 1824-1903 (Table P-PZ40)
8521	Grotius, Hugo, 1583-1645 (Table P-PZ39)
8523.G4	Gryphius, Andreas, 1616-1664 (Table P-PZ40)
8523.G45	Grzegorz z Sambora, ca. 1523-1573 (Table P-PZ40)
8523.G455	Guarini, Battista, 1538-1612 (Table P-PZ40)
8523.G457	Guarino, Veronese, 1374-1460 (Table P-PZ40)

Individual authors or works
Modern, 1350- -- Continued

8523.G46	Guidiccioni, Lelio, 1570-1643 (Table P-PZ40)
8523.G5	Gunnarsen, Halvard, d. 1608 (Table P-PZ40)
	Gwalther, Rudolf, 1519-1586 see PA8595.W3123
8523.H35	Halford, Sir Henry, bart., 1766-1844 (Table P-PZ40)
8523.H4	Hall, Joseph, bp. of Norwich, 1574-1656 (Table P-PZ40)
8523.H68	Harmonius Marsus, Joannes, ca. 1477-ca. 1552 (Table P-PZ40)
8523.H72	Hasištejnský z Lobkovic, Bohuslav, 1461-1510 (Table P-PZ40)
8523.H85	Hawkesworth, Walter, d. 1606 (Table P-PZ40)
8524.H3	Hebenstreit, Franz, 1747-1795 (Table P-PZ40)
8525	Heinsius, Daniel, 1580-1655 (Table P-PZ39)
8526.H4	Heinsius, Nicolaas, 1620-1681 (Table P-PZ40)
8527.H365	Henning, Marcus (Table P-PZ40)
8527.H37	Henríquez, Miguel, b. 1582 (Table P-PZ40)
8527.H4	Hessus, Helius Eobanus, 1488-1540 (Table P-PZ40)
8527.H45	Heymerick, Arnold, ca. 1424-1491 (Table P-PZ40)
8527.H48	Hilarion, Veronensis, ca. 1440-ca. 1484 (Table P-PZ40)
8527.H5	Hiltprand, Michael, d. 1590 (Table P-PZ40)
8527.H58	Holberg, Ludvig, baron, 1684-1754 (Table P-PZ40)
8527.H6	Holdsworth, Edward, 1684-1746 (Table P-PZ40)
8527.H7	Horatius, Romanus, fl. 1450 (Table P-PZ40)
8527.H8	Hossche, Sidronius de, 1596-1653 (Table P-PZ40)
8527.H86	Hozjusz, Stanisław, 1504-1579 (Table P-PZ40)
8527.H9	Hussovianus, Nicolaus, fl. 1523-1525 (Table P-PZ40)
	Hutten, Ulrich von, 1488-1523
8530	Collected works. By date
8532.A-Z	Translations. By language, A-Z
8533.A-Z	Individual works, A-Z
8535	Biography and criticism
	Cf. BR350.H8 Reformation
(8537)	Iacobus Nicholai, de Dacia
	see PA8540.J32
8537.I42	Imberdis, Jean (Table P-PZ40)
8537.I52	In globum aerostaticum
8537.I88	Istvánffy, Miklós, 1538-1615 (Table P-PZ40)
8538	Iturriaga, José Mariano de, 1717-1787 (Table P-PZ39)
8540.J3	Jacobini, Domenico Maria, cardinal, 1837-1900 (Table P-PZ40)
8540.J32	Jacobus Nicholai, de Dacia, 14th century (Table P-PZ40)
8540.J35	Janus Pannonius, bp., 1434-1472 (Table P-PZ40)
	Janus Secundus see PA8580
8540.J58	Joannes, Visliciensis, ca. 1485-1516 (Table P-PZ40)
	Johannes Secundus see PA8580
8540.J65	Joncre, Joannes (Table P-PZ40)

Individual authors or works

Modern, 1350- -- Continued

8540.J67	Jordaens, Wilhelm (Table P-PZ40)
8540.J7	Jourdan, Adrien, père, 1617-1692 (Table P-PZ40)
8540.J85	Jungius, Joachim, 1587-1657 (Table P-PZ40)
8540.K24	Karner, Egyed, 1662-1708 (Table P-PZ40)
8540.K26	Karytski, Mikahil Aľiaksandravich, 1714-1791 (Table P-PZ40)
8540.K37	Ker, John, d. 1741 (Table P-PZ40)
8540.K4	Kerckmeister, Johannes, fl. 1466-1485 (Table P-PZ40)
8540.K5	Kiel, Corneille van, d. 1607 (Table P-PZ40)
8540.K53	King, Edward, 1612-1637 (Table P-PZ40)
8540.K55	King, William, 1685-1763 (Table P-PZ40)
	Kirchmeyer, Thomas see PA8555.N3
8540.K57	Klonowitz, Sebastian Fabian, ca. 1545-1602 (Table P-PZ40)
8540.K58	Klotz, Christian Adolph, 1738-1771 (Table P-PZ40)
8540.K583	Knapiusz, Grzegorz, 1564-1639 (Table P-PZ40)
8540.K585	Kniaźnin, Franciszek Dionizy, 1750-1807 (Table P-PZ40)
8540.K587	Knickknackius, Gripholdus (Table P-PZ40)
8540.K588	Knobelsdorf, Eustathius von, 1519-1571 (Table P-PZ40)
8540.K6	Kochanowski, Jan, 1530-1584 (Table P-PZ40)
	For Kochanowski's Polish works see PG7157.K6+
8540.K8	Krzycki, Andrzej, 1482-1537 (Table P-PZ40)
8540.K9	Kynaston, Herbert, 1809-1878 (Table P-PZ40)
8540.L2	La Croix, Demetrius de (Table P-PZ40)
	Lanckvelt, Joris van, 1487-1558 see PA8547.M2
8540.L3	Landino, Cristoforo, 1424-1504 (Table P-PZ40)
8540.L4	Landívar, Rafael, 1731-1793 (Table P-PZ38)
	Cf. PQ7499.L3 Spanish works
8540.L44	Landor, Walter Savage, 1775-1864 (Table P-PZ40)
	Langeveld, Joris van, 1487-1558 see PA8547.M2
8540.L6	La Rue, Charles de, 1643-1725 (Table P-PZ40)
8540.L615	Latino, Juan, 16th century (Table P-PZ40)
8540.L6157	Laudatio dramatica clarissimae Firleiorum familiae
8540.L616	Laudivio, Zacchia, de Vezzano, fl. 1473 (Table P-PZ40)
8540.L618	Lazzarelli, Ludovico, 1450-1500 (Table P-PZ40)
8540.L6199	Lazzaroni, Pietro, 15th cent. (Table P-PZ40)
8540.L62	Le Brun, Laurent, 1608-1663 (Table P-PZ40)
8540.L63	Leech, John, fl. 1623 (Table P-PZ40)
8540.L633	Leeuwen, Joannes van, 19th cent. (Table P-PZ40)
8540.L635	Lefèvre, Jacques, d'Etaples (Table P-PZ40)
8540.L64	Legge, Thomas, 1535-1607 (Table P-PZ40)
8540.L65	Leland, John, 1506?-1552 (Table P-PZ40)
8540.L67	Lemnius, Simon, 1511?-1550 (Table P-PZ40)
8540.L8	Leo XIII, pope, 1810-1903 (Table P-PZ40)
	Biography see BX1374

	Individual authors or works
	Modern, 1350- -- Continued
8543.L47	L'Hospital, Michel de, 1573-1573 (Table P-PZ40)
8543.L5	Libellus de natura animaliam
8545	Lipsius, Justus, 1547-1606 (Table P-PZ39)
	Cf. B785.L4+ Philosophy
8546.L5	Llanos, Bernardino de los, 1557-1639 (Table P-PZ40)
8546.L62	Lobkowitz, Bohuslaw Hassenstein, Freiherr von, 1460 or 1461-1510 (Table P-PZ40)
8547.L5	Lopes dos Santos Valente, Antonio, 1839-1896 (Table P-PZ40)
8547.L55	Loschi, Antonio, d. 1441 (Table P-PZ40)
8547.L6	Lotichius, Johann Peter, 1598-1669 (Table P-PZ40)
8547.L7	Lotichius, Petrus, 1528-1560 (Table P-PZ40)
8547.L8	Lucarus, Nicolaus, d. 1515 (Table P-PZ40)
8547.L82	Luder, Peter, 15th century (Table P-PZ40)
8547.L83	Leucht, Johannes, 16th cent. (Table P-PZ40)
8547.L83	Ludovico da Fabriano, b. ca. 1335 (Table P-PZ40)
8547.M18	Macquelyn, Michael Jacobus, 1771-1852 (Table P-PZ40)
8547.M2	Macropedius, Georgius, 1487-1558 (Table P-PZ40)
8547.M25	Magno, Pietro (Table P-PZ40)
8547.M26	Maidstone, Richard, d. 1396 (Table P-PZ40)
8547.M264	Maier, Michael, 1568?-1622 (Table P-PZ40)
8547.M267	Maittaire, Michael, 1667-1747 (Table P-PZ40)
8547.M27	Maldonado, Juan (Table P-PZ40)
8547.M3	Mambrun, Pierre, 1601-1661 (Table P-PZ40)
8547.M4	Mameranus, Nicolaus, 16th century (Table P-PZ40)
8547.M43	Mancinus, Dominicus, fl. 1478-1491 (Table P-PZ40)
8547.M44	Mansi, Giovan Domenico, 1692-1769 (Table P-PZ40)
8547.M45	Mantova Benavides, Marco, conte, 1489-1582 (Table P-PZ40)
8547.M5	Manuzio, Paolo, 1512-1574 (Table P-PZ40)
	Manzolli, Pietro Angelo see PA8555.P3
8547.M5376	Marrasio, Giovanni, 1405-ca. 1457 (Table P-PZ40)
8547.M54	Martin, Francois, 1639-1726 (Table P-PZ40)
8547.M55	Martirano, Coriolano, d. 1558 (Table P-PZ40)
8547.M554	Marullo Tarcaniota, Michele, d. 1500 (Table P-PZ40)
8547.M555	Marulus, Marcus, 1450-1524 (Table P-PZ40)
8547.M556	Marzio, Galeotto, 1427-1497 (Table P-PZ40)
8547.M56	Masen, Jacob, 1601-1681 (Table P-PZ40)
8547.M574	Masselot, Jean, 1657-1710 (Table P-PZ40)
8547.M58	Massimi, Pacifico, ca. 1400-ca. 1500 (Table P-PZ40)
8547.M6	Mathevon de Curnieu, Antoine, 1740-1807 (Table P-PZ40)
8547.M68	May, Thomas, 1595-1650 (Table P-PZ40)
8547.M72	Medius, Thomas, 15th century (Table P-PZ40)

	Individual authors or works
	Modern, 1350- -- Continued
8550	Melanchthon, Philipp, 1497-1560 (Table P-PZ39)
	Epigrammata, Declamationes, etc.
	Cf. BR335+ Reformation
8552.M2	Melissus, Paul, 1539-1602 (Table P-PZ40)
8552.M4	Mensa philosophica
8552.M42	Mercurius rusticans
8552.M435	Mewe, William, ca. 1603-1669 (Table P-PZ40)
8552.M44	Meyer, Liévin de, 1655-1730 (Table P-PZ40)
8552.M445	Mézières, Philippe de, 1327?-1405 (Table P-PZ40)
	Milton, John, 1608-1674 see PR3571
8552.M48	Mochius, Petrus (Table P-PZ40)
8552.M487	Moggi, Moggio, 14th cent. (Table P-PZ40)
8552.M495	Molza, Francesco Maria, 1489-1544 (Table P-PZ40)
8552.M5	Montalti, Cesare (Table P-PZ40)
8552.M512	Montano, Benito Arias, 1527-1598 (Table P-PZ40)
8552.M522-.M5223	Montevergine (Abbey). Biblioteca. Manuscript. Scaffale, XXIII, 171 (Table P-PZ42)
8552.M524	Montmoret, Humbert de, d. 1525 (Table P-PZ40)
8552.M525	Montreuil, Jean de, d. 1418 (Table P-PZ40)
8552.M55	Moraes, Ignacio de, 16th century (Table P-PZ40)
8552.M6	Morata, Olympia Fulvia, 1526-1555 (Table P-PZ40)
8553	More, Sir Thomas, Saint, 1478-1535
	Cf. DA334.M8 Biography
	Cf. HX810.5 Utopias
8553.A2	Collected works
8555.M2	Morlini, Girolamo, 16th century (Table P-PZ40)
8555.M24	Morus, Philippus, 1539 or 1540-1578 (Table P-PZ40)
8555.M3	Mosellanus, Petrus, 1493?-1524 (Table P-PZ40)
8555.M5	Muret, Marc Antoine, 1526-1585 (Table P-PZ40)
8555.M6	Murmellius, Johannes, d. 1517 (Table P-PZ40)
8555.M65	Mussonius, Petrus (Table P-PZ40)
8555.M7	Mutianus Rufus, Conradus, 1471-1526 (Table P-PZ40)
8555.N25	Naldi, Naldo, 1439-ca. 1520 (Table P-PZ40)
8555.N27	Nannius, Petrus, 1500-1557 (Table P-PZ40)
8555.N3	Naogeorgus, Thomas, 1511-1563 (Table P-PZ40)
8555.N38	Naudé, Gabriel, 1600-1653 (Table P-PZ40)
8555.N4	Navagero, Andrea, 1483-1529 (Table P-PZ40)
8555.N55	Neuhusius, Reinerus, 17th century (Table P-PZ40)
8555.N565	Niavis, Paulus, 1460-1514 (Table P-PZ40)
8555.N57	Nichols, William, 1655-1716 (Table P-PZ40)
8555.N575	Nicolaus Hermanni, d. 1391 (Table P-PZ40)
8555.N58	Nigronus, Joannes (Table P-PZ40)
8555.N6	Nogarola, Isotta, 1420?-1466 (Table P-PZ40)
8555.N85	Nuñez de Acosta, Duarte (Table P-PZ40)
8555.O42	Oláh, Miklós, 1493-1568 (Table P-PZ40)

	Individual authors or works
	Modern, 1350- -- Continued
8555.O64	Opuscalum fabularum (Table P-PZ40)
8555.O67	Orsaeus, Johannes, 1576-1626 (Table P-PZ40)
8555.O8	Owen, John, 1560?-1622 (Table P-PZ40)
8555.P23	Pacheco, Francisco, 1539-1599 (Table P-PZ40)
8555.P28	Paganus, Petrus, 1532-1576 (Table P-PZ40)
8555.P286	Paladino, Paolo, 15th cent. (Table P-PZ40)
8555.P29	Paleario, Aonio, 1503-1570 (Table P-PZ40)
8555.P3	Palingenius, Marcellus, Stellatus, fl. 1528 (Table P-PZ40)
8555.P32	Palladinus, Jacobus, de Theramo, bp. of Spoleto, 1349-1417 (Table P-PZ40)
8555.P322	Palladio, Domizio (Table P-PZ40)
8555.P34	Parmenius, Stephanus, Budaeus, d. 1583 (Table P-PZ40)
8555.P344	Parrasio, Aulo Giano, 1470-1534 (Table P-PZ40)
8555.P35	Pascoli, Giovanni, 1855-1912 (Table P-PZ40)
8555.P4	Passerat, Jean, 1534-1602 (Table P-PZ40)
8555.P42	Paterson, Ninian, d. 1688 (Table P-PZ40)
8555.P424	Pau, Jeroni, d. 1497 (Table P-PZ40)
8555.P43	Paulus, Crosnensis (Paweł z Krosna), d. 1517? (Table P-PZ40)
8555.P433	Peacham, Henry, 1576?-1643? (Table P-PZ40)
8555.P4334	Pekkanen, Tuomo (Table P-PZ40)
8555.P4335	Pellisieri, Pietro, 1762-1831 (Table P-PZ40)
8555.P434	Pereira, Bento, 1605-1681 (Table P-PZ40)
8555.P44	Perrin, Aegidius, fl. ca. 1560 (Table P-PZ40)
8555.P45	Petit-Radel, Philippe, 1749-1815 (Table P-PZ40)
8555.P453	Petkowski, Kasper, 1554-1612 (Table P-PZ40)
	Petrarca, Francesco see PQ4489+
8555.P46	Petrucci, Giovanni Battista, d. 1514 (Table P-PZ40)
8555.P49	Philippus de Bergamo, d. ca. 1380 (Table P-PZ40)
	Piccolomini, Enea Sylvio see PA8556
	Pico della Mirandola, Giovanni, 1463-1494 see B785.P5+
8555.P6	Pico della Mirandola, Giovanni Francesco, 1470-1533 (Table P-PZ40)
8555.P63	Pietro, da Ripalta, 1340-1374? (Table P-PZ40)
8555.P7	Pirckheimer, Wilibald, 1470-1530 (Table P-PZ40)
8555.P73	Pires, Diogo, 1517-1607? (Table P-PZ40)
8555.P75	Pisani, Ugolino, fl. 1430-1440 (Table P-PZ40)
8555.P8	Pitcairne, Archibald, 1652-1713 (Table P-PZ40)
8555.P87	Pittorio, Ludovic, b. 1454 (Table P-PZ40)
8556	Pius, II, pope, 1405-1464
8556.A6-.Z4	Separate works
	e.g.
8556.C3	Carmen Sapphicum
8556.D4	De duobus amantibus, sive Euryalus et Lucretia
	Biography see BX1308

Individual authors or works

Modern, 1350- -- Continued

8557.P44	Placcius, Vincent, 1642-1699 (Table P-PZ40)
8557.P48	Placentius, Johannes, 1500?-1550? (Table P-PZ40)
8557.P5	Pleurre, Etienne de, 1585-1635 (Table P-PZ40)
8557.P55	Plinius, Basilius, d. 1605 (Table P-PZ40)
8557.P63	Poema en honor de San Ignacio de Loyola
	Poggio-Bracciolini, 1380-1459 see PA8477.B76
8557.P7	Polignac, Melchior de, cardinal, 1661-1741 (Table P-PZ40)
	Poliziano, Angelo, 1454-1494
8560	Collected works
8562.A-Z	Translations. By language, A-Z
8563.A-Z	Special works, A-Z
8565	Biography and criticism
8570.P47	Pompilius, Paulus, 1453 or 1454-1490 or 1491 (Table P-PZ40)
8570.P485	Poniński, Antoni, d. 1744 (Table P-PZ40)
8570.P5	Pontano, Giovanni Gioviano, 1426-1503 (Table P-PZ40)
8570.P6	Porée, Charles, 1675-1741 (Table P-PZ40)
8570.P8	Prat de Saba, Onofre, 1733?-1810 (Table P-PZ40)
8570.P82	Problemata Ivdicra & historiolae ridiculae
8570.P823	Probo, Marco, 1455-1499 (Table P-PZ40)
8570.P84	Purkircher, György, 1530-1578 (Table P-PZ40)
8570.P85	Pusculus, Ubertinus, fl. 1500 (Table P-PZ40)
8570.Q28	Quatrario, Giovanni, 1336-1402 (Table P-PZ40)
8570.Q3	Quattromani, Sertorio, 1541-1611 (Table P-PZ40)
	Cf. PQ4632.Q38 Italian literature
8570.Q44	Querno, Camillo, 1470-1530 (Table P-PZ40)
8570.Q6	Quillet, Claude, 1602-1661 (Table P-PZ40)
8570.Q63	Quinziano Stoa, Giovanni Francesco, 1484?-1557 (Table P-PZ40)
8570.Q64	Quirini, Lauro, ca. 1420-ca. 1475 (Table P-PZ40)
8570.R14	Radvanas, Jonas (Table P-PZ40)
8570.R16	Rakovský, Martin, 1535-1579 (Table P-PZ40)
8570.R2	Ramirez, Jerónimo, fl. ca. 1550 (Table P-PZ40)
8570.R3	Ramsay, Allen Beville, 1872- (Table P-PZ40)
8570.R35	Rapicio, Andrea, d. 1573 (Table P-PZ40)
8570.R4	Rapin, René, 1621-1687 (Table P-PZ40)
	Including his Hortorum libri IV
8570.R42	Ravaud, Abraham, 1600-1646 (Table P-PZ40)
8570.R433	Ravisius Textor, Joannes, ca. 1480-1524 (Table P-PZ40)
8570.R44	Régnier, Jacques, 1589-1653 (Table P-PZ40)
8570.R45	Reis, Antonio dos, 1690-1738 (Table P-PZ40)
	Rena, Andrea della, 1478-1517 see PA8485.D637
8570.R47	Resende, André de, 1498-1573 (Table P-PZ40)
8570.R48	Rettenbacher, Simon, 1634-1706 (Table P-PZ40)
8570.R5	Reuchlin, Johann, 1455-1522 (Table P-PZ40)

Individual authors or works
Modern, 1350- -- Continued

8570.R6	Reynard the Fox (Latin versions)
8570.R7	Rhodiginus, Lodovicus Caelius, 1450-1520 (Table P-PZ40)
	Including his Lectionum antiquarum libri XXX
8570.R716	Richards, G.P. (George Pierce) (Table P-PZ40)
8570.R72	Rimbaud, Arthur, 1854-1891 (Table P-PZ40)
8570.R73	Rinuccio, of Arezzo, 15th century (Table P-PZ40)
8570.R76	Roberti, Giovanni Battista, 1719-1786 (Table P-PZ40)
8570.R8	Rodrigues de Mello, Jose, 1704-1783 (Table P-PZ40)
8570.R83	Rorario, Girolame, 1485-1556 (Table P-PZ40)
8570.R84	Rosini, Carlo Maria, 1748-1836 (Table P-PZ40)
8570.R844	Ross, John, 1563?-1607 (Table P-PZ40)
	Rossus, Johannes, 1563?-1607 see PA8570.R844
8570.R845	Rota, Berardino, 1508-1575 (Table P-PZ40)
8570.R846	Rottendorff, Bernhard, 1594-1671 (Table P-PZ40)
8570.R85	Roussel, Carolus Joannes (Table P-PZ40)
8570.R87	Rubigallus, Paulus, d. 1577? (Table P-PZ40)
8570.R9	Ruggle, George, 1575-1622 (Table P-PZ38)
	Author of "Ignoramus"
8570.R95	Ruiz de Moros, Pedro, 1506-1571 (Table P-PZ40)
8570.R97	Rysiński, Salomon, da. 1560-1625 (Table P-PZ40)
8570.S2	Sabellico, Marco Antonio Coccio, called, 1436-1506 (Table P-PZ40)
8570.S22	Sacco, Catone, 1394?-1463 (Table P-PZ40)
8570.S24	Sainte-Marthe, Scévole de, 1536-1623 (Table P-PZ40)
8570.S25	Salmon Macrin, Jean, 1490-1557 (Table P-PZ40)
	Sambucus, Joannes, 1531-1584 see PA8595.Z75
8570.S257	Sánchez, Francisco, ca. 1550-ca. 1623 (Table P-PZ40)
8570.S259	Sanderus, Antoine, 1586-1664 (Table P-PZ40)
8570.S3	Sannazaro, Jacopo, 1458-1530 (Table P-PZ40)
	For Italian works see PQ4633
8570.S35	Santa Clara, Francisco de Paula, 1836-1902 (Table P-PZ40)
8570.S4	Santeul, Jean de, 1630-1697 (Table P-PZ40)
8570.S43	Sapidus, Johannes, 1490-1561 (Table P-PZ40)
8570.S45	Sarbiewski, Maciej Kazimierz, 1595-1640 (Table P-PZ40)
8570.S5	Sautel, Pierre Just, 1613-1662 (Table P-PZ40)
8570.S53	Sbrulius, Richardus, d. 1480 (Table P-PZ40)
8570.S54	Scala, Bartolomeo, 1430-1497 (Table P-PZ40)
8575.S2	Scaliger, Joseph Juste, 1540-1609 (Table P-PZ40)
8575.S3	Scaliger, Julius Caesar, 1484-1558 (Table P-PZ40)
	Schede, Paul see PA8552.M2
	Schelhorn, Johann Georg, 1694-1773 see AC14
8577.S2	Schemering, Daniel, ca. 1615-ca. 1630 (Table P-PZ40)
8577.S23	Schesaeus, Christianus, 1535?-1585 (Table P-PZ40)
8577.S234	Schmidlin, Johannes Lorenz, 1626-1692 (Table P-PZ40)

Individual authors or works
Modern, 1350- -- Continued

8577.S235	Schnur, C. Harry (Table P-PZ40)
8577.S237	Schonens, Andreas, 1552-1615 (Table P-PZ40)
8577.S239	Schottennius, Hermannus (Table P-PZ40)
8577.S3	Schrijver, Pieter, 1576-1660 (Table P-PZ40)
8577.S33	Sclarici dal Gambaro, Tommaso, ca. 1455-ca. 1526 (Table P-PZ40)
8577.S36	Scurzi, Giandomenico, ca. 1571-ca. 1650 (Table P-PZ40)
8580	Secundus, Joannes Nicolai, 1511-1536 (Table P-PZ39)
8585.S25	Seneca, Tommaso, ca. 1390-1472 (Table P-PZ40)
8585.S3	Sergardi, Lodovico, 1660-1726 (Table P-PZ40)
8585.S35	Serón Antonio, 16th century (Table P-PZ40)
8585.S37	Settle, Elkanah, 1648-1724 (Table P-PZ40)
8585.S397	Sigonio, Silvestro (Table P-PZ40)
8585.S4	Silos, Giuseppe, d. 1674 (Table P-PZ40)
8585.S45	Silvestri, Domenico (Table P-PZ40)
	Sisgoreus Sibenicensis, Georgius see PA8585.S5
8585.S5	Šižgorić Šibenčanin, Juraj, fl. 1477-1487 (Table P-PZ40)
8585.S64	Smolinski, Jan, 16th-17th centuries (Table P-PZ40)
8585.S643	Sommer, Johannes, 1559-1622 (Table P-PZ40)
8585.S65	Spes aurei saeculi
8585.S66	Spinoso, Paolo, d. 1481 (Table P-PZ40)
8585.S67	Stagneus, Carolus (Table P-PZ40)
8585.S675	Stanisław, ze Skalbmierza, d. 1431 (Table P-PZ40)
8585.S678	Stefonio, Bernardino, 1560-1620 (Table P-PZ40)
8585.S68	Stellini, Jacopo, 1699-1770 (Table P-PZ40)
8585.S684	Stieröxel, István (Table P-PZ40)
8585.S687	Stobaeus, Andreas, 1642-1714 (Table P-PZ40)
8585.S69	Streithagen, Peter von, 1595-1670 (Table P-PZ40)
8585.S7	Strozzi, Tito Vespasiano, 1425?-1505 (Table P-PZ40)
8585.S78	Stubbe, Edmund, fl. 1618 (Table P-PZ40)
8585.S8	Stymmelius, Christophorus, 1525-1588 (Table P-PZ40)
8585.S85	Susenbrotus (Table P-PZ40)
8585.S9	Swedenborg, Emmanuel, 1688-1772 (Table P-PZ40)
	Cf. B4468.S8+ Philosophy
	Cf. BX8711+ New Jerusalem Church
8585.S95	Szymonowicz, Szymon, 1558-1629 (Table P-PZ40)
	For Szymonowicz's Polish works see PG7157.S95+
8585.T26	Tasso, Torquato, 1544-1595 (Table P-PZ40)
8585.T3	Taubmann, Friedrich, 1565-1613 (Table P-PZ40)
8585.T35	Taunay, Theodoro Maria, 1798-1880 (Table P-PZ40)
8585.T4	Teive, Diogo de, 1513 or 1514-ca. 1565 (Table P-PZ40)
8585.T44	Telesio, Antonio, 1482-1533? (Table P-PZ40)
8585.T47	Themata medica de beanorvm
8585.T48	Theses de hasione et hasibili qvalitate

Individual authors or works
Modern, 1350- -- Continued
Thoresby, John, d. 1373
For the Lay folks' catechism, a Middle English verse
translation of his instruction for the people see
PR2019.L37

8585.T5	Thorius, Raphael, d. 1625 (Table P-PZ40)
8585.T515	Thou, Jacques-Auguste de, 1553-1617 (Table P-PZ40)
8585.T52	Tiara, Petrus, 1514-1586 (Table P-PZ40)
8585.T55	Tizio, Sigismondo, 1458-1528 (Table P-PZ40)
	Tixier, Jean, seigneur de Ravisy, d. 1524 see PA8570.R433
8585.T65	Tory, Geoffroy, 1480-1533 (Table P-PZ40)
8585.T7	Tractatus varii de pulicibus
8585.T75	Traversagni, Lorenzo Guglielmo, 1425-1503 (Table P-PZ40)
8585.T77	Tribraco, Gaspare, 1439-ca. 1493 (Table P-PZ40)
8585.T775	Trithemius, Johannes, 1462-1516 (Table P-PZ40)
8585.T78-.T783	Triumphus divi Michaelis Archangeli Bavarici (Table P-PZ43)
8585.T79	Tucci, Stefano, 1540-1597 (Table P-PZ40)
8585.T8	Turnèbe, Adrien, 1512-1565 (Table P-PZ40)
8585.T86	Typographiae Calissiensis studium honoris. illustrissimi principis et reverendissimi domini d. Lavrenty Gembicki
	Ugolino, Michele see PA8585.V45
8585.U72	Upmarck, Johan, 1664-1743 (Table P-PZ40)
8585.U8	Urbanus VIII, pope, 1568-1644 (Table P-PZ40)
	For biography see BX1343
8585.U83	Urceo, Antonio, 1446-1500 (Table P-PZ40)
8585.V17	Valencia, Pedro de, 1555-1620 (Table P-PZ40)
8585.V2	Valeriano Bolzani, Giovanni Pierio, 1477-1558 (Table P-PZ40)
8585.V215	Valla, Lorenzo, 1406-1457 (Table P-PZ40)
8585.V22	Valle, Girolamo della, fl. 1509 (Table P-PZ40)
8585.V23	Vanière, Jacques, 1664-1739 (Table P-PZ40)
8585.V25	Varadier de Saint Andiol, Gaspard, 1624-1712 (Table P-PZ40)
8585.V277	Vavasseur, François, 1605-1681 (Table P-PZ40)
8585.V28	Vavřinec z Březové, ca. 1365-ca. 1438 (Table P-PZ40)
8585.V3	Vegius, Mapheus, d. 1458 (Table P-PZ40)
8585.V35	Velmatius, Joannes Maria, fl. 1530 (Table P-PZ40)
8585.V36	Venator, Balthasar, 1594-1664 (Table P-PZ40)
8585.V39	Verardi, Carlo, 1440-1500 (Table P-PZ40)
8585.V395	Verelius, Olof, 1618-1682 (Table P-PZ40)
8585.V397	Vergerio, Pietro Paulo, the Elder, 1370-1444 (Table P-PZ40)
8585.V4	Vergilius, Polydoras, d. 1555 (Table P-PZ40)

Individual authors or works

Modern, 1350- -- Continued

8585.V45	Verino, Ugolino, 1438-1516 (Table P-PZ40)
8585.V58	Vico, Giambattista, 1668-1744 (Table P-PZ40)
8585.V6	Vida, Marco Girolamo, bp. of Alba, d. 1566 (Table P-PZ40)
	De arte poetica see PN1040
	Sacchia (poem on the game of chess) see GV1449
8585.V63	Vilches, Juan de, d. 1566 (Table P-PZ40)
8585.V64	Villani, Filippo, d. 1405 (Table P-PZ40)
8585.V8	Viriati, Santo (Table P-PZ40)
8585.V85	Vitalis, Janus, 1490?-1560? (Table P-PZ40)
	Vitellius, Iacobus, 1587-1648 see PA8485.C519
8588	Vives, Juan Luis, 1492-1540 (Table P-PZ37)
	Cf. B785.V6+ Philosophy
8589.V55	Vladeraccus, Petrus, 1571-1618 (Table P-PZ40)
8589.V6	Volpi, Giovanni Antonio, 1686-1766 (Table P-PZ40)
8590	Vossius, Gerardus Joannes, 1577-1649 (Table P-PZ39)
8595.V3	Vossius, Isaac, 1618-1689 (Table P-PZ40)
	Vulpius, Joannes Antonius see PA8589.V6
8595.W25	Wakefield, Gilbert, 1756-1801 (Table P-PZ40)
8595.W3	Walle, Jacques van de, 1599-1690 (Table P-PZ40)
8595.W3123	Walther, Rudolph, 1519-1586 (Table P-PZ40)
8595.W3127	Warwick, Anne Dudley, Countess of, d. 1588 (Table P-PZ40)
8595.W325	Weerdt, Josse de, d. 1625 (Table P-PZ40)
8595.W4	Wellesley, Richard Colley Wellesley, marquis, 1760-1842 (Table P-PZ40)
8595.W45	Westmorland, Mildmay Fane, earl of, 1601-1666 (Table P-PZ40)
	Weston, Elizabeth Jane, 1582-1612 see PA8595.W454
8595.W454	Westonia, Elizabetha Johanna, 1582-1612 (Table P-PZ40)
8595.W46	Whittington, Robert, fl. 1490-1548 (Table P-PZ40)
8595.W49	Wilde, George, Bp. of Derry, 1610-1665 (Table P-PZ40)
8595.W494	Willet, Andrew, 1562-1621 (Table P-PZ40)
8595.W5	Wimpheling, Jacob, 1450-1528 (Table P-PZ40)
8595.Z26	Zacharie de Lisieux, père, 1582-1661 (Table P-PZ40)
8595.Z3	Zamagna, Bernardo, 1735-1820 (Table P-PZ40)
8595.Z32	Zanchi, Basilio, 1501-1588 (Table P-PZ40)
8595.Z35	Zappone, Almericus (Table P-PZ40)
8595.Z54	Zilioli, Ziliolo, 15th century (Table P-PZ40)
8595.Z75	Zsámboki, János, 1531-1584 (Table P-PZ40)

.x	General works
.x2A-.x2Z	By region or country, A-Z

0	Collections
2	General works
3	Grammar
4	Phonology
5	Morphology
6	Syntax
7	Other
8	Dictionaries
9	Local
(9.9)	Particular authors
	see the author

0	Collections
1	General works
3	Dictionaries
4.A-Z	Local, A-Z
	Under each (using succesive Cutter numbers):
	(1) *Collections*
	(2) *General works*
	(3) *Special*
	(4) *Dictionaries*
(4.9)	Particular authors
	see the author

TABLES

.xA2	Comprehensive or Ilias and Odyssea. By date
.xA22	Selections from Ilias and Odyssea. By date
.xA3	Ilias. By date
.xA4	Odyssea. By date
.xA5	Minor works. By date
.xA6	Batrachomyomachia. By date
.xA7	Hymni. By date
	Paraphrases. Tales, etc.
.xZ3	Ilias and Odyssea. By date
.xZ4	Ilias. By date
.xZ5	Odyssea. By date
.xZ6	Batrachomyomachia. By date
.xZ9	Parodies. By date
(.xZ99)	Dramatization. Fiction
	see the author

.x date	Comprehensive (the three main works, entire or portions). By date
.xA3	Selections: passages, thoughts, etc. By date
.xA5	Aeneis. By date
	Including translations of portions, or books
.xA7	Paraphrases, tales, etc. By date
(.xA8)	Dramatization, fiction, etc.
	see the author
.xA9	Parodies, travesties, etc. By date
.xB7	Bucolica (or Bucolica and Georgica). By date
.xB8	Parodies, travesties, etc. By date
.xG4	Georgica. By date
(.xZ5)	Appendix Vergiliana
	see PA6956

TABLES

.A1A-.A1Z	Comprehensive (the three main works, entire or portions). By translator, A-Z
.A3A-.A3Z	Selections: passages, thoughts, etc. By translator or compiler, A-Z, anonymous selections by date
.A5A-.A5Z	Aeneis. By translator, A-Z
	Including translations of portions, or books
.A7	Paraphrases, tales, etc.
(.A8)	Dramatization, fiction, etc.
	see the author
.A9	Parodies, travesties, etc.
.B7	Bucolica (or Bucolica and Georgica)
.B8	Parodies, travesties, etc.
.G4	Georgica
(.Z5)	Appendix Vergiliana
	see PA6956

0	Collections
5	Theory. Method. Relations
	Study and teaching. History
7	General
8.A-Z	By region or country, A-Z
9.A-Z	By school, A-Z
10	General works
	Grammar
13	Treatises
17	Textbooks. Exercises, etc.
	Phonology
21	General works
(23)	Pronunciation
	see PA267
25	Accent
31	Orthography
36	Morphology. Inflection. Accidence
	Parts of speech (Morphology and syntax)
41	Noun
43	Adjective. Comparison
44	Article
45	Pronoun
47	Verb
49	Particles
	Syntax
51	General works
53	Sentence
57	Other
(60)	Grammatical usage of particular authors
	see PA6 91
63	Style. Composition. Rhetoric
64	Machine translating
	Including research
66	Prosody. Metrics. Rhythmics
	Etymology
71	General works
73	Foreign elements
75	Semantics
77	Synonymy
78.A-Z	Particular words, A-Z
81	Dictionaries
	For research on word frequency, etc., in connection with machine translating, see PA6 64
91	Treatises on particular works or authors

TABLES

	General and miscellaneous
1.A-.Z3	Collections. By editor
1.Z5	Anthologies. Selections. Specimens
	Poetry
2.A2	By various translators
2.A5-Z	By individual tranlators, A-Z
	Drama
	General, or Tragedy alone
	Collected or selected plays
3.A2	By various translators
3.A5-.Z3	By individual translators, A-Z
3.Z5	Selections, specimens, etc.
3.Z7	Stories, paraphrases, etc.
3.Z8A-.Z8Z	Comedy. By translator, A-Z
	Prose
4.A-.Z3	General and miscellaneous
4.Z5	Selections, specimens, etc.
	Oratory
5.A-.Z3	Comprehensive collections
5.Z5	Selected orations
7.A-Z	By subject, A-Z
7.E7	Epigrams

	General and miscellaneous
1.A1-.A79	Collections
1.A8-Z	Anthologies. Selections. By translator or editor, A-Z
	Poetry
2.A2	Early, to 1800/1850
2.A5-Z	Later, 1800/1850-
3	Drama. Comedy
4	Prose

.A1A-.A1Z	Comprehensive, or Iliad and Odyssey. By translator, A-Z
.A15A-.A15Z	Selections. Passages. Thoughts. By translator, A-Z
	Iliad. Ἰλιάς
.A2A-.A2Z	Complete. By translator, A-Z
.A3A-.A3Z	Selected books. By translator, A-Z
.A35A-.A35Z	Portions (from several books). By translator, A-Z
.A38A-.A38Z	Selections. Passages. Thoughts. By translator, A-Z
.A4A-.A4Z	Particular books. By translator, A-Z
	Odyssey. Ὀδύσσεια
.A5A-.A5Z	Complete. By translator, A-Z
.A6A-.A6Z	Selected books. By translator, A-Z
.A7A-.A7Z	Portions (from several books). By translator, A-Z
.A75A-.A75Z	Selections. Passages. Thoughts. By translator, A-Z
.A8A-.A8Z	Particular books. By translator, A-Z
.A9A-.A9Z	Minor works (Collected and selected)
.B3A-.B3Z	Batrachomyomachia
.H8A-.H8Z	Hymns (Collected and selected)
	Particular hymns
.H81	In Apollinem. Hymn to Apollo. Εἰς Ἀπόλλωνα. By date
	Authorship ascribed to Cynaethus, of Chios
.H81A-.H81Z	Criticism
.H83	In Cererem. Hymn to Demeter. Εἰς Δήμητραν. By date
.H83A-.H83Z	Criticism
.H84	Hymn to Dionysus. Εἰς Διόνυσον. By date
.H84A-.H84Z	Criticism
.H85	In Mercurium. Εἰς Ἑρμῆν. By date
.H85A-.H85Z	Criticism
.H87	In Venerem. Hymn to Aphrodite. Εἰς Ἀφροδίτην. By date
.H87A-.H87Z	Criticism
	Paraphrases, tales, etc.
	For children's books, see PZ8.1; PZ25; PZ35; etc.
.Z3	Iliad and Odyssey
.Z4	Iliad. Ἰλιάς
.Z5	Odyssey. Ὀδύσσεια
.Z6	Batrachomyomachia
(.Z8)	Dramatization
	see classification for author
.Z9	Parodies

.A1	Complete works
.A2	Selected works from Moralia and Vitae
	Moralia
.M6	Complete. By date
.M7	Selected, and abridged. By date
.M8A-.M8Z	Separate treatises. By Latin title, A-Z, and date
	Vitae parallelae
.V6	Complete. By date
.V7	Selected, and abridged. By date
.V8A-.V8Z	Separate treatises. By biographee, A-Z, and date

TABLES

1	Collected works. By date
1A2	Selected works (Moralia and Vitae). By date
1A3	Moralia (Collected or Selected). By date
1A5-1Z	Moralia (Particular treatises, A-Z, by Latin title)
	Subarrange by date
2	Vitae (Collected or Selected). By date
2A5-2Z	Vitae (Particular lives, A-Z, by pair or single)
	Subarrange by date

.A1	Collected or selected works. By date
.A5-.Z	Particular works, A-Z, by original title
	Metamorphoses (Golden ass)
.M3	Complete
.M4	Selections
	Episodes
	Psyche
.M5	Translations and adaptations
.M6	Versions (metrical)
.M7	Dramatizations
.M72-.M79	Other

TABLES

.A1	Works, or translations of Gallic War
.A2	Gallic War (selected books)
	Gallic War (particular books)
.A21	I
.A22	II
.A23	III
.A24	IV
.A25	V
.A26	VI
.A27	VII
.A28	VIII
.B3	Bellum civile
.B4	Bellum africum
.B6	Bellum alexandrinum
.B8	Bellum hispaniense

TABLE FOR TRANSLATIONS OF MARCUS TULLIUS CICERO (2 NOS.)

1.A1	Collected works
1.A2	Selected works (from various groups)
1.A25	Selections. Passages. Thoughts
	Particular groups
	Orations
1.A3	Comprehensive
1.A4	Selected
1.A5-Z	Single orations, by original title, A-Z
2.A1	Rhetorical
2.A2	Philosophical
2.A5-Z	Single works, A-Z, by original title
	For single orations see PA14 1.A5+
	Letters (Epistulae)
2.E5	General and "Ad familiares"
2.E6	Ad Atticum
2.E7	Ad Brutum
2.E8	Ad Quintum fratrem

TABLES

.x	Collected or selected works
.xA15	Selections. Passages. Thoughts
	Particular groups
	Orations
.xA2	Comprehensive or selected
.xA21-.xA39	Single orations, by original title
.xA5	Rhetorical
.xA6	Philosophical
.xA7-.xZ	Single works, A-Z, by original title
	For single orations see PA14a .xA21+

.A1	Comprehensive (or selections from Odes and other works)
.A3	Carmina
.A5	Epodae
.E5	Epistulae
.E6	Ars poetica
.S3	Satirae

TABLES

TABLE FOR TRANSLATIONS OF TITUS MACCIUS
PLAUTUS (2 NOS.)

1.A-Z	Collected plays. By translator, A-Z
2.A3	Selected plays
2.A5	Selections
2.A6-.V	Single plays (by original title and translator)
2.Z5	Paraphrases and tales
2.Z7	Imitations. Adaptations

TABLE FOR TRANSLATIONS OF TITUS MACCIUS PLAUTUS (CUTTER NO.)

.x	Collected plays. By date
.xA3	Selected plays. By date
.xA5	Selections. By date
.xA6-.xV	Single plays
	Subarrange each by play by date
.xZ5	Paraphrases and tales. By date
.xZ7	Imitations. Adaptations. By date

1.A1	Collected and selected works (prose, or prose and tragedies)
1.A3-Z	Single prose works (by original title, A-Z, and by translator)
2.A1	Collected and selected tragedies
2.A3-.Z3	Single tragedies (by original title, A-Z)
2.Z4	Pseudo-Seneca. Octavia
2.Z5	Imitations. Adaptations
2.Z7	Parodies. Travesties

.x	Collected and selected works (prose, or prose and tragedies)
.xA3-.xZ2	Single prose works (by original title, A-Z)
.xZ3	Collected and selected tragedies
.xZ31-.xZ39	Single tragedies (by original title, A-Z)
.xZ4	Pseudo-Seneca. Octavia
.xZ5	Imitations. Adaptations
.xZ7	Parodies. Travesties

TABLES

.A1	Collected works
.A2	Selected works
.A25	Selections. Passages. Thoughts
.A3	Annales
.A5	Historiae
.A7	Opera minora
.A8	Agricola
.D4	Dialogus
.G4	Germania

TABLE FOR TRANSLATIONS OF CORNELIUS TACITUS (CUTTER NO.)

.x	Collected works
.xA2	Selected works
.xA25	Selections. Passages. Thoughts
.xA3	Annales
.xA5	Historiae
.xA7	Opera minora
.xA8	Agricola
.xD4	Dialogus
.xG4	Germania

.A1A-.A1Z	Collected and selected plays, by translator, A-Z
	Subarrange anonymous translations, and translations by various hands, by date
.A5-.P5	Single plays, by original title, A-P
.Z5	Paraphrases and tales
.Z7	Imitations. Adaptations

A

Abbreviations: P305.2
  Comparative lexicography: P365+
Ability testing
  Philology: P53.4
Ablaut
  Indo-European (Indo-Germanic)
    philology: P601
Aboriginal Australians
  Communication. Mass media:
    P94.5.A85+
Absolute constructions
  Comparative grammar: P291.2
Academic language: P120.A24
Academic writing
  Discourse analysis: P302.18
  Style and composition: P301.5.A27
Accent
  Greek language: PA269
    New Testament Greek: PA825
  Indo-European (Indo-Germanic)
    philology: P597
  Latin language: PA2119
  Medieval and modern Greek
    language: PA1065
  Phonetics: P231
Acceptability
  Sociology and philology: P40.5.A22+
Accidence
  Classical philology: PA141+
  Greek language: PA283+
    New Testament Greek: PA836
  Latin language: PA2133+
  Medieval and modern Greek
    language: PA1076
Accidents
  Communication: P96.A22+
Achaemenian inscriptions: P943.A5
Acoustic phonetics: P221.5
Acquisition of language: P118+
Acreontic poetry
  Byzantine literature
    Collections: PA5181
Acronyms: P305.2
  Comparative lexicography: P365+

Adjective
  Comparative grammar: P273
  Greek language: PA325
    New Testament Greek: PA843
  Indo-European philology: P641
    Comparison: P627
  Latin language: PA2201
    Comparison: PA2147
  Medieval and modern Greek
    language: PA1082
Adjuncts
  Comparative grammar: P299.A32
Adjustment (Psychology)
  Sociolinguistics: P40.5.A25+
Adverb
  Comparative grammar: P284
  Greek language: PA353
  Indo-European (Indo-Germanic)
    philology: P657
  Latin language: PA2273
Advertising
  Style and composition: P301.5.A38
Aequian dialect: PA2481
Aesthetics
  Communication. Mass media: P93.4
Africa
  Mass media: P96.A37+
African Americans
  Communication. Mass media:
    P94.5.A37+
Age factors
  Language acquisition: P118.65
Agreement
  Comparative grammar: P299.A35
Agriculture in literature
  Classical literature: PA3015.A37
  Greek literature: PA3015.A37
Aids
  Study and teaching
    Philology: P53.15
AIDS (Disease)
  Mass media: P96.A39+
Air in literature
  Roman literature: PA6029.A57
Albania
  Mass media: P96.A4+
Alcoholism in mass media: P96.A42+

Fiction
  Roman literature
    Literary history: PA6091
Field theory
  Linguistic analysis: P128.F5
  Semantics: P325.5.F54
Fieldwork
  Linguistic analysis: P128.F53
  Semiotics: P99.4.F53
Figures of speech
  Latin language: PA2318.F54
  Psycholinguistics: P37.5.F53
  Sociology and philology: P40.5.F54+
  Style and composition: P301.5.F53
Finiteness
  Comparative grammar: P299.F56
Fish in literature
  Classical literature: PA3015.N4F5
  Greek literature: PA3015.N4F5
Fluency
  Study and teaching
    Philology: P53.4115
Focus
  Comparative grammar: P299.F63
  Semantics: P325.5.F63
Folk literature
  Greek literature
    Literary history: PA3285
Folk poetry
  Byzantine literature
    History and criticism: PA5155
Folk songs
  Byzantine literature
    Collections: PA5185
  Greek literature
    Literary history: PA3109
Folklore
  Communication. Mass media:
    P96.F65+
Food in literature
  Classical literature: PA3015.F63
  Greek literature: PA3015.F63
  Roman literature: PA6029.F66
Forecasting
  Communication. Mass media:
    P96.F67+
  Semantics: P325.5.F67

Foreign study
  Linguistics: P53.41155
Foreign workers
  Communication. Mass media:
    P94.5.A45+
Forgeries
  Classical literature: PA3014.F6
  Greek literature: PA3014.F6
  Roman literature: PA3014.F6
Formalization
  Linguistic analysis: P128.F67
Forms of address
  Sociology and philology: P40.5.F67+
Frames
  Discourse analysis: P302.36
  Semantics: P325.5.F72
  Study and teaching
    Philology: P53.4116
Freedmen in literature
  Roman literature: PA6030.S6
French-Canadians
  Communication. Mass media:
    P94.5.F74+
Frequency
  Linguistic analysis: P128.F73
Friendship in literature
  Classical literature: PA3015.F7
  Greek literature: PA3015.F7
  Medieval and modern Latin literature
    History and criticism: PA8065.F75
  Roman literature: PA6029.F75
Function words
  Comparative grammar: P283+
Functional discourse grammar: P167
Functional sentence perspective: P298
Functionalism
  Structural linguistics: P147
Future life in literature
  Roman literature: PA6029.F87

G

Gays
  Communication. Mass media:
    P94.5.G38+
Gender
  Comparative grammar: P240.7

INDEX

Prosody
  Medieval and modern Greek
    language: PA1106
  Study and teaching
    Philology: P53.68
Proto-Indo-European language: P572
Prototype
  Linguistic analysis: P128.P74
  Semantics: P325.5.P74
Pschological aspects
  Bilingualism: P115.4
Psychic trauma in mass media:
  P96.P73+
Psycholinguistics: P37+
Psychological aspects
  Communication. Mass media:
    P96.P75+
  Discourse analysis: P302.8
  Lexicology: P326.5.P75
  Semantics: P325.5.P78
  Semiotics: P99.4.P78
  Study and teaching
    Philology: P53.7
  Style and composition: P301.5.P75
  Vocabulary: P305.18.P79
  Written communication: P211.6
Psychology and philology: P37+
Psychology in literature
  Classical literature: PA3015.P78
  Greek literature: PA3015.P78
Public opinion
  Communication. Mass media:
    P96.P83+
Public service interpreting: P306.947
Public welfare
  Communication. Mass media:
    P96.P84+
Publicity
  Communication. Mass media:
    P96.P85+
Punctuation
  Discourse analysis: P302.813
  Latin language: PA2318.P8
  Style and composition: P301.5.P86
Punishment in literature
  Classical literature: PA3015.P8
  Greek literature: PA3015.P8

Q

Quantifiers
  Comparative grammar: P299.Q3
Quantity
  Indo-European (Indo-Germanic)
    philology: P591
Questioning
  Communication. Mass media: P95.52
Quotation
  Discourse analysis: P302.814
Quotation in literature
  Classical literature: PA3014.Q7
  Greek literature: PA3014.Q7

R

Rabbinic Greek language: PA700+
Race relations
  Communication. Mass media:
    P94.5.M55+
Racism
  Language: P120.R32
Radicalism
  Communication. Mass media:
    P96.R32+
Raetian language: P1091
Rape in mass media: P96.R35+
Ratings
  Communication. Mass media:
    P96.R36+
Readers
  Greek language: PA260
  Latin language: PA2095
  Medieval and modern Greek
    language: PA1103
Reading
  Psycholinguistics: P37.5.R42
  Study and teaching
    Philology: P53.75
Realism in literature
  Classical literature: PA3014.R4
  Greek literature: PA3014.R4
Realization
  Linguistic analysis: P128.R43
Reciprocals
  Comparative grammar: P299.R38

INDEX

V

Vampires
  Communication. Mass media:
    P96.V35+
Variation
  Language: P120.V37
  Lexicography: P327.5.V37
Variation in language
  Study and teaching: P53.88
Venetic language: P1075
Verb
  Comparative grammar: P281
  Greek language: PA337+
    New Testament Greek: PA847
  Indo-European (Indo-Germanic)
    philology: P649
    Conjugation: P625
  Latin language: PA2215+
    Conjugation: PA2150+
  Medieval and modern Greek
    language: PA1087+
Verbal self-defense
  Discourse analysis: P302.87
Verner's law
  Indo-European (Indo-Germanic)
    philology: P607
Versification
  Greek language: PA413
  Latin language: PA2333
Vestianian dialect: PA2491
Vietnam War
  Communication. Mass media:
    P96.V46+
Villains
  Communication. Mass media:
    P96.V48+
Violence
  Communication. Mass media:
    P96.V5+
Vision
  Greek literature: PA3015.V57
Visual communication: P93.5+
Visual poetry
  Medieval and modern Latin literature
    Literary history: PA8063.V57
Vocabulary: P305+

Vocabulary
  Classical philology: PA184
  Greek language: PA406
  Latin language: PA2320
Vocabulary teaching
  Philology: P53.9
Vocational guidance
  Communication. Mass media: P91.6
  Philology: P60+
  Translating and interpreting: P306.6
Voice
  Greek language: PA341
  Latin language: PA2235
  Medieval and modern Greek
    language: PA1087.93
Voice quality
  Phonetics: P236.5
Voiōtia (Greece) in literature
  Classical literature: PA3015.V64
  Greek literature: PA3015.V64
Volscian dialect: PA2493
Vowel gradation
  Indo-European (Indo-Germanic)
    philology: P601
Vowel harmony
  Comparative grammar: P234
Vowels
  Comparative grammar: P233
  Greek language: PA275
  Indo-European (Indo-Germanic)
    philology: P599+
  Latin language: PA2127
Voyages, Imaginary
  Communication. Mass media:
    P96.V68+
Vulgar Latin language: PA2601+
Vulgar Latin literature: PA2701+

W

War
  Communication. Mass media:
    P96.W35+
War in literature
  Classical literature: PA3015.W46
  Greek literature: PA3015.W46
  Roman literature: PA6029.W37

472

INDEX

X

Xenophobia
  Communication. Mass media:
    P96.X45+

Y

Young adults
  Communication. Mass media:
    P94.5.Y68+
Youth
  Language: P120.Y68
Youth in mass media: P94.5.Y72+
Yuezhi language: P929

Z

Zaire
  Communication. Mass media:
    P96.Z34+
Zero
  Linguistic analysis: P128.Z47
Zionism
  Communication. Mass media:
    P96.Z56+